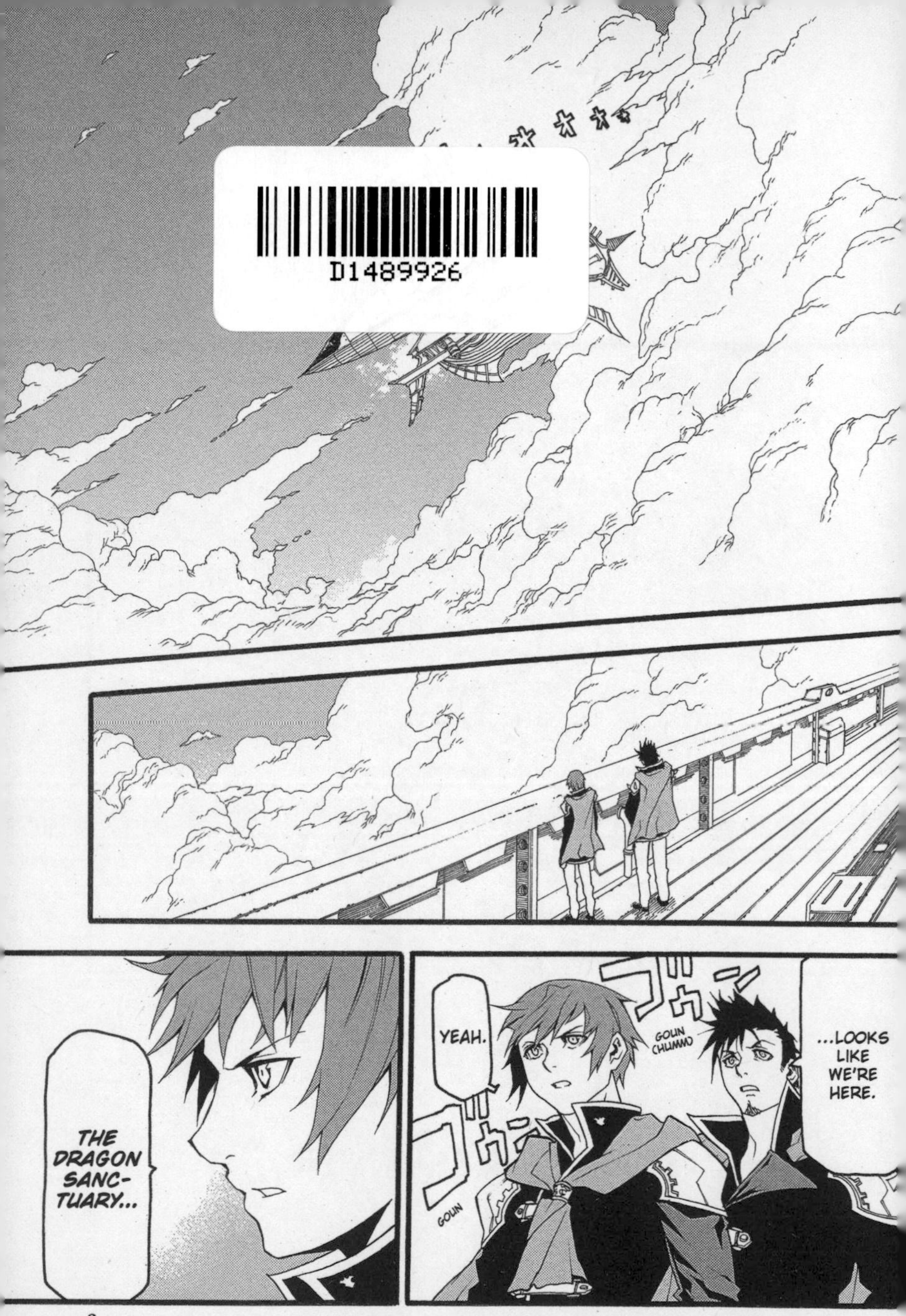
...LOOKS LIKE WE'RE HERE.
GOUN (HUMMM)
YEAH.
GOUN
THE DRAGON SANCTUARY...

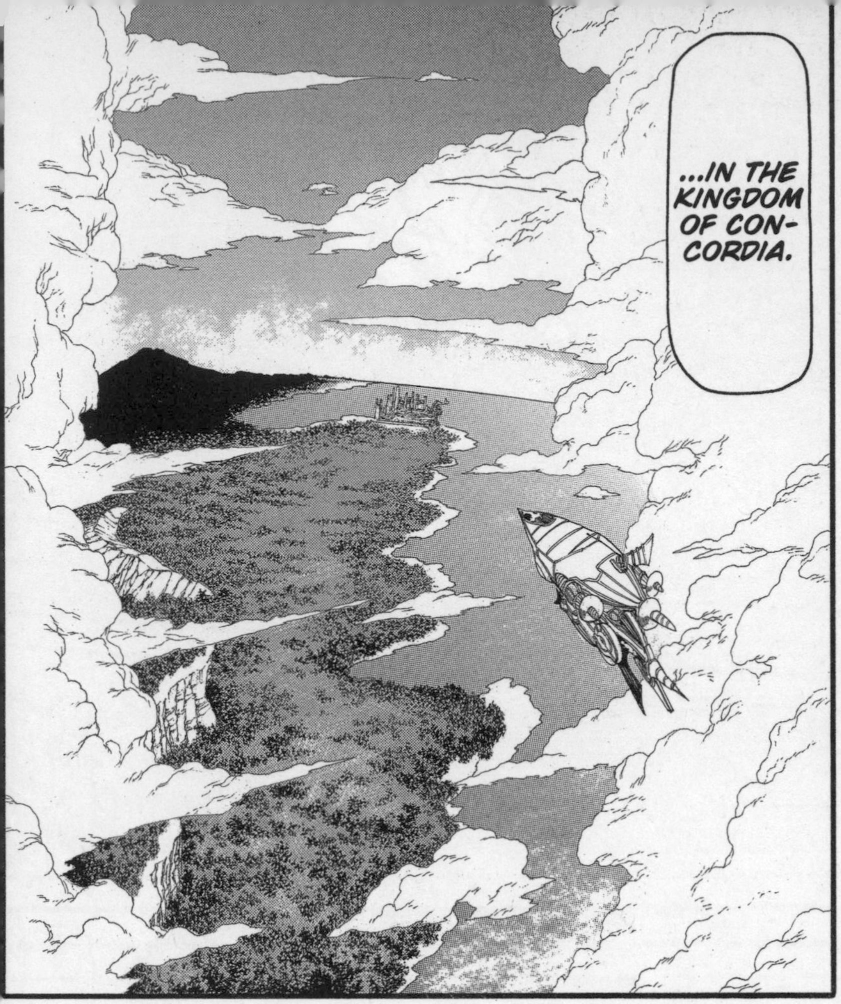
...IN THE KINGDOM OF CON-CORDIA.

CHAPTER 5: CHANCE ENCOUNTERS

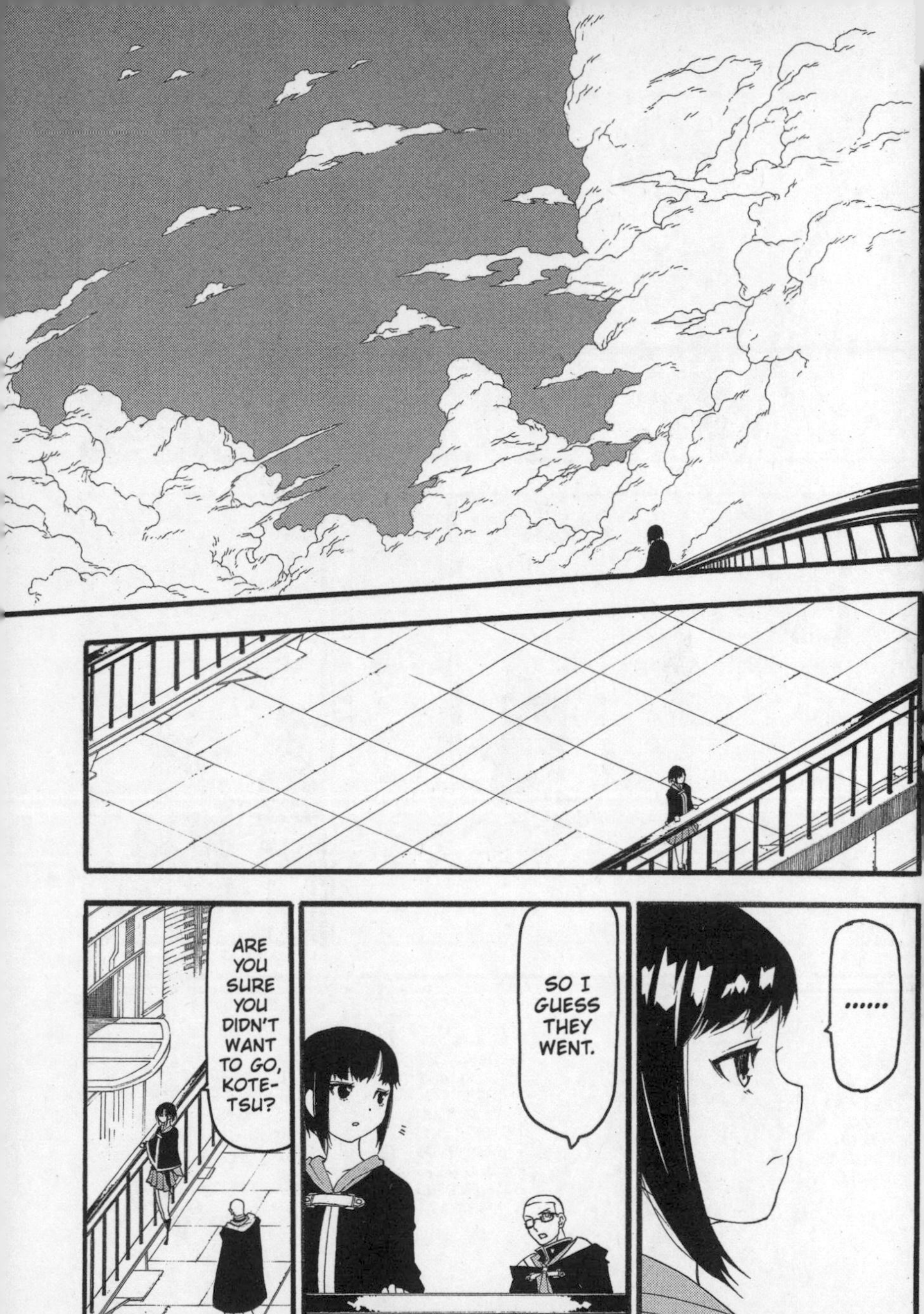
......
SO I GUESS THEY WENT.
ARE YOU SURE YOU DIDN'T WANT TO GO, KOTE-TSU?

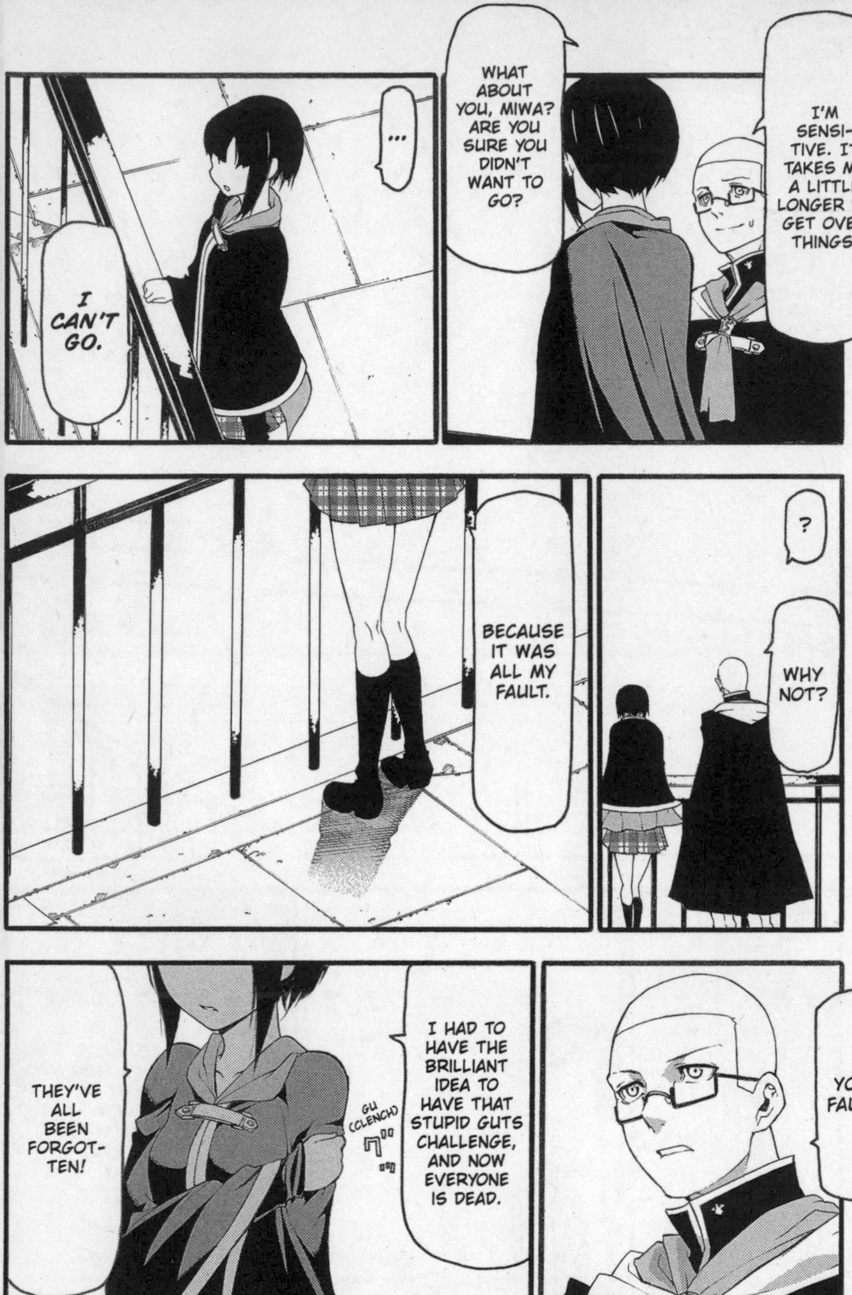
I'M SENSI-TIVE. IT TAKES ME A LITTLE LONGER TO GET OVER THINGS.
WHAT ABOUT YOU, MIWA? ARE YOU SURE YOU DIDN'T WANT TO GO?
...
I CAN'T GO.
?
WHY NOT?
BECAUSE IT WAS ALL MY FAULT.
YOUR FAULT?
I HAD TO HAVE THE BRILLIANT IDEA TO HAVE THAT STUPID GUTS CHALLENGE, AND NOW EVERYONE IS DEAD.
GU (CLENCH)
THEY'VE ALL BEEN FORGOT-TEN!

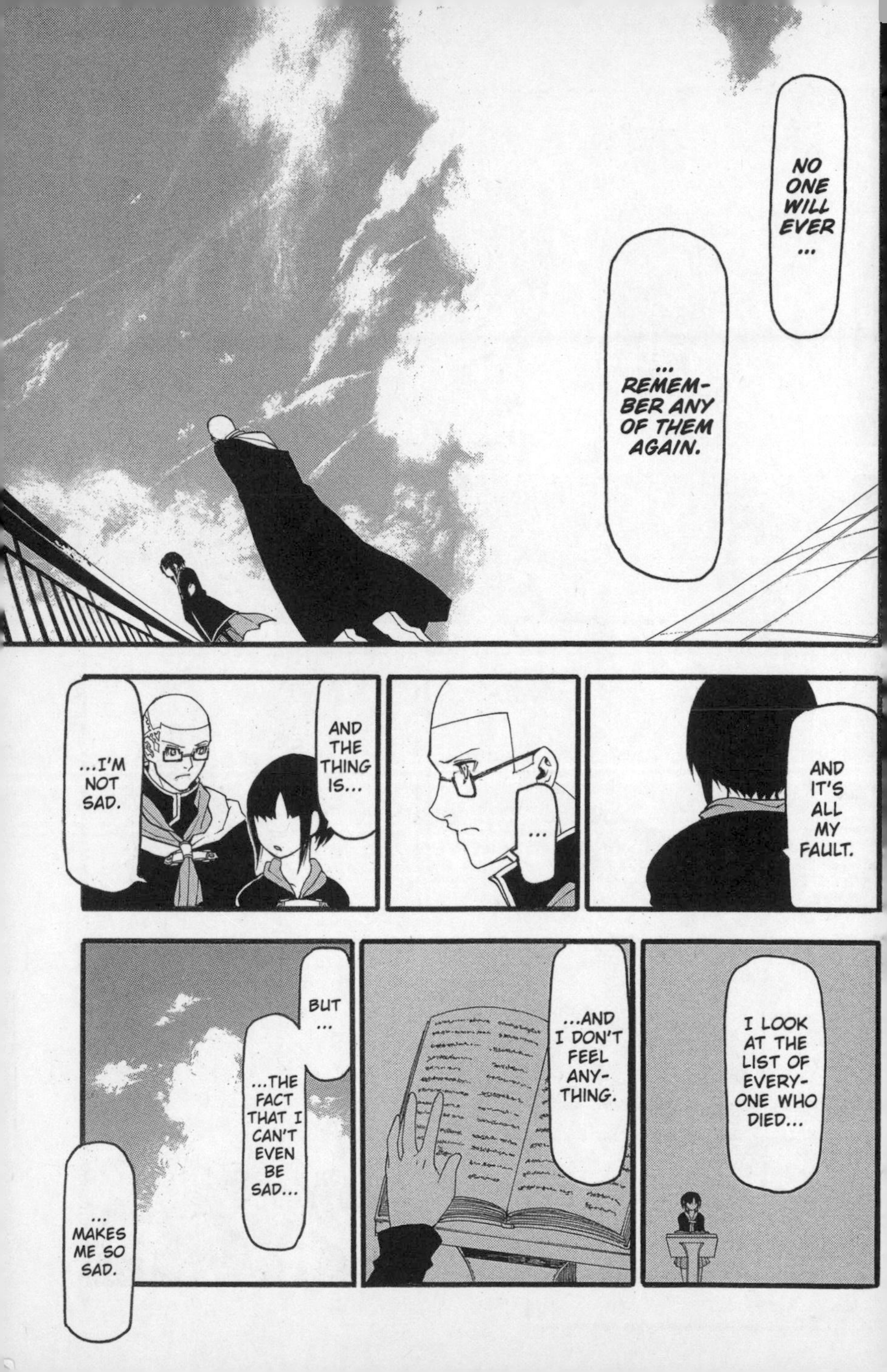
NO ONE WILL EVER...
...REMEMBER ANY OF THEM AGAIN.
AND IT'S ALL MY FAULT.
...
AND THE THING IS...
...I'M NOT SAD.
I LOOK AT THE LIST OF EVERYONE WHO DIED...
...AND I DON'T FEEL ANYTHING.
BUT...
...THE FACT THAT I CAN'T EVEN BE SAD...
...MAKES ME SO SAD.

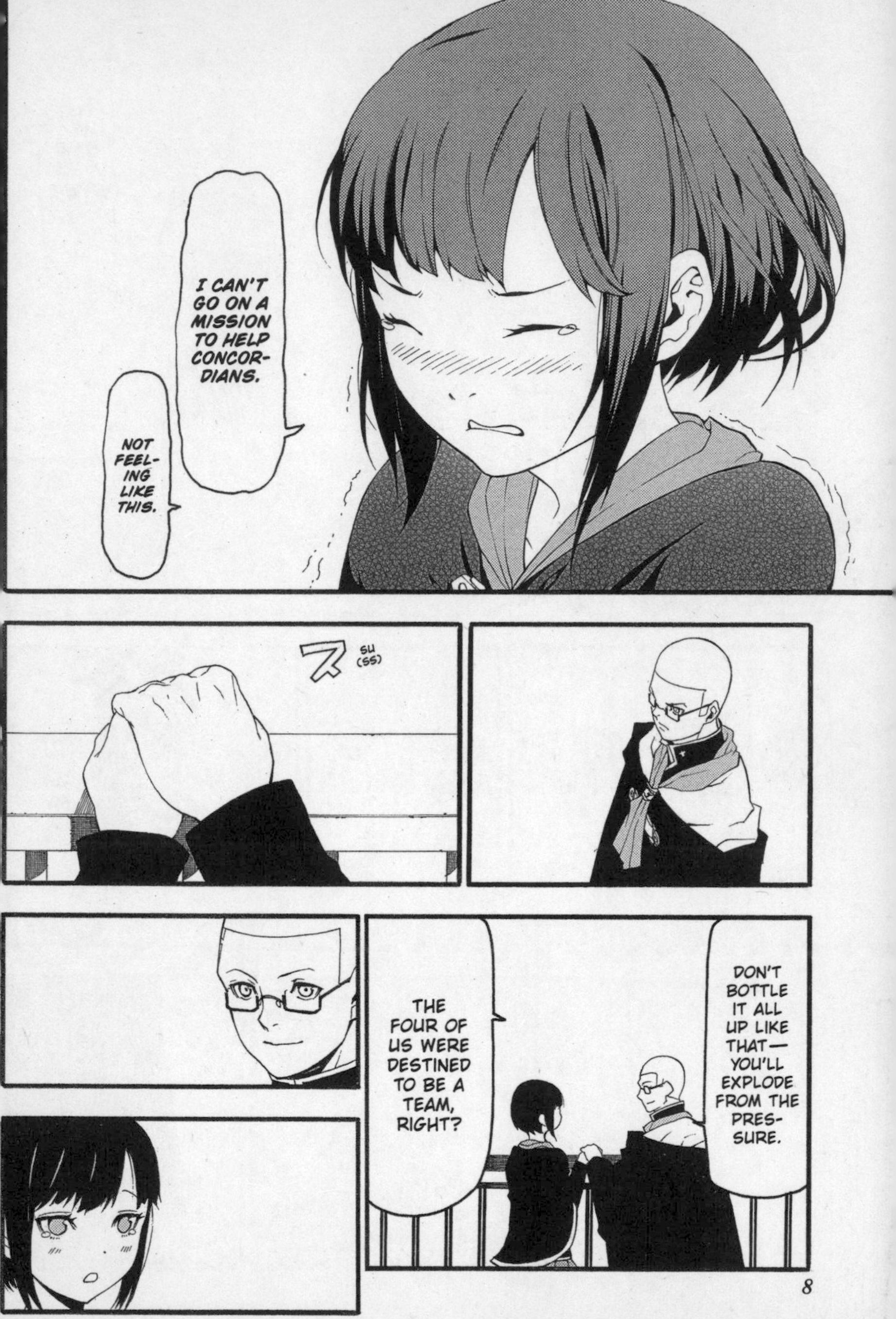
I CAN'T GO ON A MISSION TO HELP CONCORDIANS.
NOT FEELING LIKE THIS.
SU (SS)
DON'T BOTTLE IT ALL UP LIKE THAT—YOU'LL EXPLODE FROM THE PRESSURE.
THE FOUR OF US WERE DESTINED TO BE A TEAM, RIGHT?

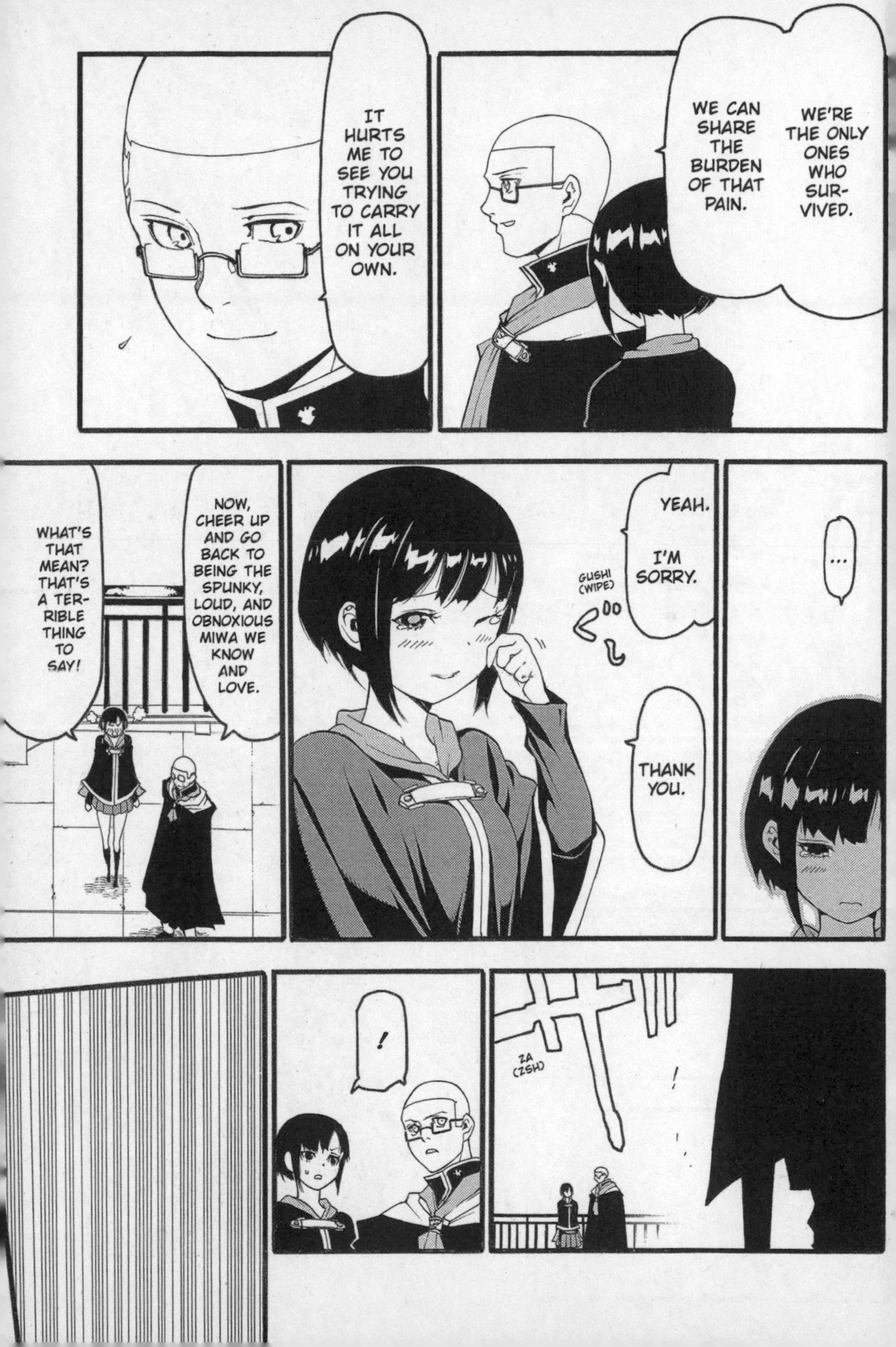
WE'RE THE ONLY ONES WHO SURVIVED.
WE CAN SHARE THE BURDEN OF THAT PAIN.
IT HURTS ME TO SEE YOU TRYING TO CARRY IT ALL ON YOUR OWN.
...
YEAH.
I'M SORRY.
GUSHI (WIPE)
THANK YOU.
NOW, CHEER UP AND GO BACK TO BEING THE SPUNKY, LOUD, AND OBNOXIOUS MIWA WE KNOW AND LOVE.
WHAT'S THAT MEAN? THAT'S A TERRIBLE THING TO SAY!
ZA (ZSH)
!
!

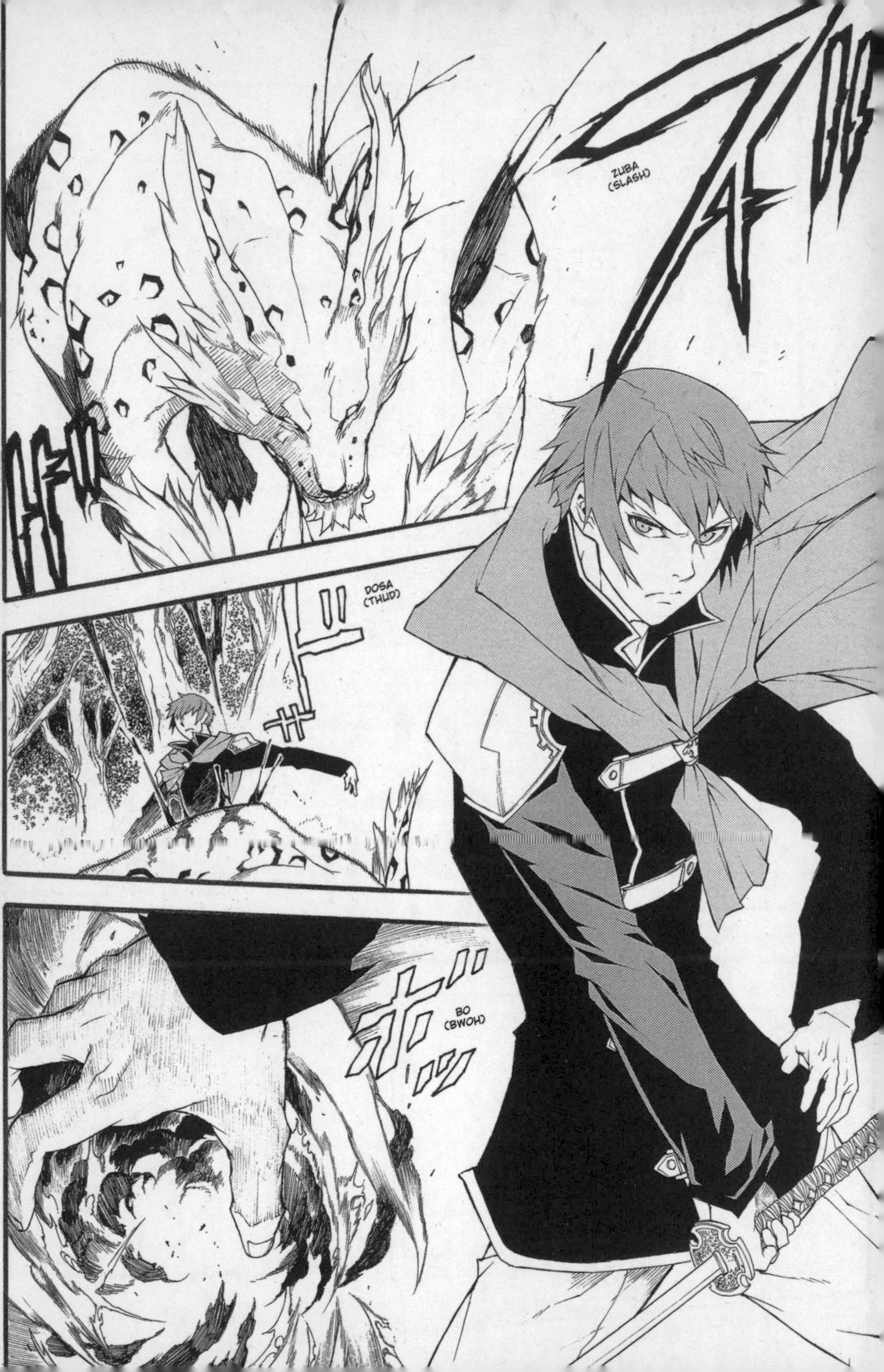
ZUBA (SLASH)
DOSA (THUD)
BO (BWOH)

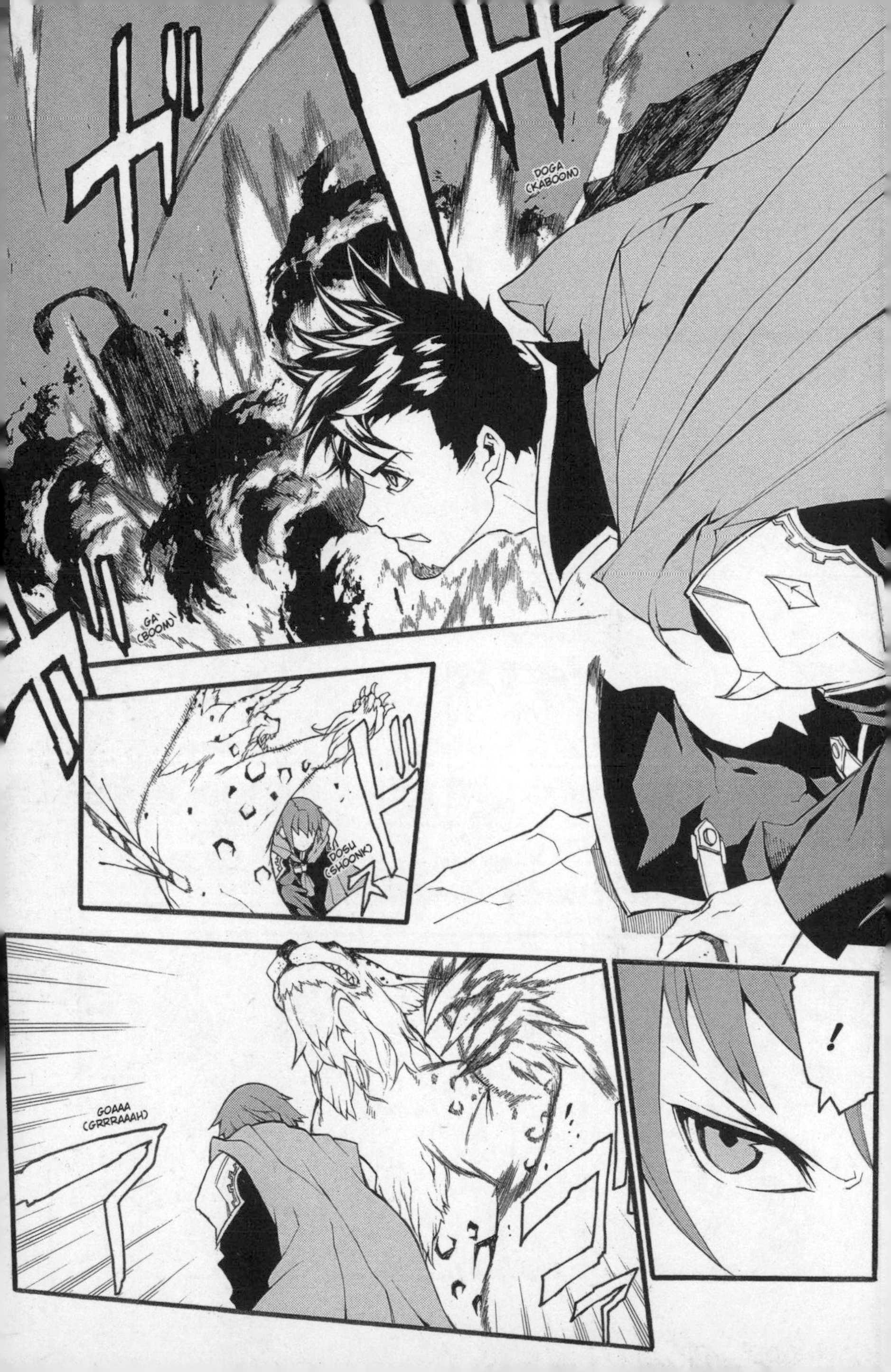
DOGA (KABOOM)
GA (BOOM)
DOGU (SHOONK)
!
GOAAA (GRRRAAAH)

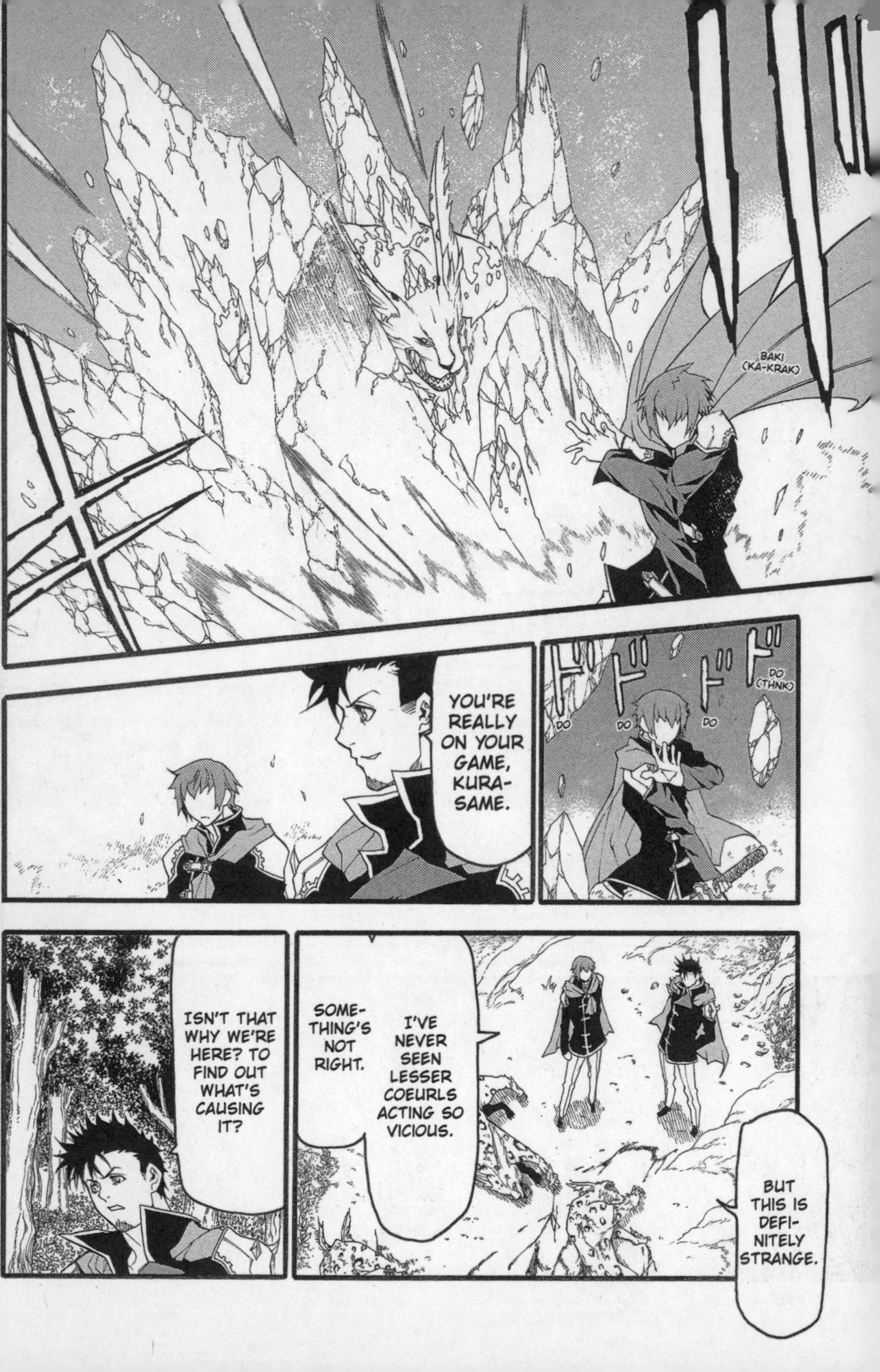
BAKI (KA-KRAK)
DO (THNK)
DO
DO
DO
YOU'RE REALLY ON YOUR GAME, KURA-SAME.
SOME-THING'S NOT RIGHT. I'VE NEVER SEEN LESSER COEURLS ACTING SO VICIOUS.
BUT THIS IS DEFI-NITELY STRANGE.
ISN'T THAT WHY WE'RE HERE? TO FIND OUT WHAT'S CAUSING IT?

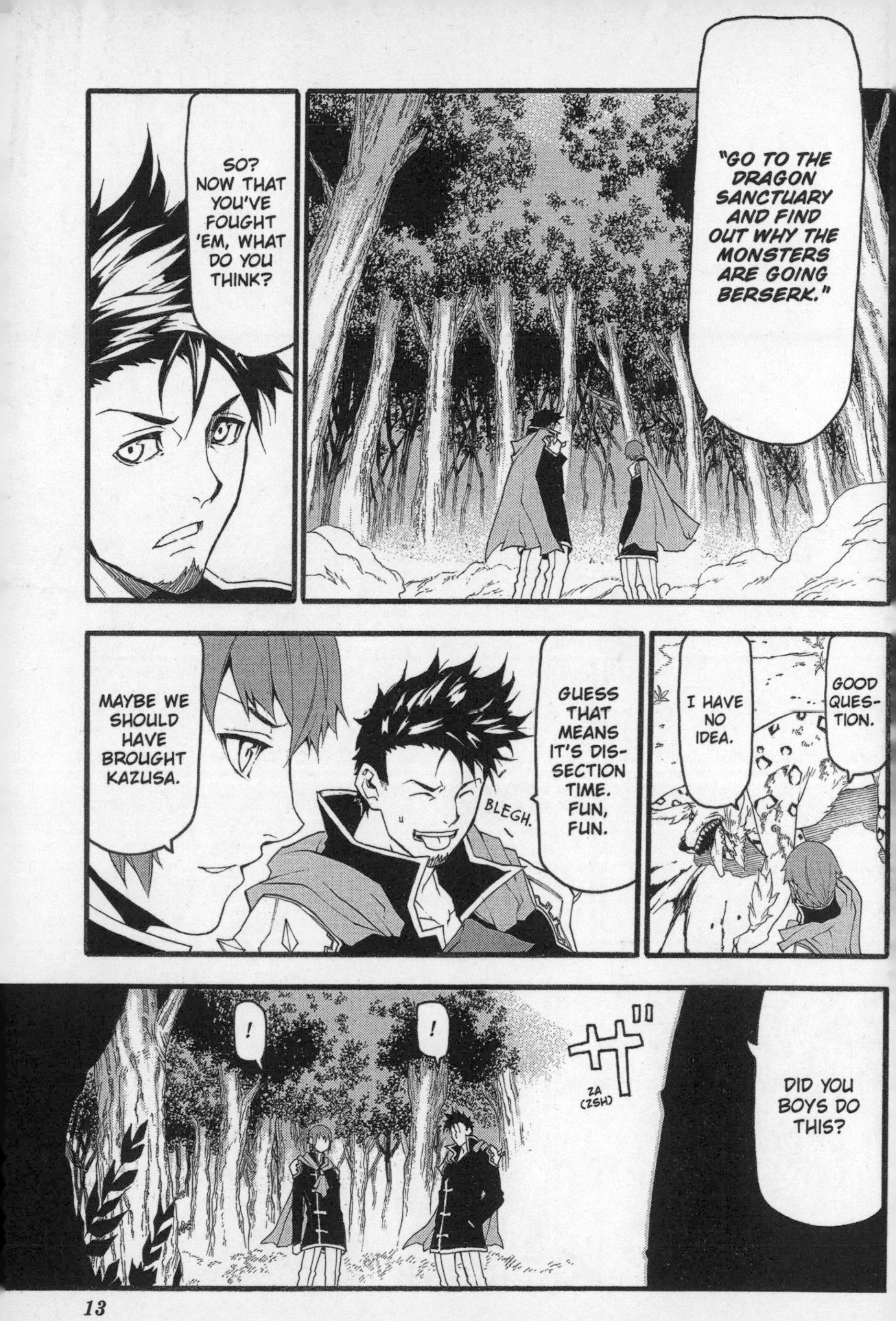
"GO TO THE DRAGON SANCTUARY AND FIND OUT WHY THE MONSTERS ARE GOING BERSERK."
SO? NOW THAT YOU'VE FOUGHT 'EM, WHAT DO YOU THINK?
GOOD QUES-TION.
I HAVE NO IDEA.
GUESS THAT MEANS IT'S DIS-SECTION TIME. FUN, FUN.
BLEGH.
MAYBE WE SHOULD HAVE BROUGHT KAZUSA.
DID YOU BOYS DO THIS?
ZA (ZSH)
!
!

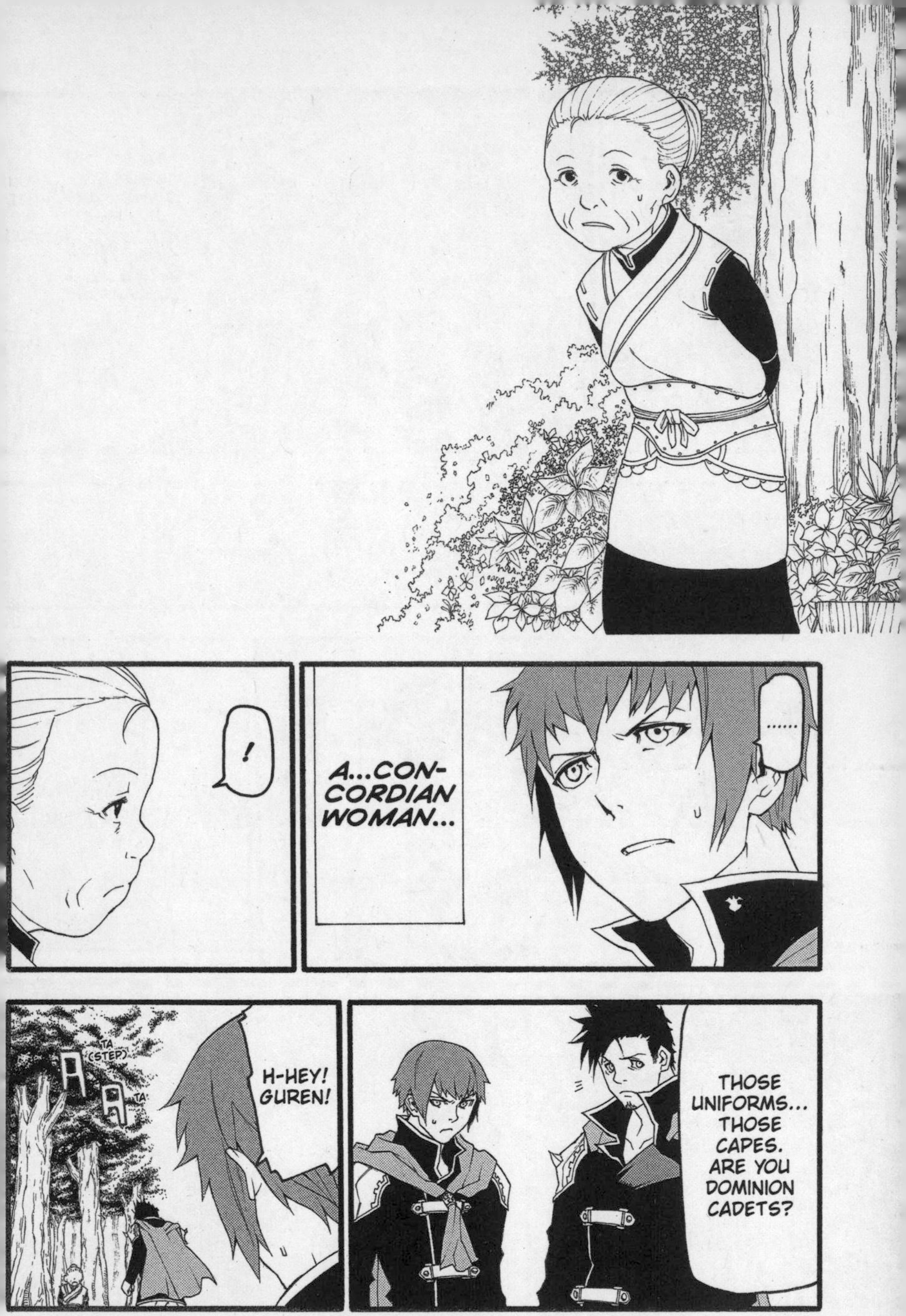
......
A...CON-CORDIAN WOMAN...
!
THOSE UNIFORMS... THOSE CAPES. ARE YOU DOMINION CADETS?
H-HEY! GUREN!
TA (STEP)
TA

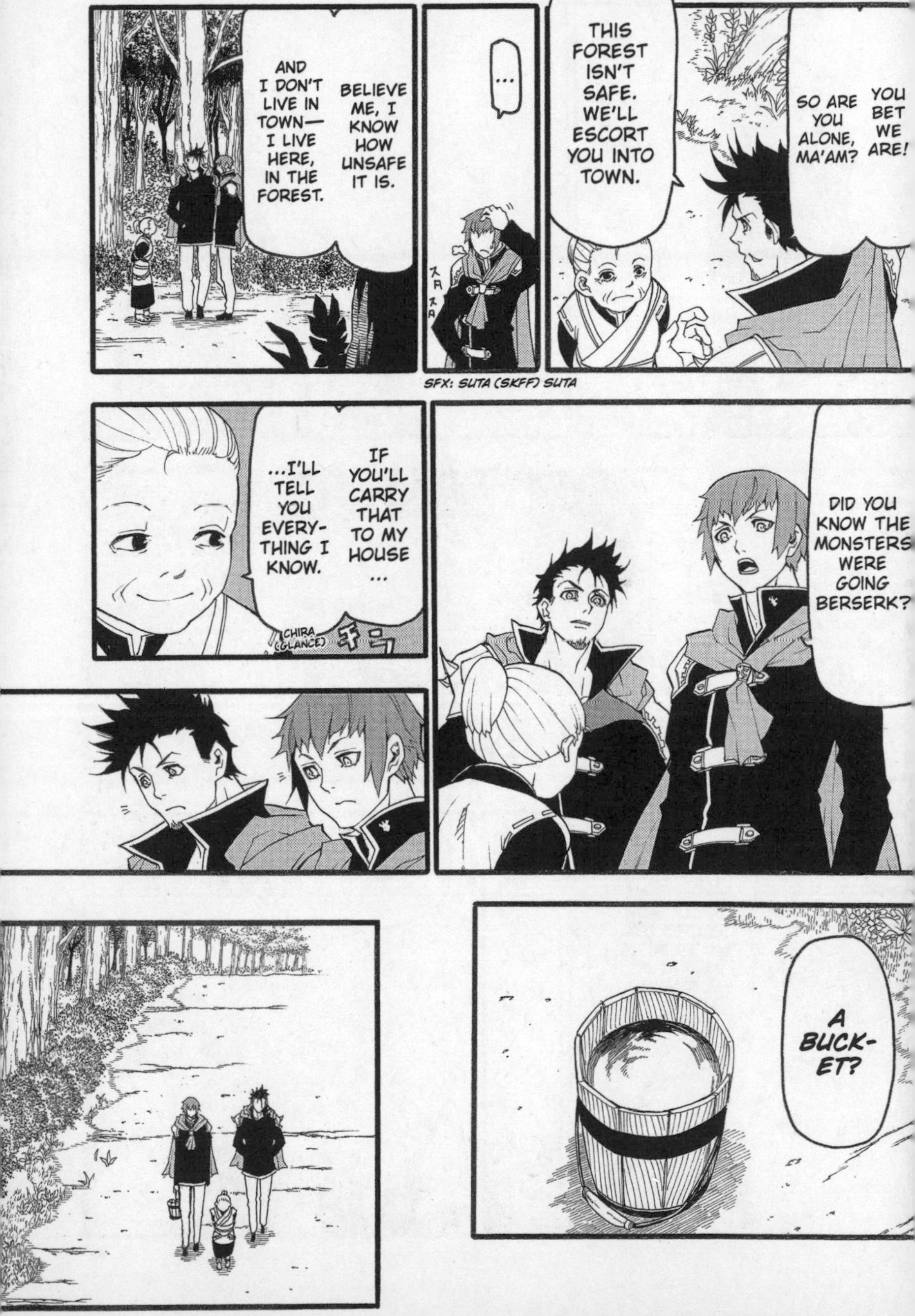
YOU BET WE ARE!
SO ARE YOU ALONE, MA'AM?
THIS FOREST ISN'T SAFE. WE'LL ESCORT YOU INTO TOWN.
...
SFX: SUTA (SKFF) SUTA
BELIEVE ME, I KNOW HOW UNSAFE IT IS.
AND I DON'T LIVE IN TOWN— I LIVE HERE, IN THE FOREST.
DID YOU KNOW THE MONSTERS WERE GOING BERSERK?
IF YOU'LL CARRY THAT TO MY HOUSE ...
...I'LL TELL YOU EVERYTHING I KNOW.
CHIRA (GLANCE)
A BUCKET?

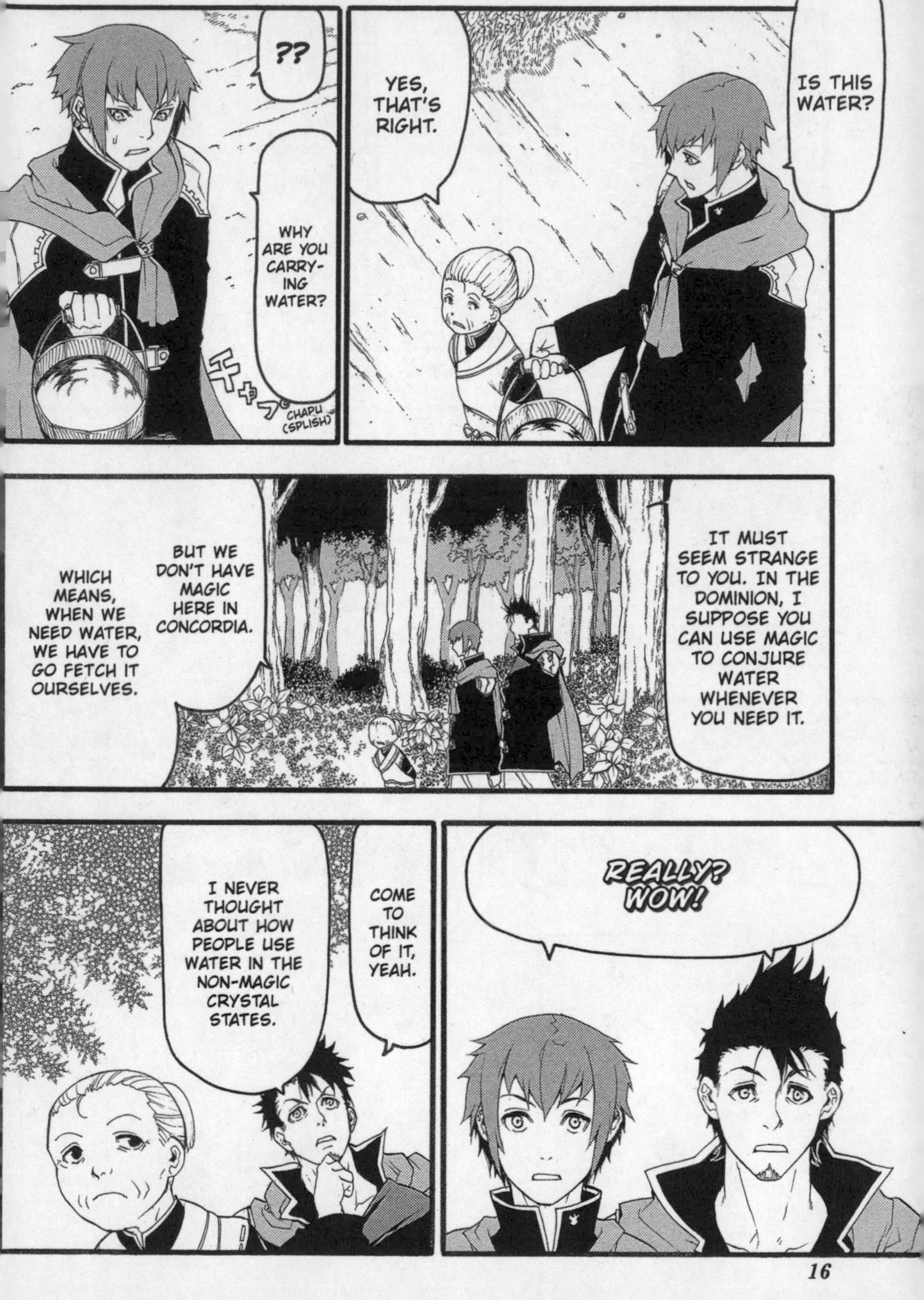
IS THIS WATER?
YES, THAT'S RIGHT.
??
WHY ARE YOU CARRY-ING WATER?
チャプ
CHAPU (SPLISH)
IT MUST SEEM STRANGE TO YOU. IN THE DOMINION, I SUPPOSE YOU CAN USE MAGIC TO CONJURE WATER WHENEVER YOU NEED IT.
BUT WE DON'T HAVE MAGIC HERE IN CONCORDIA.
WHICH MEANS, WHEN WE NEED WATER, WE HAVE TO GO FETCH IT OURSELVES.
REALLY? WOW!
COME TO THINK OF IT, YEAH.
I NEVER THOUGHT ABOUT HOW PEOPLE USE WATER IN THE NON-MAGIC CRYSTAL STATES.

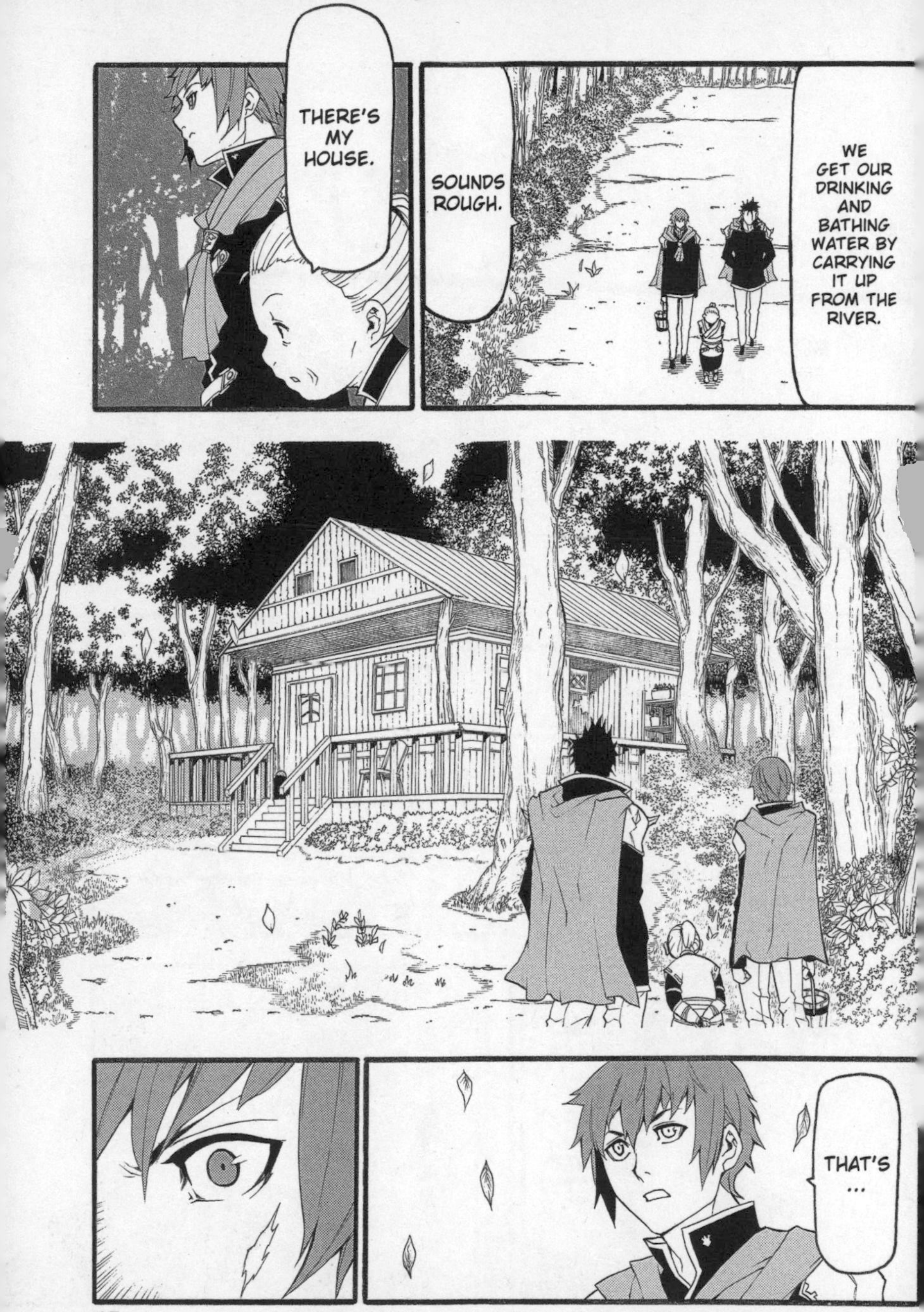
WE GET OUR DRINKING AND BATHING WATER BY CARRYING IT UP FROM THE RIVER.
SOUNDS ROUGH.
THERE'S MY HOUSE.
THAT'S ...

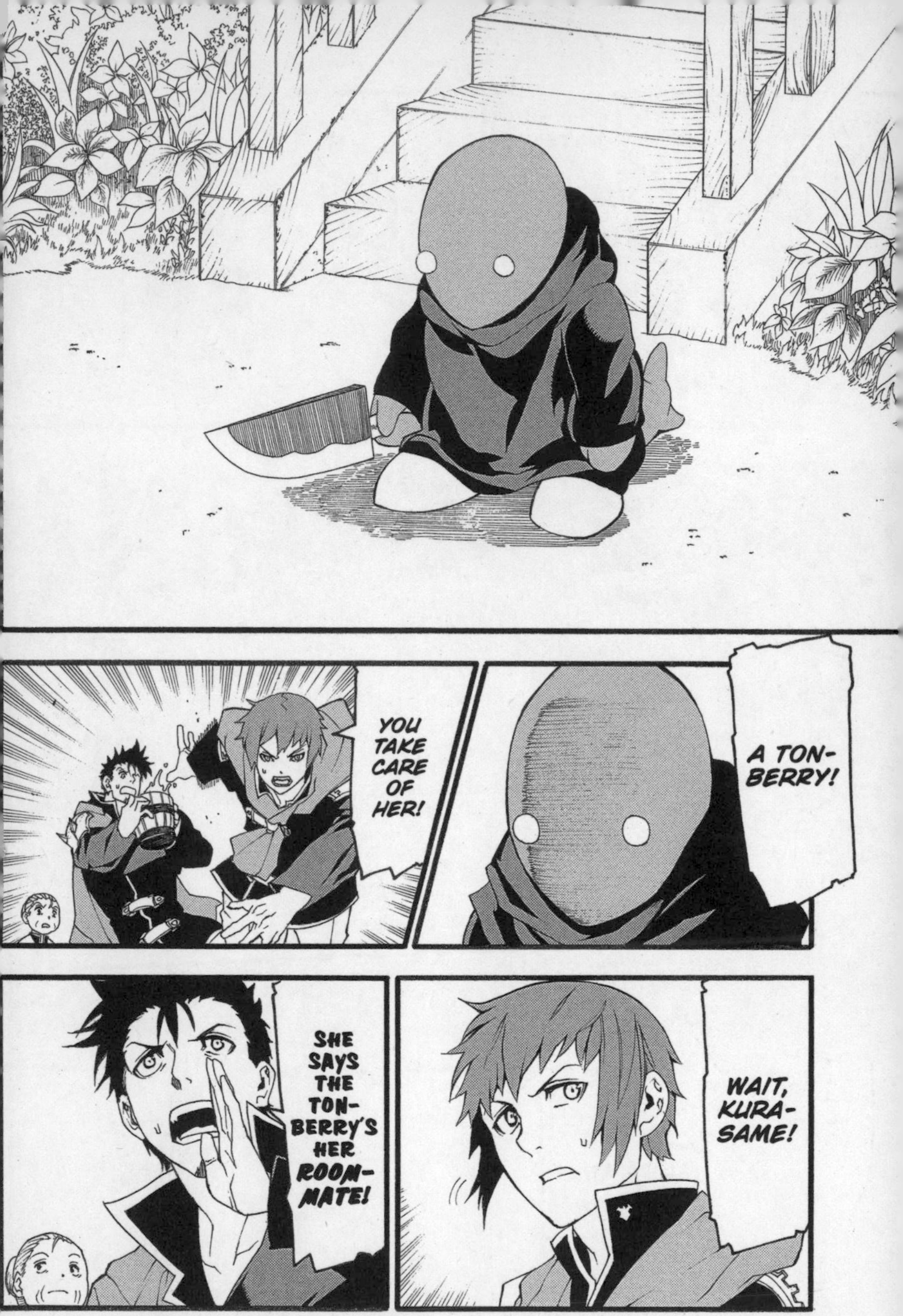
A TON-BERRY!
YOU TAKE CARE OF HER!
WAIT, KURA-SAME!
SHE SAYS THE TON-BERRY'S HER ROOM-MATE!

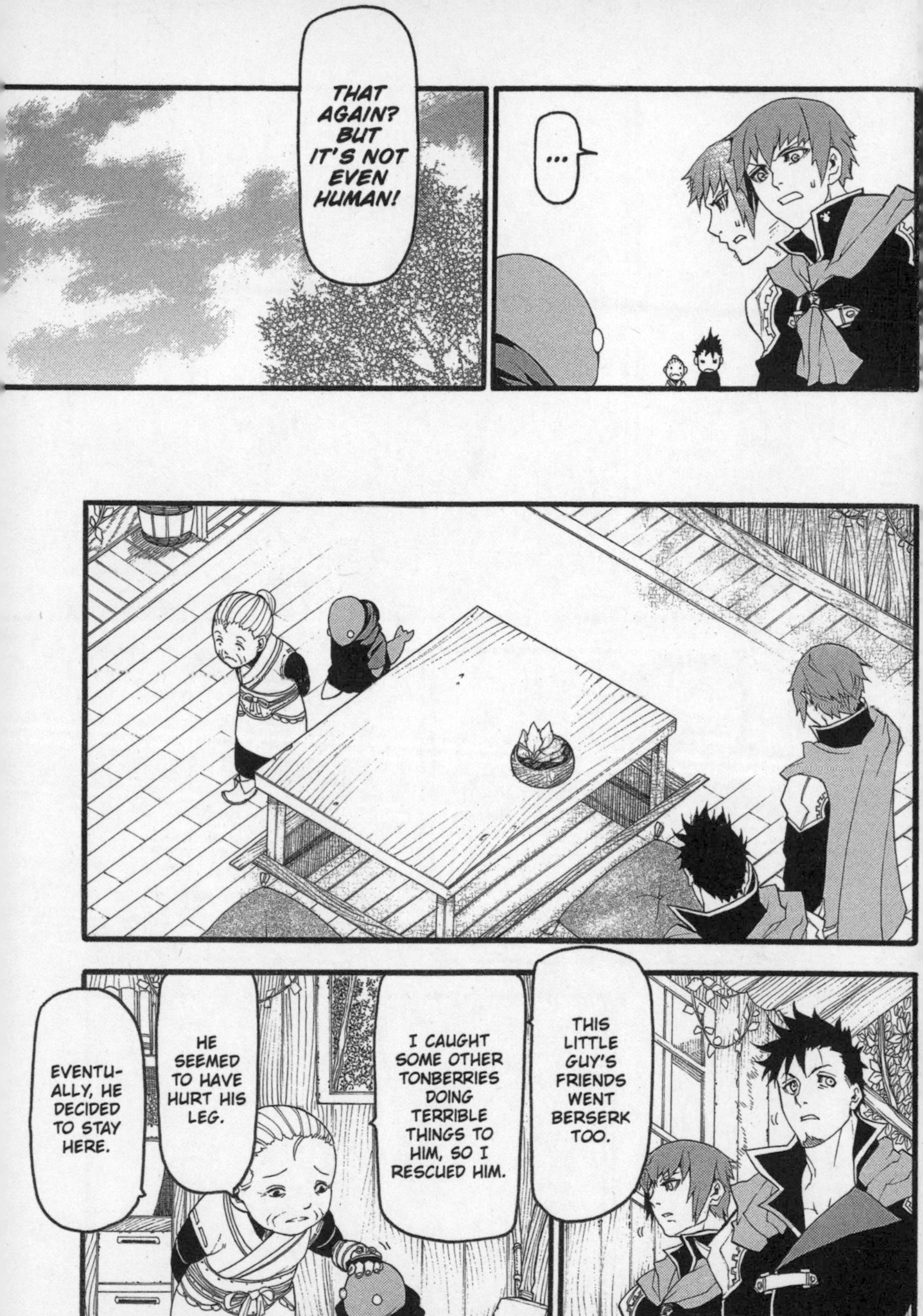
...
THAT AGAIN? BUT IT'S NOT EVEN HUMAN!
THIS LITTLE GUY'S FRIENDS WENT BERSERK TOO.
I CAUGHT SOME OTHER TONBERRIES DOING TERRIBLE THINGS TO HIM, SO I RESCUED HIM.
HE SEEMED TO HAVE HURT HIS LEG.
EVENTU-ALLY, HE DECIDED TO STAY HERE.

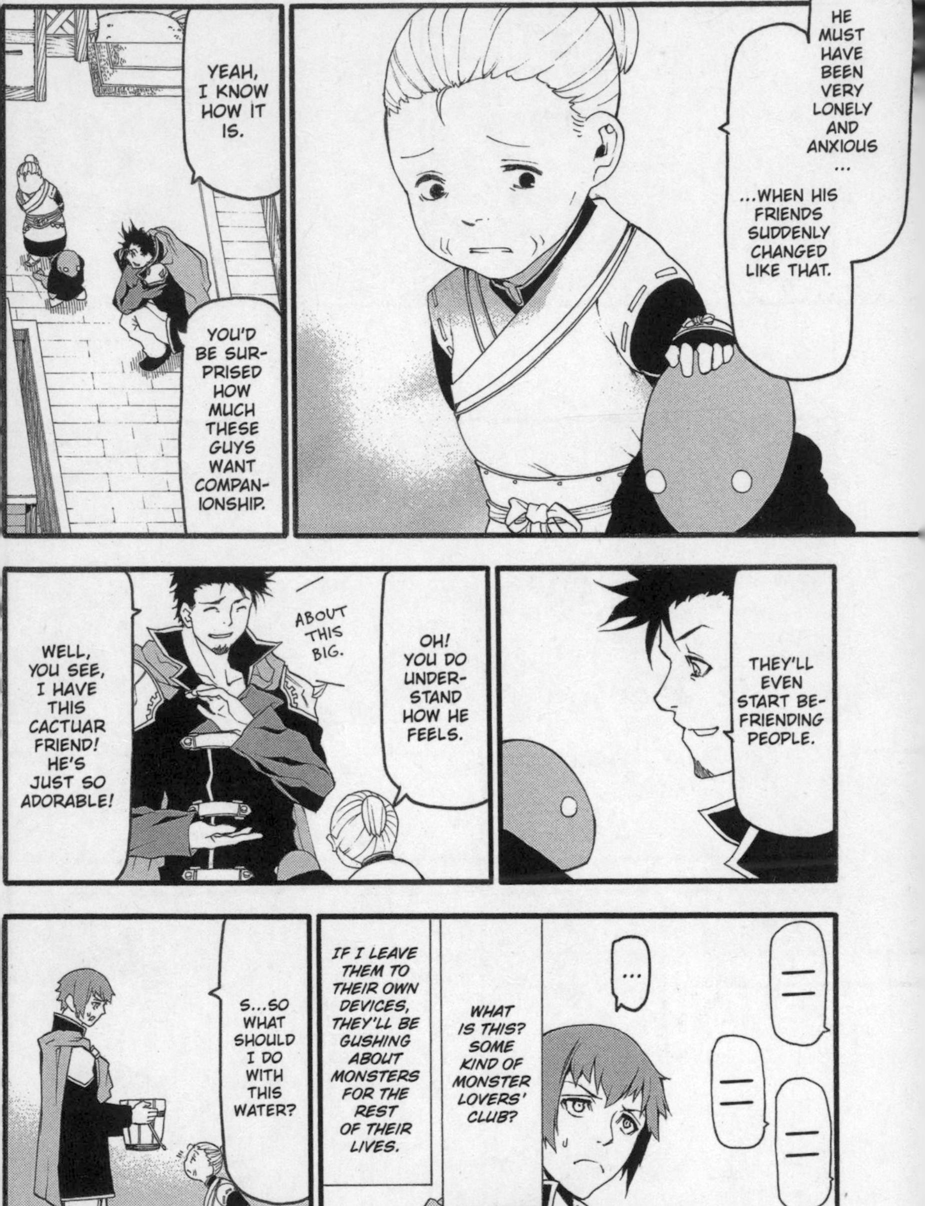
HE MUST HAVE BEEN VERY LONELY AND ANXIOUS...
...WHEN HIS FRIENDS SUDDENLY CHANGED LIKE THAT.
YEAH, I KNOW HOW IT IS.
YOU'D BE SURPRISED HOW MUCH THESE GUYS WANT COMPANIONSHIP.
THEY'LL EVEN START BEFRIENDING PEOPLE.
OH! YOU DO UNDERSTAND HOW HE FEELS.
ABOUT THIS BIG.
WELL, YOU SEE, I HAVE THIS CACTUAR FRIEND! HE'S JUST SO ADORABLE!
...
WHAT IS THIS? SOME KIND OF MONSTER LOVERS' CLUB?
IF I LEAVE THEM TO THEIR OWN DEVICES, THEY'LL BE GUSHING ABOUT MONSTERS FOR THE REST OF THEIR LIVES.
S...SO WHAT SHOULD I DO WITH THIS WATER?

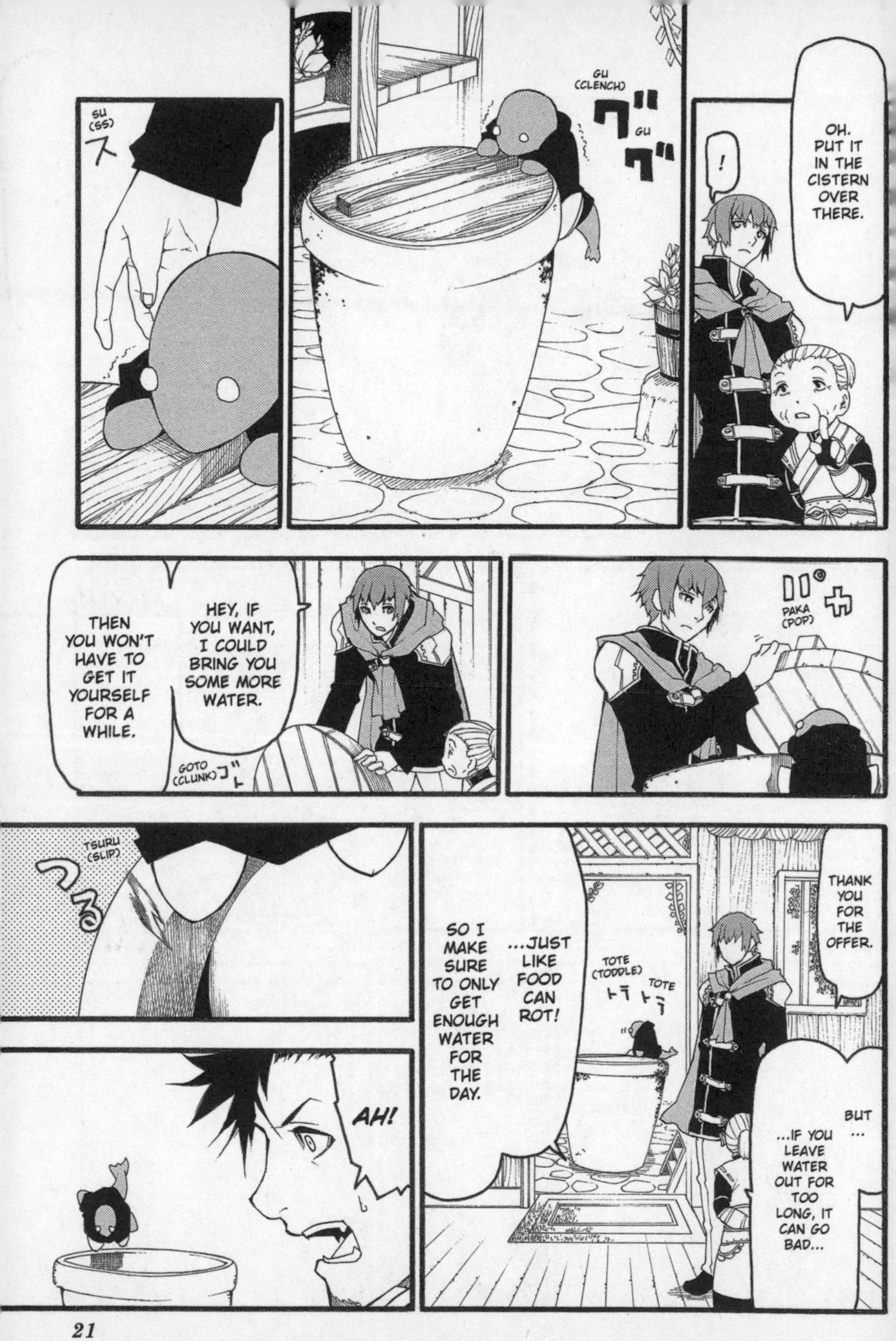
!
OH. PUT IT IN THE CISTERN OVER THERE.
GU (CLENCH) グ
GU グ
SU (SS) ス
PAKA (POP)
HEY, IF YOU WANT, I COULD BRING YOU SOME MORE WATER.
THEN YOU WON'T HAVE TO GET IT YOURSELF FOR A WHILE.
GOTO (CLUNK) ゴト
THANK YOU FOR THE OFFER.
BUT...
...IF YOU LEAVE WATER OUT FOR TOO LONG, IT CAN GO BAD...
TOTE (TODDLE) トテ
TOTE トテ
...JUST LIKE FOOD CAN ROT!
SO I MAKE SURE TO ONLY GET ENOUGH WATER FOR THE DAY.
TSURU (SLIP) つる
AH!

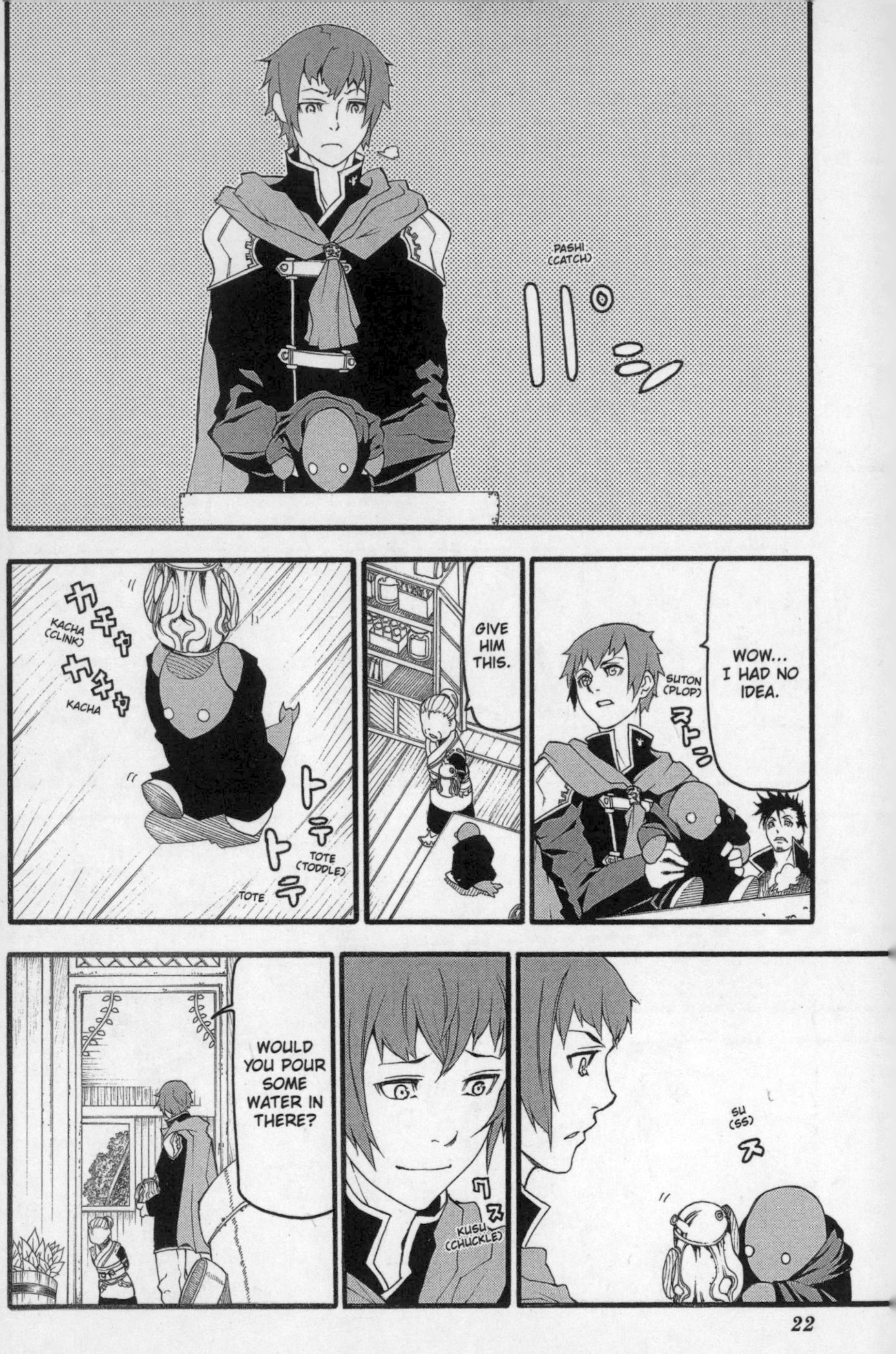
PASHI (CATCH)
WOW... I HAD NO IDEA.
SUTON (PLOP)
GIVE HIM THIS.
KACHA (CLINK)
KACHA
TOTE (TODDLE)
TOTE
SU (SS)
KUSU (CHUCKLE)
WOULD YOU POUR SOME WATER IN THERE?

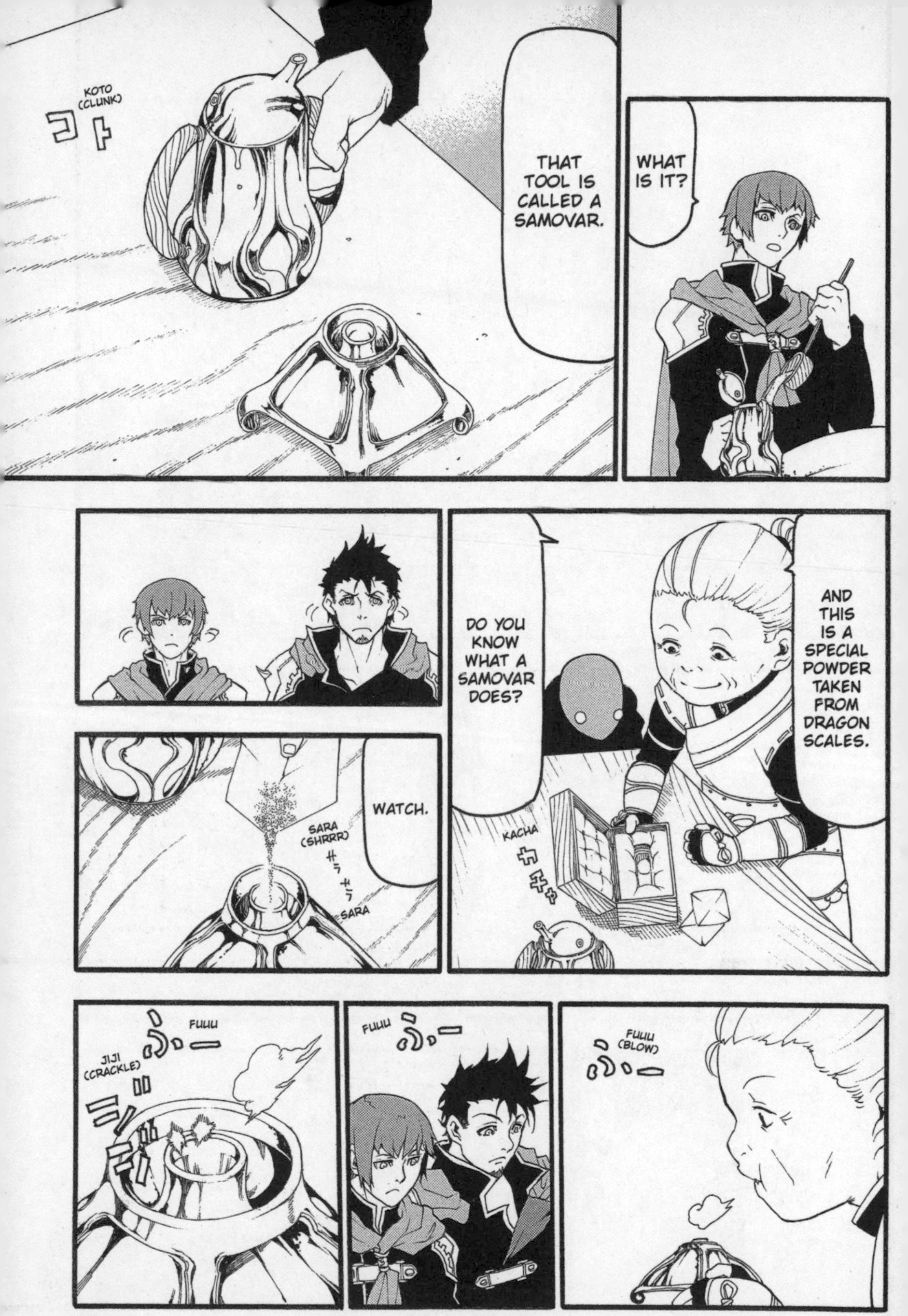
WHAT IS IT?
THAT TOOL IS CALLED A SAMOVAR.
KOTO (CLUNK)
AND THIS IS A SPECIAL POWDER TAKEN FROM DRAGON SCALES.
DO YOU KNOW WHAT A SAMOVAR DOES?
KACHA
WATCH.
SARA (SHRRR)
SARA
FUUU (BLOW)
FUUU
FUUU
JIJI (CRACKLE)

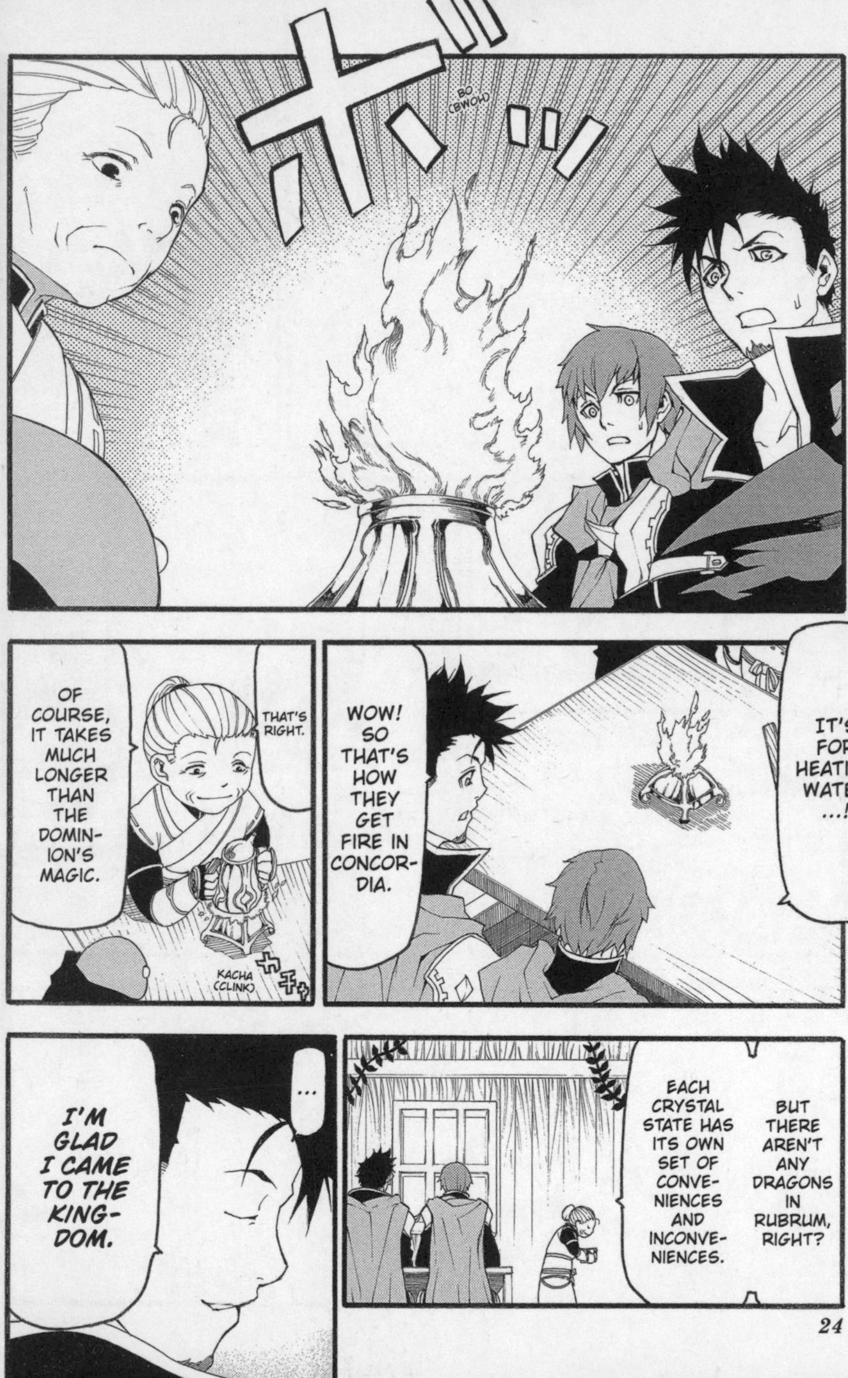
BO (BWOH)
IT'S FOR HEATING WATER ...!
WOW! SO THAT'S HOW THEY GET FIRE IN CONCORDIA.
THAT'S RIGHT.
OF COURSE, IT TAKES MUCH LONGER THAN THE DOMINION'S MAGIC.
KACHA (CLINK)
BUT THERE AREN'T ANY DRAGONS IN RUBRUM, RIGHT?
EACH CRYSTAL STATE HAS ITS OWN SET OF CONVENIENCES AND INCONVENIENCES.
...
I'M GLAD I CAME TO THE KINGDOM.

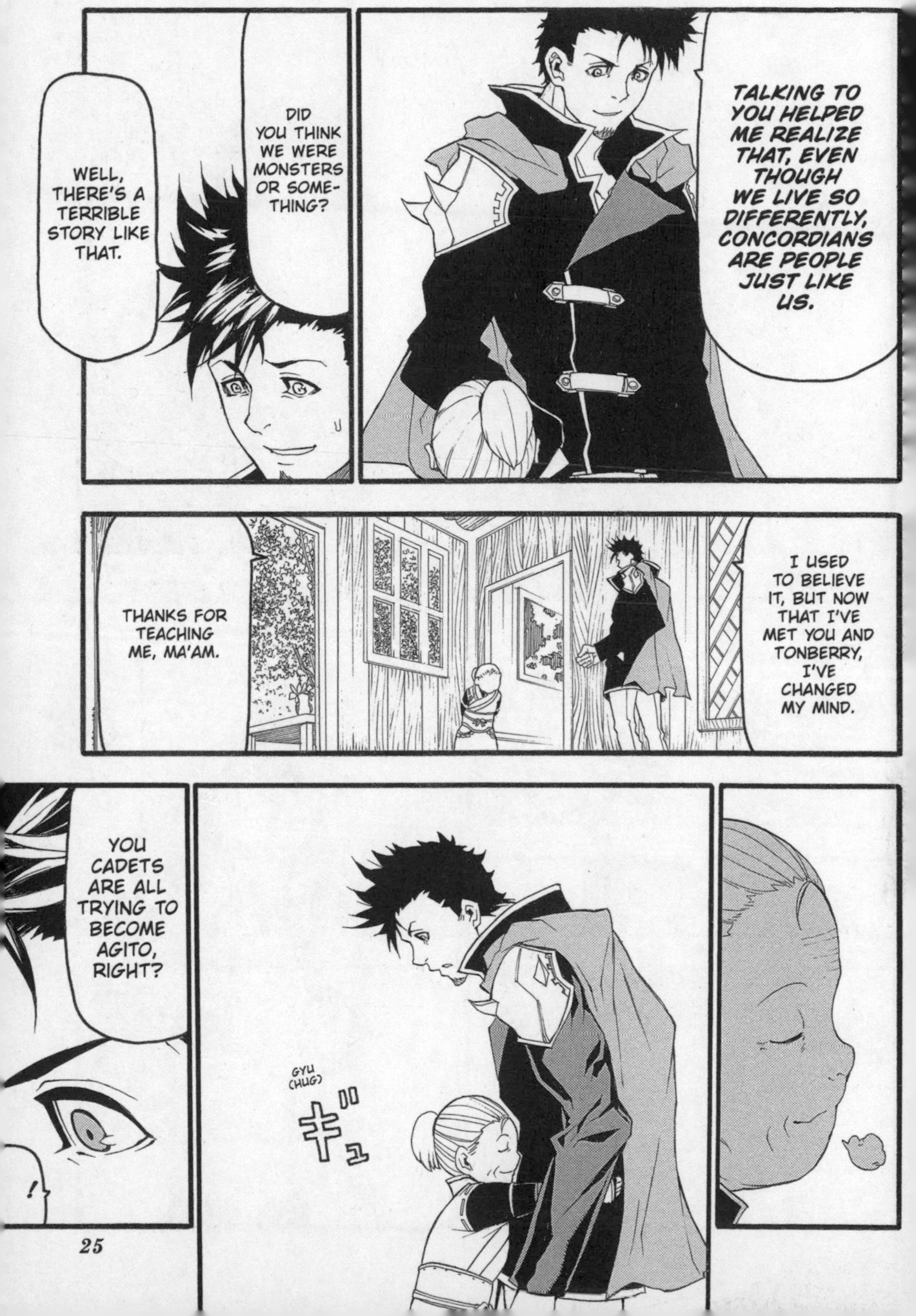
TALKING TO YOU HELPED ME REALIZE THAT, EVEN THOUGH WE LIVE SO DIFFERENTLY, CONCORDIANS ARE PEOPLE JUST LIKE US.
DID YOU THINK WE WERE MONSTERS OR SOME-THING?
WELL, THERE'S A TERRIBLE STORY LIKE THAT.
I USED TO BELIEVE IT, BUT NOW THAT I'VE MET YOU AND TONBERRY, I'VE CHANGED MY MIND.
THANKS FOR TEACHING ME, MA'AM.
GYU (HUG)
YOU CADETS ARE ALL TRYING TO BECOME AGITO, RIGHT?
!

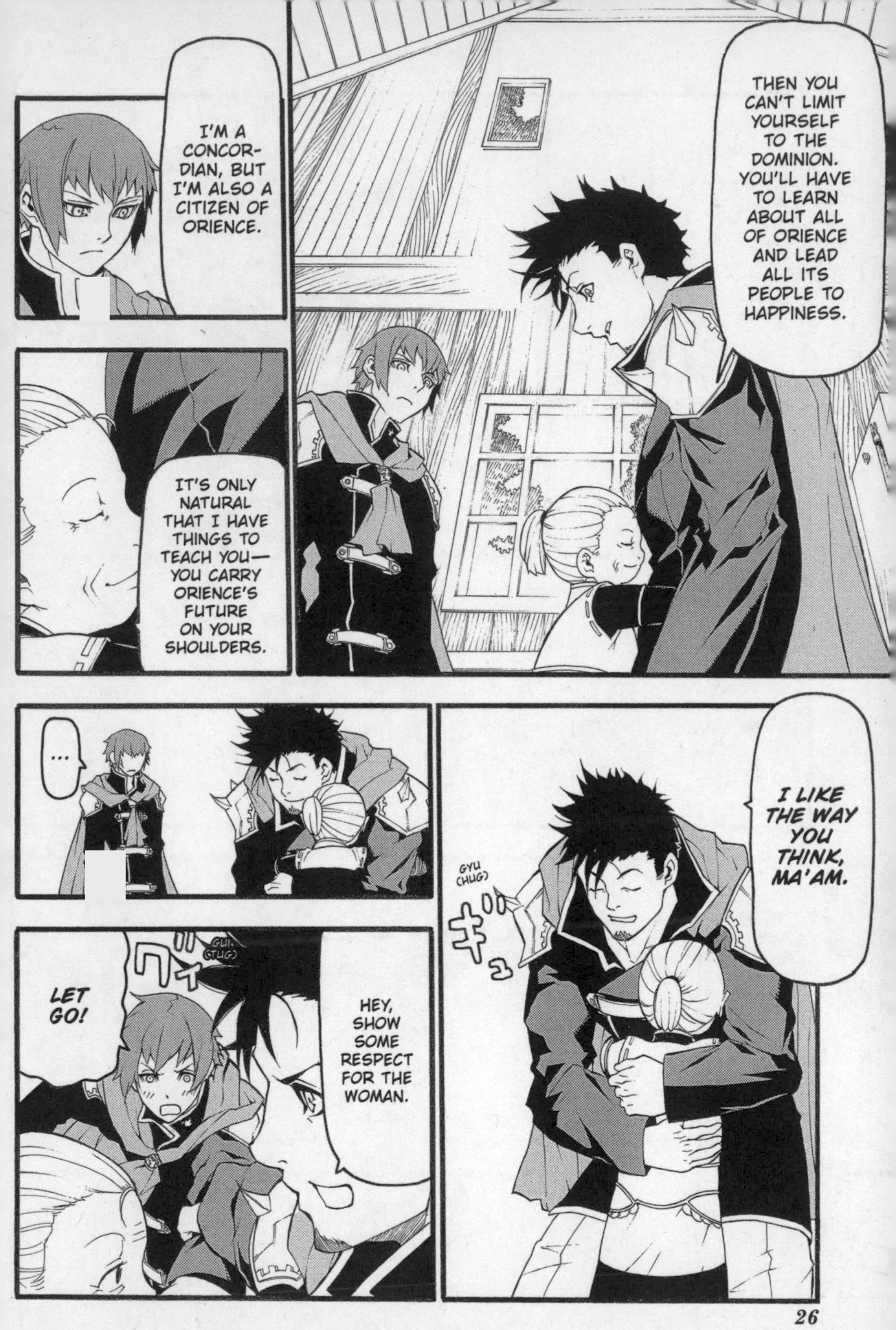
THEN YOU CAN'T LIMIT YOURSELF TO THE DOMINION. YOU'LL HAVE TO LEARN ABOUT ALL OF ORIENCE AND LEAD ALL ITS PEOPLE TO HAPPINESS.
I'M A CONCORDIAN, BUT I'M ALSO A CITIZEN OF ORIENCE.
IT'S ONLY NATURAL THAT I HAVE THINGS TO TEACH YOU—YOU CARRY ORIENCE'S FUTURE ON YOUR SHOULDERS.
I LIKE THE WAY YOU THINK, MA'AM.
GYU (HUG)
...
GUI (TUG)
HEY, SHOW SOME RESPECT FOR THE WOMAN.
LET GO!

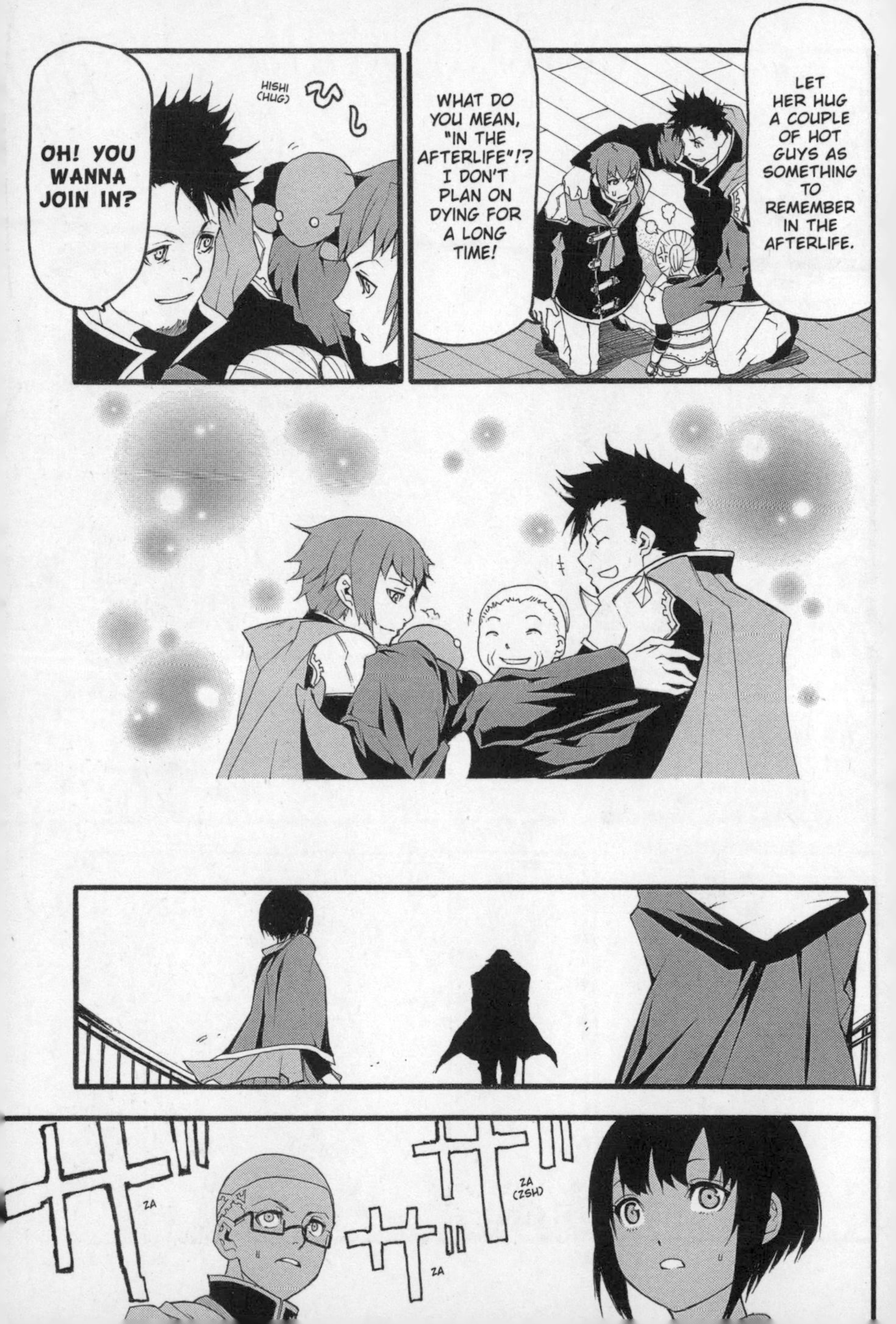
LET HER HUG A COUPLE OF HOT GUYS AS SOMETHING TO REMEMBER IN THE AFTERLIFE.
WHAT DO YOU MEAN, "IN THE AFTERLIFE"!? I DON'T PLAN ON DYING FOR A LONG TIME!
HISHI (HUG)
OH! YOU WANNA JOIN IN?
ZA (ZSH)
ZA
ZA

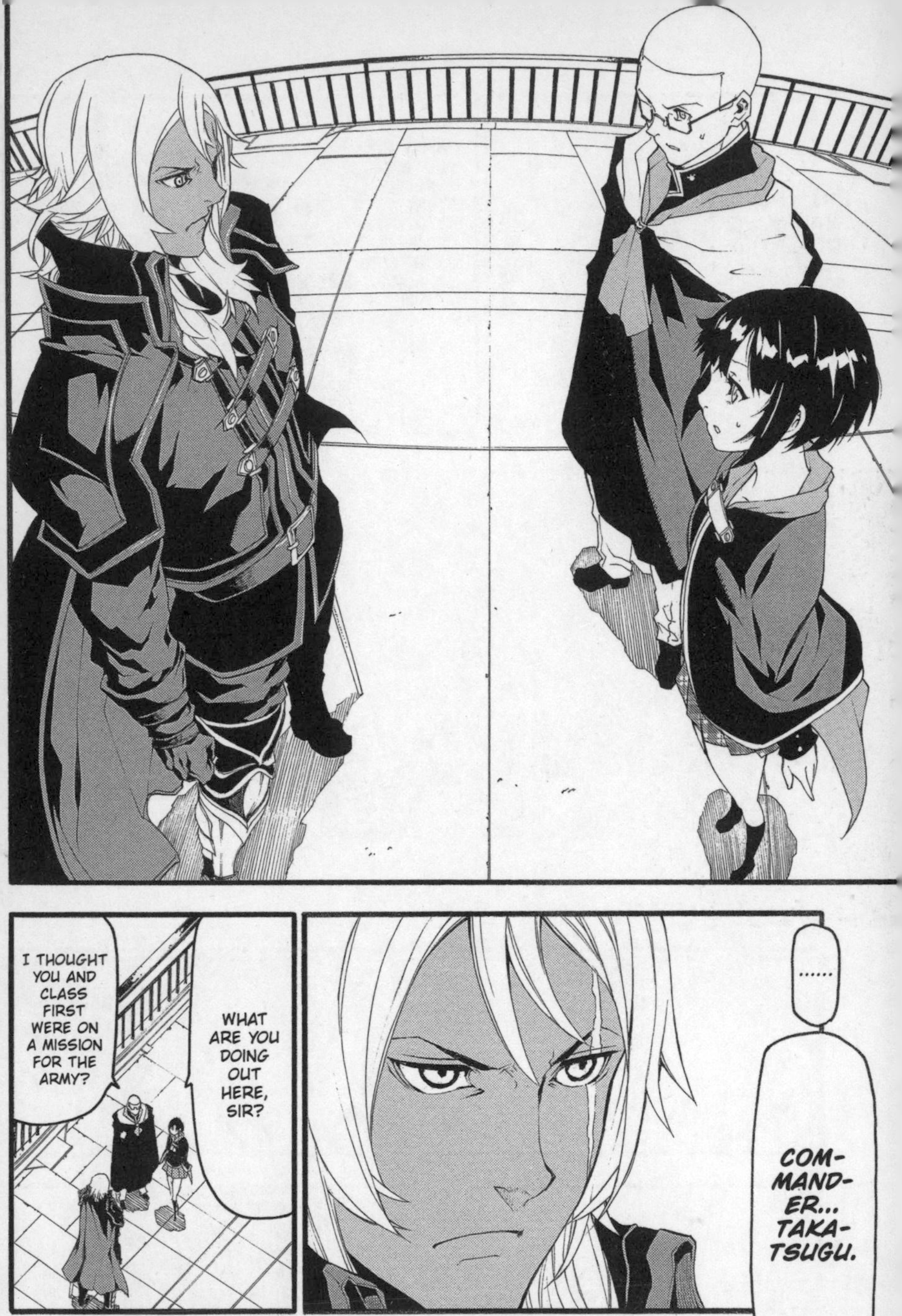
......
COMMANDER... TAKATSUGU.
WHAT ARE YOU DOING OUT HERE, SIR?
I THOUGHT YOU AND CLASS FIRST WERE ON A MISSION FOR THE ARMY?

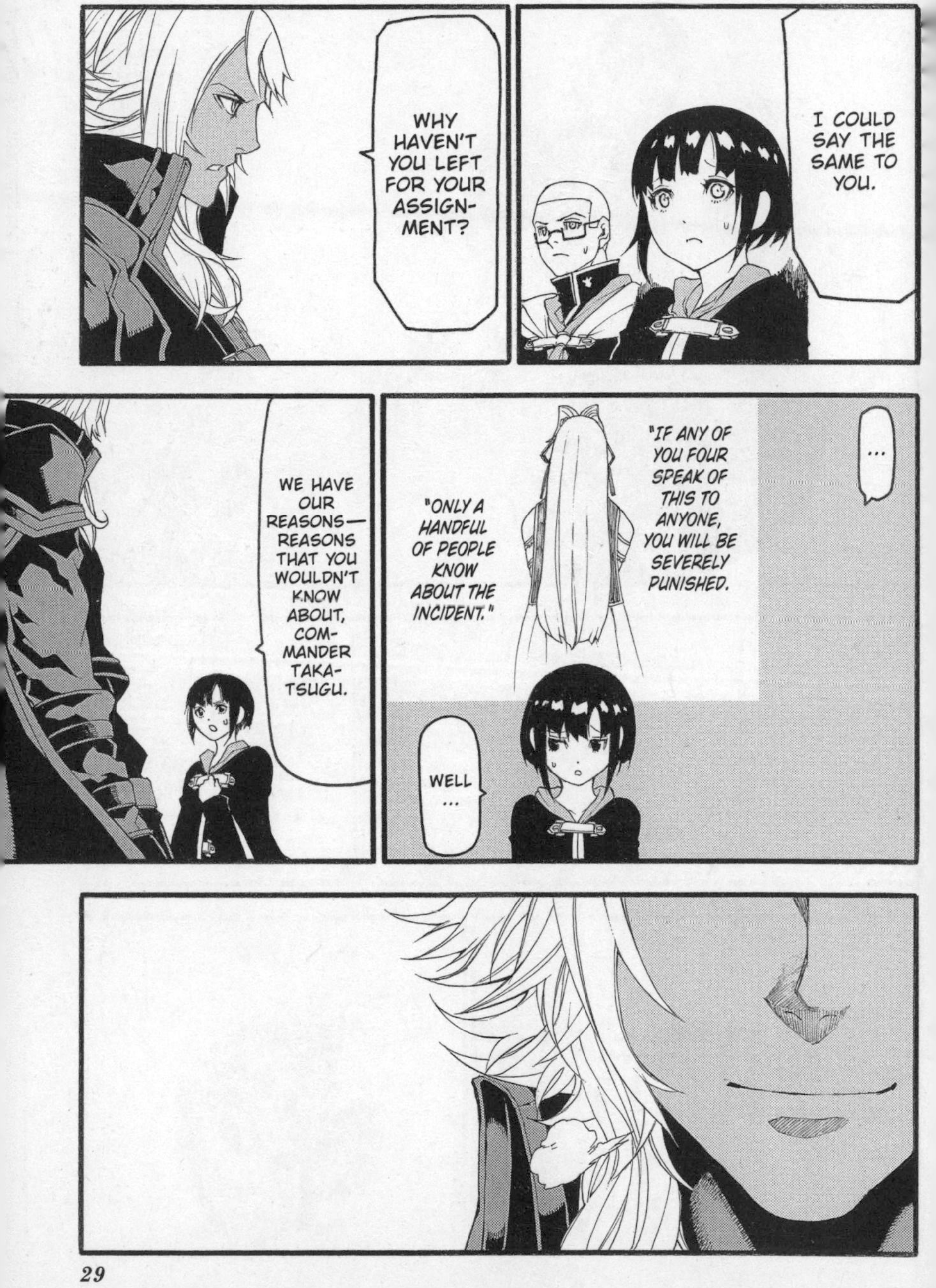
WHY HAVEN'T YOU LEFT FOR YOUR ASSIGNMENT?
I COULD SAY THE SAME TO YOU.
WE HAVE OUR REASONS—REASONS THAT YOU WOULDN'T KNOW ABOUT, COMMANDER TAKATSUGU.
"ONLY A HANDFUL OF PEOPLE KNOW ABOUT THE INCIDENT."
"IF ANY OF YOU FOUR SPEAK OF THIS TO ANYONE, YOU WILL BE SEVERELY PUNISHED.
...
WELL ...

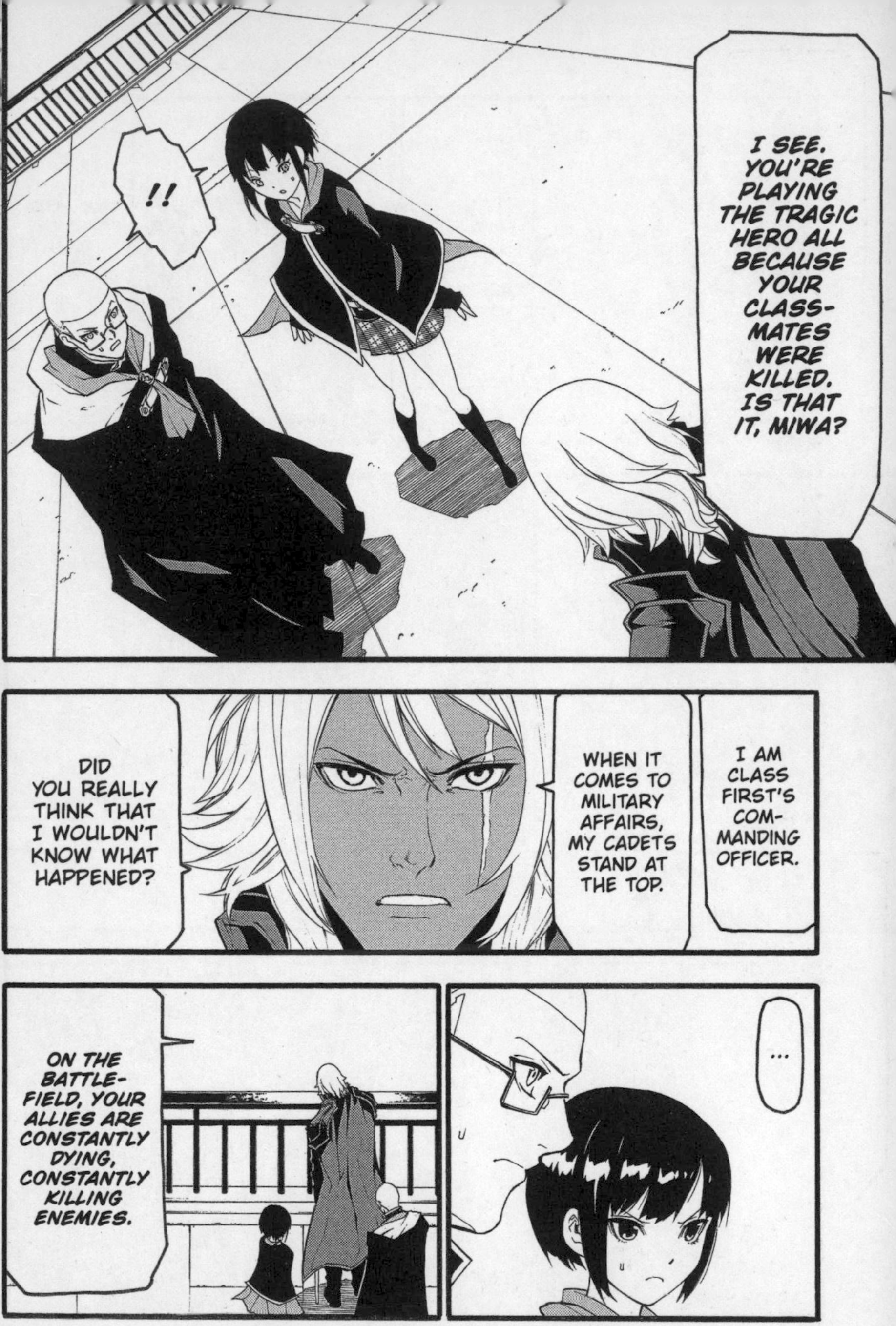
I SEE. YOU'RE PLAYING THE TRAGIC HERO ALL BECAUSE YOUR CLASS-MATES WERE KILLED. IS THAT IT, MIWA?
!!
I AM CLASS FIRST'S COM-MANDING OFFICER.
WHEN IT COMES TO MILITARY AFFAIRS, MY CADETS STAND AT THE TOP.
DID YOU REALLY THINK THAT I WOULDN'T KNOW WHAT HAPPENED?
...
ON THE BATTLE-FIELD, YOUR ALLIES ARE CONSTANTLY DYING, CONSTANTLY KILLING ENEMIES.

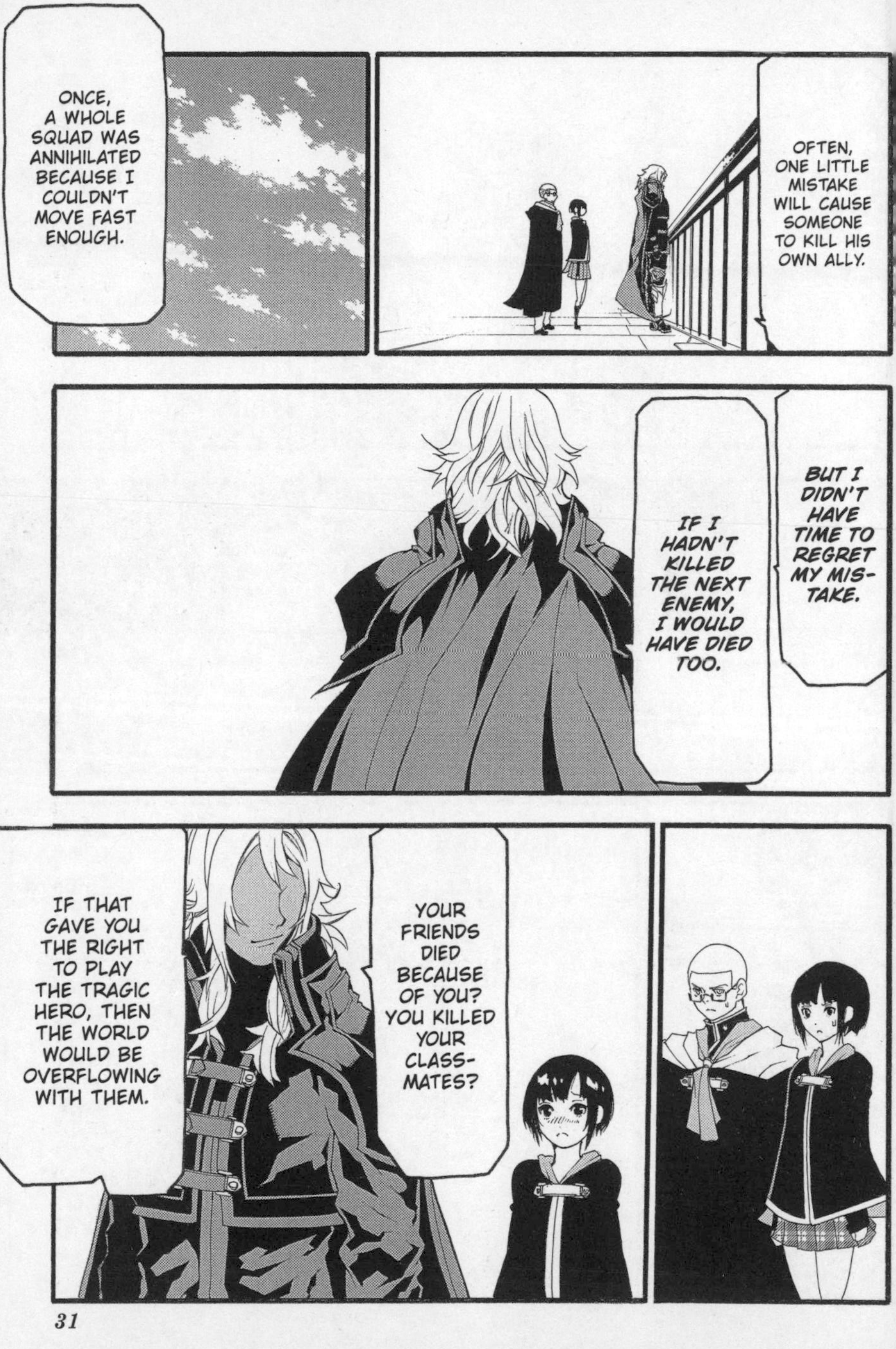
OFTEN, ONE LITTLE MISTAKE WILL CAUSE SOMEONE TO KILL HIS OWN ALLY.
ONCE, A WHOLE SQUAD WAS ANNIHILATED BECAUSE I COULDN'T MOVE FAST ENOUGH.
BUT I DIDN'T HAVE TIME TO REGRET MY MIS-TAKE.
IF I HADN'T KILLED THE NEXT ENEMY, I WOULD HAVE DIED TOO.
YOUR FRIENDS DIED BECAUSE OF YOU? YOU KILLED YOUR CLASS-MATES?
IF THAT GAVE YOU THE RIGHT TO PLAY THE TRAGIC HERO, THEN THE WORLD WOULD BE OVERFLOWING WITH THEM.

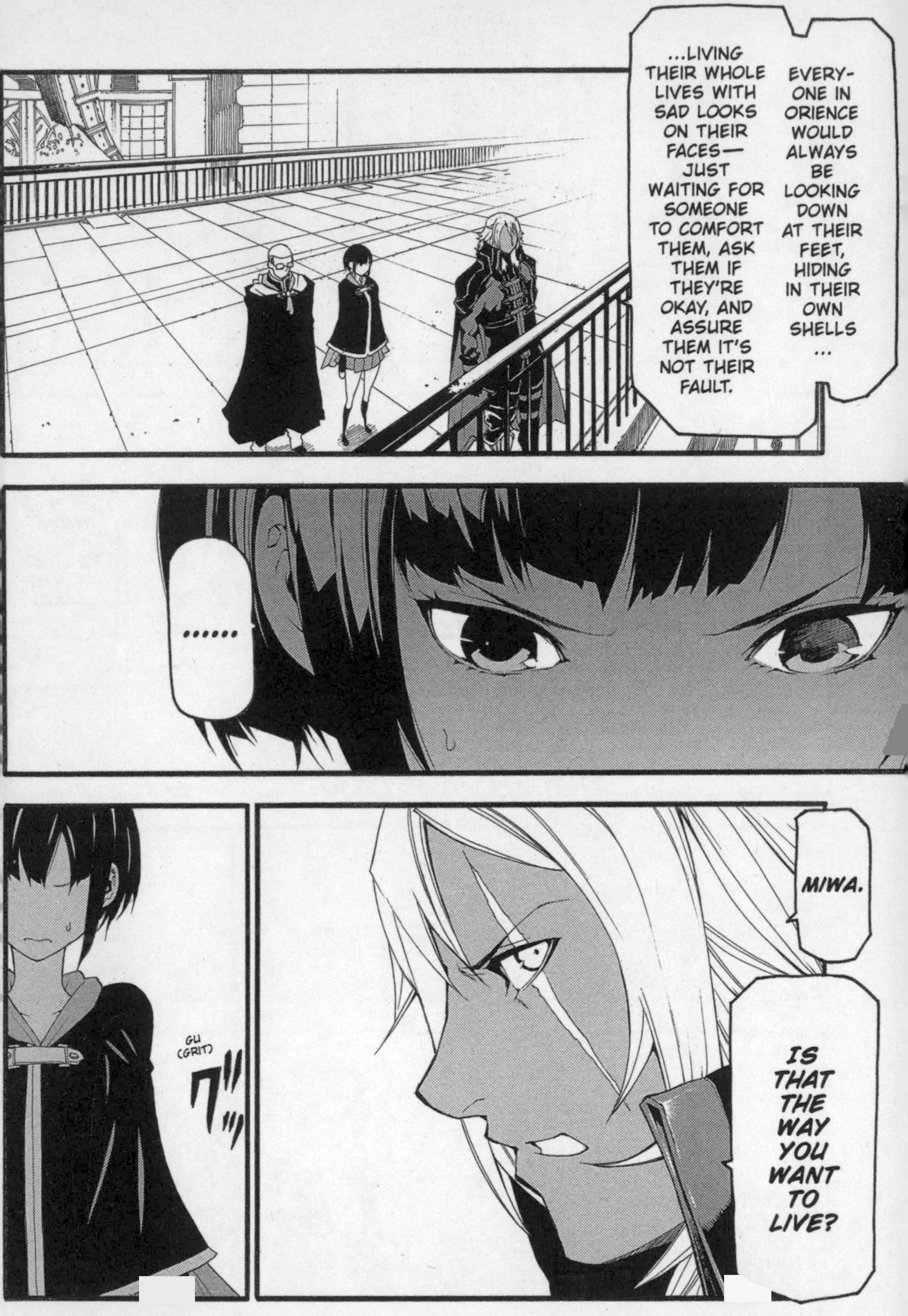
EVERYONE IN ORIENCE WOULD ALWAYS BE LOOKING DOWN AT THEIR FEET, HIDING IN THEIR OWN SHELLS...
...LIVING THEIR WHOLE LIVES WITH SAD LOOKS ON THEIR FACES—JUST WAITING FOR SOMEONE TO COMFORT THEM, ASK THEM IF THEY'RE OKAY, AND ASSURE THEM IT'S NOT THEIR FAULT.
......
MIWA.
IS THAT THE WAY YOU WANT TO LIVE?
GU (GRIT)

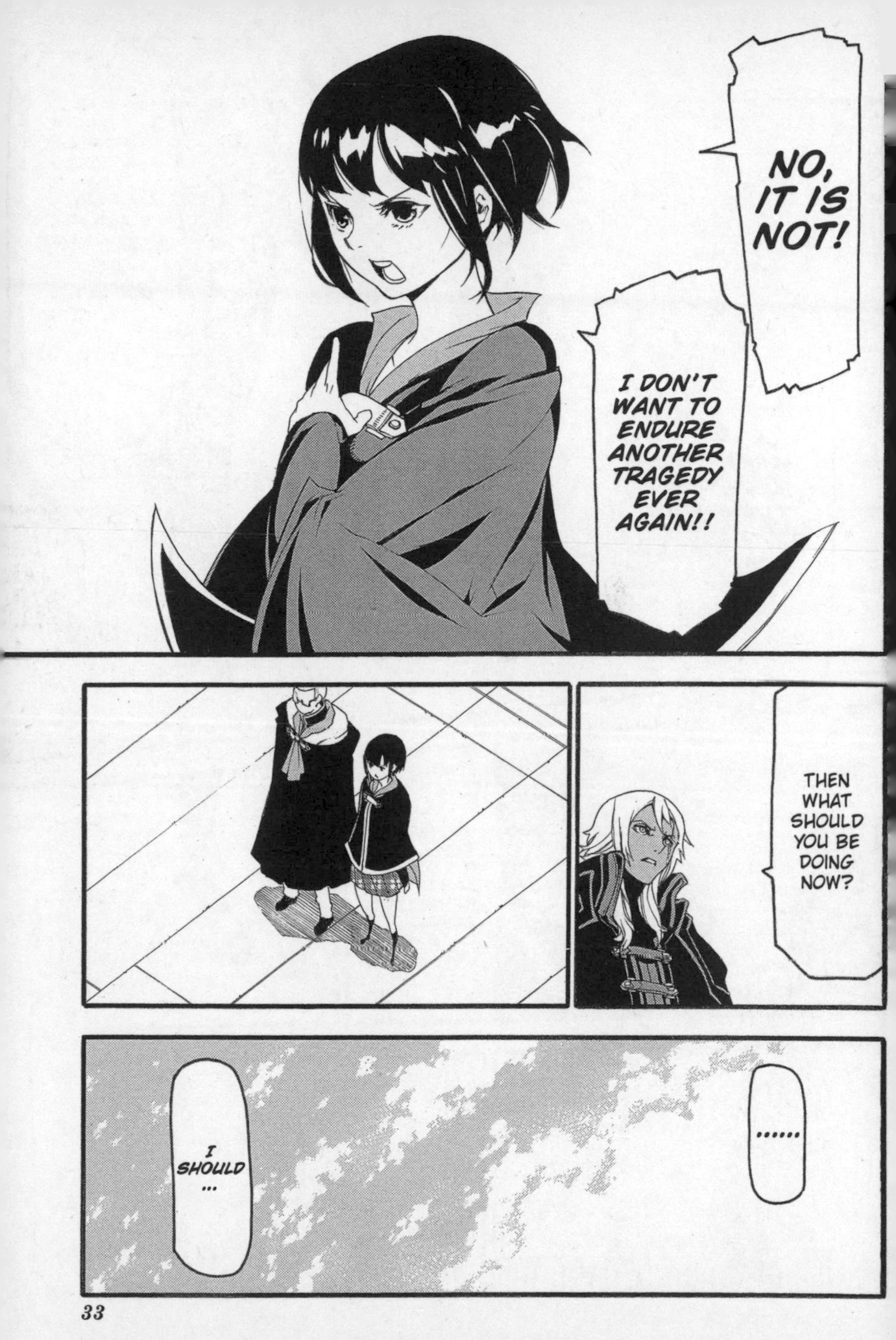
NO, IT IS NOT!
I DON'T WANT TO ENDURE ANOTHER TRAGEDY EVER AGAIN!!
THEN WHAT SHOULD YOU BE DOING NOW?
......
I SHOULD ...

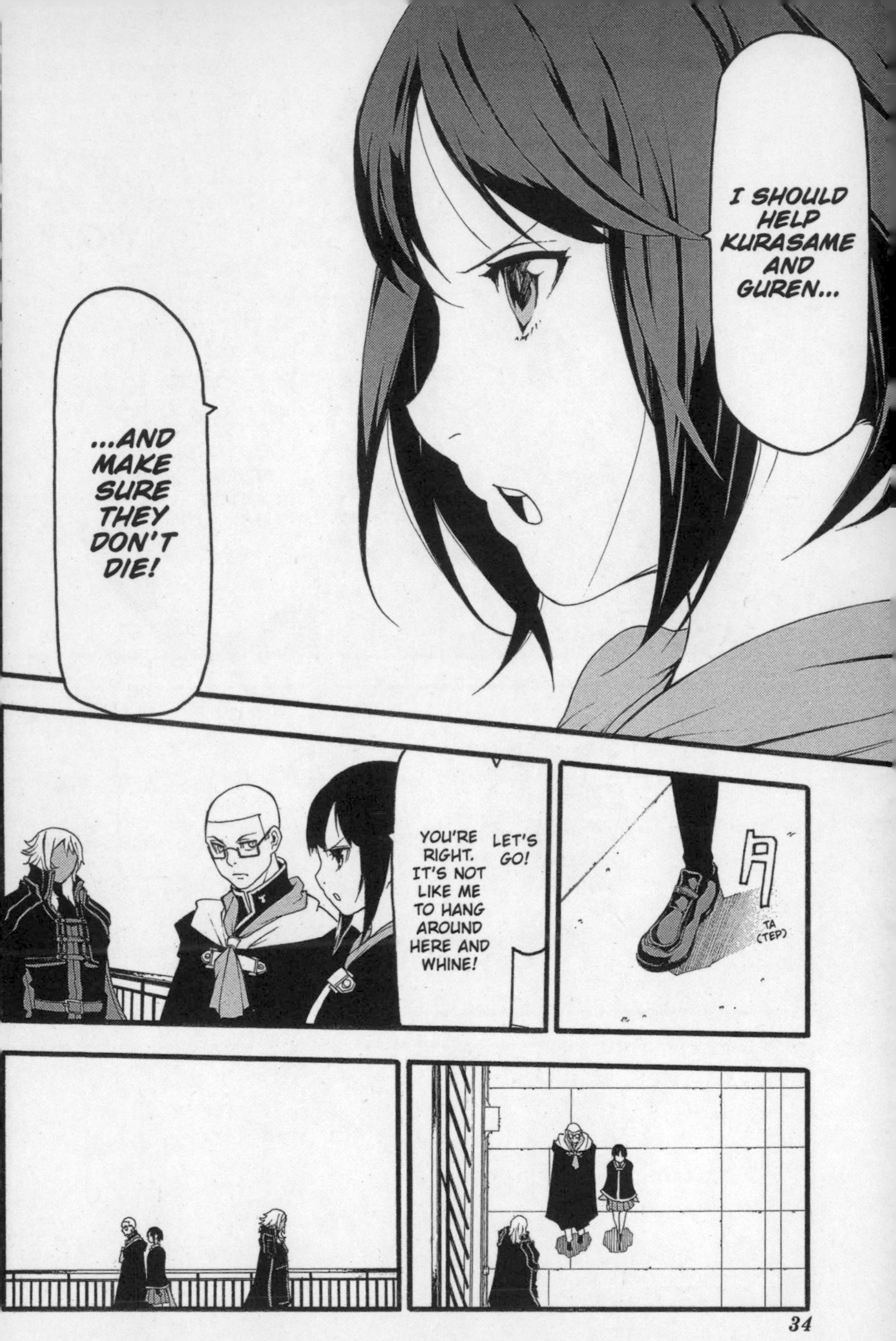
I SHOULD HELP KURASAME AND GUREN...
...AND MAKE SURE THEY DON'T DIE!
TA (TEP)
YOU'RE RIGHT. IT'S NOT LIKE ME TO HANG AROUND HERE AND WHINE!
LET'S GO!

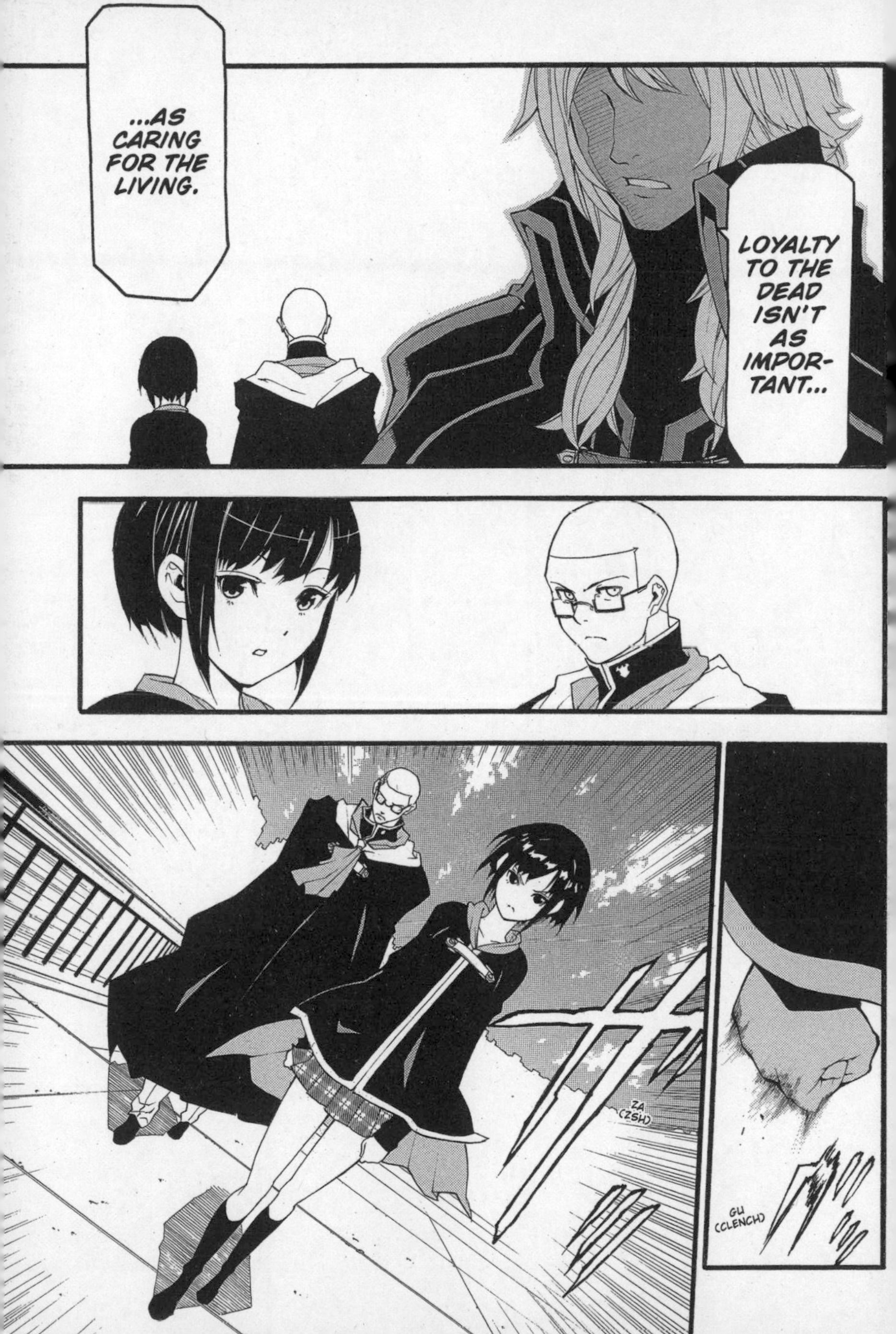
LOYALTY TO THE DEAD ISN'T AS IMPORTANT...
...AS CARING FOR THE LIVING.
GU (CLENCH)
ZA (ZSH)

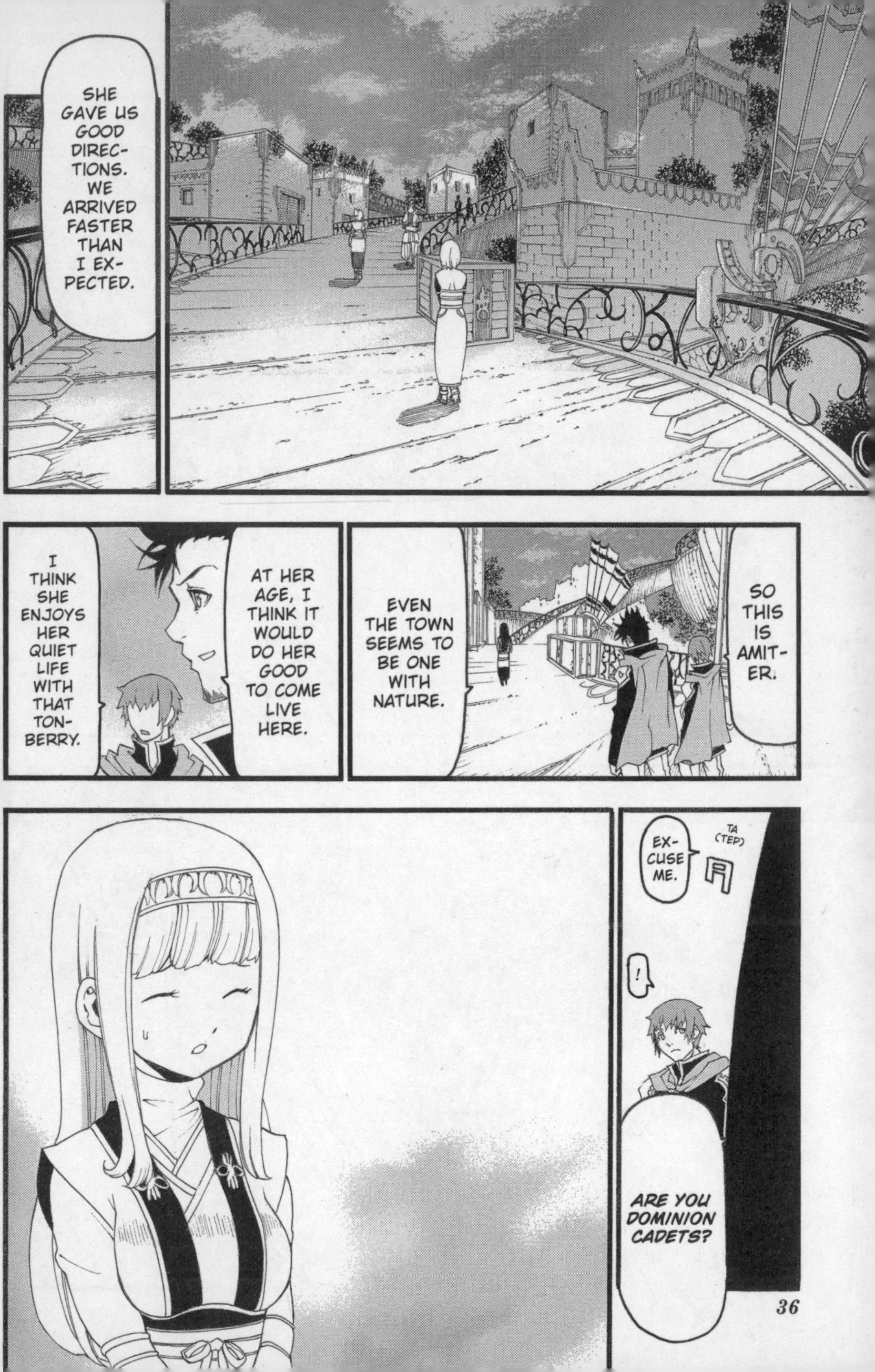

SHE GAVE US GOOD DIREC- TIONS. WE ARRIVED FASTER THAN I EX- PECTED.
SO THIS IS AMIT- ER.
EVEN THE TOWN SEEMS TO BE ONE WITH NATURE.
AT HER AGE, I THINK IT WOULD DO HER GOOD TO COME LIVE HERE.
I THINK SHE ENJOYS HER QUIET LIFE WITH THAT TON- BERRY.
EX- CUSE ME.
TA (TEP)
!
ARE YOU DOMINION CADETS?

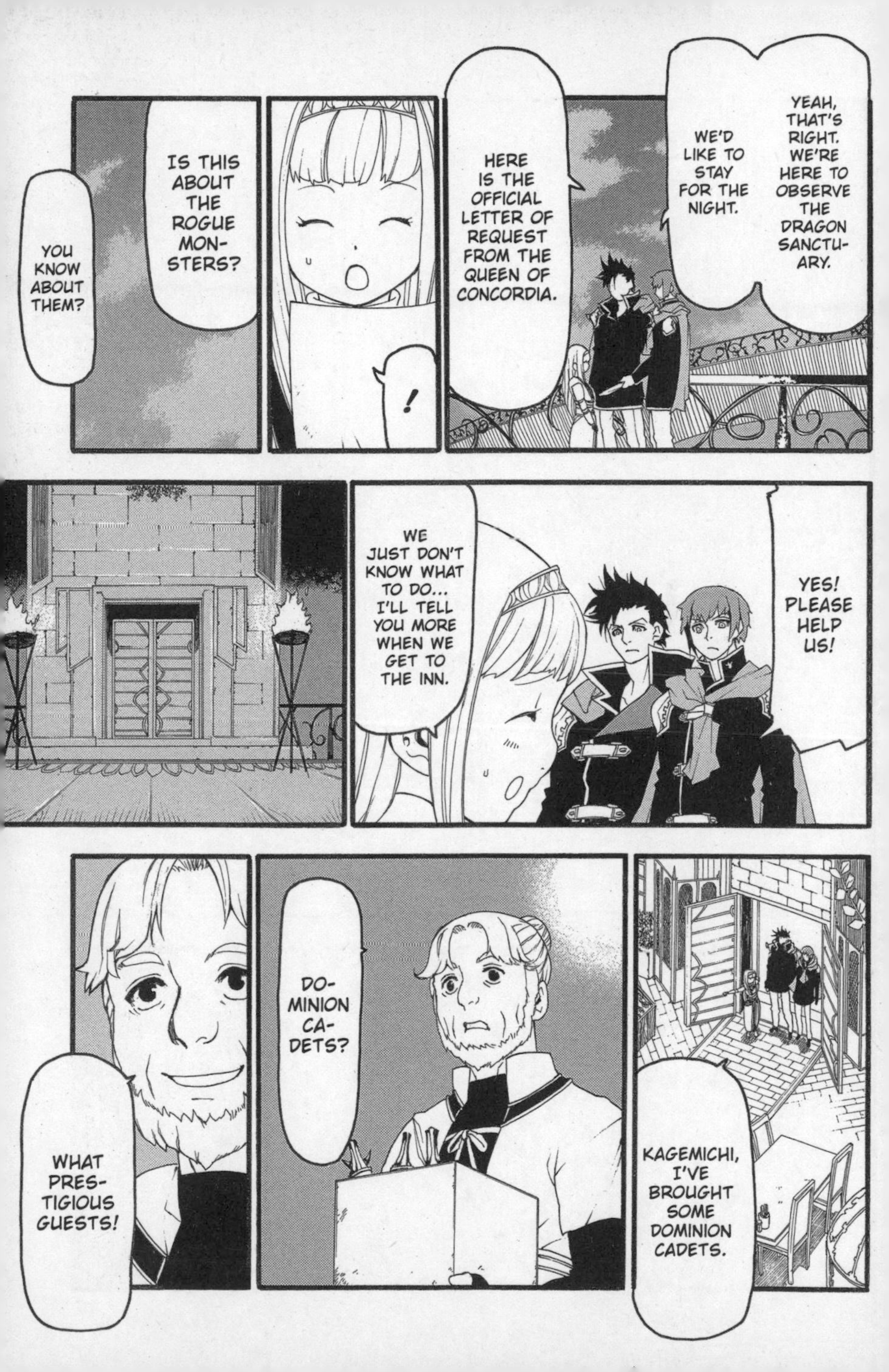
YEAH, THAT'S RIGHT. WE'RE HERE TO OBSERVE THE DRAGON SANCTUARY.
WE'D LIKE TO STAY FOR THE NIGHT.
HERE IS THE OFFICIAL LETTER OF REQUEST FROM THE QUEEN OF CONCORDIA.
!
IS THIS ABOUT THE ROGUE MONSTERS?
YOU KNOW ABOUT THEM?
YES! PLEASE HELP US!
WE JUST DON'T KNOW WHAT TO DO... I'LL TELL YOU MORE WHEN WE GET TO THE INN.
KAGEMICHI, I'VE BROUGHT SOME DOMINION CADETS.
DOMINION CADETS?
WHAT PRESTIGIOUS GUESTS!

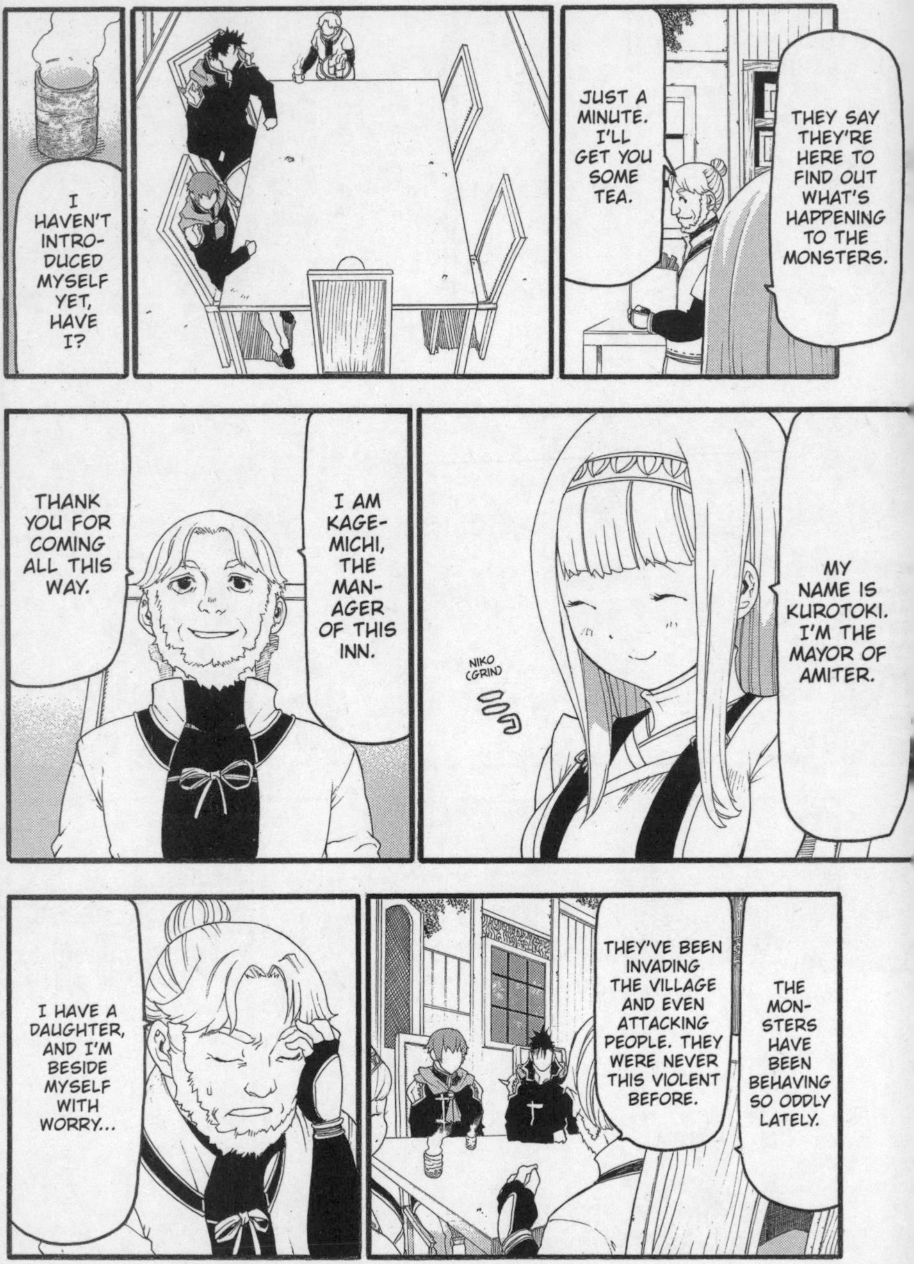
THEY SAY THEY'RE HERE TO FIND OUT WHAT'S HAPPENING TO THE MONSTERS.
JUST A MINUTE. I'LL GET YOU SOME TEA.
I HAVEN'T INTRODUCED MYSELF YET, HAVE I?
MY NAME IS KUROTOKI. I'M THE MAYOR OF AMITER.
NIKO (GRIN)
I AM KAGEMICHI, THE MANAGER OF THIS INN.
THANK YOU FOR COMING ALL THIS WAY.
THE MONSTERS HAVE BEEN BEHAVING SO ODDLY LATELY.
THEY'VE BEEN INVADING THE VILLAGE AND EVEN ATTACKING PEOPLE. THEY WERE NEVER THIS VIOLENT BEFORE.
I HAVE A DAUGHTER, AND I'M BESIDE MYSELF WITH WORRY...

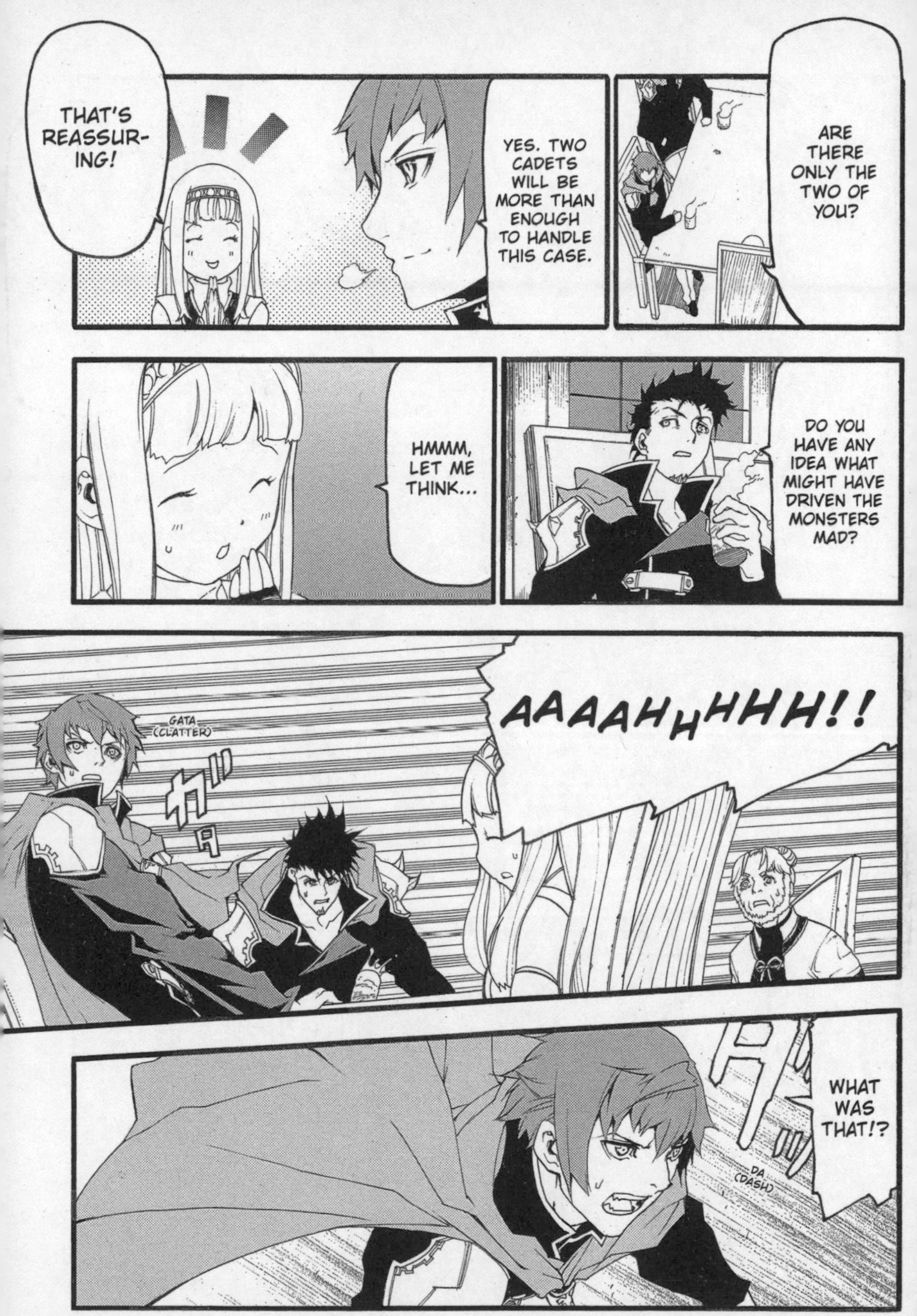
ARE THERE ONLY THE TWO OF YOU?
YES. TWO CADETS WILL BE MORE THAN ENOUGH TO HANDLE THIS CASE.
THAT'S REASSURING!
DO YOU HAVE ANY IDEA WHAT MIGHT HAVE DRIVEN THE MONSTERS MAD?
HMMM, LET ME THINK...
AAAAHHHHH!!
GATA (CLATTER)
WHAT WAS THAT!?
DA (DASH)

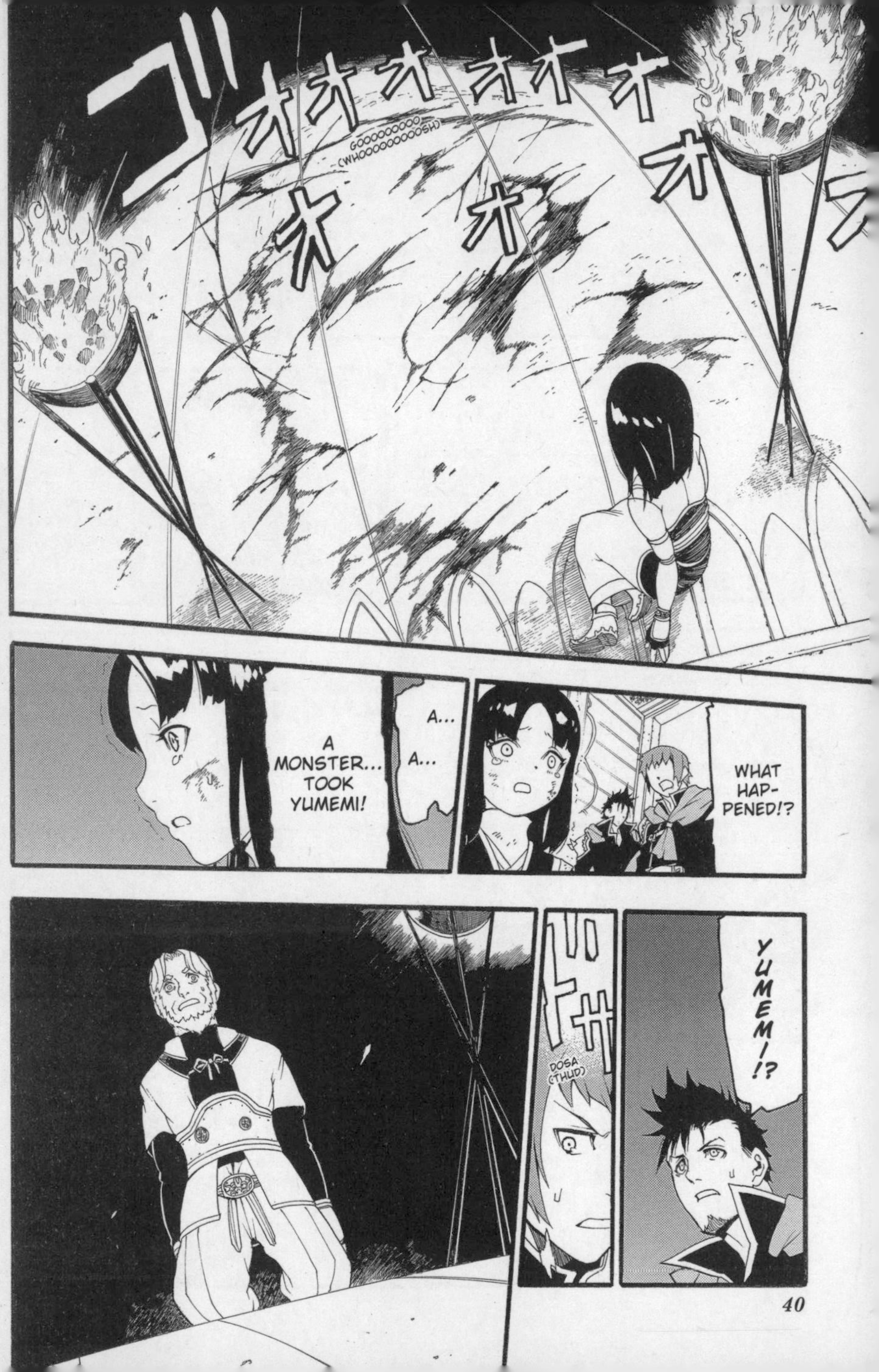
GOOOOOOOOOO
(WHOOOOOOOOOOOSH)
WHAT HAP-PENED!?
A... A...
A MONSTER... TOOK YUMEMI!
YUMEMI!?
DOSA (THUD)

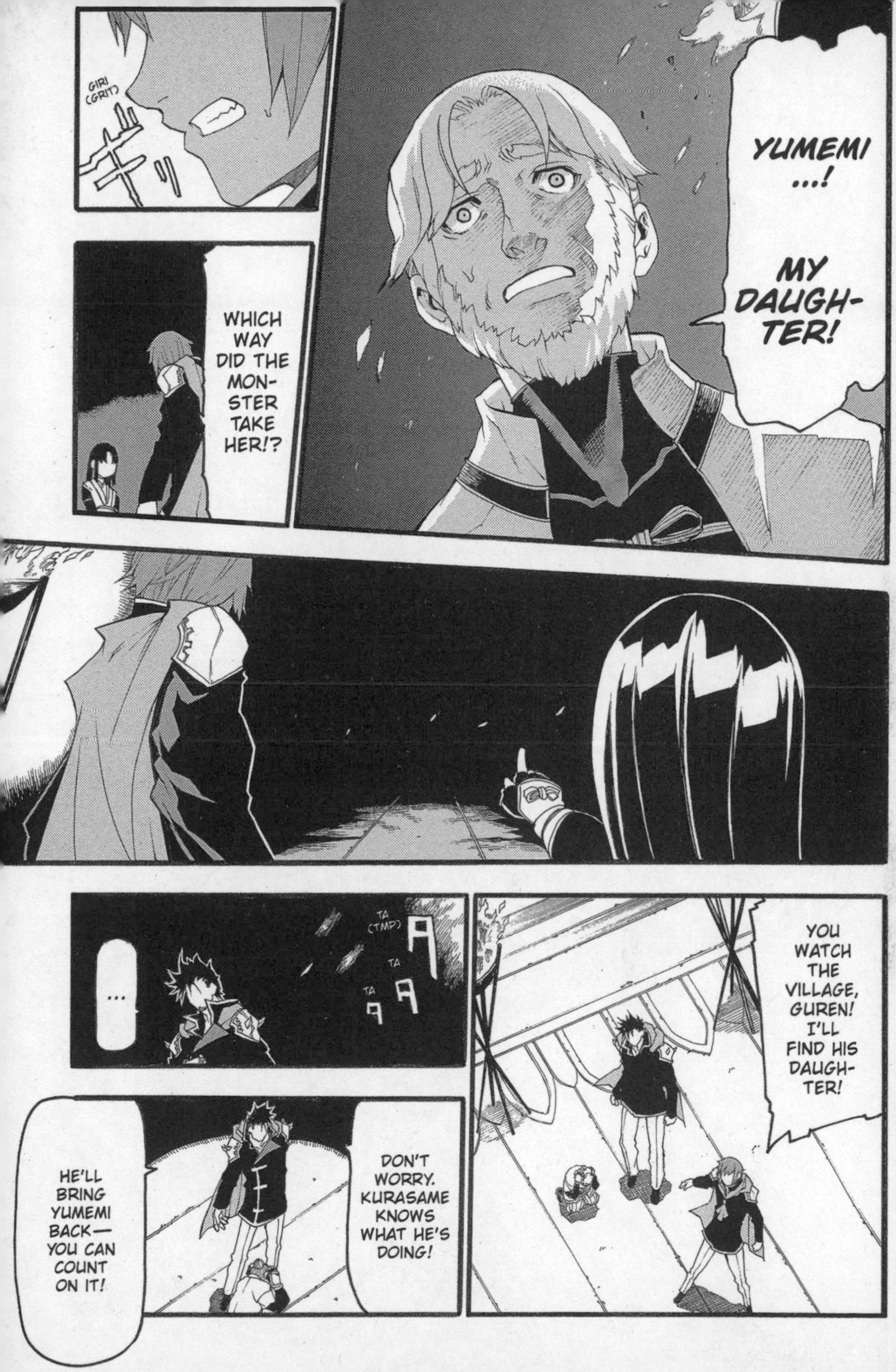
YUMEMI ...!
MY DAUGHTER!
GIRI (GRIT)
WHICH WAY DID THE MONSTER TAKE HER!?
YOU WATCH THE VILLAGE, GUREN! I'LL FIND HIS DAUGHTER!
...
TA (TMP)
TA
TA
DON'T WORRY. KURASAME KNOWS WHAT HE'S DOING!
HE'LL BRING YUMEMI BACK—YOU CAN COUNT ON IT!

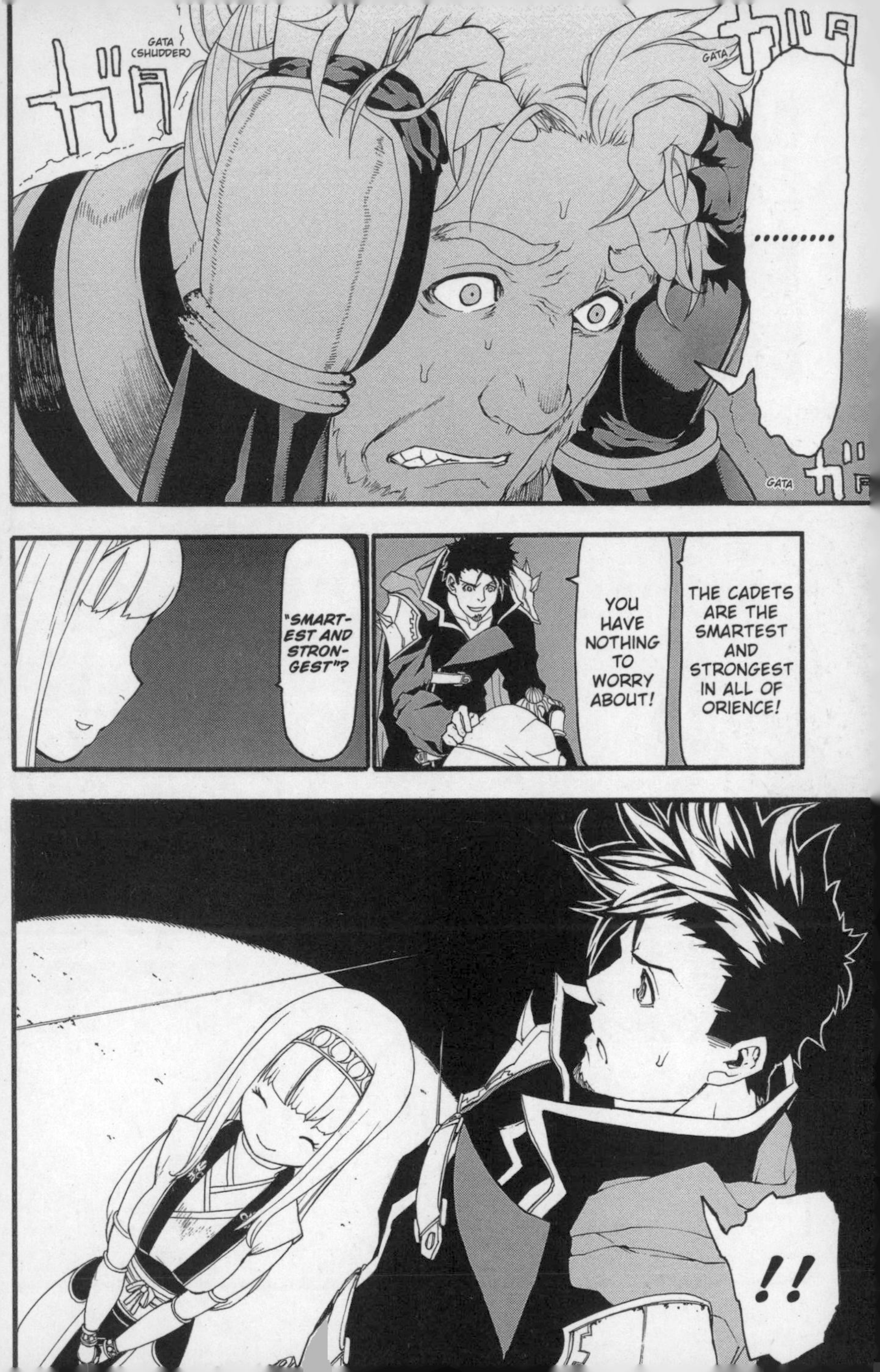
GATA
....
GATA
GATA (SHUDDER)
THE CADETS ARE THE SMARTEST AND STRONGEST IN ALL OF ORIENCE!
YOU HAVE NOTHING TO WORRY ABOUT!
"SMART-EST AND STRON-GEST"?
!!

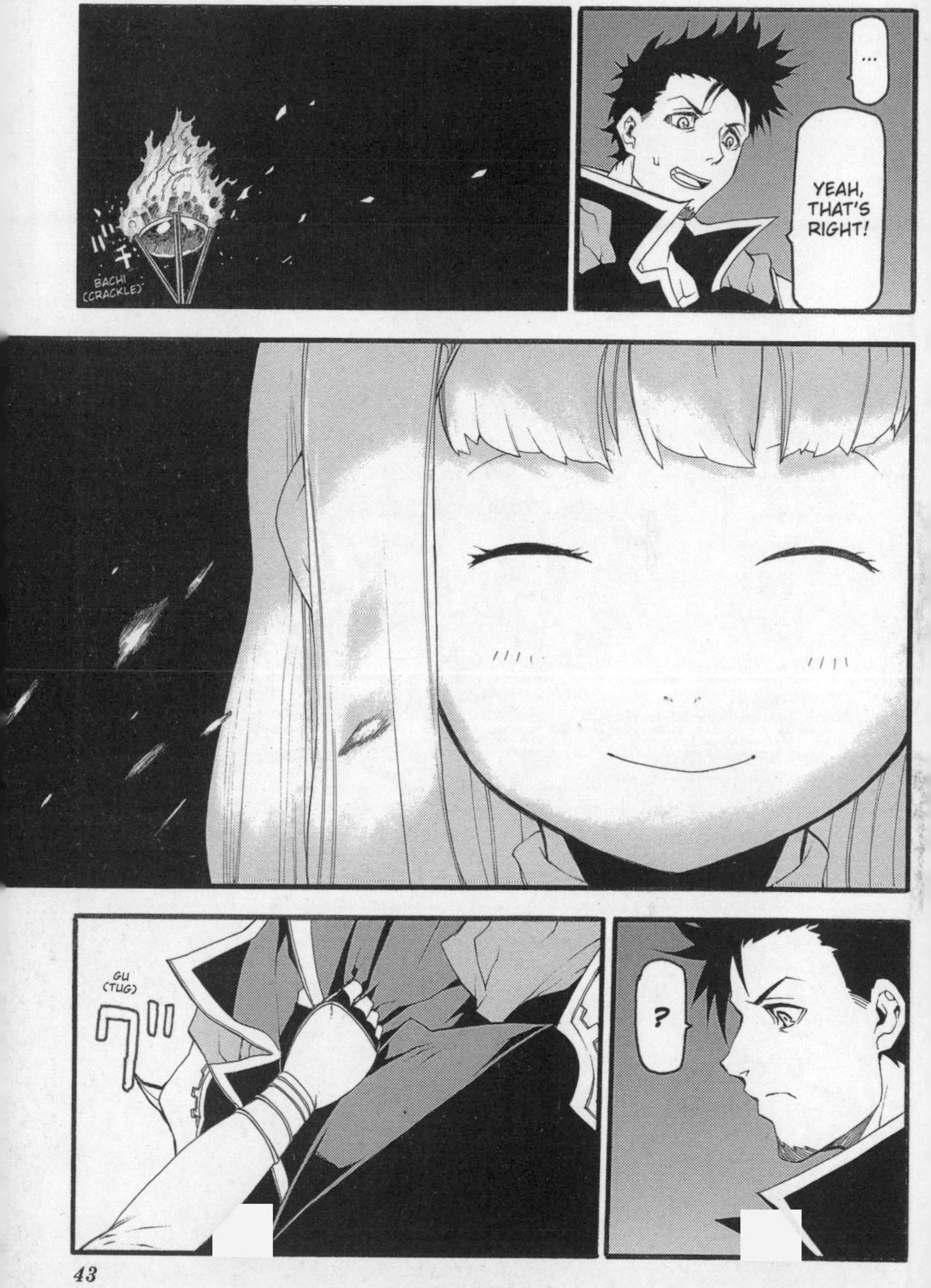
...
YEAH, THAT'S RIGHT!
バチ
BACHI (CRACKLE)
?
グッ
GU (TUG)

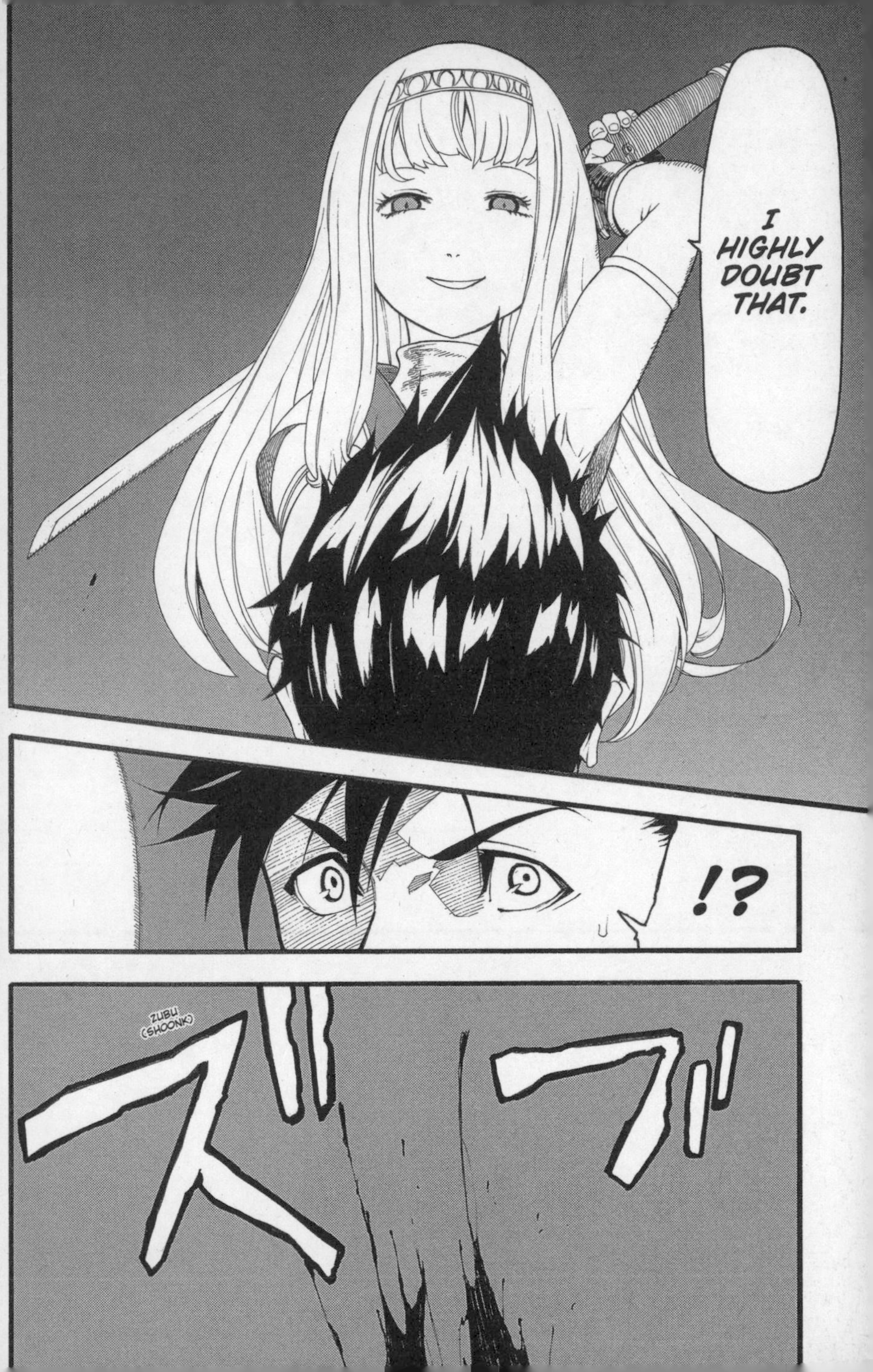
I HIGHLY DOUBT THAT.
!?
ZUBU (SHOONK)
ズブ

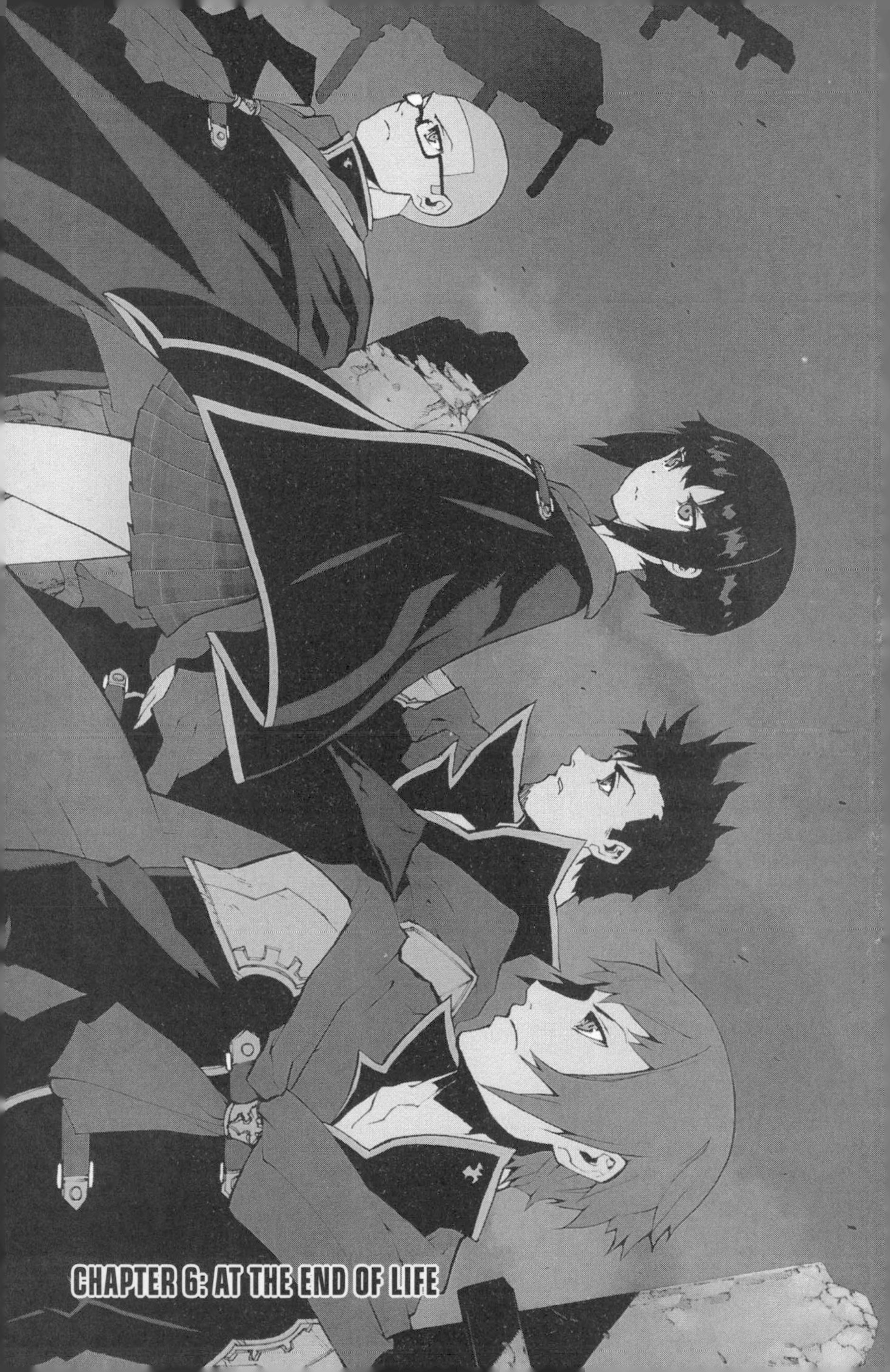

CHAPTER 6: AT THE END OF LIFE

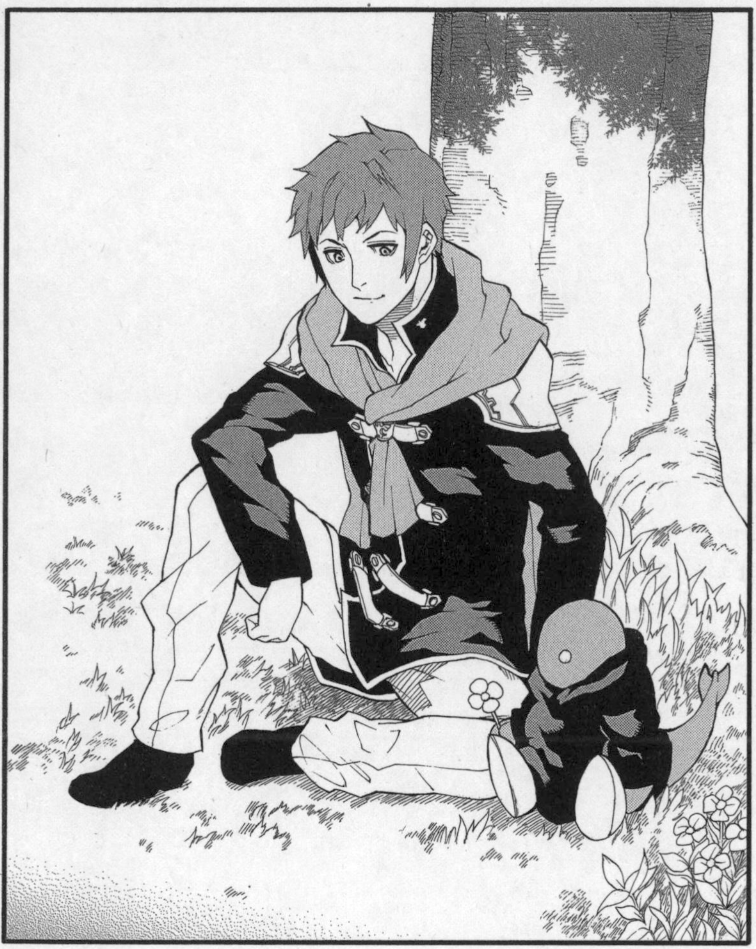

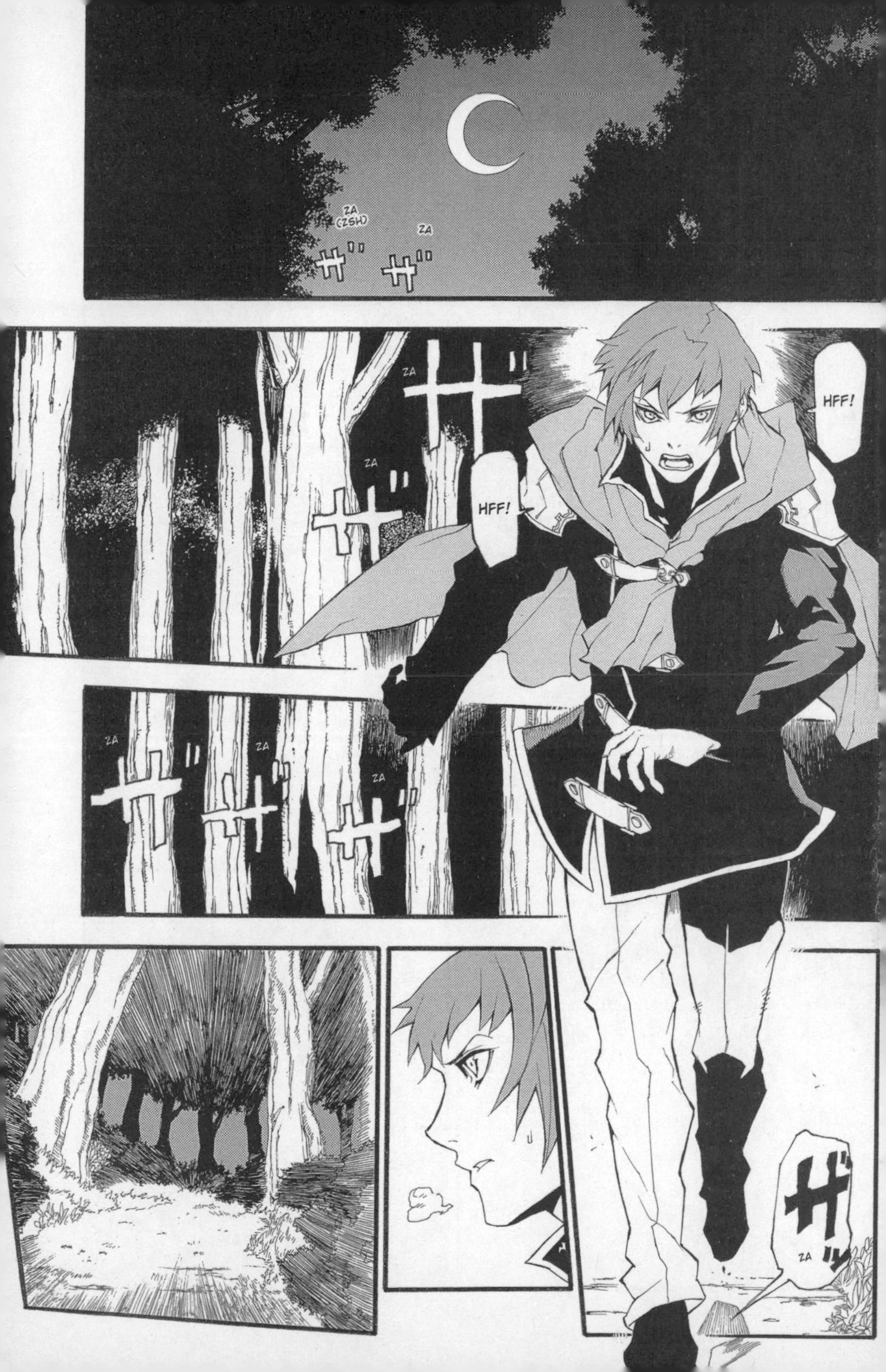
ZA (ZSH)
ザッ
ZA
ザッ
HFF!
ZA
ザッ
ZA
ザッ
HFF!
ZA
ザッ
ZA
ザッ
ZA
ザッ
ZA
ザッ

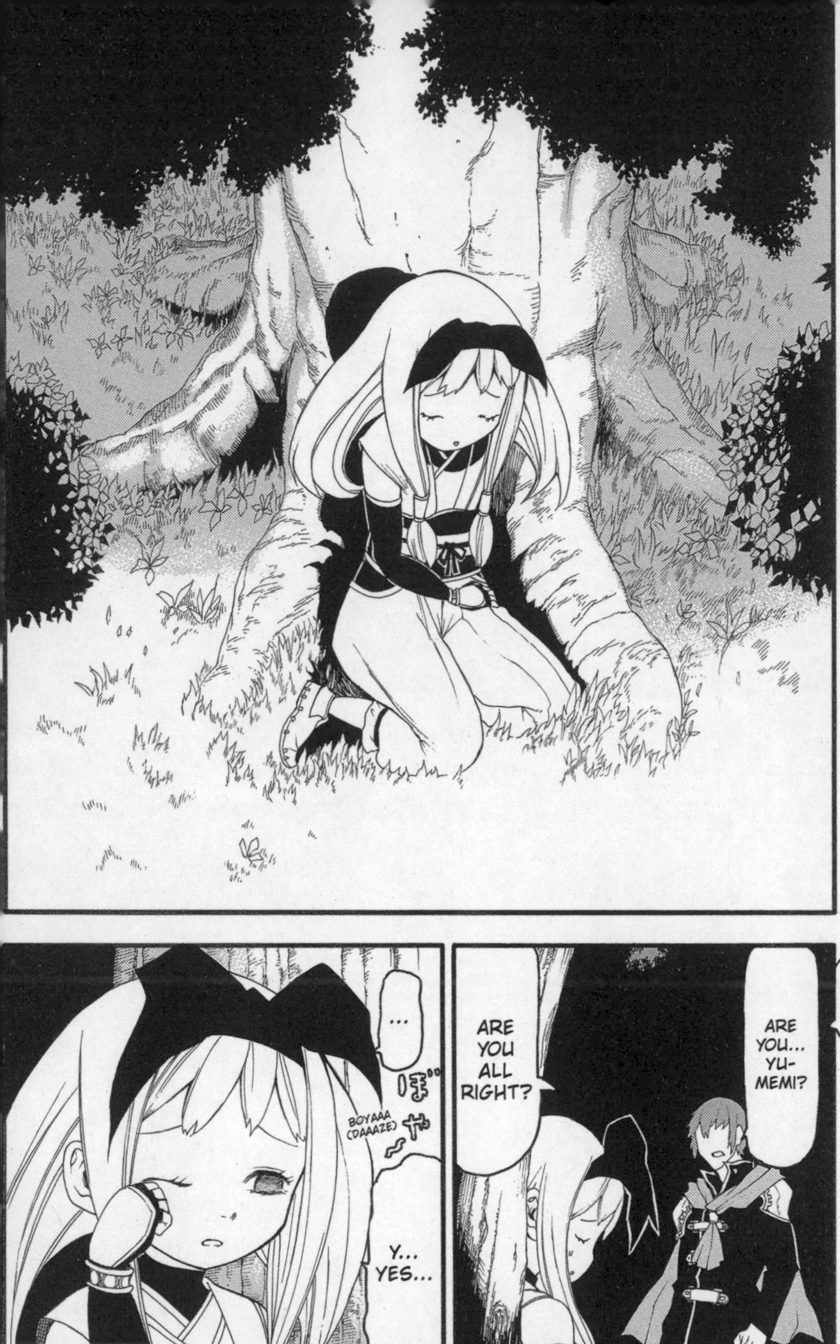
...
ARE YOU... YU-MEMI?
ARE YOU ALL RIGHT?
...
BOYAAA (DAAAZE)
Y... YES...

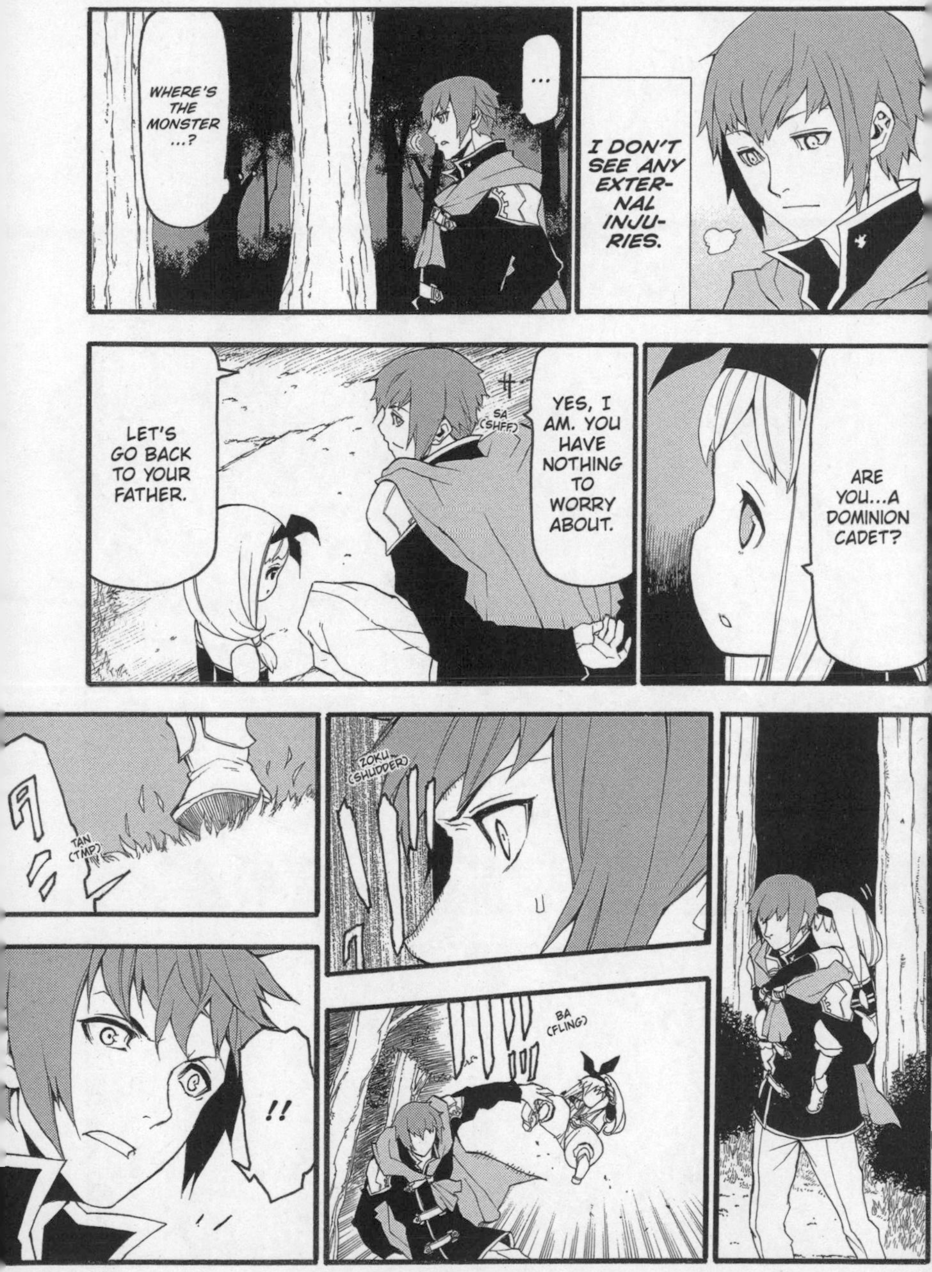
I DON'T SEE ANY EXTERNAL INJURIES.
...
WHERE'S THE MONSTER ...?
ARE YOU...A DOMINION CADET?
YES, I AM. YOU HAVE NOTHING TO WORRY ABOUT.
SA (SHFF)
LET'S GO BACK TO YOUR FATHER.
ZOKU (SHUDDER)
TAN (TMP)
BA (FLING)
!!

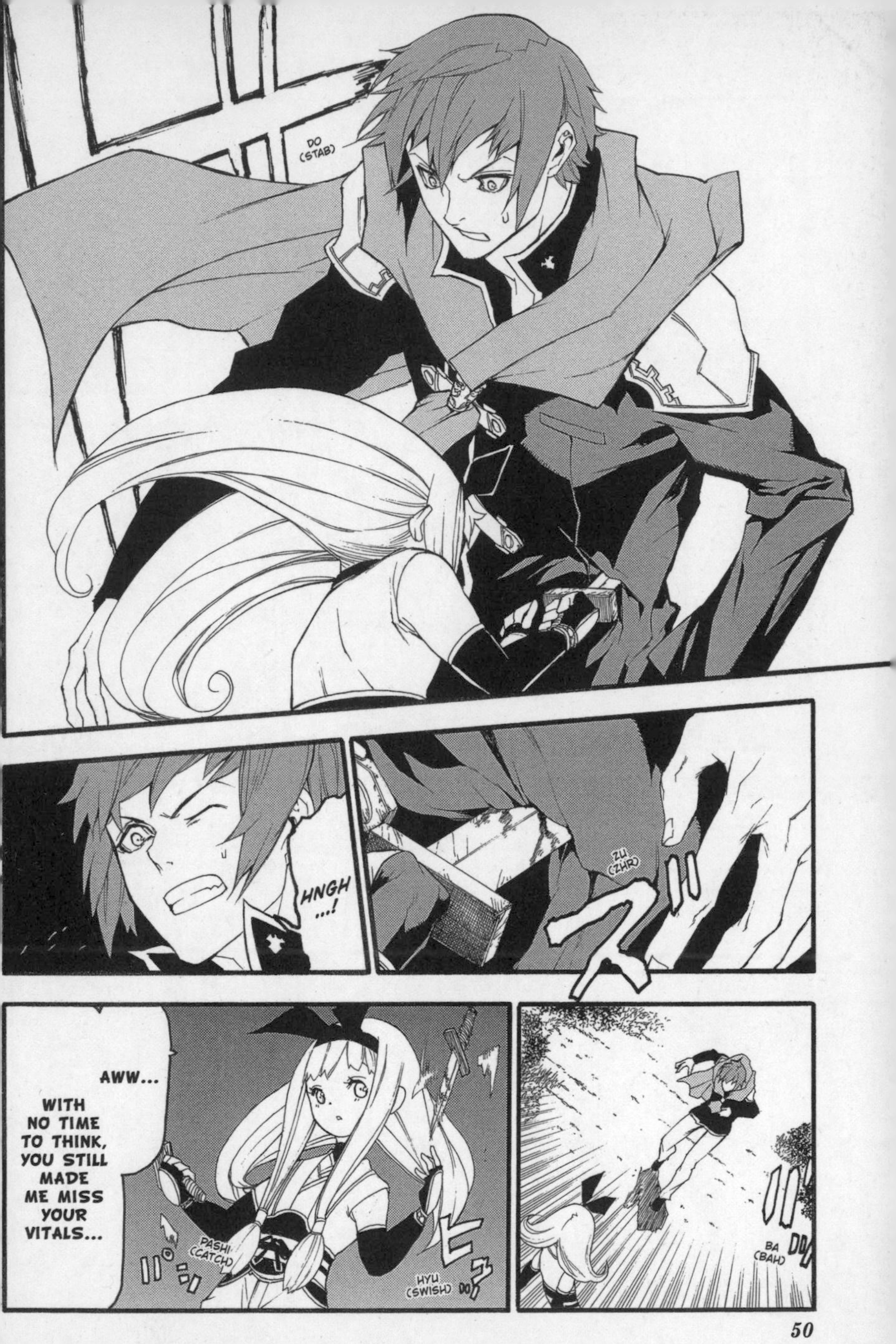
DO (STAB)
ZU (ZHR)
HNGH ...!
BA (BAH)
AWW...
WITH NO TIME TO THINK, YOU STILL MADE ME MISS YOUR VITALS...
PASHI (CATCH)
HYU (SWISH)

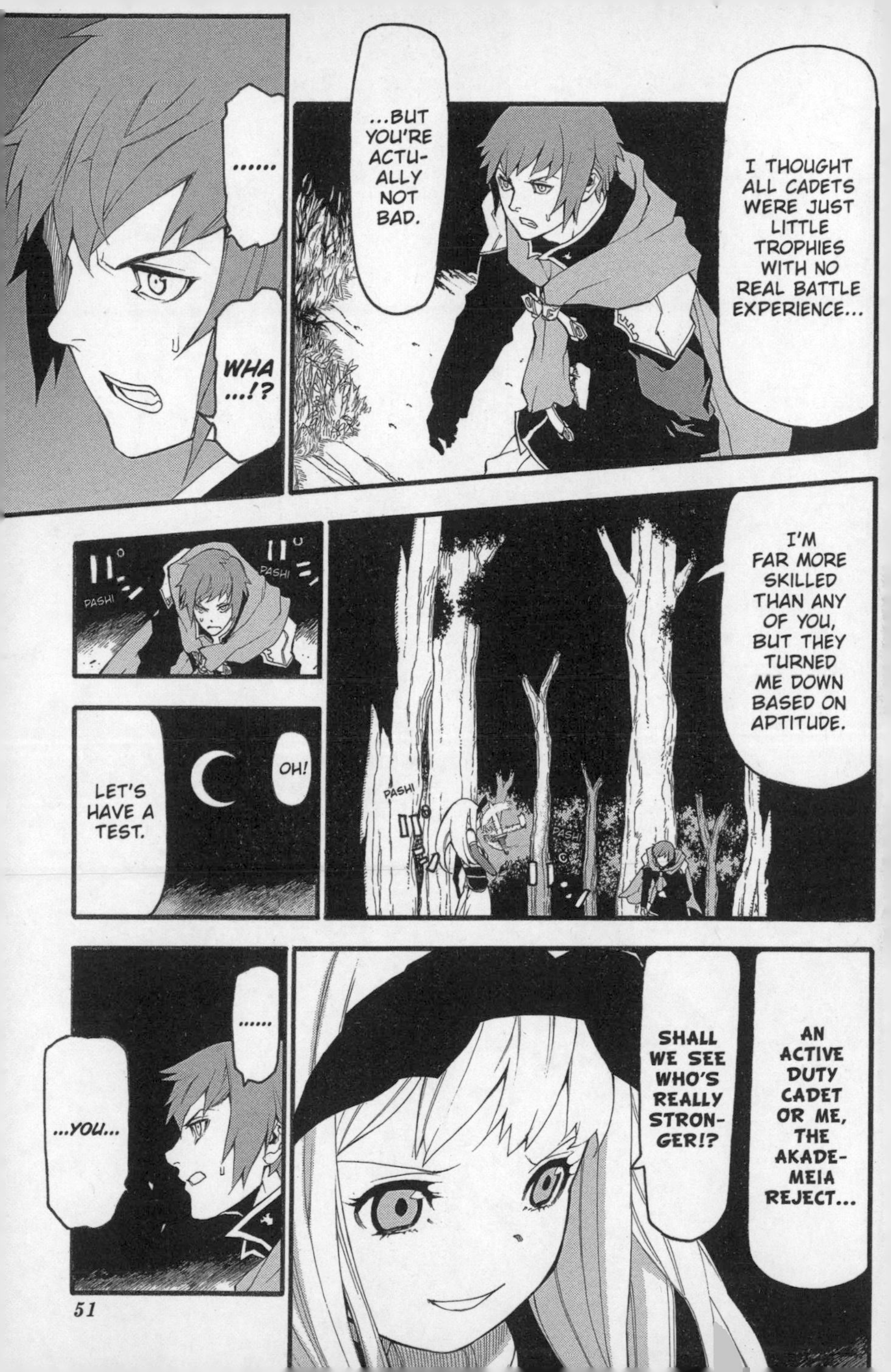
I THOUGHT ALL CADETS WERE JUST LITTLE TROPHIES WITH NO REAL BATTLE EXPERIENCE...
...BUT YOU'RE ACTU-ALLY NOT BAD.
......
WHA ...!?
I'M FAR MORE SKILLED THAN ANY OF YOU, BUT THEY TURNED ME DOWN BASED ON APTITUDE.
PASHI
PASHI
PASHI
PASHI
OH!
LET'S HAVE A TEST.
AN ACTIVE DUTY CADET OR ME, THE AKADE-MEIA REJECT...
SHALL WE SEE WHO'S REALLY STRON-GER!?
......
...YOU...

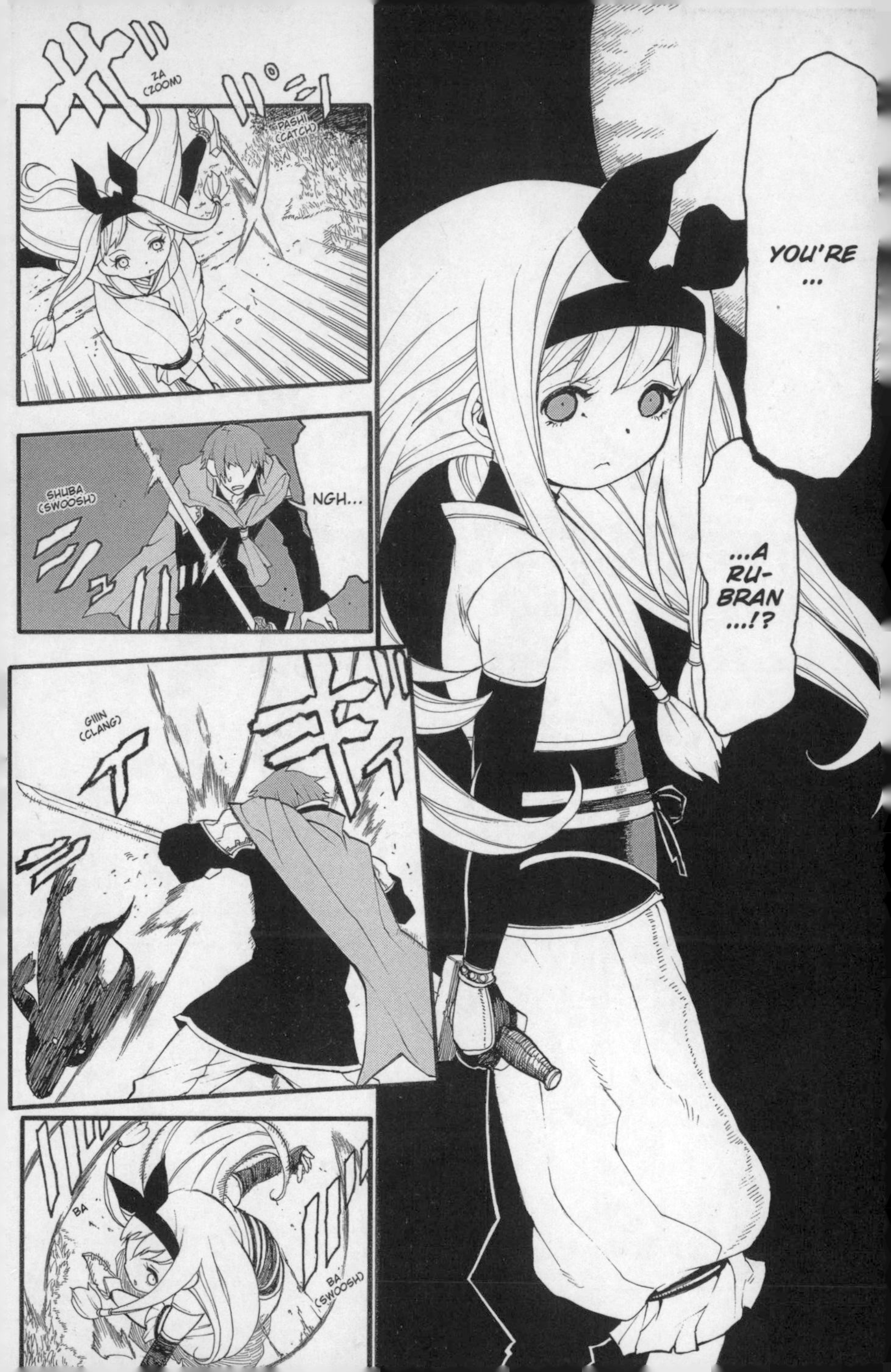
YOU'RE ...
...A RU-BRAN ...!?
ZA (ZOOM)
PASHI (CATCH)
NGH...
SHUBA (SWOOSH)
GIIIN (CLANG)
BA
BA (SWOOSH)

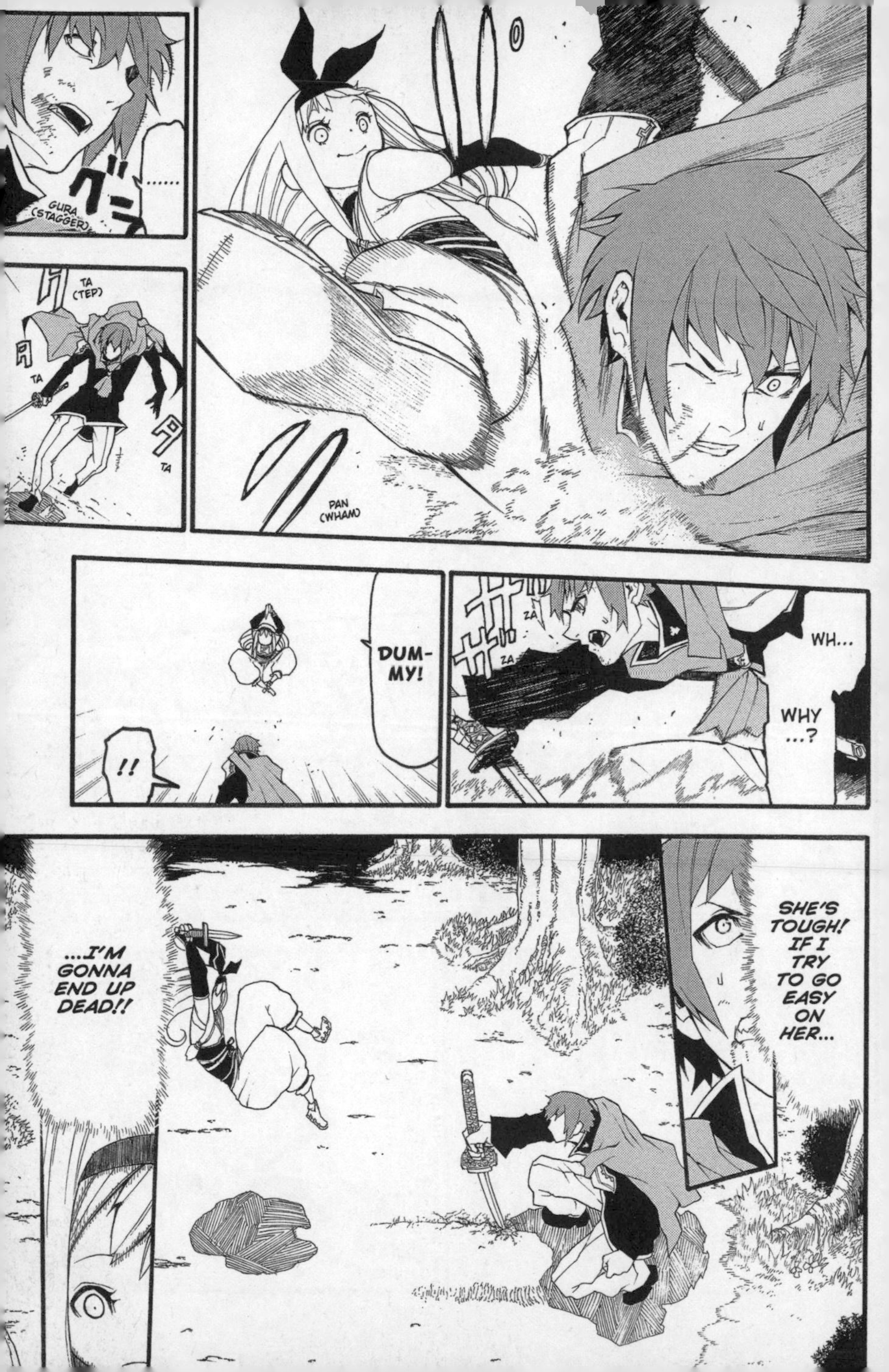
PAN (WHAM)
GURA (STAGGER)
......
TA (TEP)
TA
TA
ZA
ZA
WH...
WHY ...?
DUM-MY!
!!
SHE'S TOUGH! IF I TRY TO GO EASY ON HER...
...I'M GONNA END UP DEAD!!

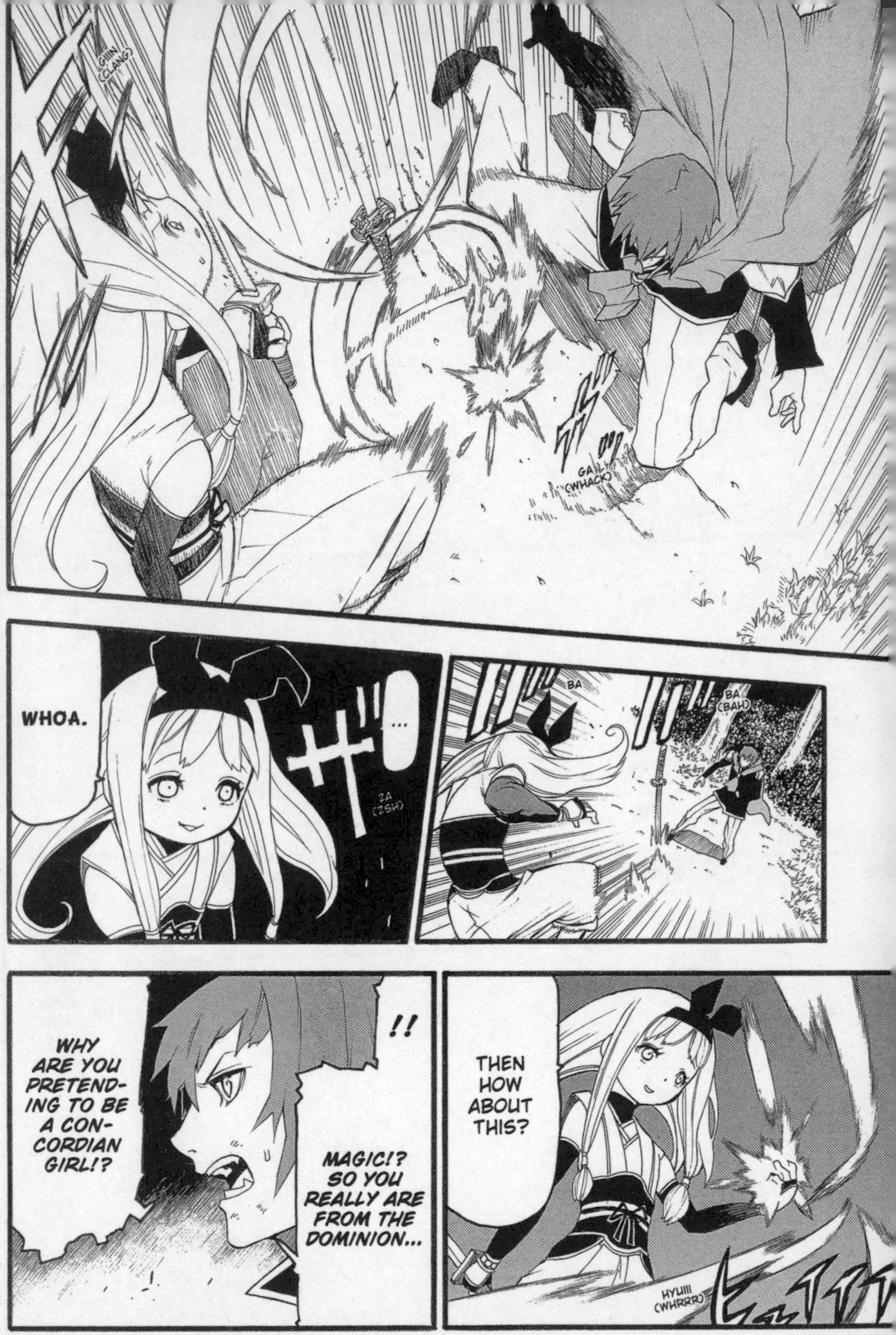
GIIIN (CLANG)
GA (WHACK)
BA
BA (BAH)
...
ZA (ZSH)
WHOA.
THEN HOW ABOUT THIS?
HYUIII (WHRRR)
!!
MAGIC!? SO YOU REALLY ARE FROM THE DOMINION...
WHY ARE YOU PRETENDING TO BE A CONCORDIAN GIRL!?

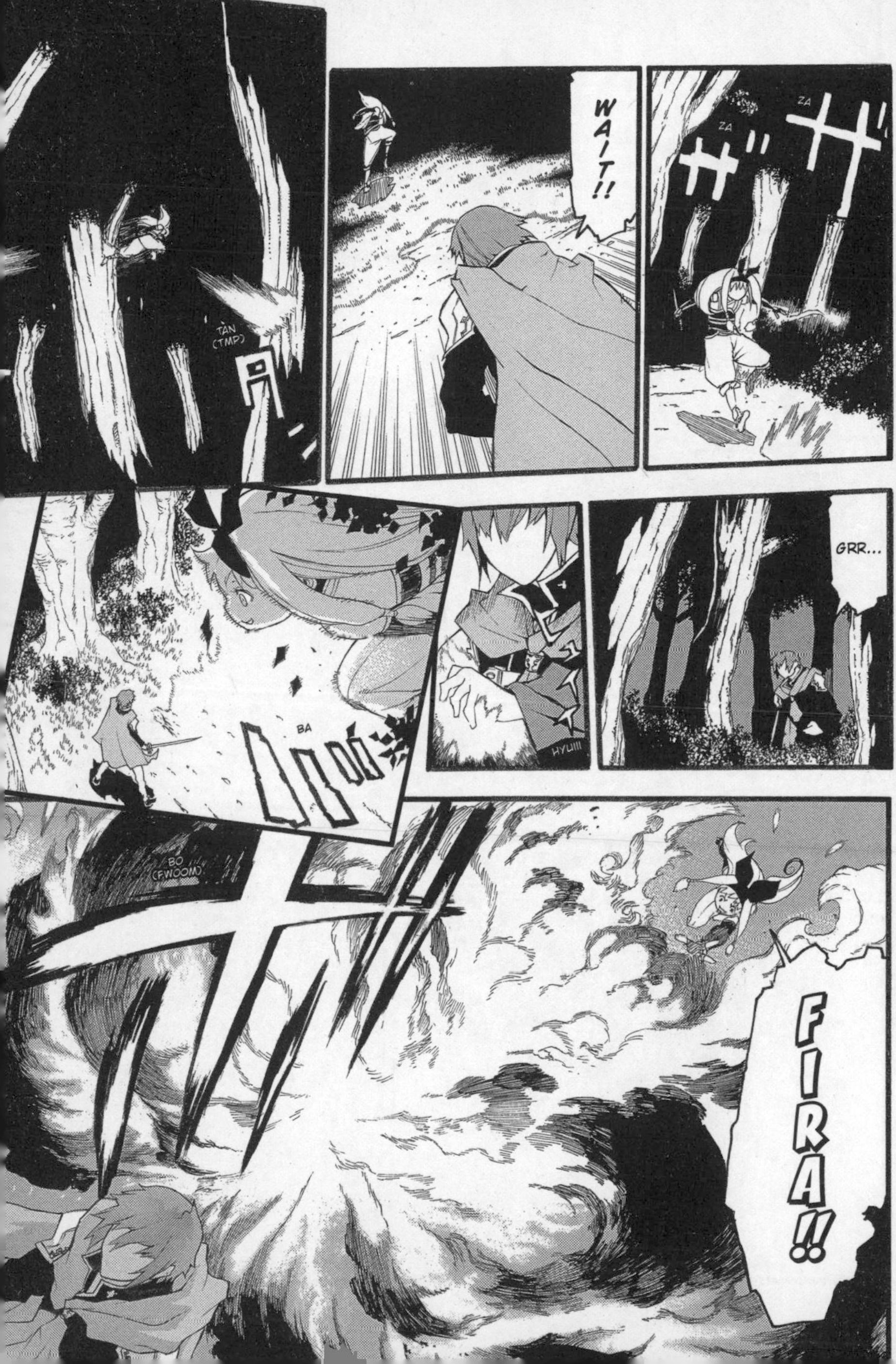
ZA
ZA
WAIT!!
TAN (TMP)
GRR...
HYUIII
BA
FIRA!!
BO (FWOOM)

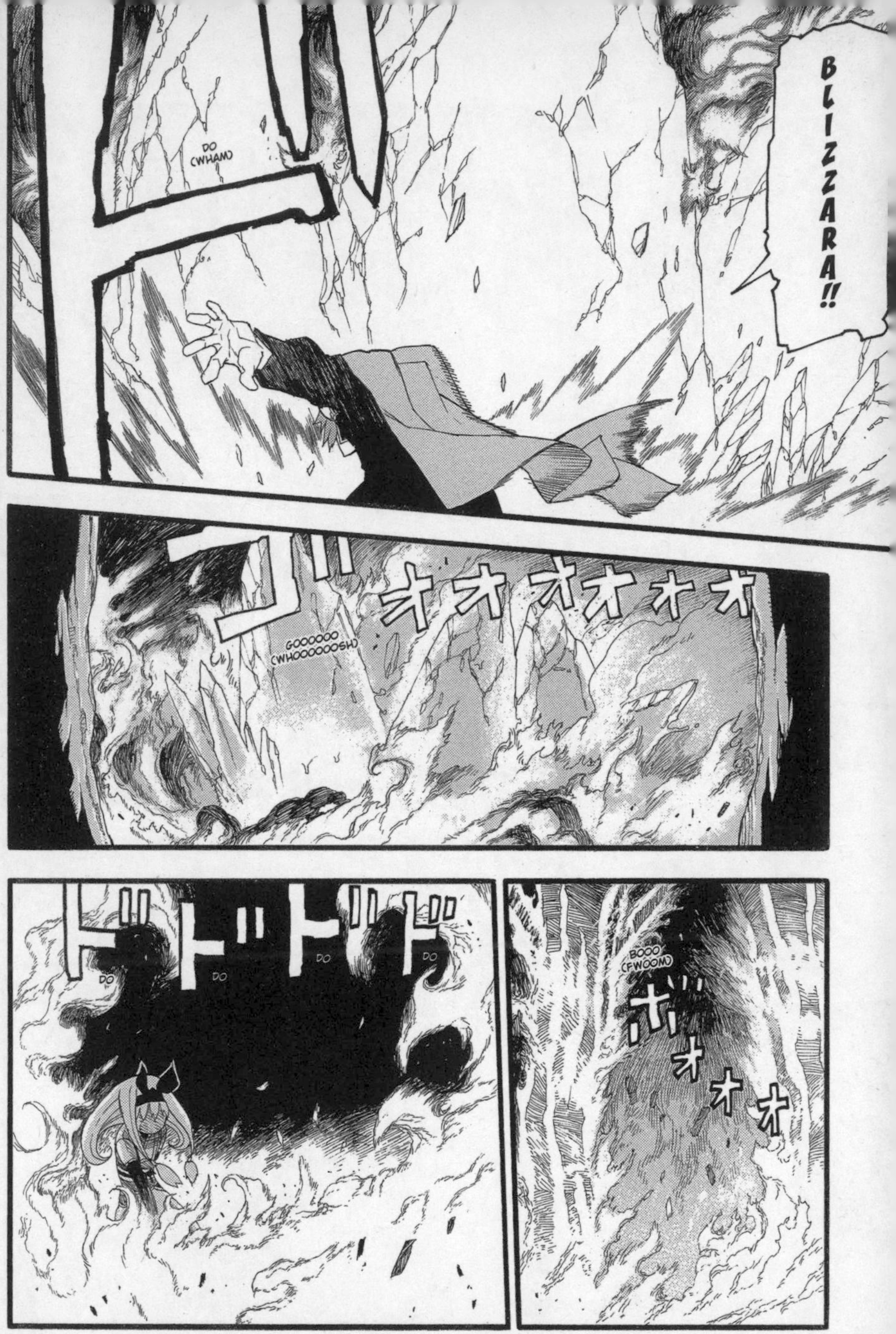
BLIZZARA!!
DO
(WHAM)
ゴオオオオオオ
GOOOOOOO
(WHOOOOOOSH)
ボオオオ
BOOO
(FWOOM)
ドドドドド
DO
DO
DO
DO

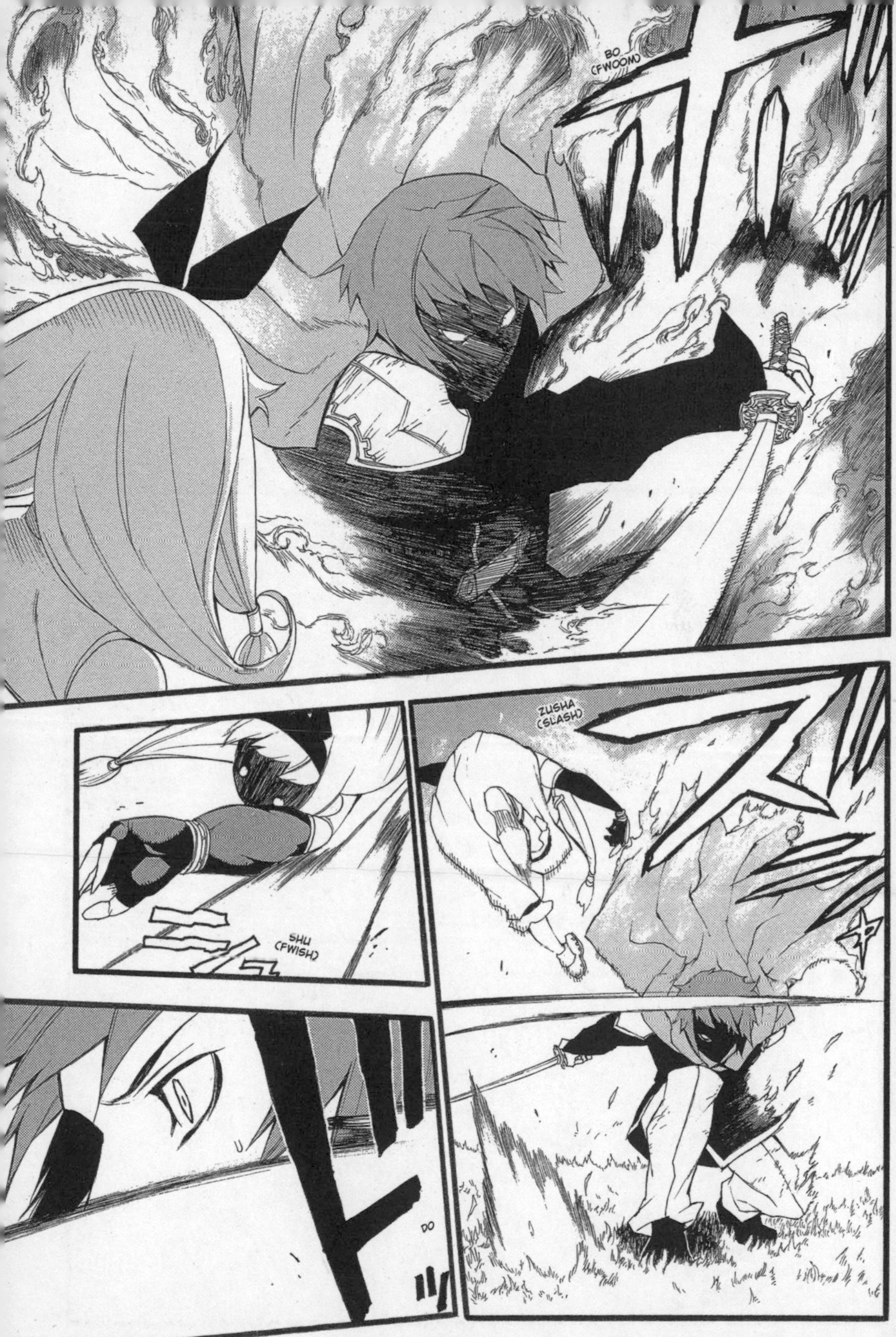
BO
(FWOOM)
ZUSHA
(SLASH)
SHU
(FWISH)
DO

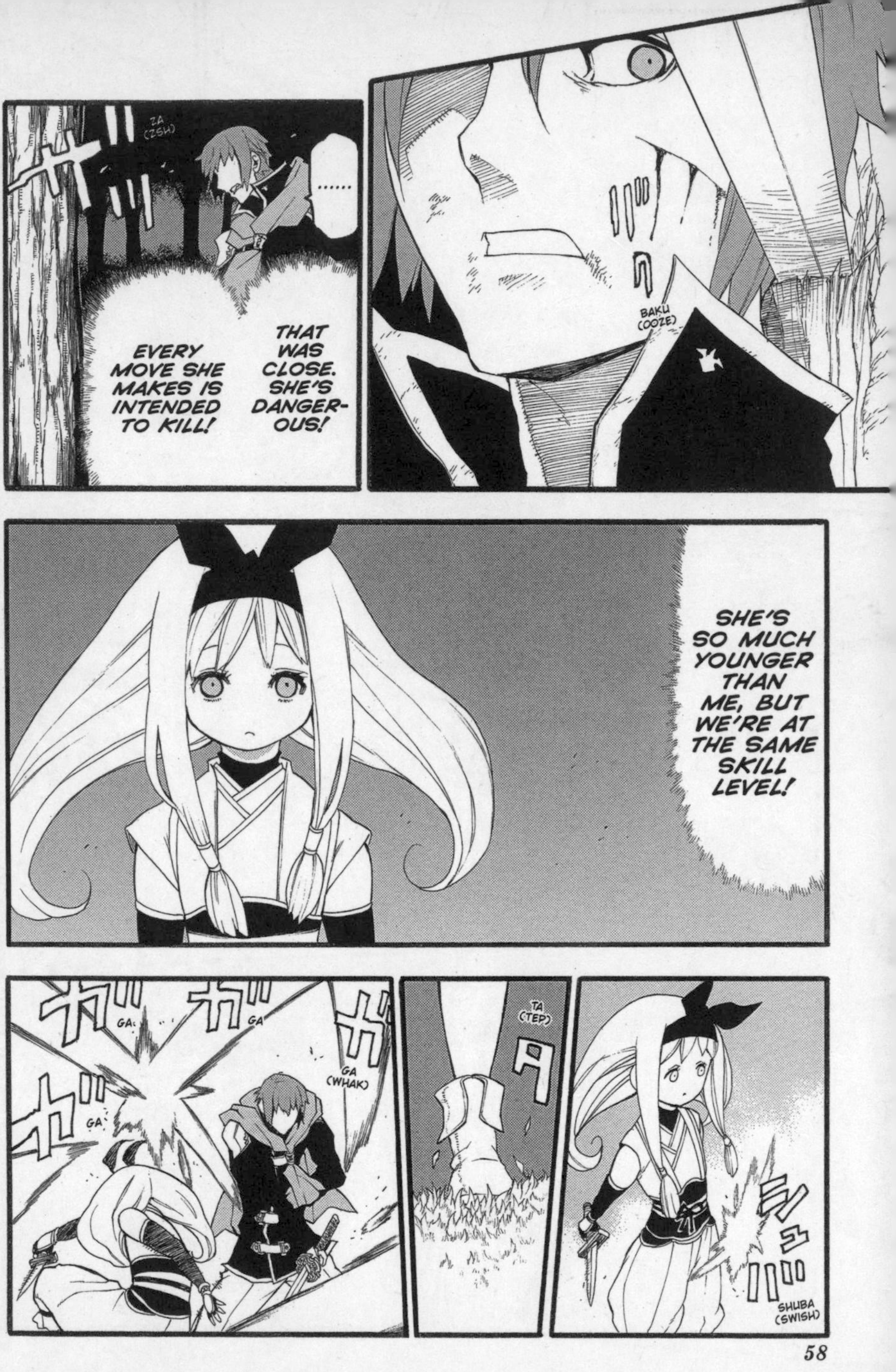
BAKU (OOZE)
ZA (ZSH)
......
THAT WAS CLOSE. SHE'S DANGER-OUS!
EVERY MOVE SHE MAKES IS INTENDED TO KILL!
SHE'S SO MUCH YOUNGER THAN ME, BUT WE'RE AT THE SAME SKILL LEVEL!
SHUBA (SWISH)
TA (TEP)
GA
GA
GA (WHAK)
GA

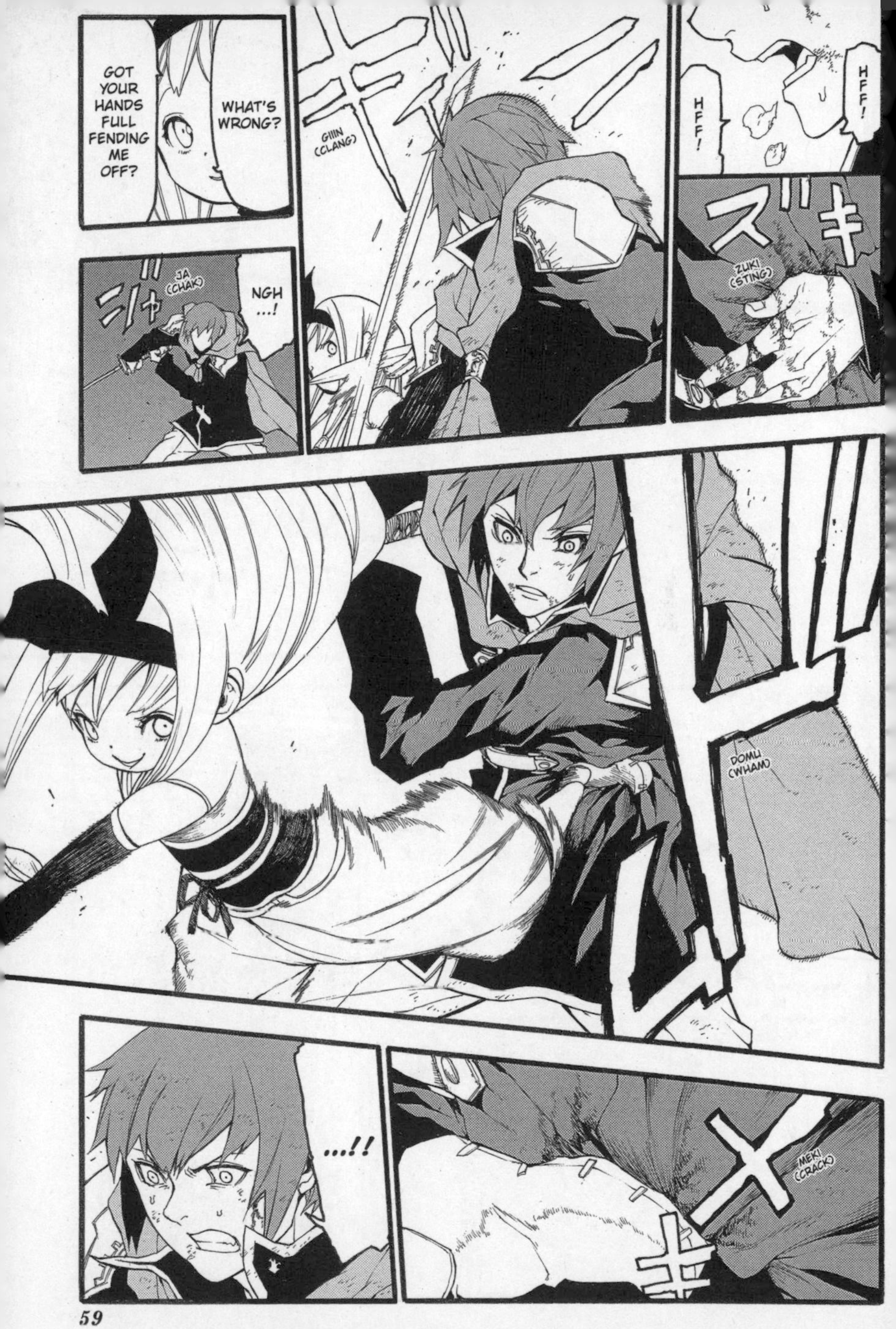
HFF!
HFF!
ZUKI (STING)
GIIN (CLANG)
WHAT'S WRONG?
GOT YOUR HANDS FULL FENDING ME OFF?
NGH ...!
JA (CHAK)
DOMU (WHAM)
MEKI (CRACK)
...!!

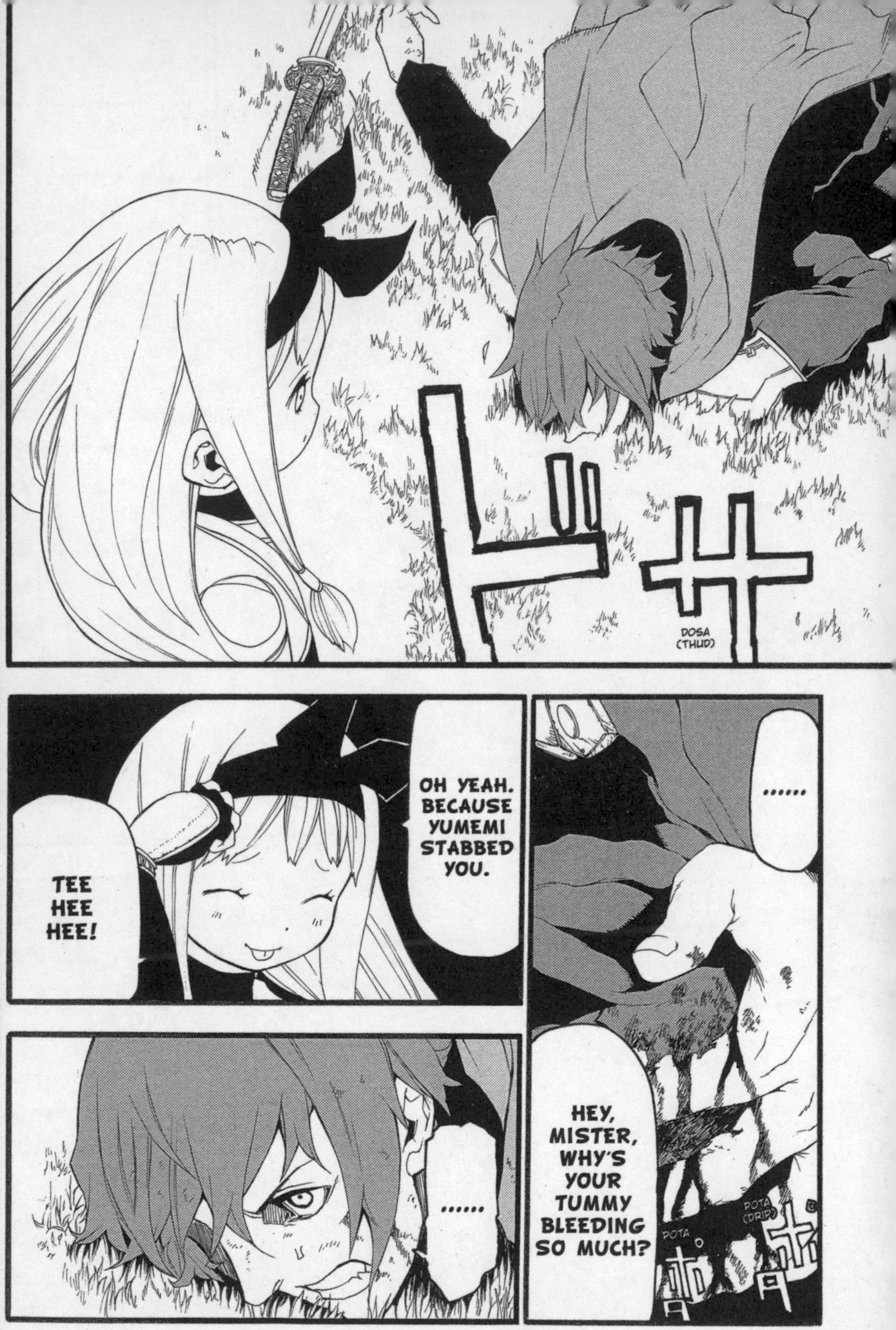
ドサッ
DOSA (THUD)
......
HEY, MISTER, WHY'S YOUR TUMMY BLEEDING SO MUCH?
POTA (DRIP)
POTA
ポタ ポタ
OH YEAH. BECAUSE YUMEMI STABBED YOU.
TEE HEE HEE!
......

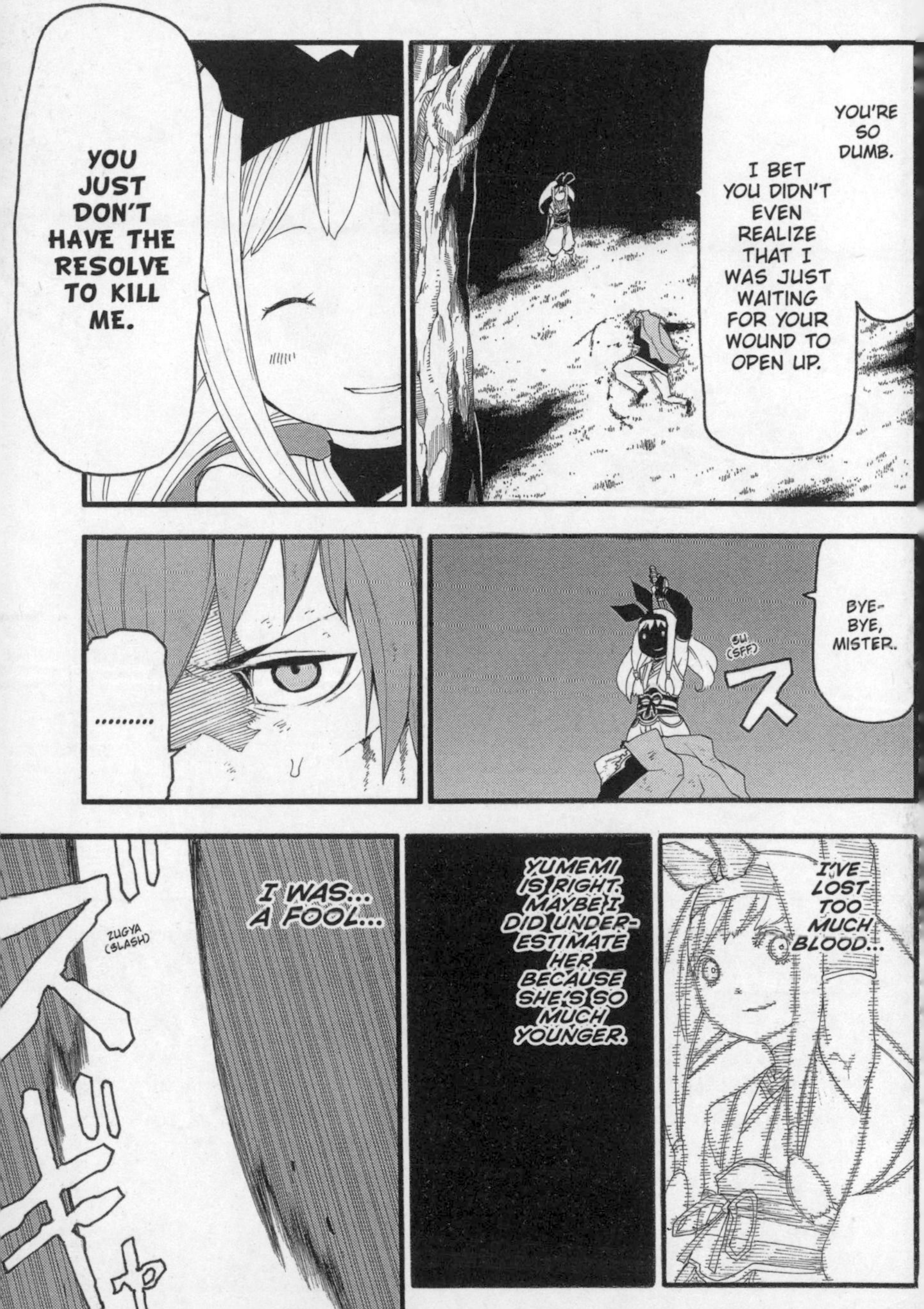
YOU'RE SO DUMB.
I BET YOU DIDN'T EVEN REALIZE THAT I WAS JUST WAITING FOR YOUR WOUND TO OPEN UP.
YOU JUST DON'T HAVE THE RESOLVE TO KILL ME.
BYE-BYE, MISTER.
SU (SFF)
....
I'VE LOST TOO MUCH BLOOD...
YUMEMI IS RIGHT. MAYBE I DID UNDER-ESTIMATE HER BECAUSE SHE'S SO MUCH YOUNGER.
I WAS... A FOOL...
ZUGYA (SLASH)

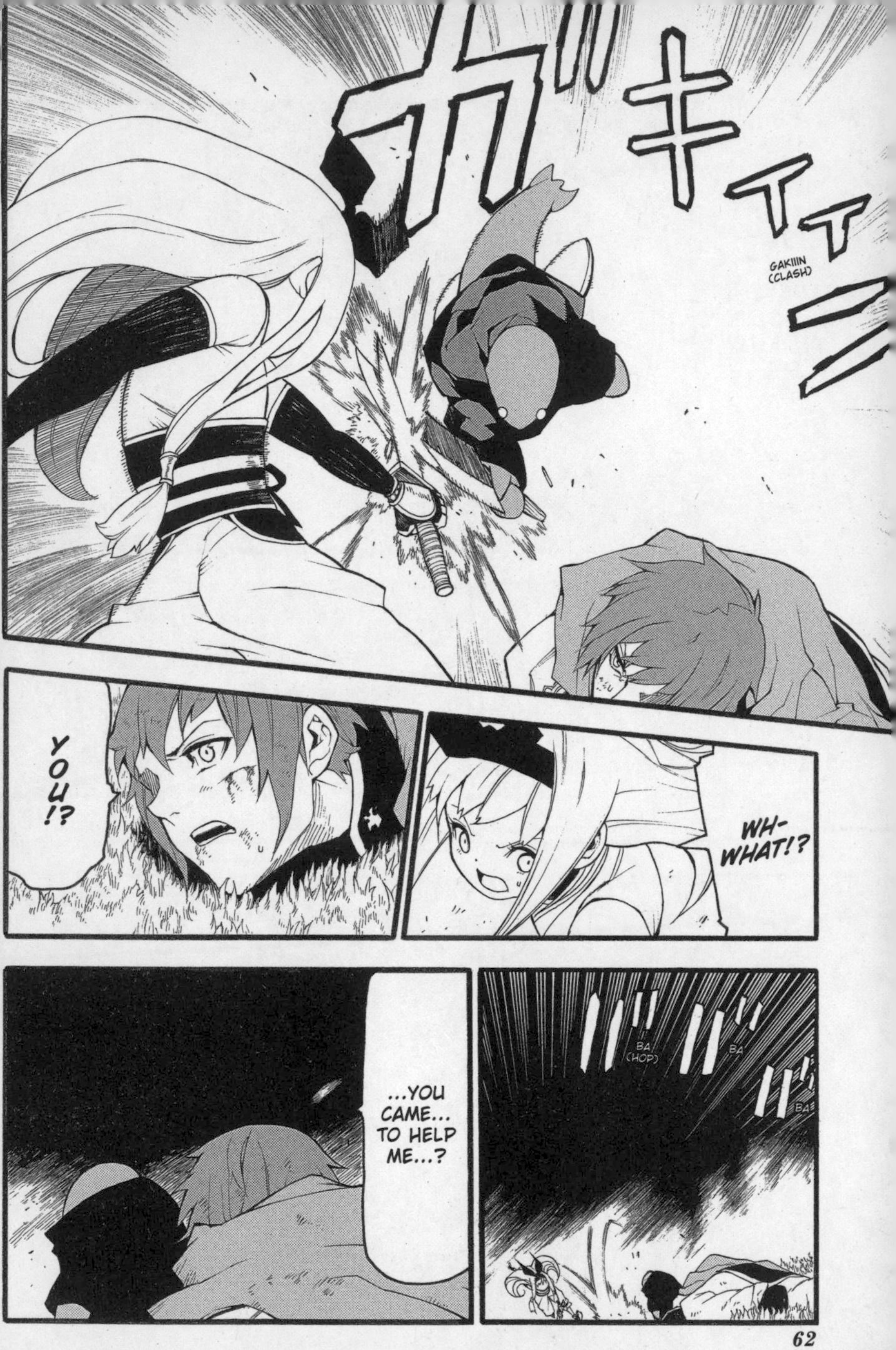
GAKIIIN (CLASH)
WH- WHAT!?
YOU!?
BA (HOP)
BA
BA
...YOU CAME... TO HELP ME...?

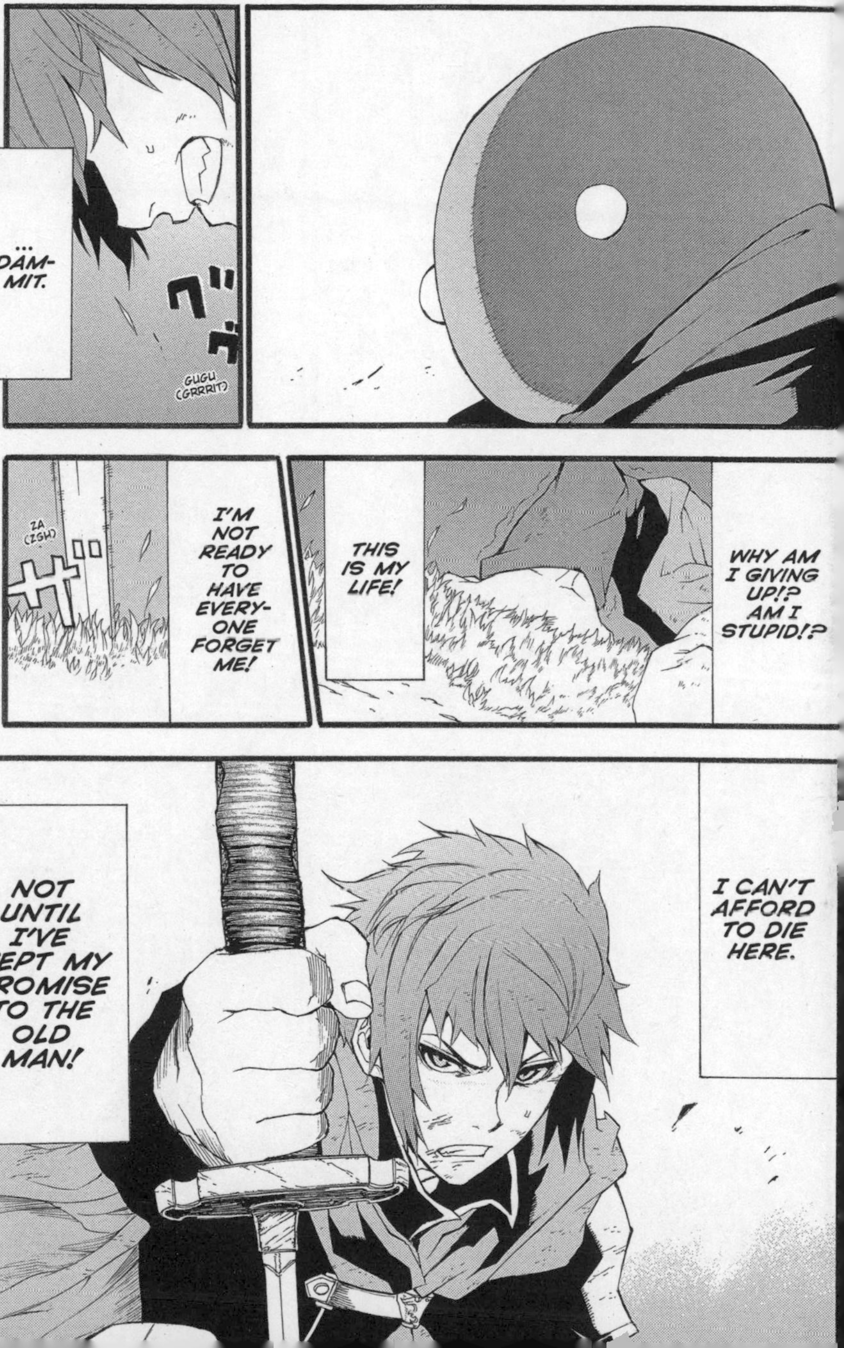

... DAMMIT.
GUGU (GRRRIT)
WHY AM I GIVING UP!? AM I STUPID!?
THIS IS MY LIFE!
I'M NOT READY TO HAVE EVERYONE FORGET ME!
ZA (ZGH)
I CAN'T AFFORD TO DIE HERE.
NOT UNTIL I'VE KEPT MY PROMISE TO THE OLD MAN!

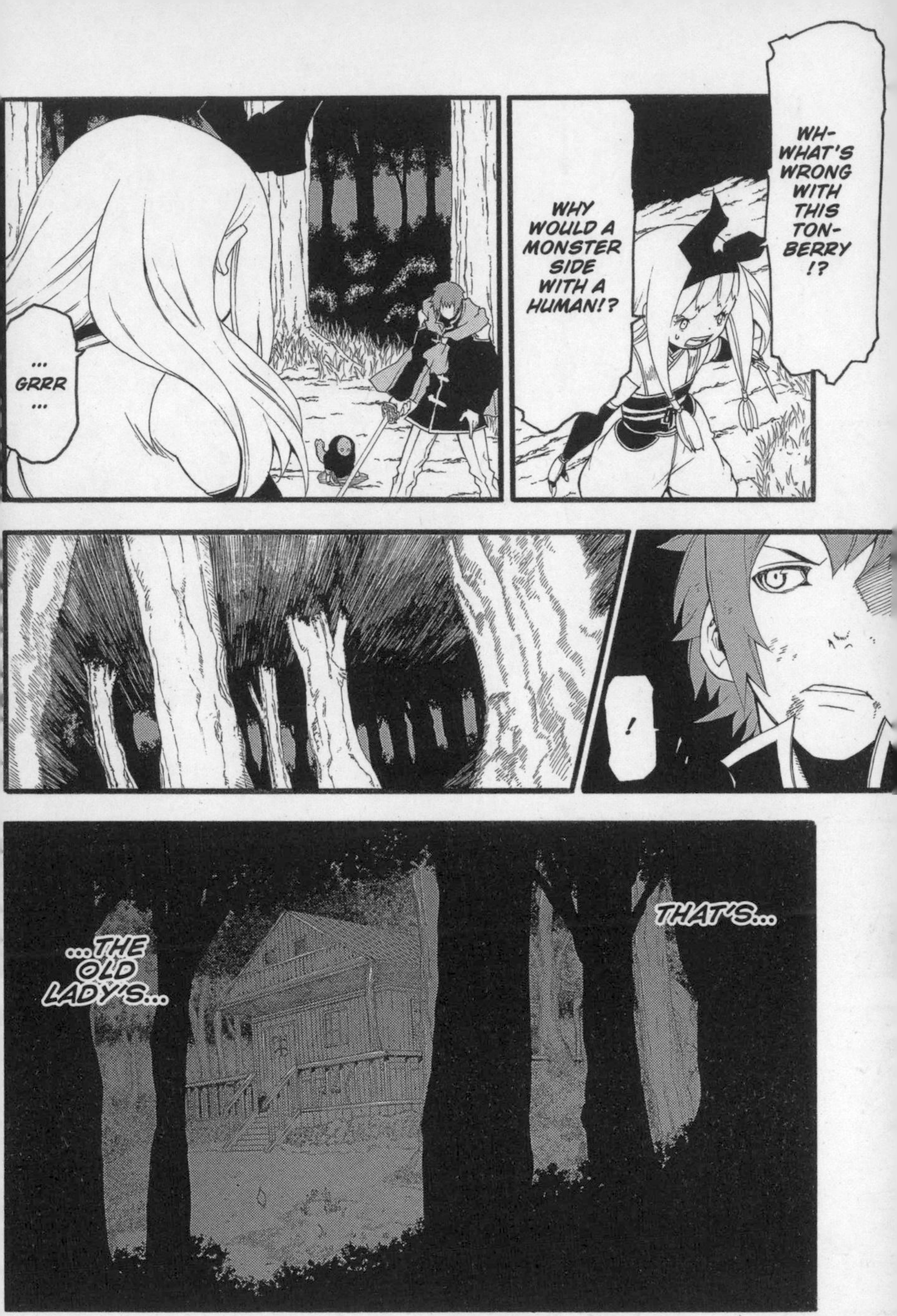
WH-WHAT'S WRONG WITH THIS TON-BERRY!?
WHY WOULD A MONSTER SIDE WITH A HUMAN!?
...GRRR...
!
THAT'S...
...THE OLD LADY'S...

UH...

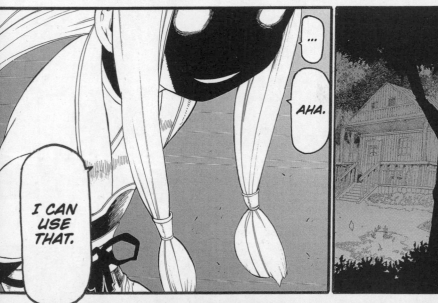

...

AHA.

I CAN
USE
THAT.

BLIZZARD!

HYUBA
(SWOOSH)

BA
(CHOP)

!

NO
ONE
IN
THAT
HOUSE
HAS
ANY-
THING
TO DO
WITH
THIS!!

NO!

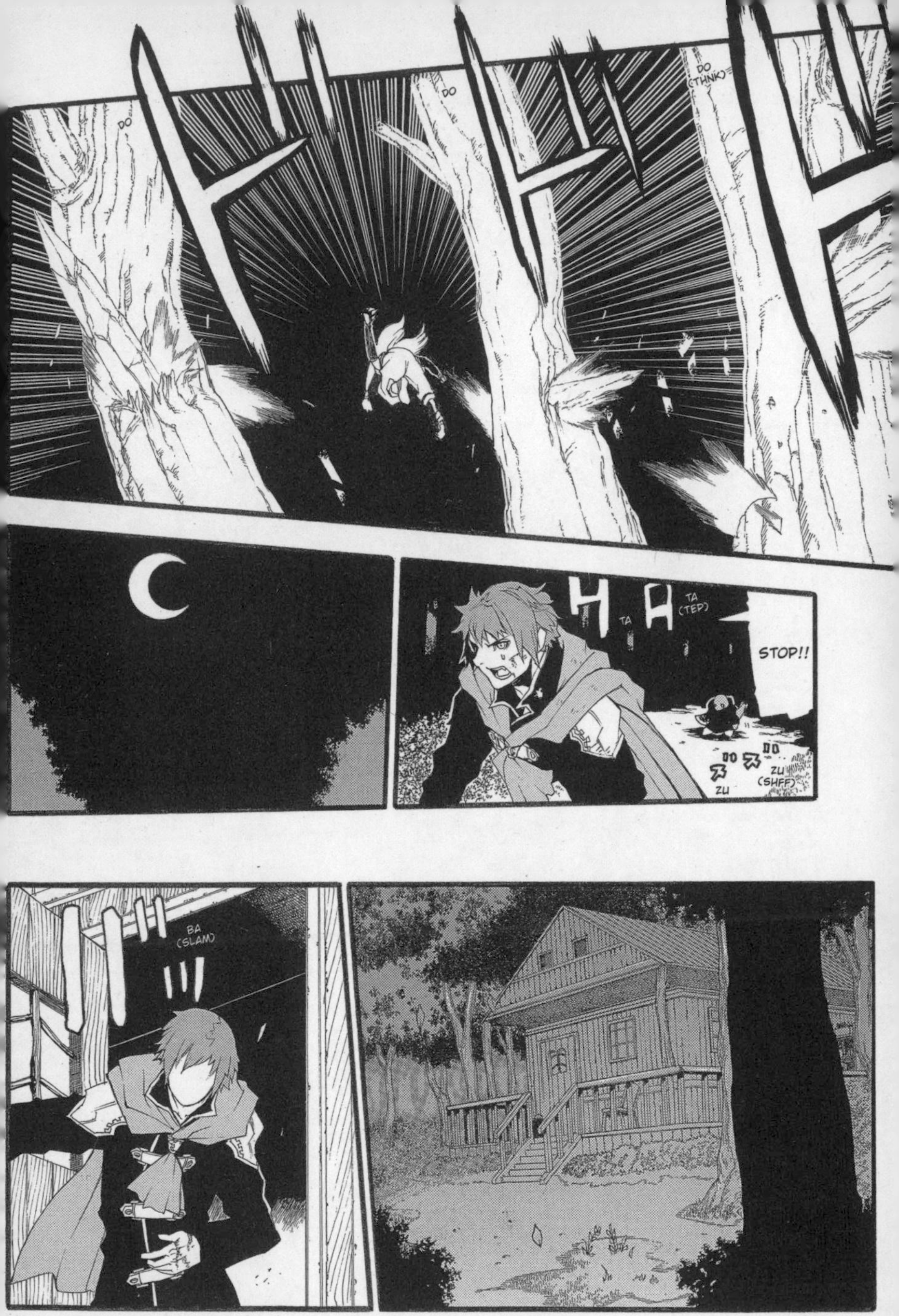
DO (THNK)
DO
DO
TA (TEP)
TA
STOP!!
ZU (SHFF)
ZU
BA (SLAM)

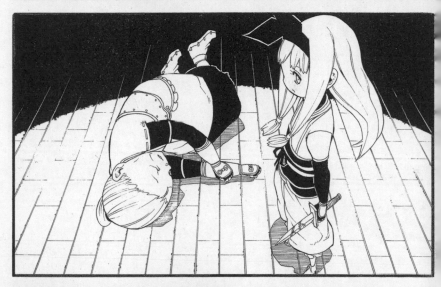

NIYA
(SMIRK)

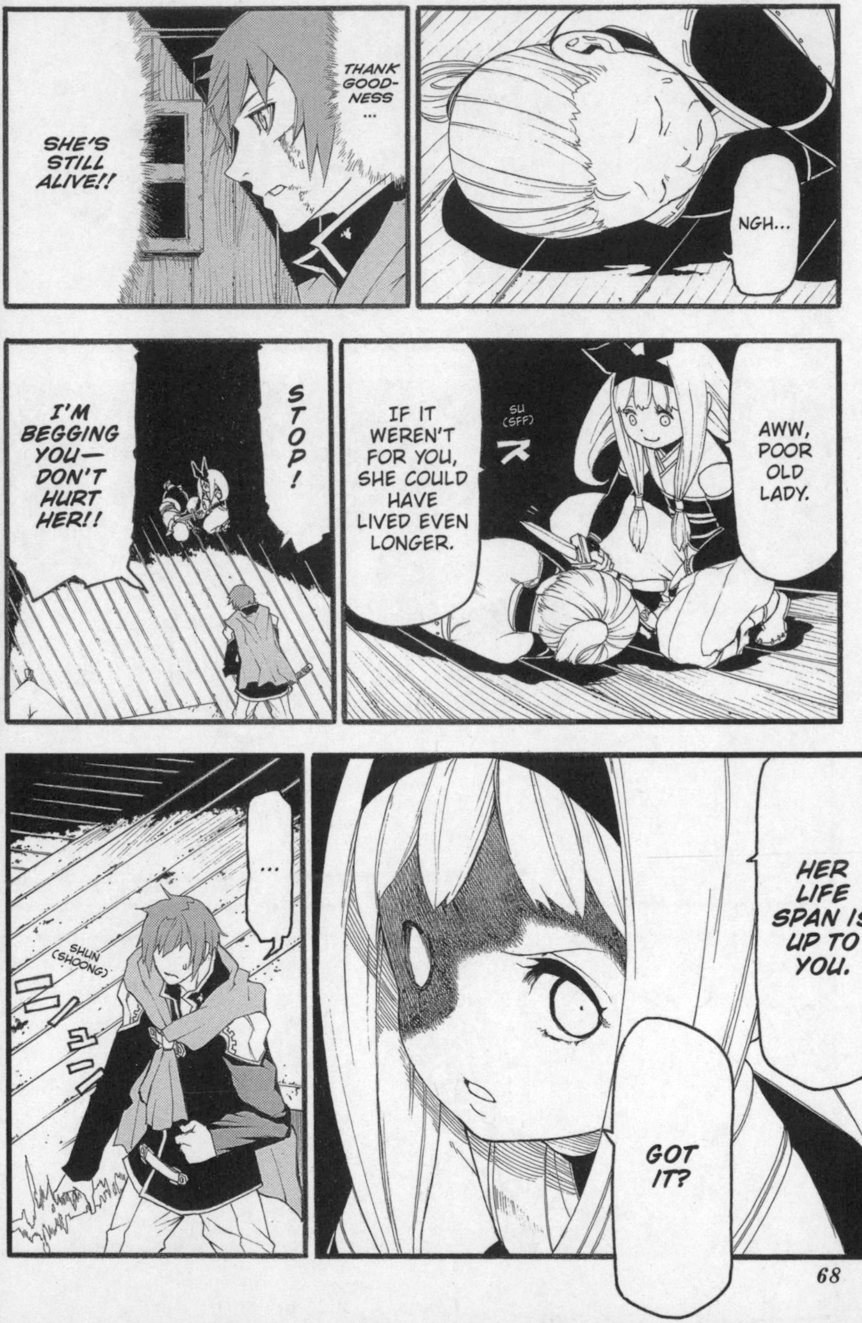
NGH...
THANK GOODNESS...
SHE'S STILL ALIVE!!
AWW, POOR OLD LADY.
SU (SFF)
IF IT WEREN'T FOR YOU, SHE COULD HAVE LIVED EVEN LONGER.
STOP!
I'M BEGGING YOU—DON'T HURT HER!!
HER LIFE SPAN IS UP TO YOU.
GOT IT?
...
SHUN (SHOONG)

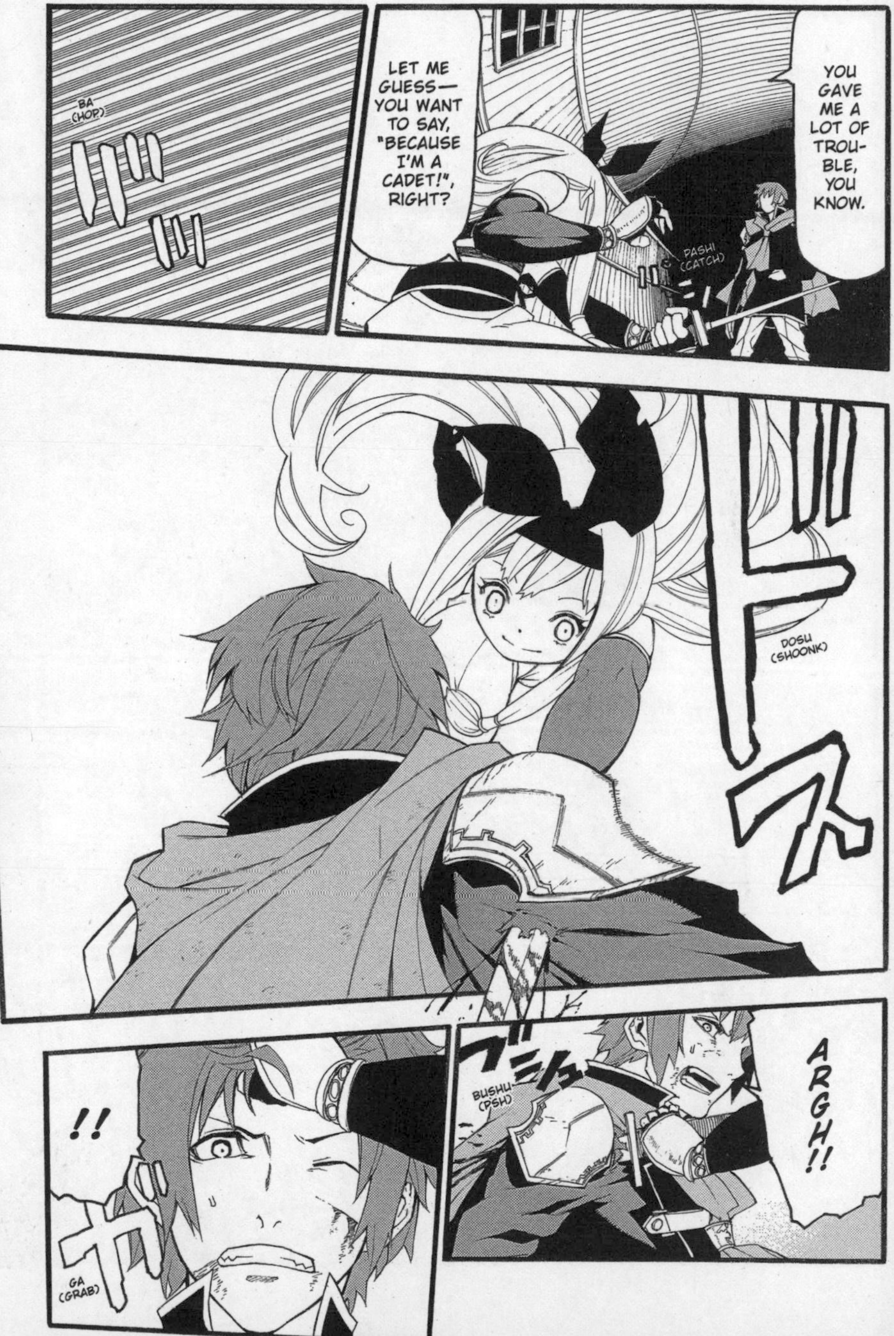
YOU GAVE ME A LOT OF TROUBLE, YOU KNOW.
LET ME GUESS—YOU WANT TO SAY, "BECAUSE I'M A CADET!", RIGHT?
PASHI (CATCH)
BA (HOP)
DOSU (SHOONK)
ARGH!!
BUSHU (PSH)
!!
GA (GRAB)

GAN
(SMASH)

...CAN'T STAND LOSING TO CADETS.

YUME-MI...

AAAUGH!!

GOKA
(SMACK)

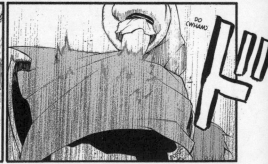

DO
(WHAM)

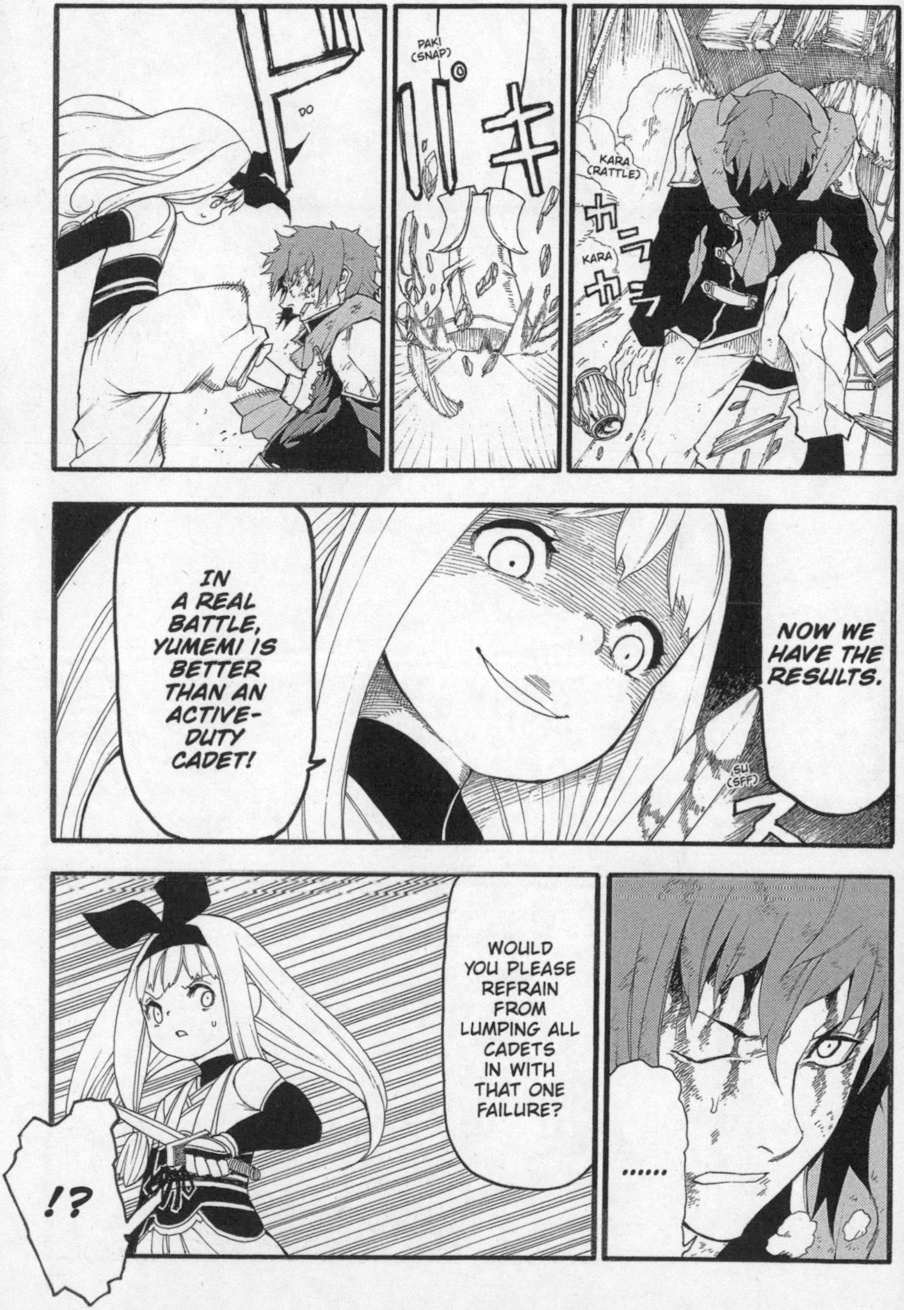
KARA (RATTLE)
KARA
PAKI (SNAP)
DO
NOW WE HAVE THE RESULTS.
SU (SFF)
IN A REAL BATTLE, YUMEMI IS BETTER THAN AN ACTIVE-DUTY CADET!
......
WOULD YOU PLEASE REFRAIN FROM LUMPING ALL CADETS IN WITH THAT ONE FAILURE?
!?

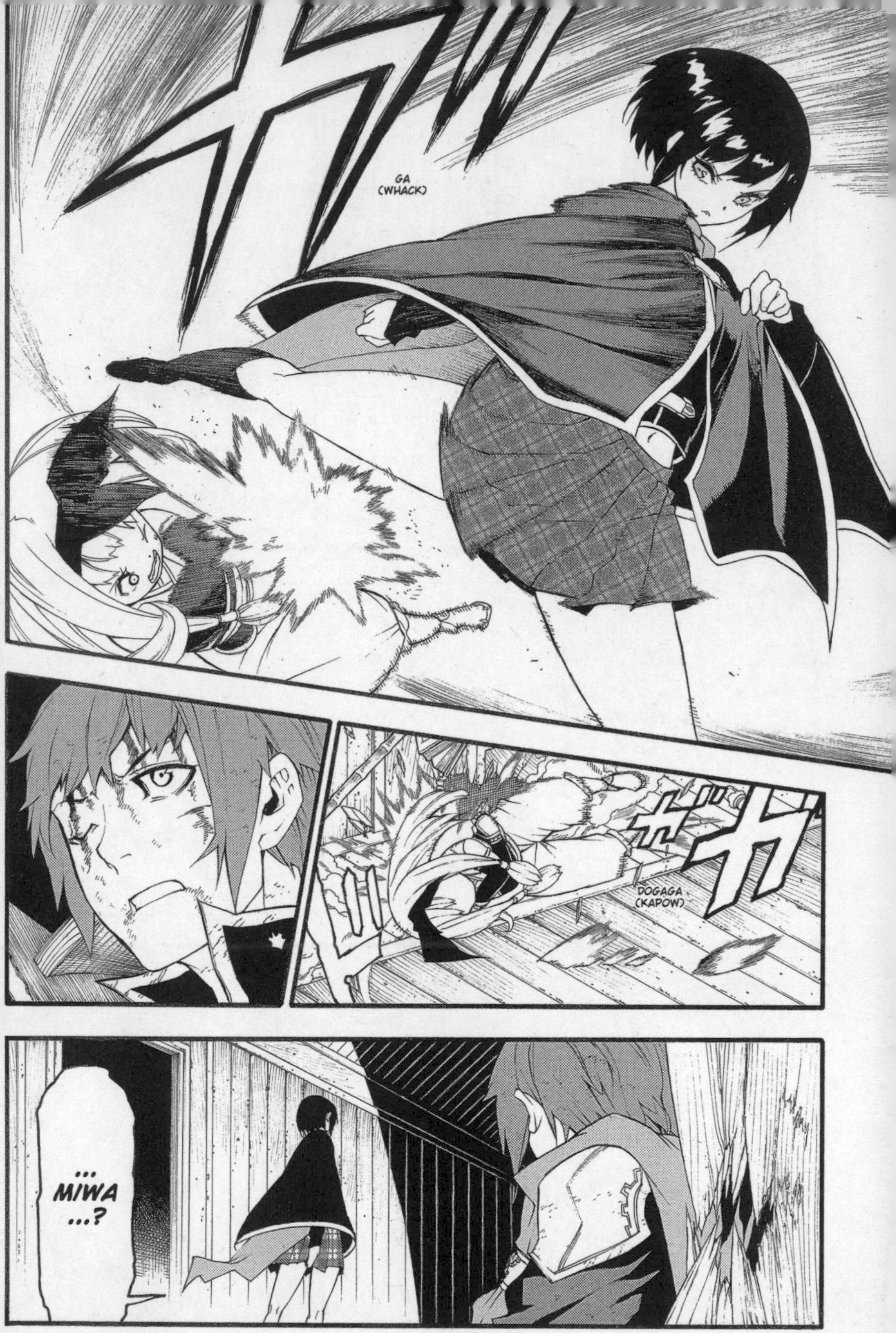
GA
(WHACK)
DOGAGA
(KAPOW)
...MIWA...?

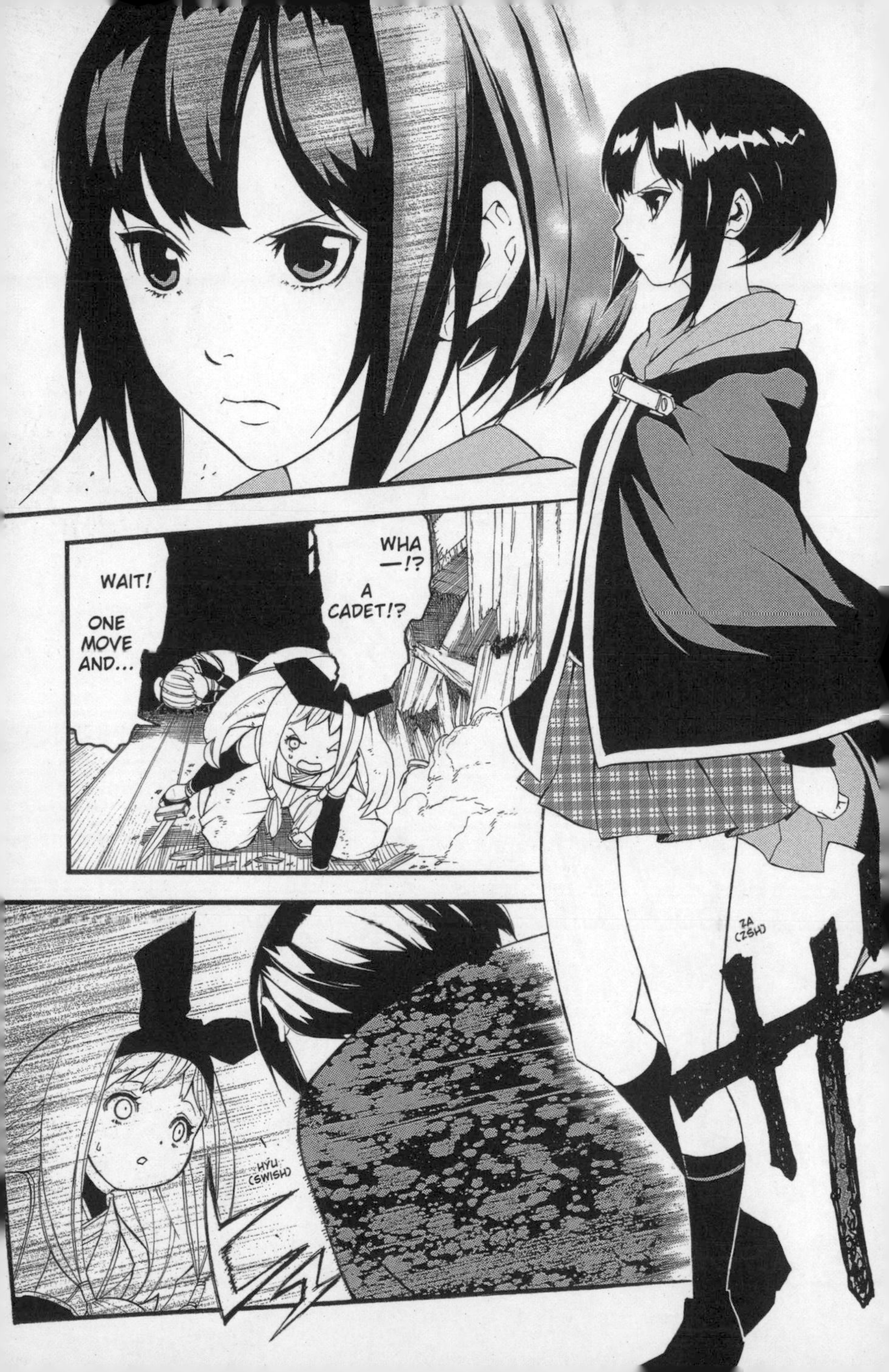
WHA—!?
A CADET!?
WAIT!
ONE MOVE AND...
ZA (ZSH)
HYU (SWISH)

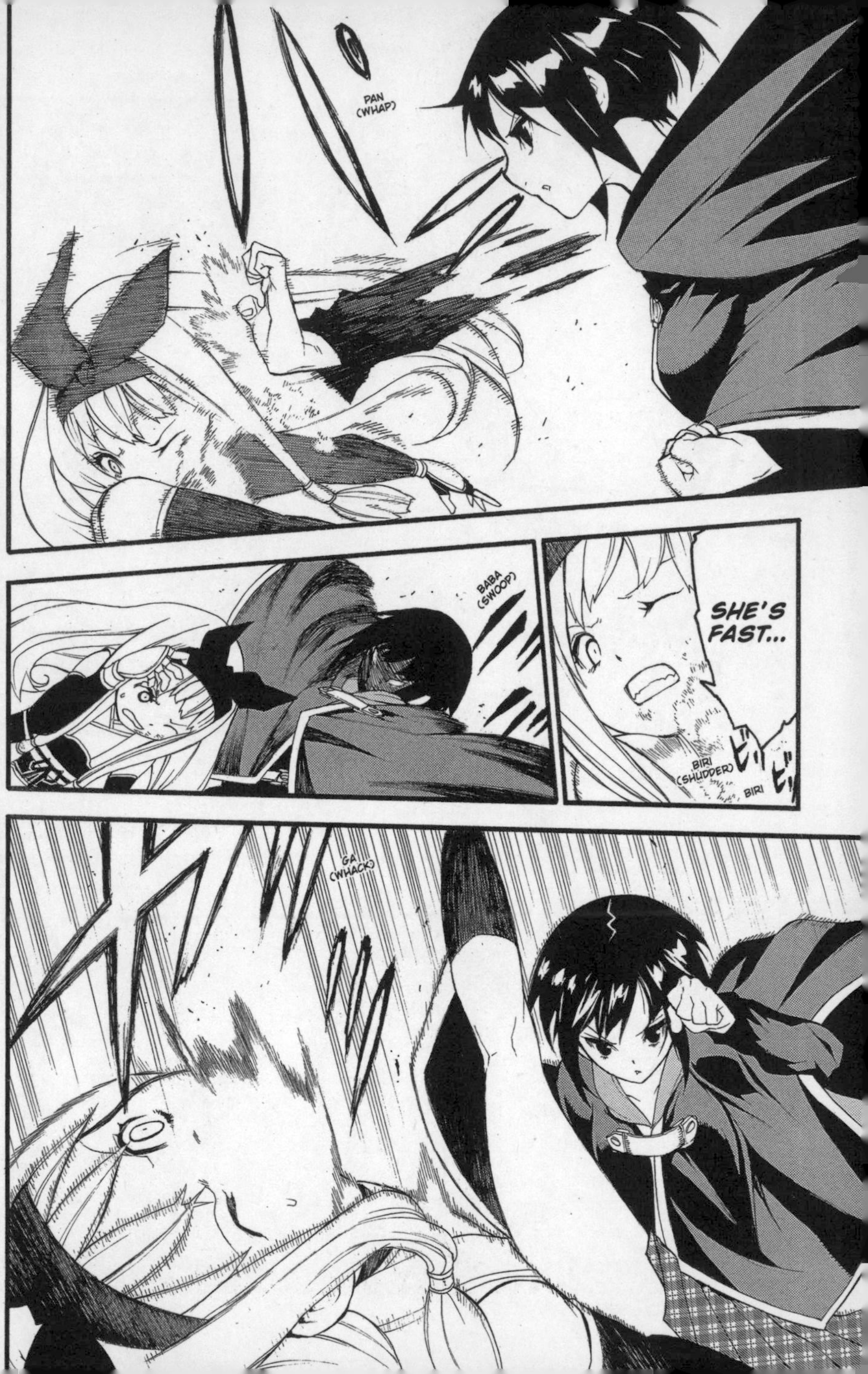
PAN
(WHAP)
SHE'S FAST...
BIRI
(SHUDDER)
BIRI
BABA
(SWOOP)
GA
(WHACK)

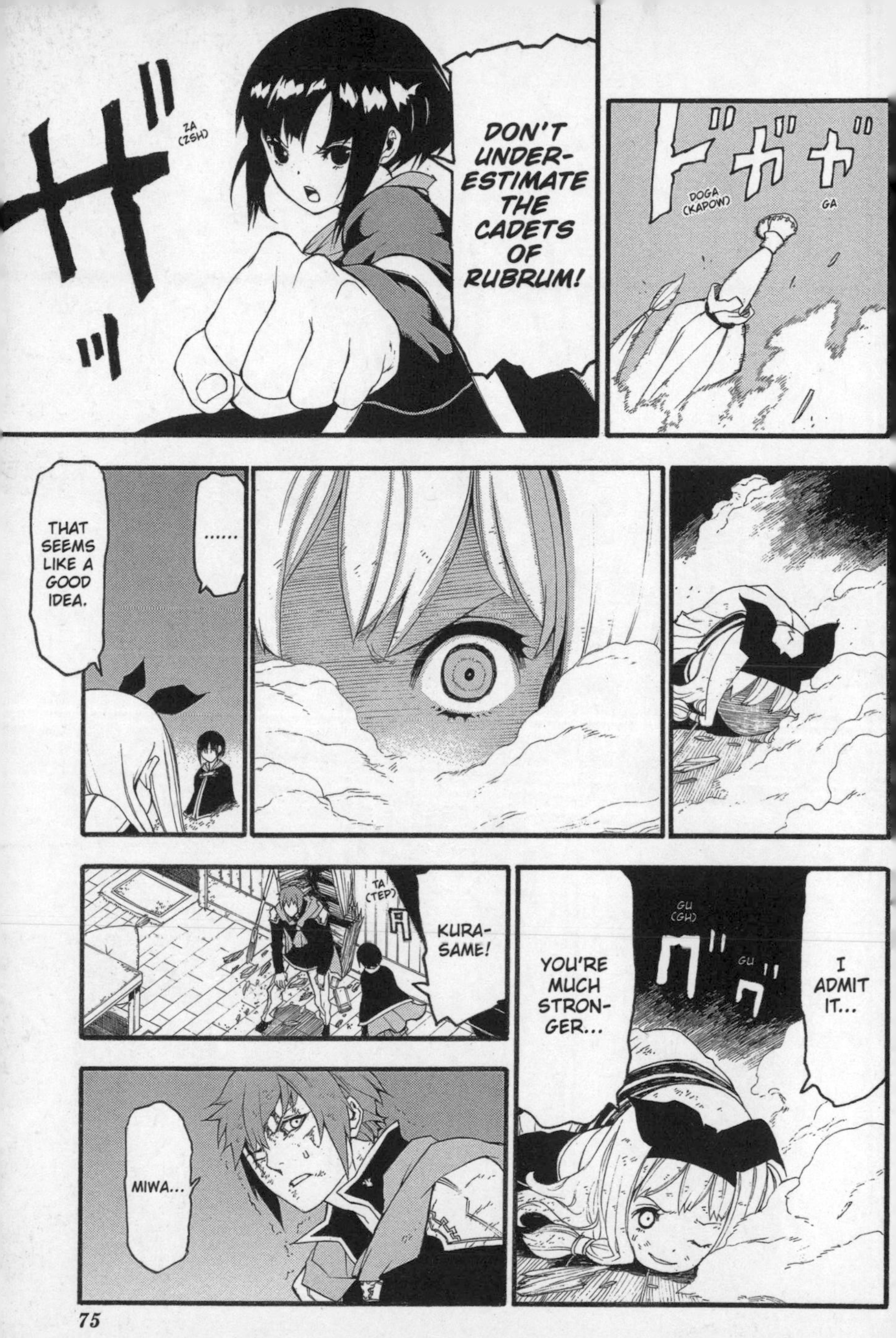

DOGA (KAPOW)
GA
ZA (ZSH)
DON'T UNDER-ESTIMATE THE CADETS OF RUBRUM!
......
THAT SEEMS LIKE A GOOD IDEA.
I ADMIT IT...
GU (GH)
GU
YOU'RE MUCH STRON-GER...
TA (TEP)
KURA-SAME!
MIWA...

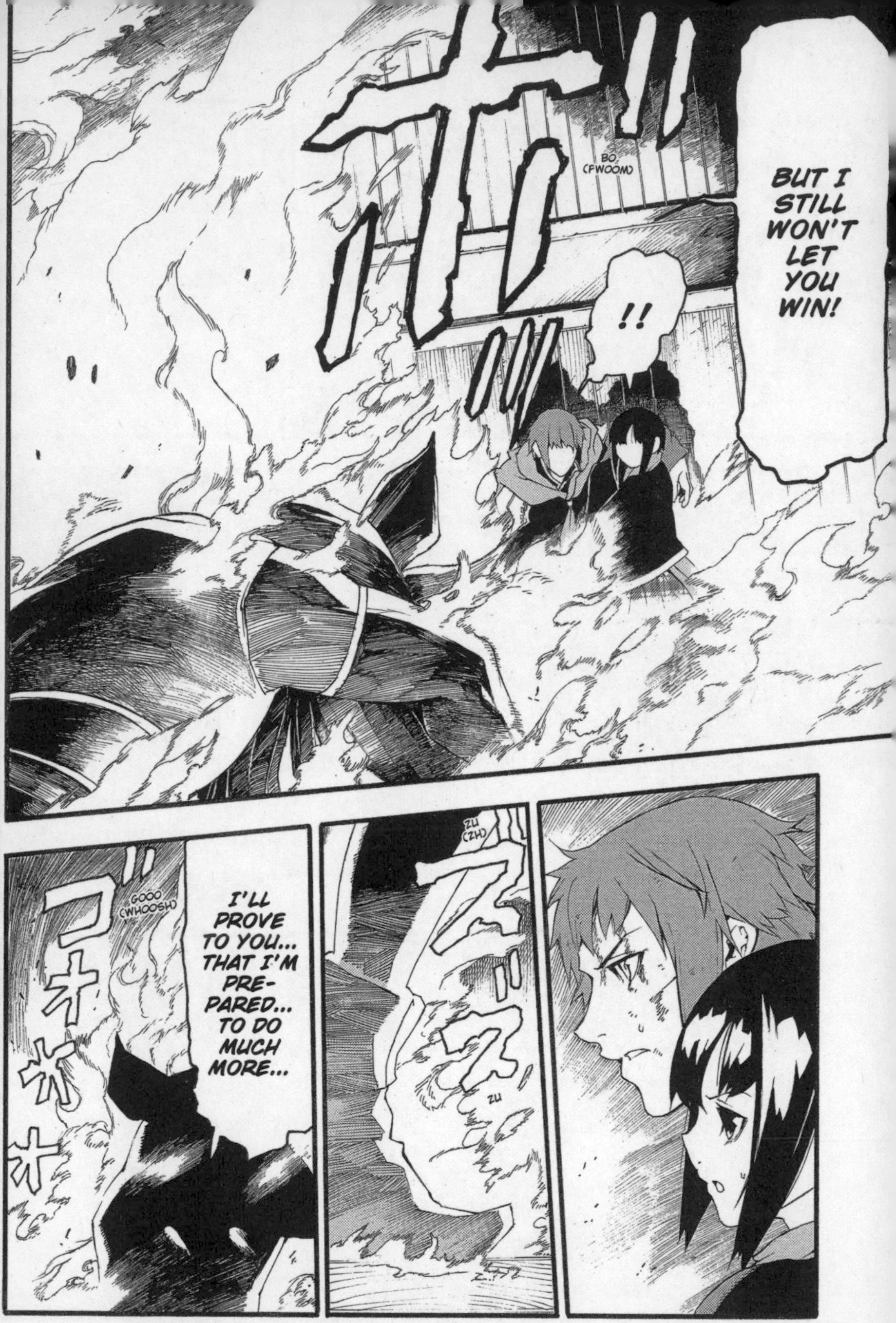
BUT I STILL WON'T LET YOU WIN!
BO (FWOOM)
!!
ZU (ZH)
ZU
I'LL PROVE TO YOU... THAT I'M PRE-PARED... TO DO MUCH MORE...
GOOO (WHOOSH)

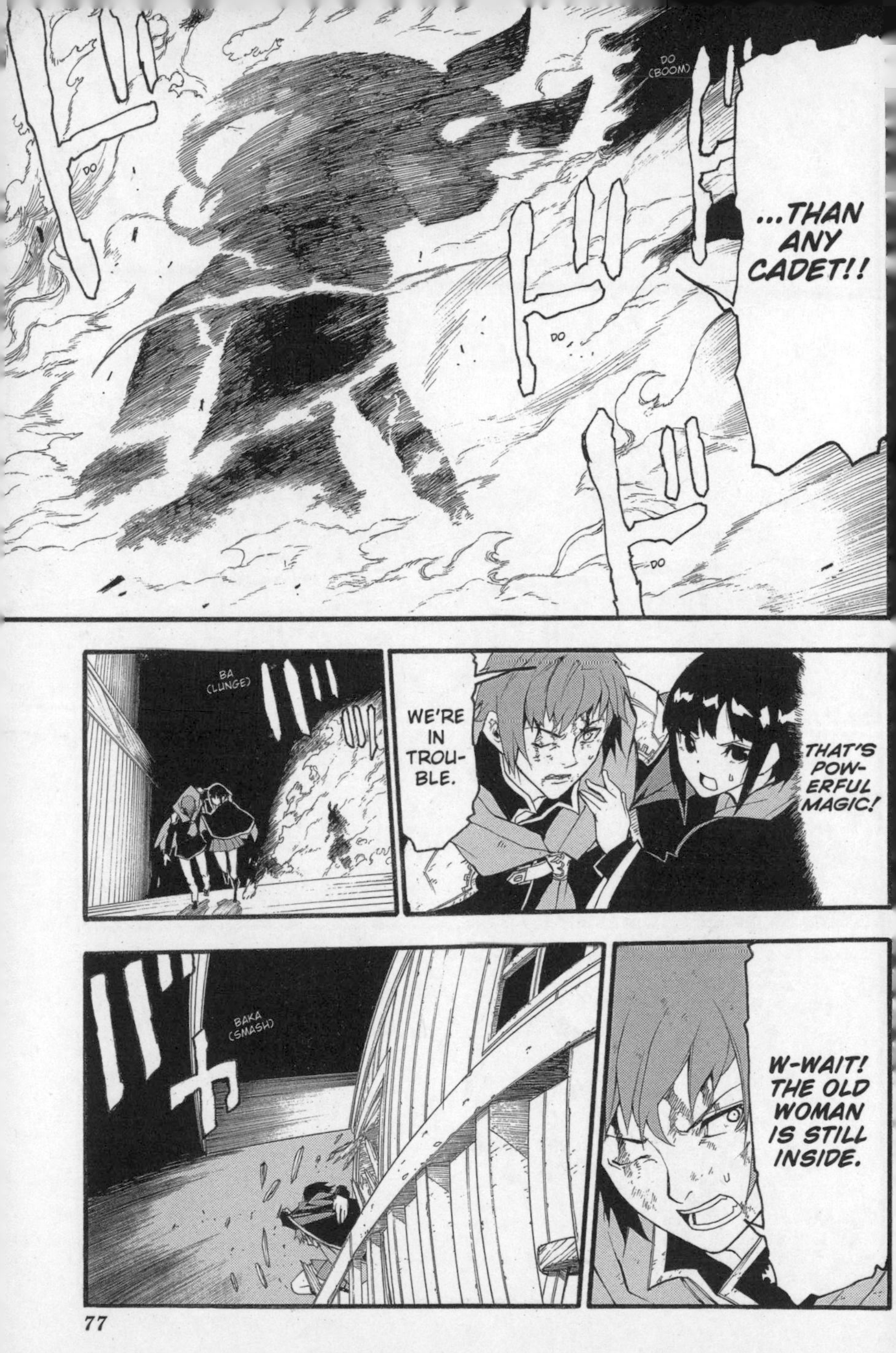
DO (BOOM)
...THAN ANY CADET!!
DO
DO
DO
THAT'S POW-ERFUL MAGIC!
WE'RE IN TROU-BLE.
BA (LUNGE)
W-WAIT! THE OLD WOMAN IS STILL INSIDE.
BAKA (SMASH)

GOA
(FWOOM)

....

ド゙ドドド
DO DO DO DO
(BOOM)

コオ
ZA
(ZSH)

ゴオオオオ
(WHOOOOOOSH)

MIWA
...!

KOKU
(NOD)

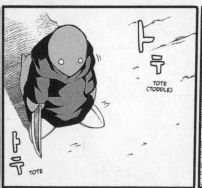

ト
テ
TOTE
(TODDLE)

ト
テ
TOTE

TA
(TEP)
TA

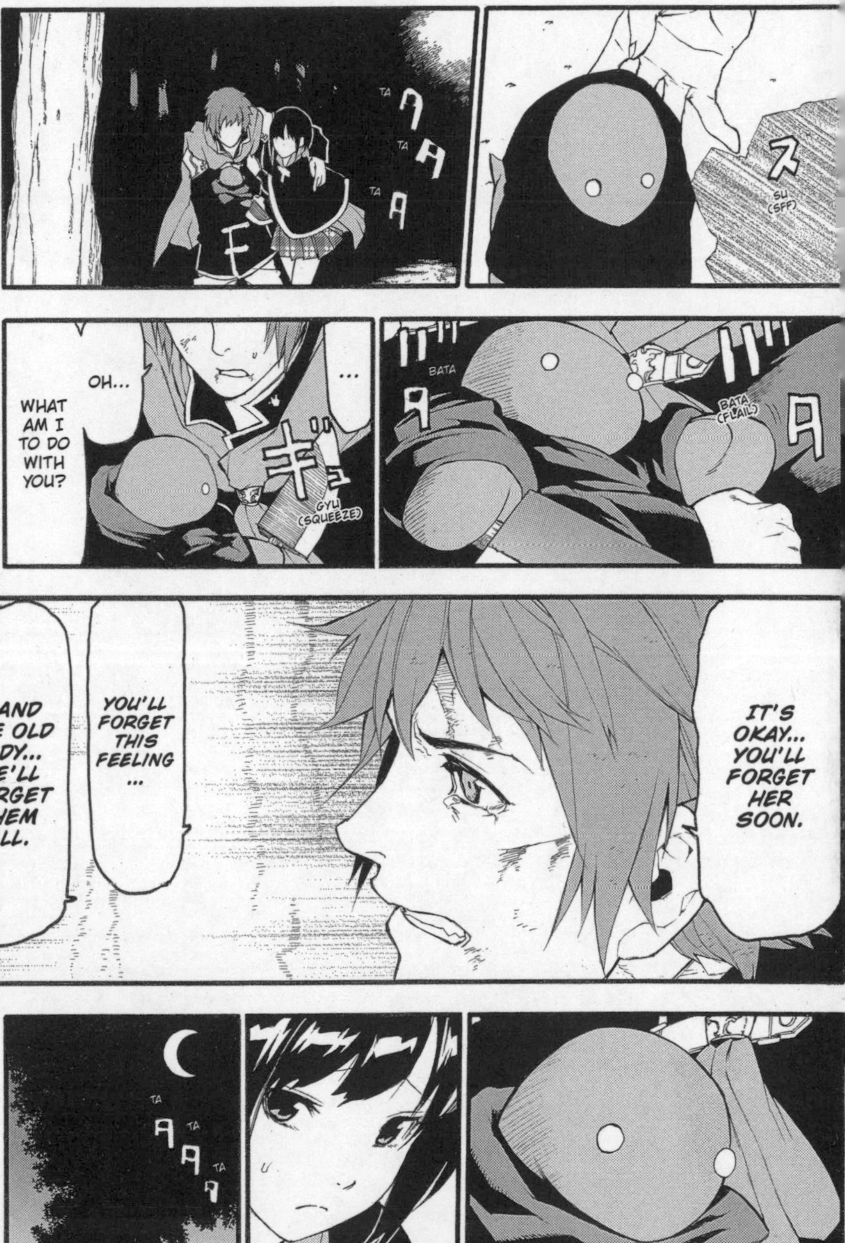
SU (SFF)
TA TA TA
BATA
BATA (FLAIL)
...
OH... WHAT AM I TO DO WITH YOU?
GYU (SQUEEZE)
IT'S OKAY... YOU'LL FORGET HER SOON.
YOU'LL FORGET THIS FEELING...
...AND THE OLD LADY... WE'LL FORGET THEM ALL.
TA TA TA

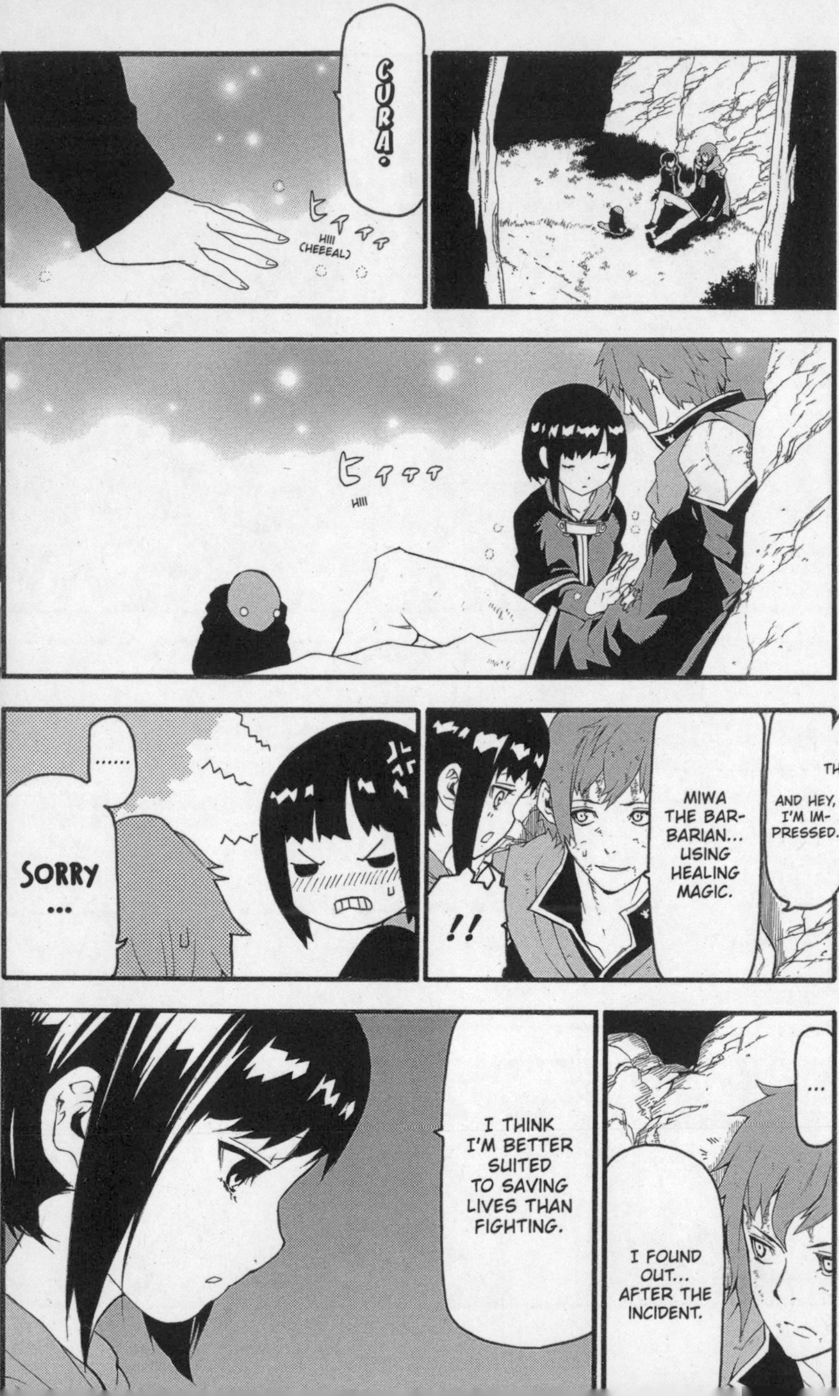
CURA.
ヒィィィ
HIII (CHEEEAL)
ヒィィィ
HIII
... THANKS.
AND HEY, I'M IM-PRESSED.
MIWA THE BAR-BARIAN... USING HEALING MAGIC.
!!
......
SORRY ...
...
I FOUND OUT... AFTER THE INCIDENT.
I THINK I'M BETTER SUITED TO SAVING LIVES THAN FIGHTING.

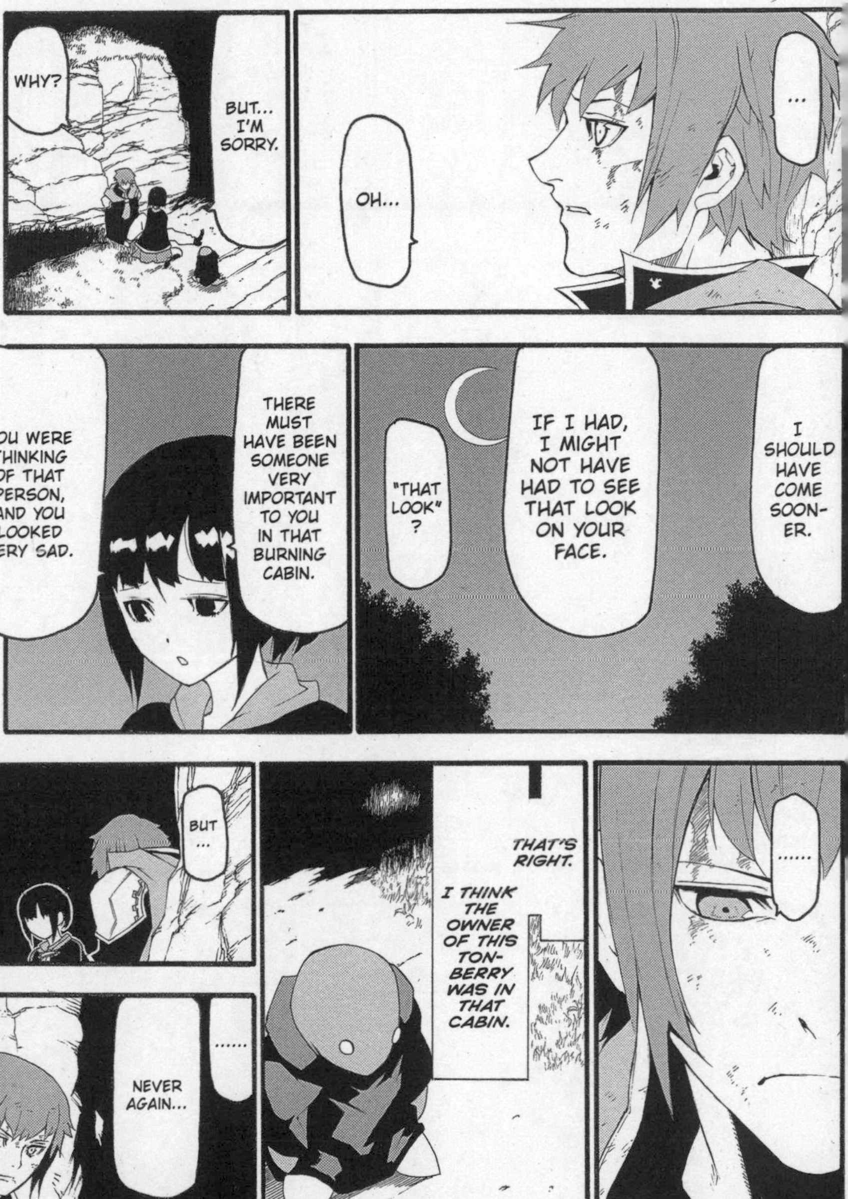
...
OH...
BUT... I'M SORRY.
WHY?
I SHOULD HAVE COME SOON-ER.
IF I HAD, I MIGHT NOT HAVE HAD TO SEE THAT LOOK ON YOUR FACE.
"THAT LOOK"?
THERE MUST HAVE BEEN SOMEONE VERY IMPORTANT TO YOU IN THAT BURNING CABIN.
YOU WERE THINKING OF THAT PERSON, AND YOU LOOKED VERY SAD.
......
THAT'S RIGHT.
I THINK THE OWNER OF THIS TON-BERRY WAS IN THAT CABIN.
BUT ...
......
NEVER AGAIN...

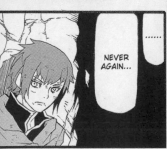

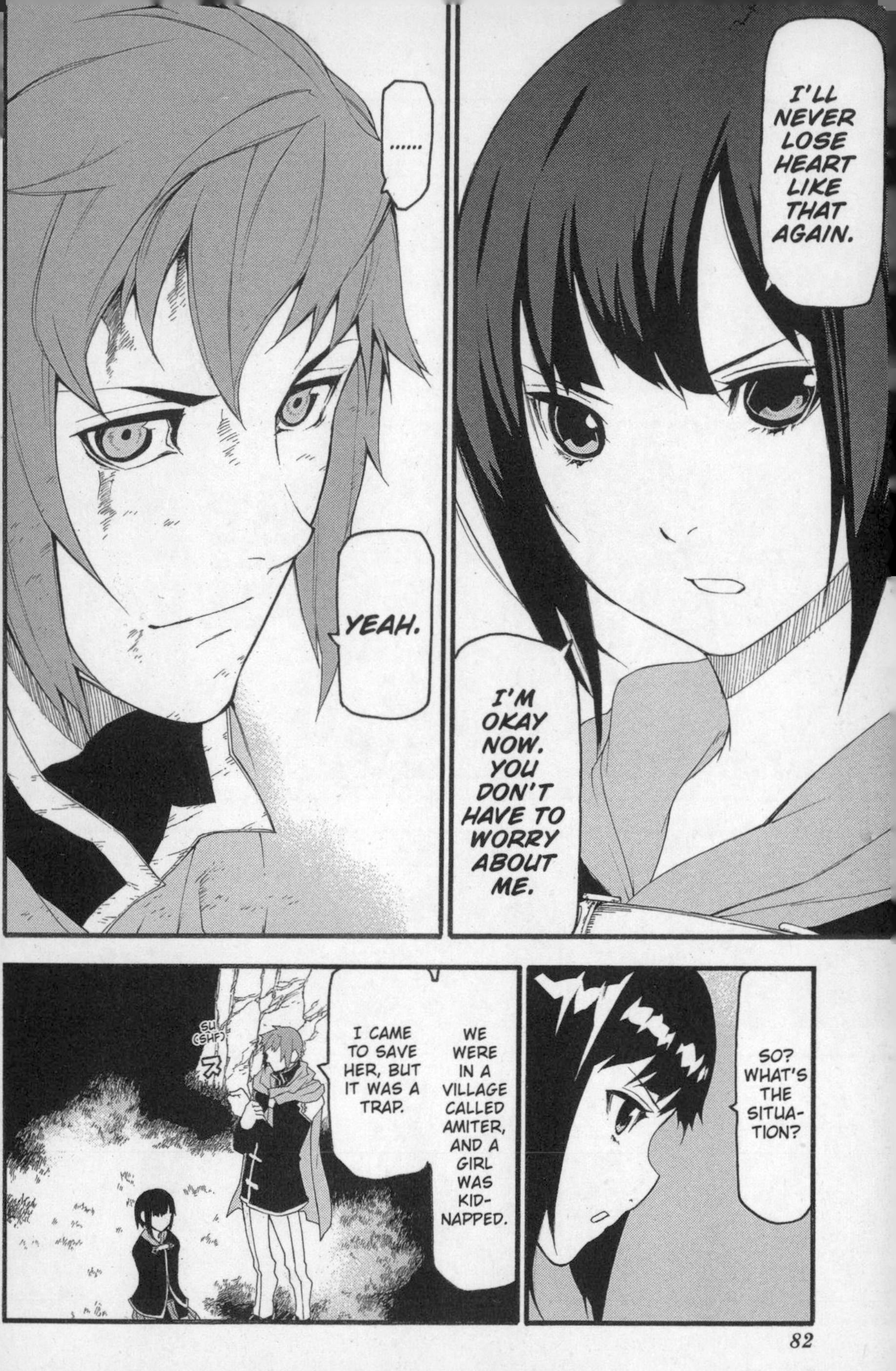
I'LL NEVER LOSE HEART LIKE THAT AGAIN.
I'M OKAY NOW. YOU DON'T HAVE TO WORRY ABOUT ME.
......
YEAH.
SO? WHAT'S THE SITUATION?
WE WERE IN A VILLAGE CALLED AMITER, AND A GIRL WAS KIDNAPPED.
I CAME TO SAVE HER, BUT IT WAS A TRAP.
SU (SHF)

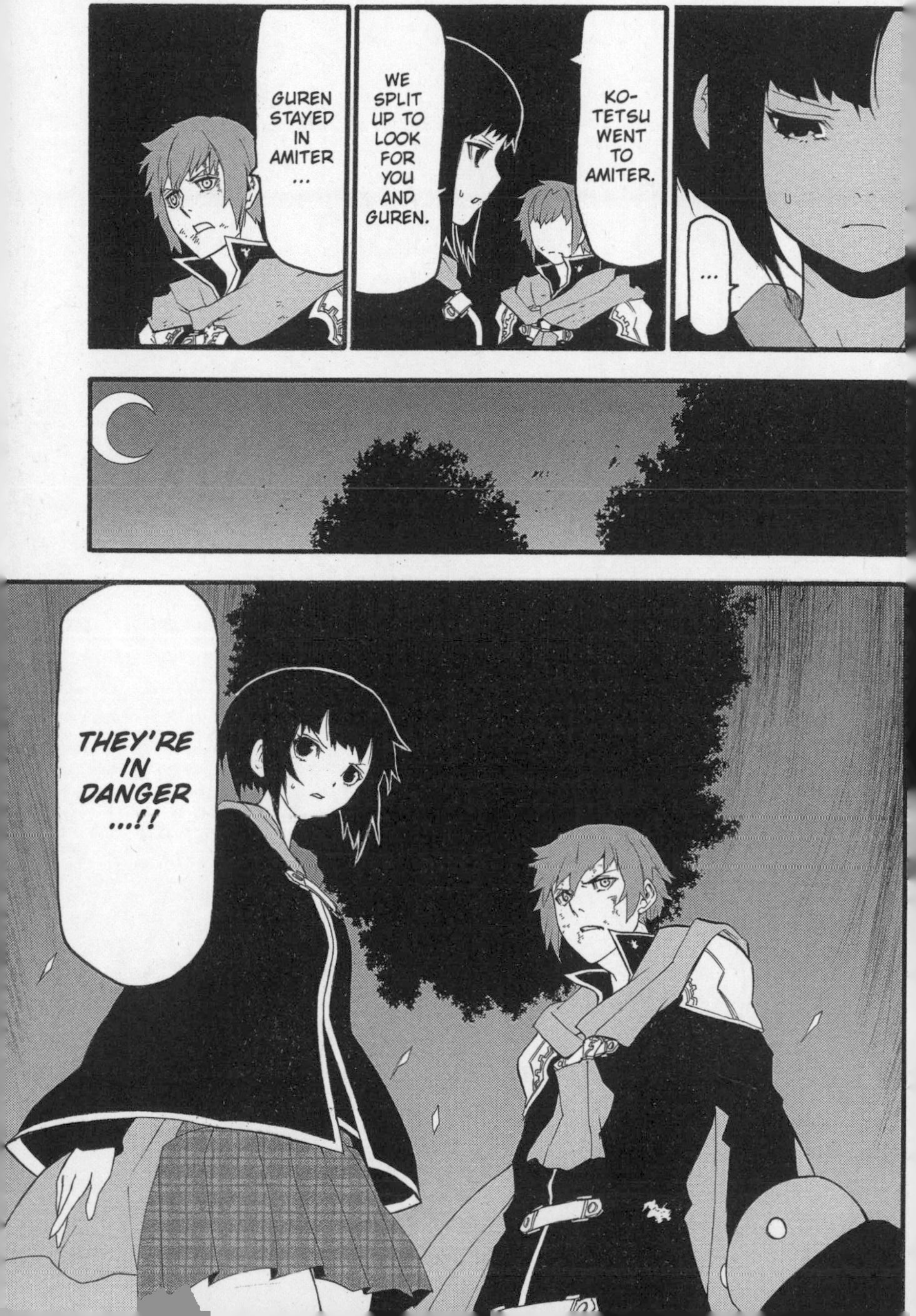
...
KO-TETSU WENT TO AMITER.
WE SPLIT UP TO LOOK FOR YOU AND GUREN.
GUREN STAYED IN AMITER ...
THEY'RE IN DANGER ...!!

FINAL FANTASY. 零式 TYPE-0™
SIDE STORY
The Ice Reaper

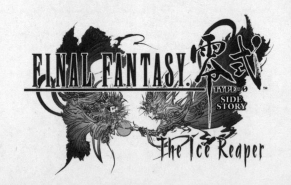

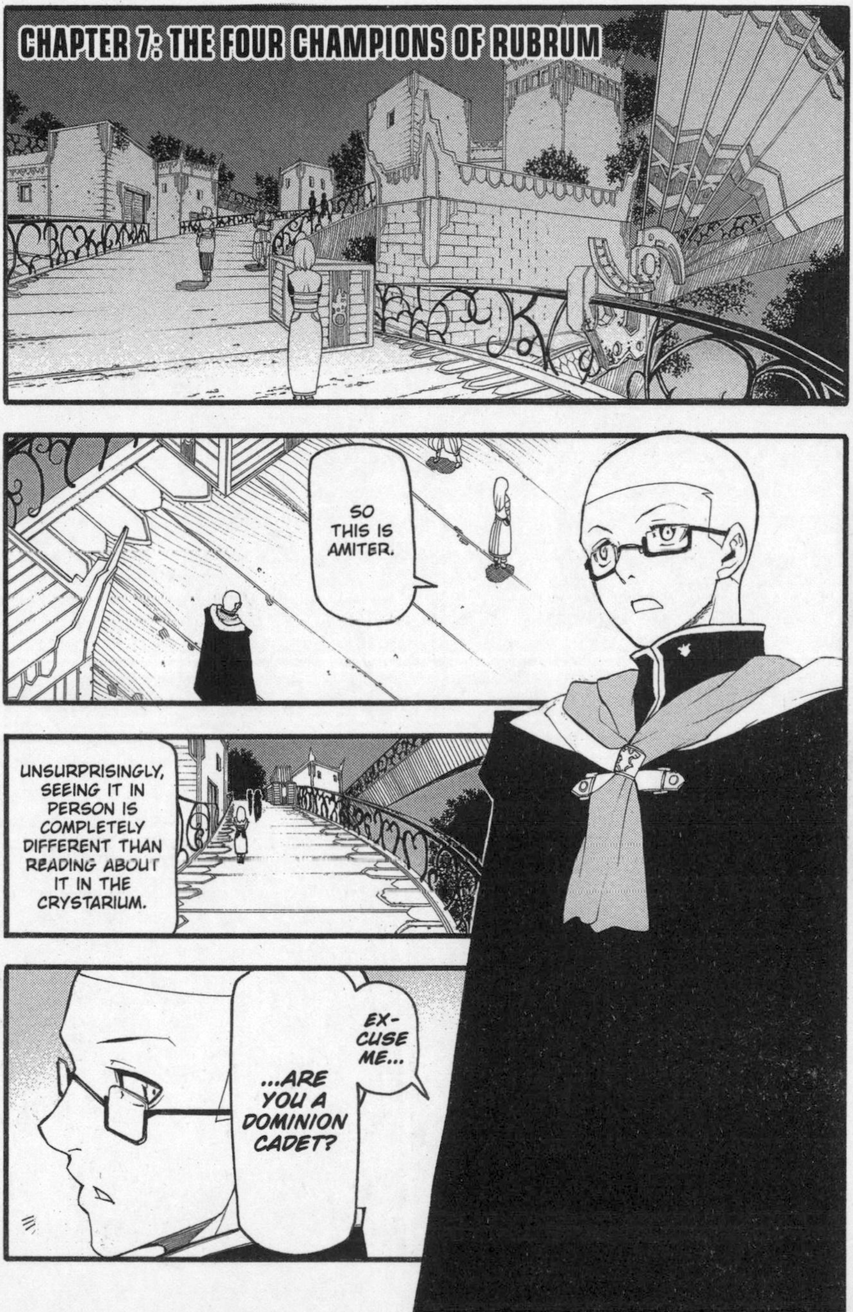
CHAPTER 7: THE FOUR CHAMPIONS OF RUBRUM
SO THIS IS AMITER.
UNSURPRISINGLY, SEEING IT IN PERSON IS COMPLETELY DIFFERENT THAN READING ABOUT IT IN THE CRYSTARIUM.
EX-CUSE ME...
...ARE YOU A DOMINION CADET?

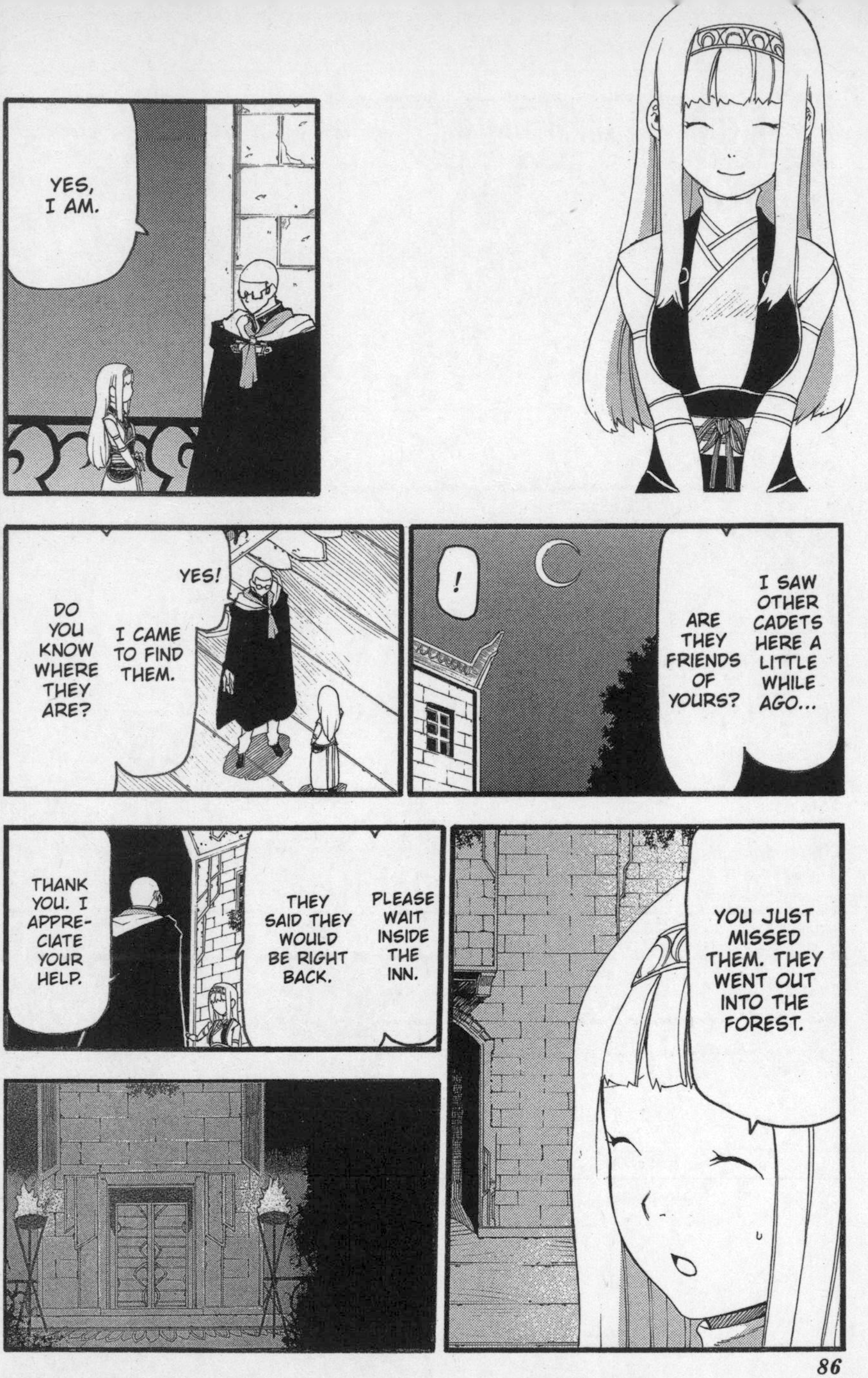
YES, I AM.
I SAW OTHER CADETS HERE A LITTLE WHILE AGO...
ARE THEY FRIENDS OF YOURS?
!
YES!
I CAME TO FIND THEM.
DO YOU KNOW WHERE THEY ARE?
YOU JUST MISSED THEM. THEY WENT OUT INTO THE FOREST.
PLEASE WAIT INSIDE THE INN.
THEY SAID THEY WOULD BE RIGHT BACK.
THANK YOU. I APPRECIATE YOUR HELP.

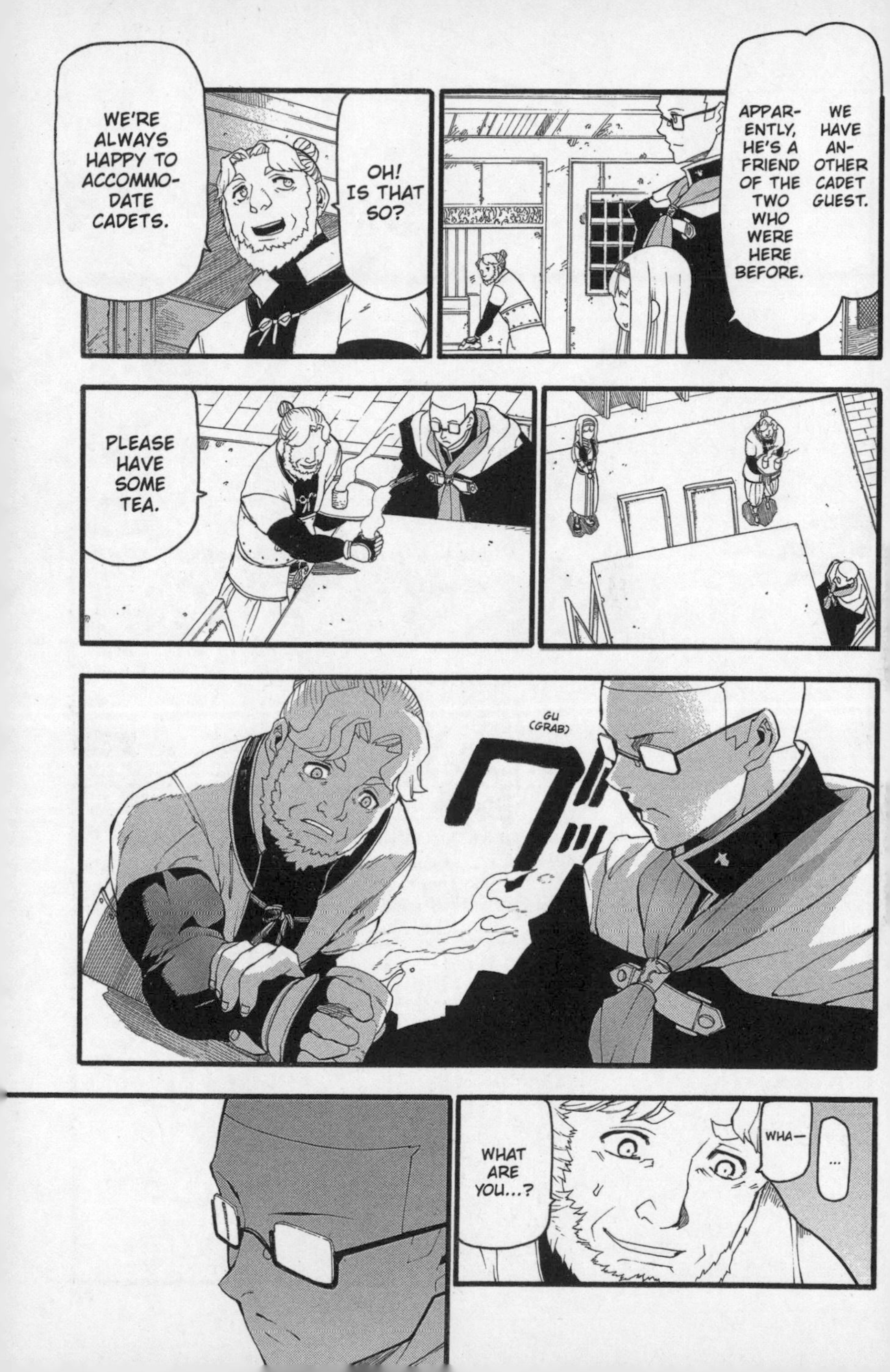
WE HAVE ANOTHER CADET GUEST.
APPARENTLY, HE'S A FRIEND OF THE TWO WHO WERE HERE BEFORE.
OH! IS THAT SO?
WE'RE ALWAYS HAPPY TO ACCOMMODATE CADETS.
PLEASE HAVE SOME TEA.
GU (GRAB)
...
WHA—
WHAT ARE YOU...?

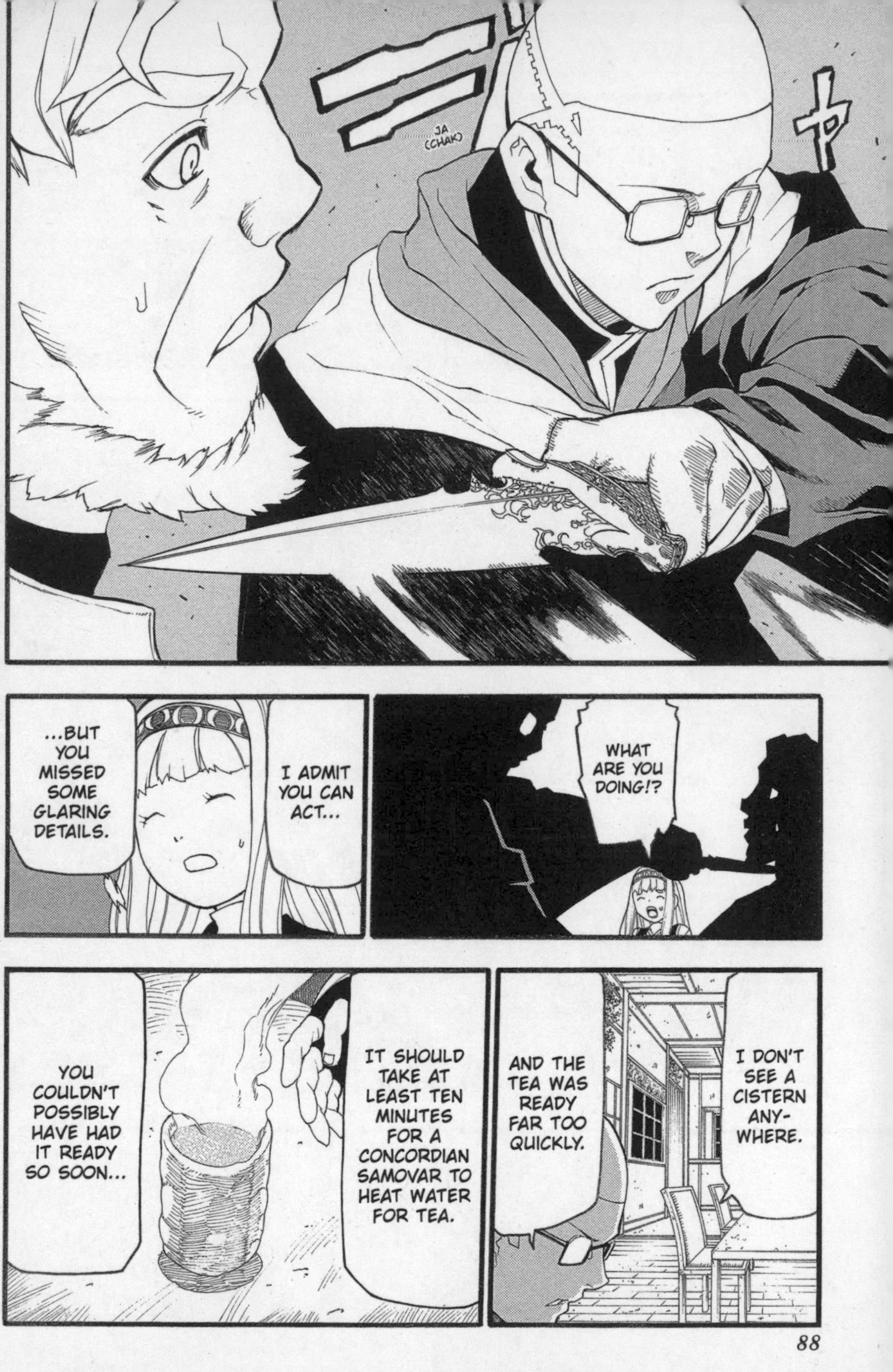
JA (CHAK)
WHAT ARE YOU DOING!?
I ADMIT YOU CAN ACT...
...BUT YOU MISSED SOME GLARING DETAILS.
I DON'T SEE A CISTERN ANY-WHERE.
AND THE TEA WAS READY FAR TOO QUICKLY.
IT SHOULD TAKE AT LEAST TEN MINUTES FOR A CONCORDIAN SAMOVAR TO HEAT WATER FOR TEA.
YOU COULDN'T POSSIBLY HAVE HAD IT READY SO SOON...

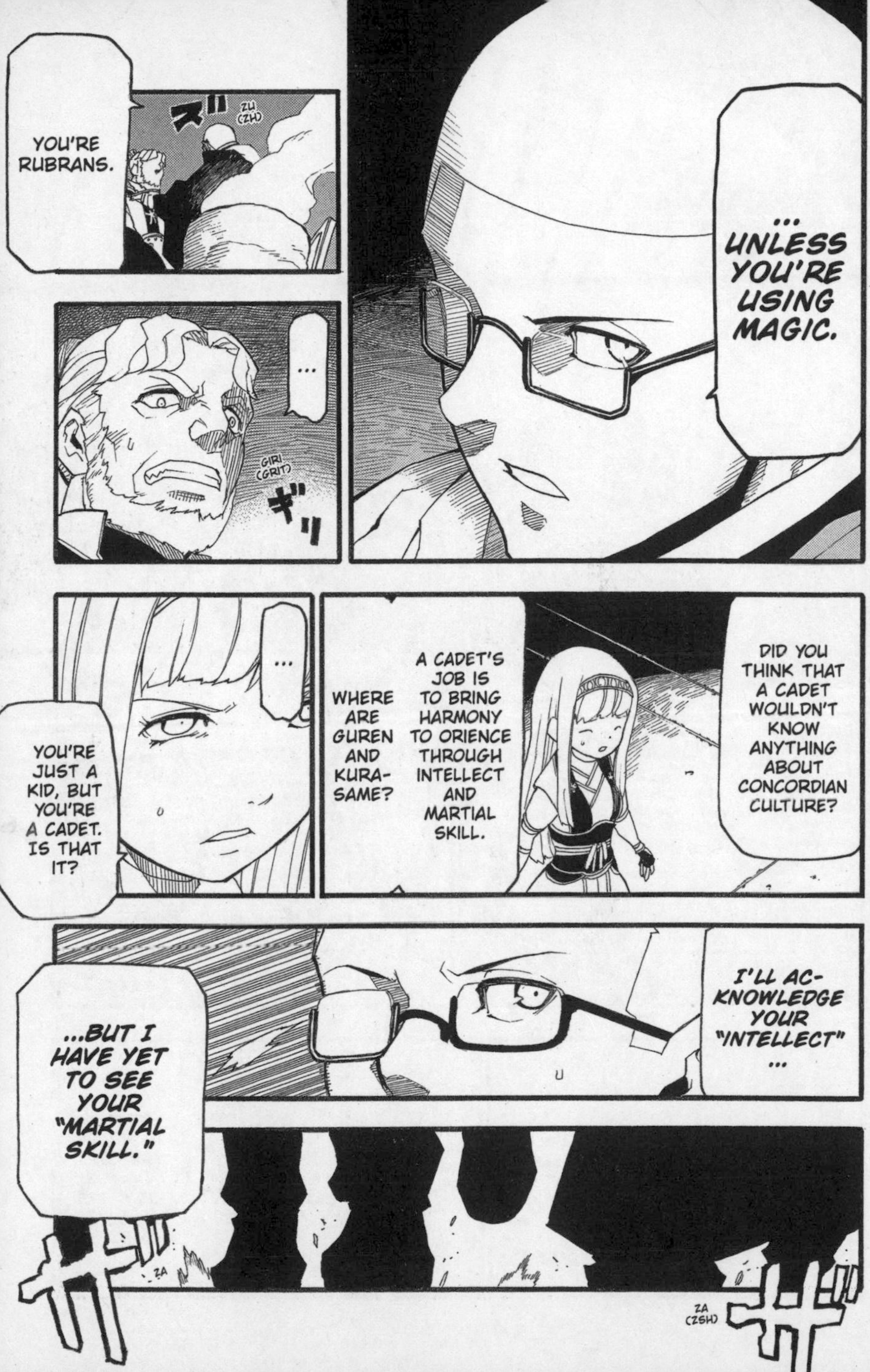
...UNLESS YOU'RE USING MAGIC.
YOU'RE RUBRANS.
ZU (ZH)
...
GIRI (GRIT)
DID YOU THINK THAT A CADET WOULDN'T KNOW ANYTHING ABOUT CONCORDIAN CULTURE?
A CADET'S JOB IS TO BRING HARMONY TO ORIENCE THROUGH INTELLECT AND MARTIAL SKILL.
WHERE ARE GUREN AND KURA-SAME?
...
YOU'RE JUST A KID, BUT YOU'RE A CADET. IS THAT IT?
I'LL AC-KNOWLEDGE YOUR "INTELLECT"...
...BUT I HAVE YET TO SEE YOUR "MARTIAL SKILL."
ZA (ZSH)
ZA

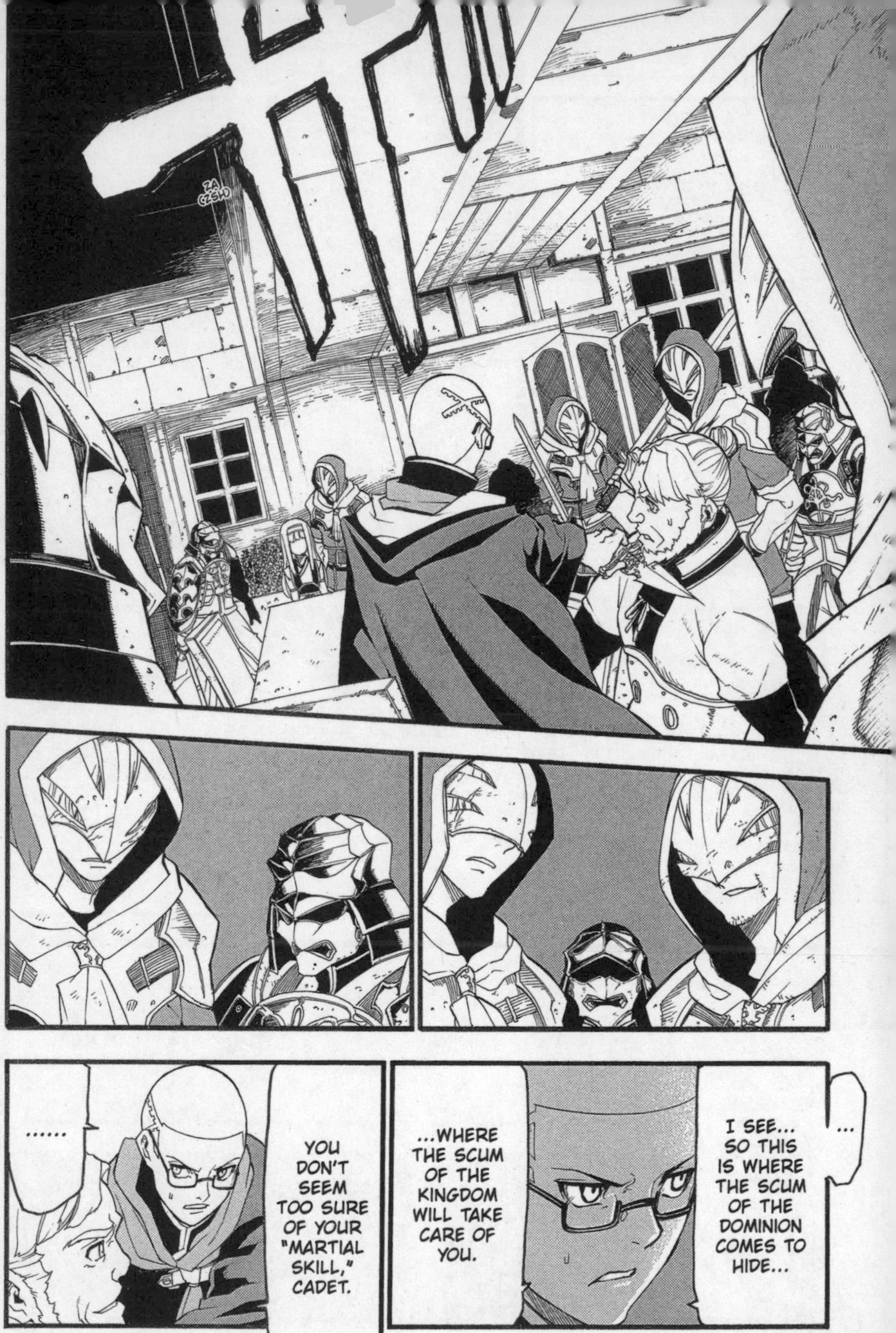
ZA (ZSH)
...
I SEE... SO THIS IS WHERE THE SCUM OF THE DOMINION COMES TO HIDE...
...WHERE THE SCUM OF THE KINGDOM WILL TAKE CARE OF YOU.
YOU DON'T SEEM TOO SURE OF YOUR "MARTIAL SKILL," CADET.
......

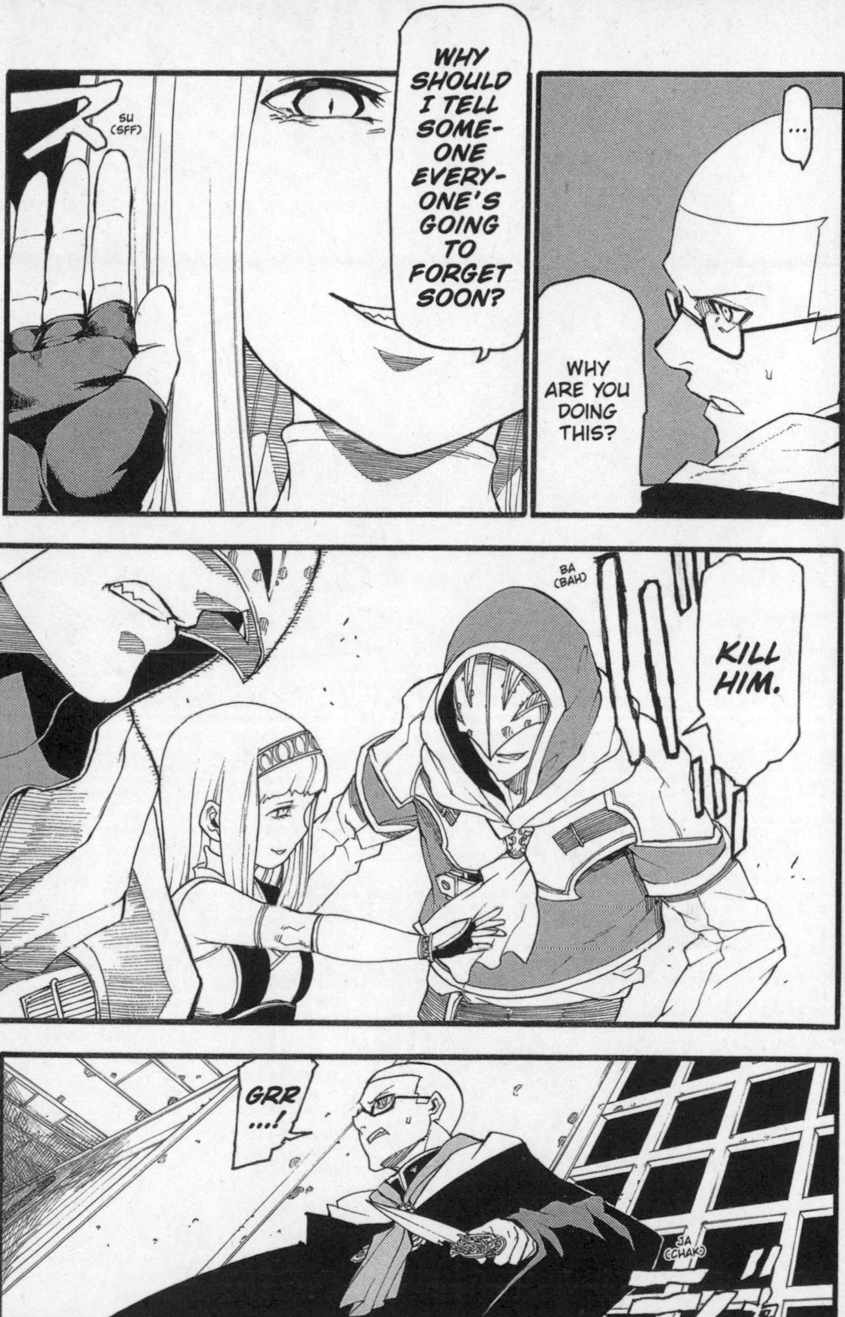
...
WHY ARE YOU DOING THIS?
WHY SHOULD I TELL SOME-ONE EVERY-ONE'S GOING TO FORGET SOON?
SU (SFF)
BA (BAH)
KILL HIM.
GRR ...!
JA (CHAK)

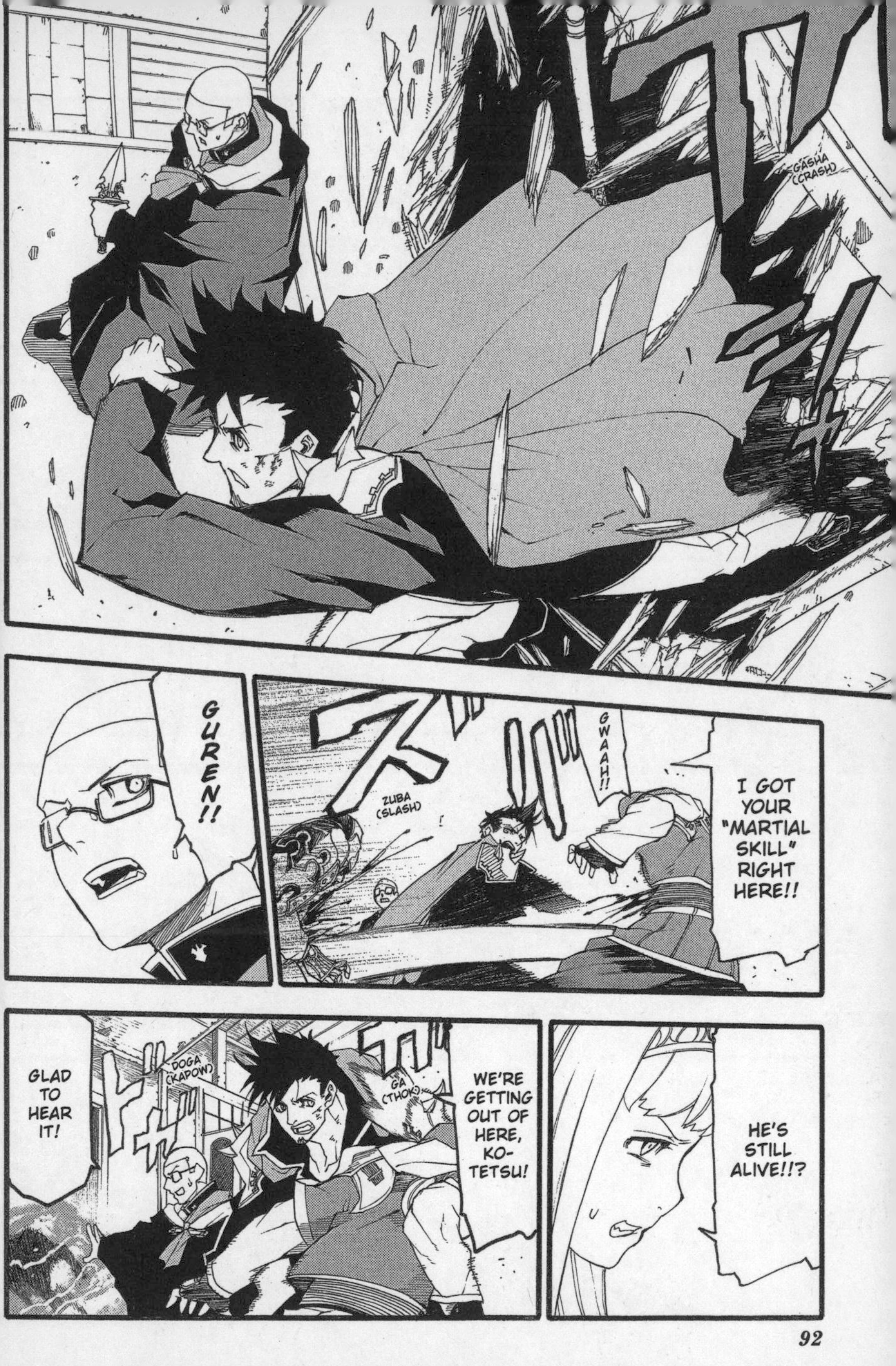
GASHA (CRASH)
I GOT YOUR "MARTIAL SKILL" RIGHT HERE!!
GWAAH!!
ZUBA (SLASH)
GUREN!!
HE'S STILL ALIVE!!?
WE'RE GETTING OUT OF HERE, KO-TETSU!
GA (THOK)
DOGA (KAPOW)
GLAD TO HEAR IT!

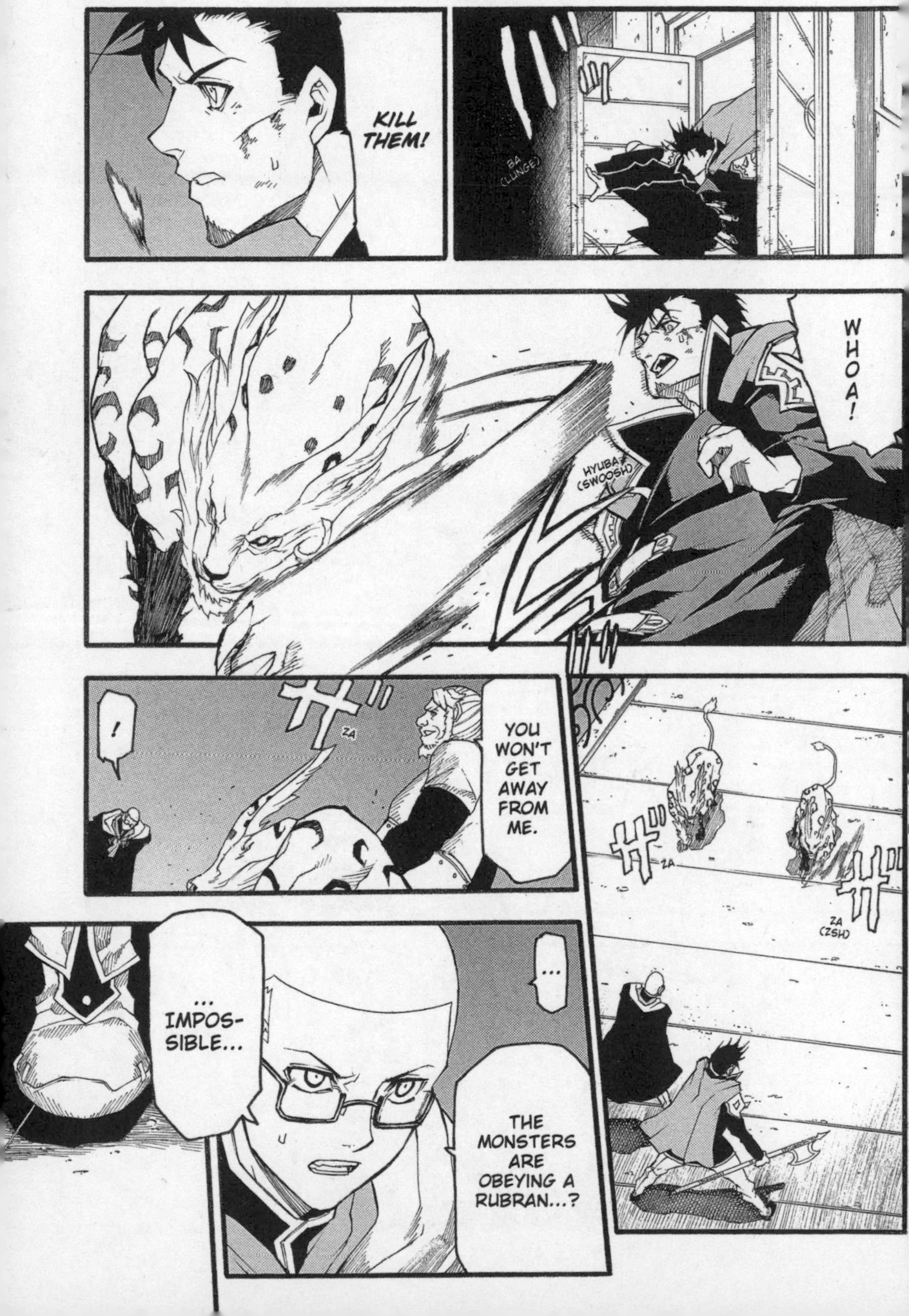
BA (LUNGE)
KILL THEM!
WHOA!
HYUBA (SWOOSH)
ZA
ZA (ZSH)
YOU WON'T GET AWAY FROM ME.
ZA
!
...
... IMPOSSIBLE...
THE MONSTERS ARE OBEYING A RUBRAN...?

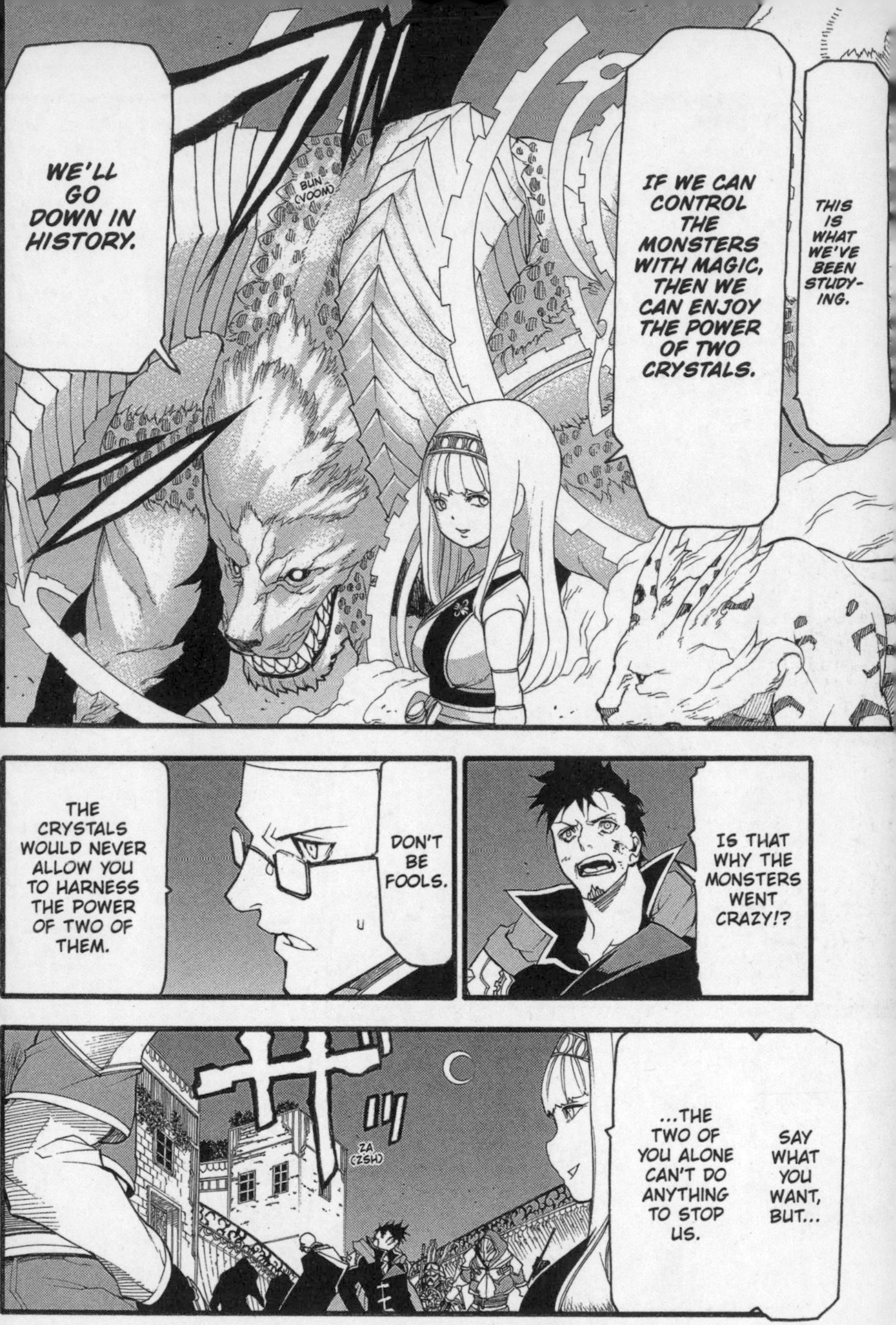
THIS IS WHAT WE'VE BEEN STUDY-ING.
IF WE CAN CONTROL THE MONSTERS WITH MAGIC, THEN WE CAN ENJOY THE POWER OF TWO CRYSTALS.
BUN (VOOM)
WE'LL GO DOWN IN HISTORY.
IS THAT WHY THE MONSTERS WENT CRAZY!?
DON'T BE FOOLS.
THE CRYSTALS WOULD NEVER ALLOW YOU TO HARNESS THE POWER OF TWO OF THEM.
SAY WHAT YOU WANT, BUT...
...THE TWO OF YOU ALONE CAN'T DO ANYTHING TO STOP US.
ZA (ZSH)

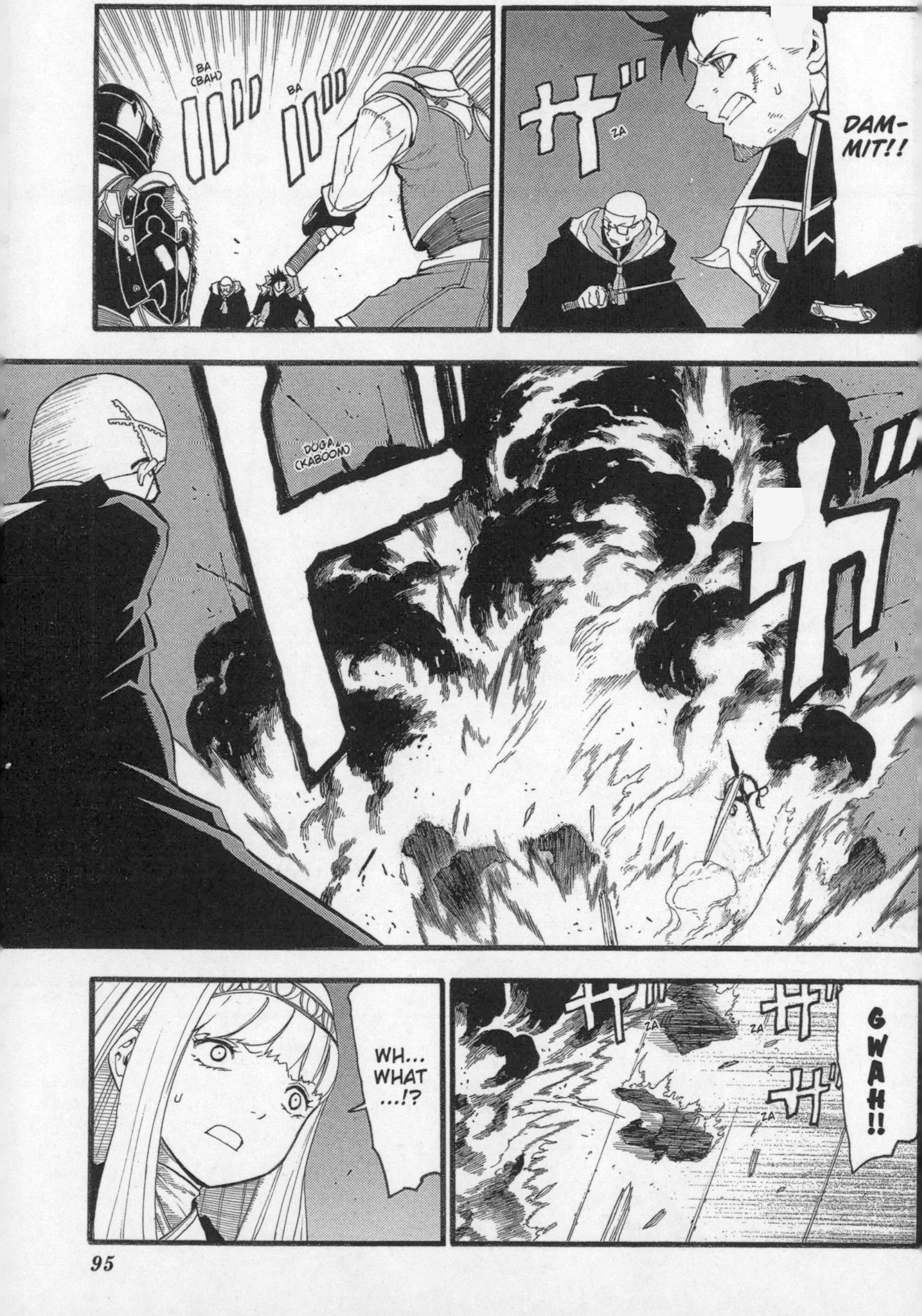
DAM-
MIT!!
ZA
BA
BA
(BAH)
DOGA
(KABOOM)
GWAH!!
ZA
ZA
ZA
WH...
WHAT
...!?

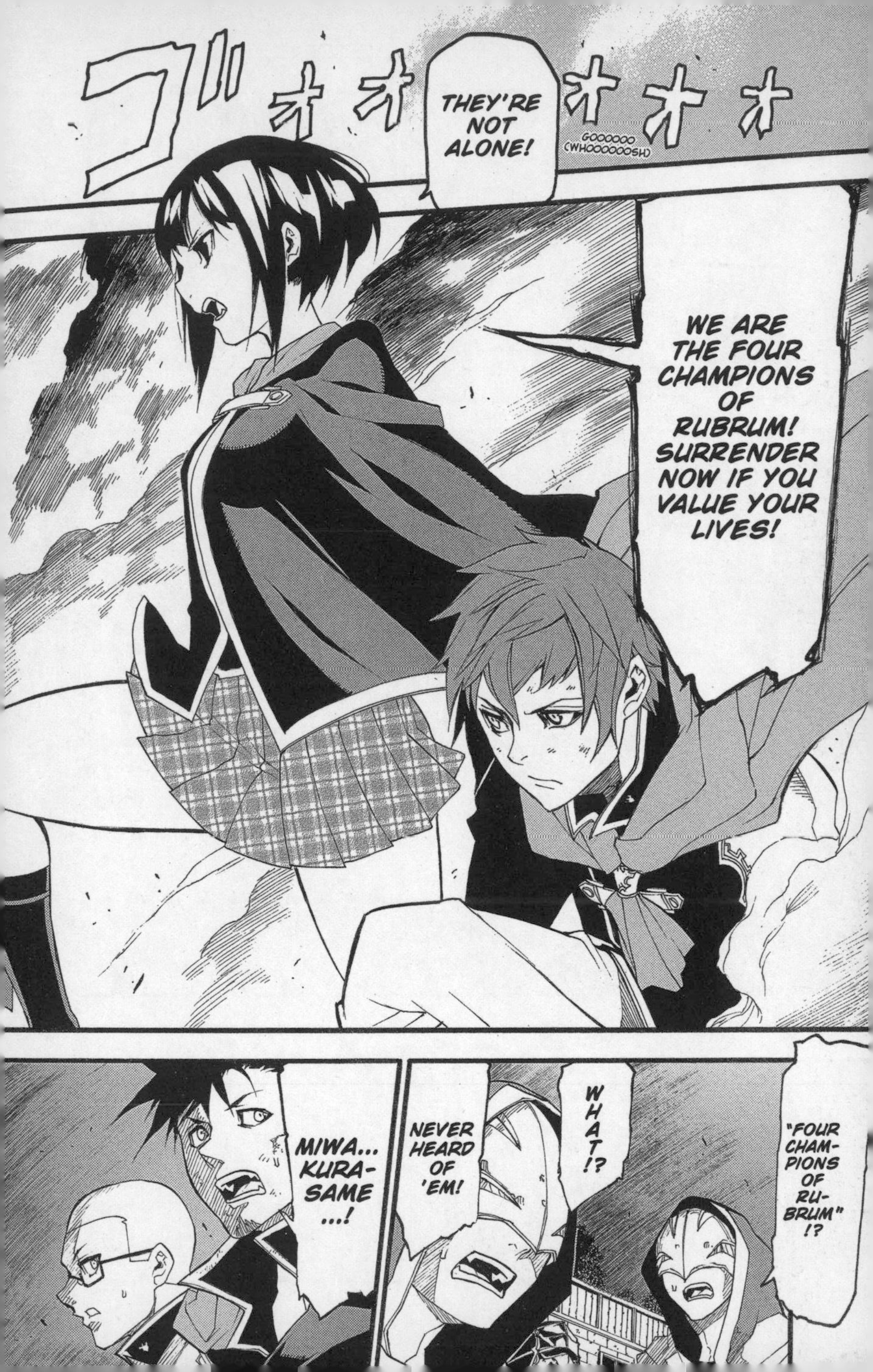
ゴオオオオオ
GOOOOOO (WHOOOOOOSH)
THEY'RE NOT ALONE!
WE ARE THE FOUR CHAMPIONS OF RUBRUM! SURRENDER NOW IF YOU VALUE YOUR LIVES!
"FOUR CHAMPIONS OF RUBRUM"!?
WHAT!?
NEVER HEARD OF 'EM!
MIWA... KURASAME ...!

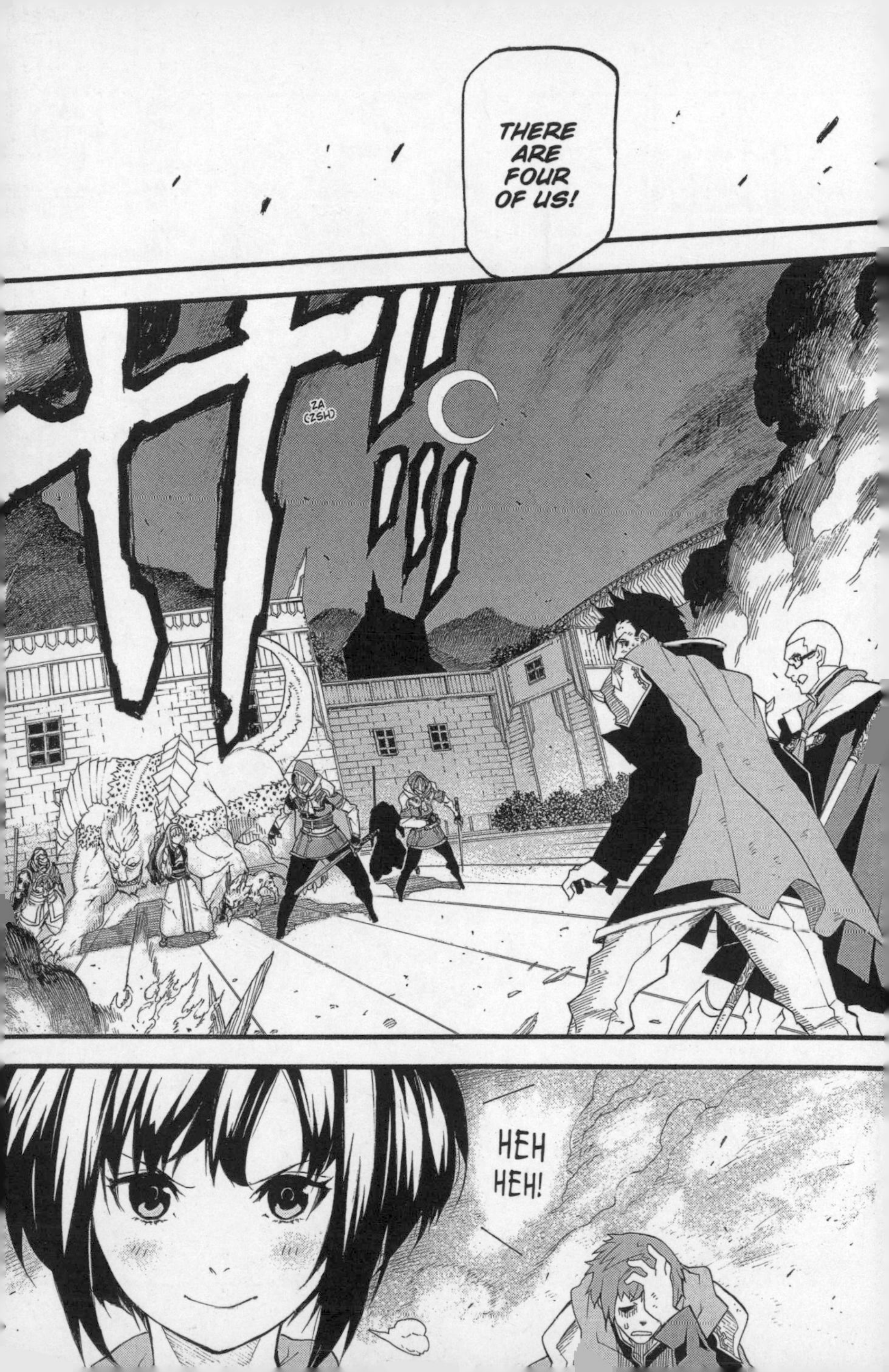
THERE ARE FOUR OF US!
ZA (ZSH)
HEH HEH!

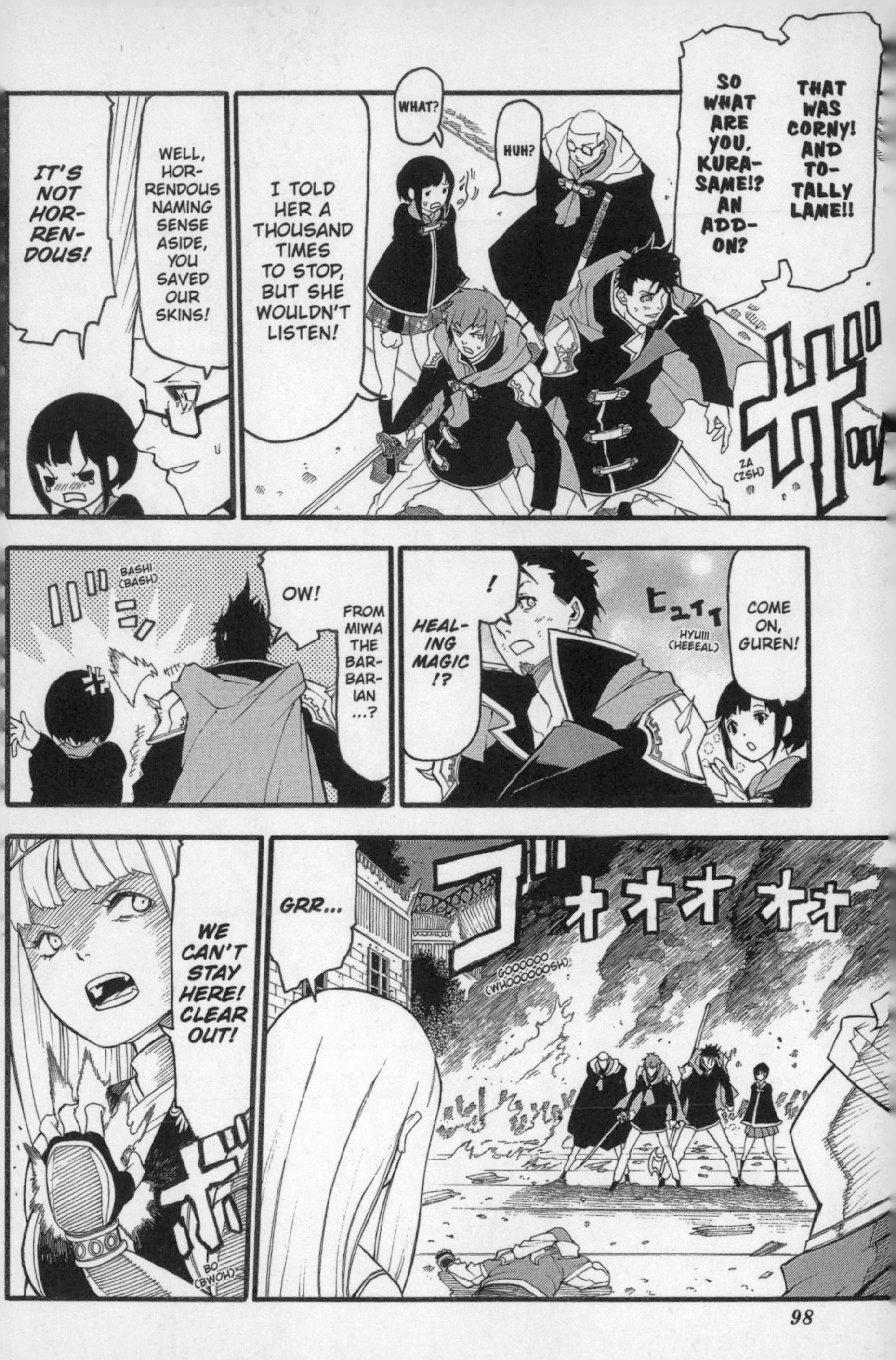
THAT WAS CORNY! AND TOTALLY LAME!!
SO WHAT ARE YOU, KURASAME!? AN ADD-ON?
HUH?
WHAT?
I TOLD HER A THOUSAND TIMES TO STOP, BUT SHE WOULDN'T LISTEN!
ZA (ZSH)
WELL, HORRENDOUS NAMING SENSE ASIDE, YOU SAVED OUR SKINS!
IT'S NOT HORRENDOUS!
COME ON, GUREN!
HYUIII (HEEEAL)
HEALING MAGIC!?
!
OW!
FROM MIWA THE BARBARIAN...?
BASHI (BASH)
GOOOOOO (WHOOOOOOSH)
GRR...
WE CAN'T STAY HERE! CLEAR OUT!
BO (BWOH)

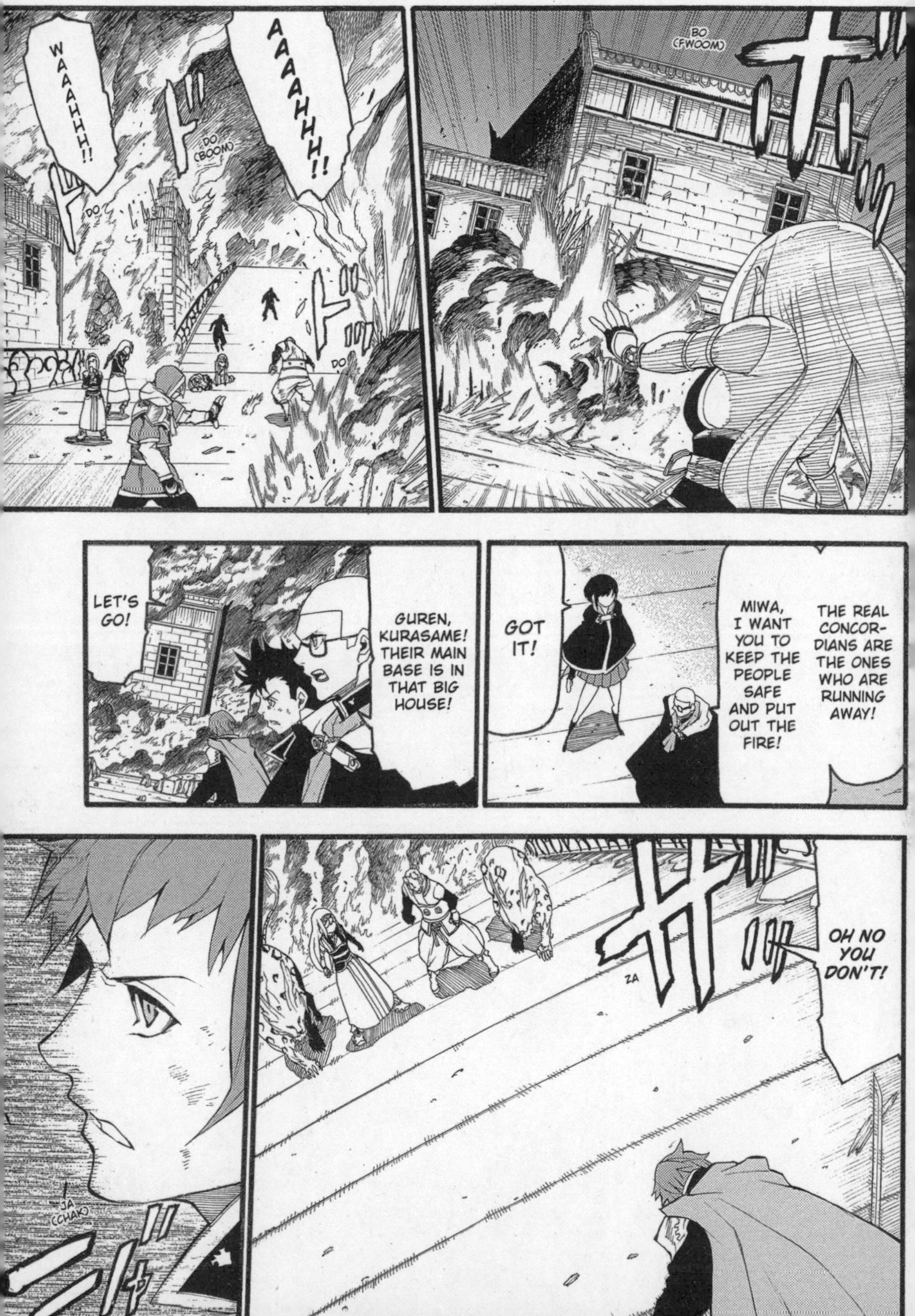
BO (FWOOM)
AAAAAHHH!!
DO (BOOM)
WAAAAHHH!!
DO
DO
THE REAL CONCORDIANS ARE THE ONES WHO ARE RUNNING AWAY!
MIWA, I WANT YOU TO KEEP THE PEOPLE SAFE AND PUT OUT THE FIRE!
GOT IT!
GUREN, KURASAME! THEIR MAIN BASE IS IN THAT BIG HOUSE!
LET'S GO!
OH NO YOU DON'T!
ZA
JA (CHAK)

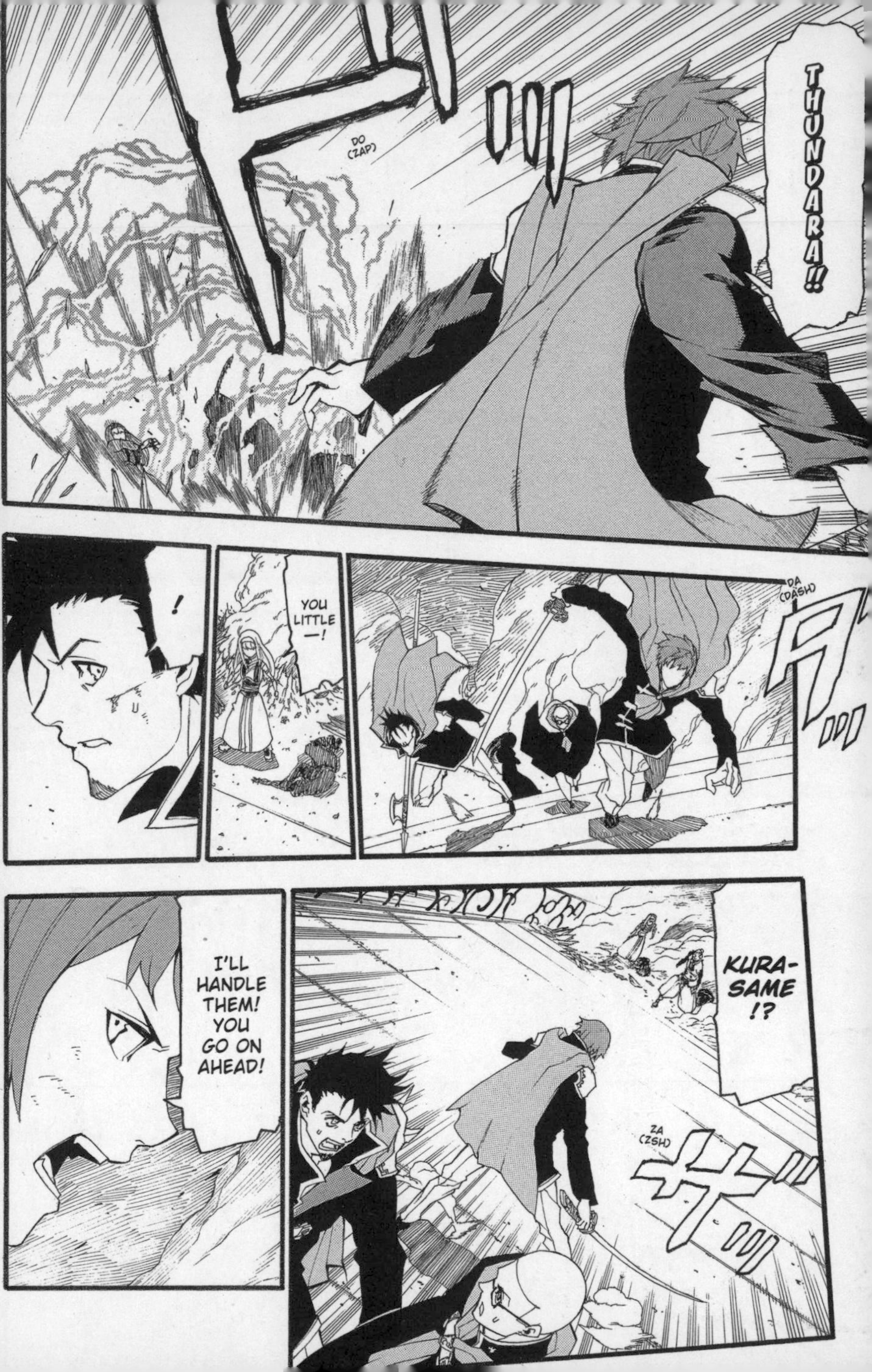
THUNDARA!!
DO (ZAP)
DA (DASH)
YOU LITTLE—!
!
KURA-SAME!?
ZA (ZSH)
I'LL HANDLE THEM! YOU GO ON AHEAD!

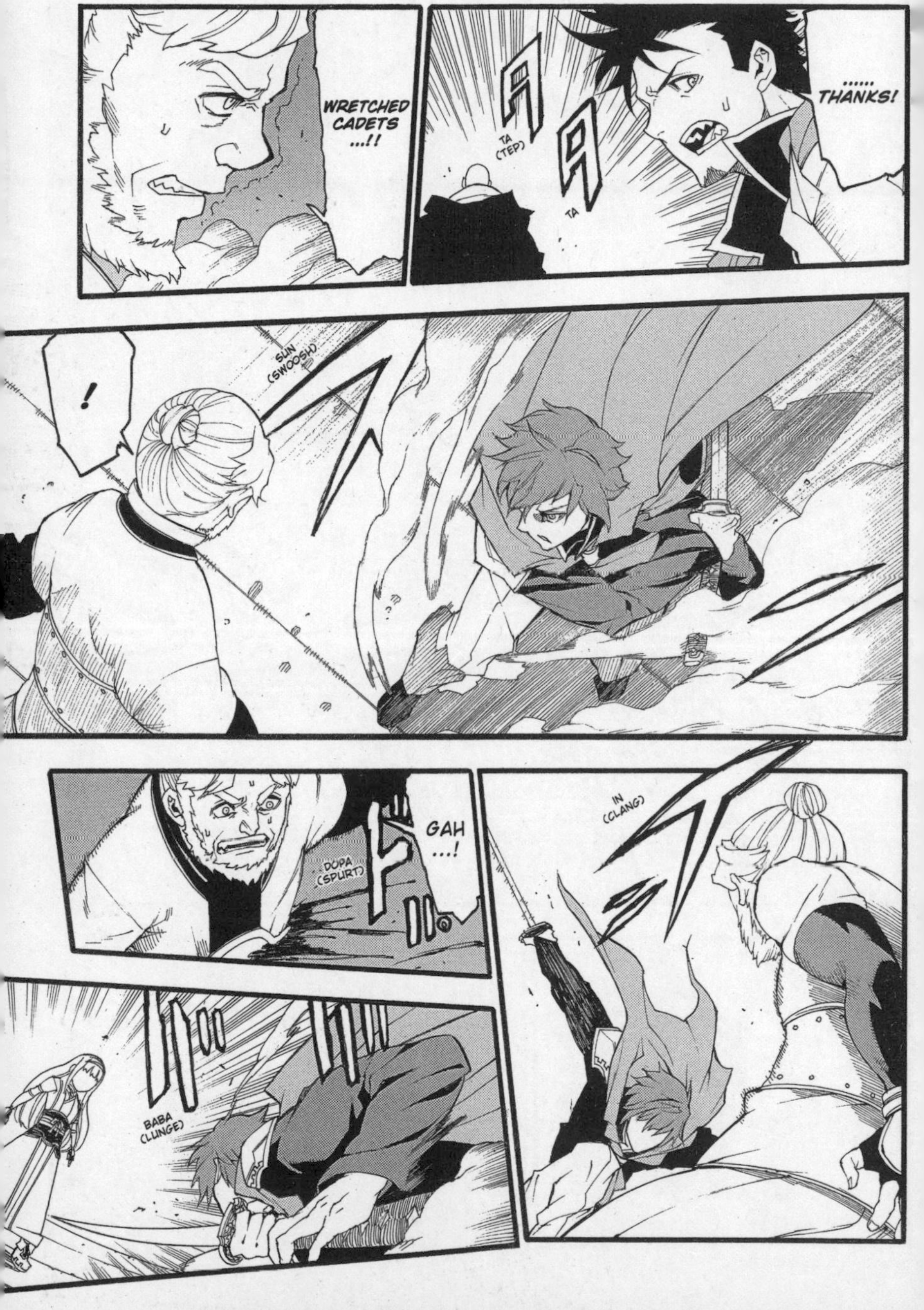
......THANKS!
TA (TEP)
TA
WRETCHED CADETS ...!!
SUN (SWOOSH)
!
IN (CLANG)
GAH ...!
DOPA (SPURT)
BABA (LUNGE)

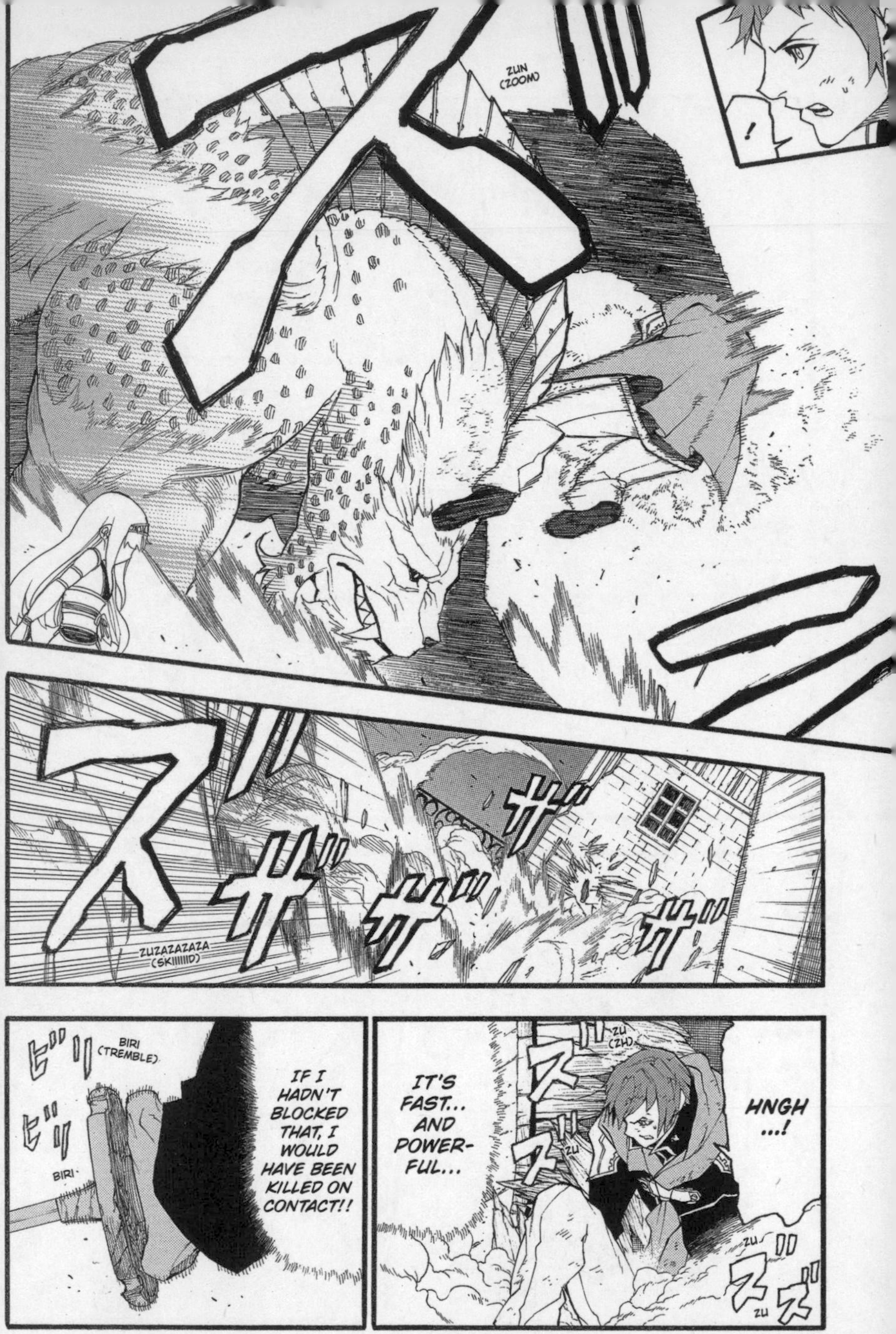

!
ZUN (ZOOM)
ZUZAZAZAZA (SKIIIIIID)
ZU (ZH)
ZU
HNGH ...!
IT'S FAST... AND POWER-FUL...
ZU
ZU
IF I HADN'T BLOCKED THAT, I WOULD HAVE BEEN KILLED ON CONTACT!!
BIRI (TREMBLE)
BIRI

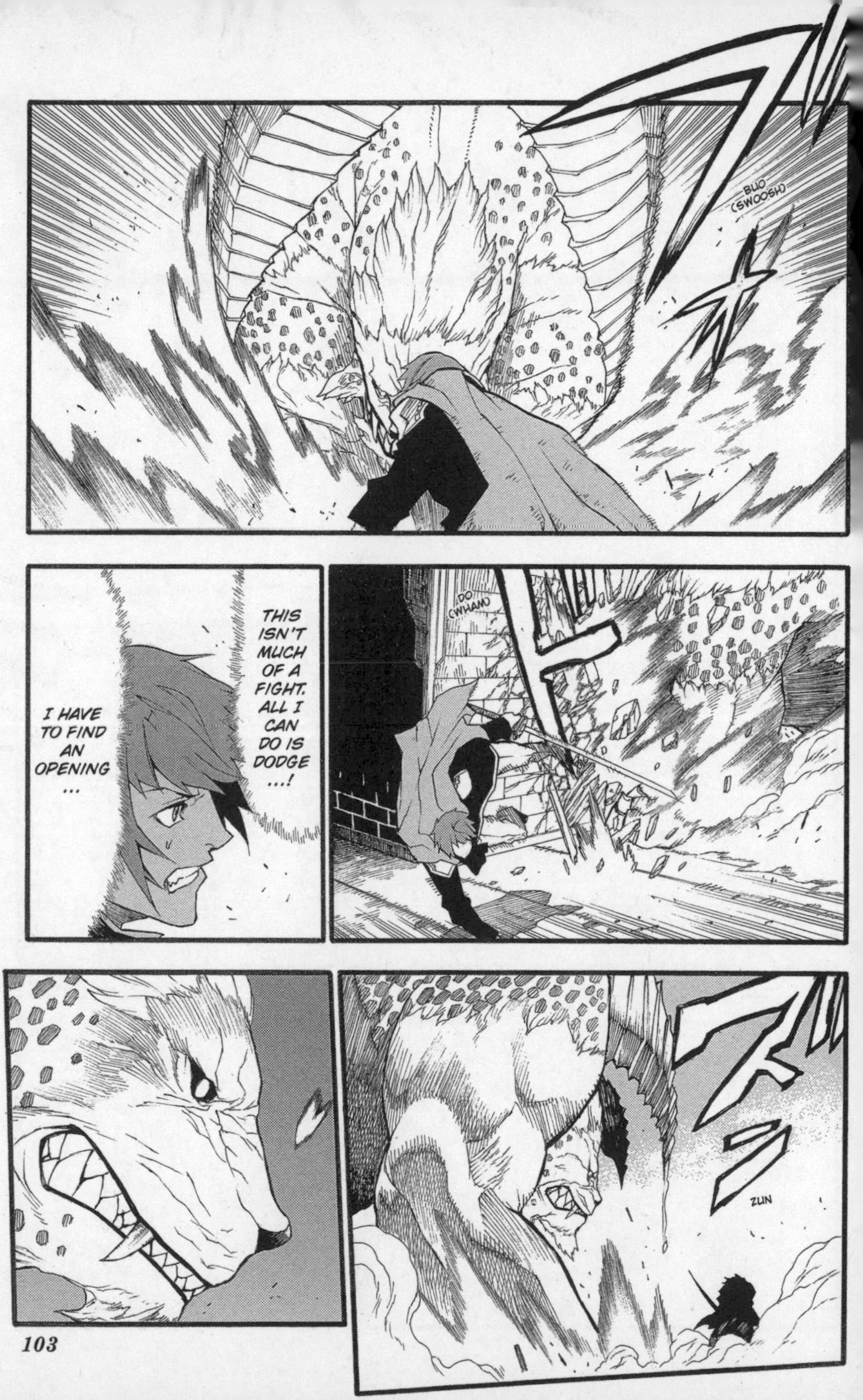
BUO (SWOOSH)
DO (WHAM)
THIS ISN'T MUCH OF A FIGHT. ALL I CAN DO IS DODGE...!
I HAVE TO FIND AN OPENING...
ZUN

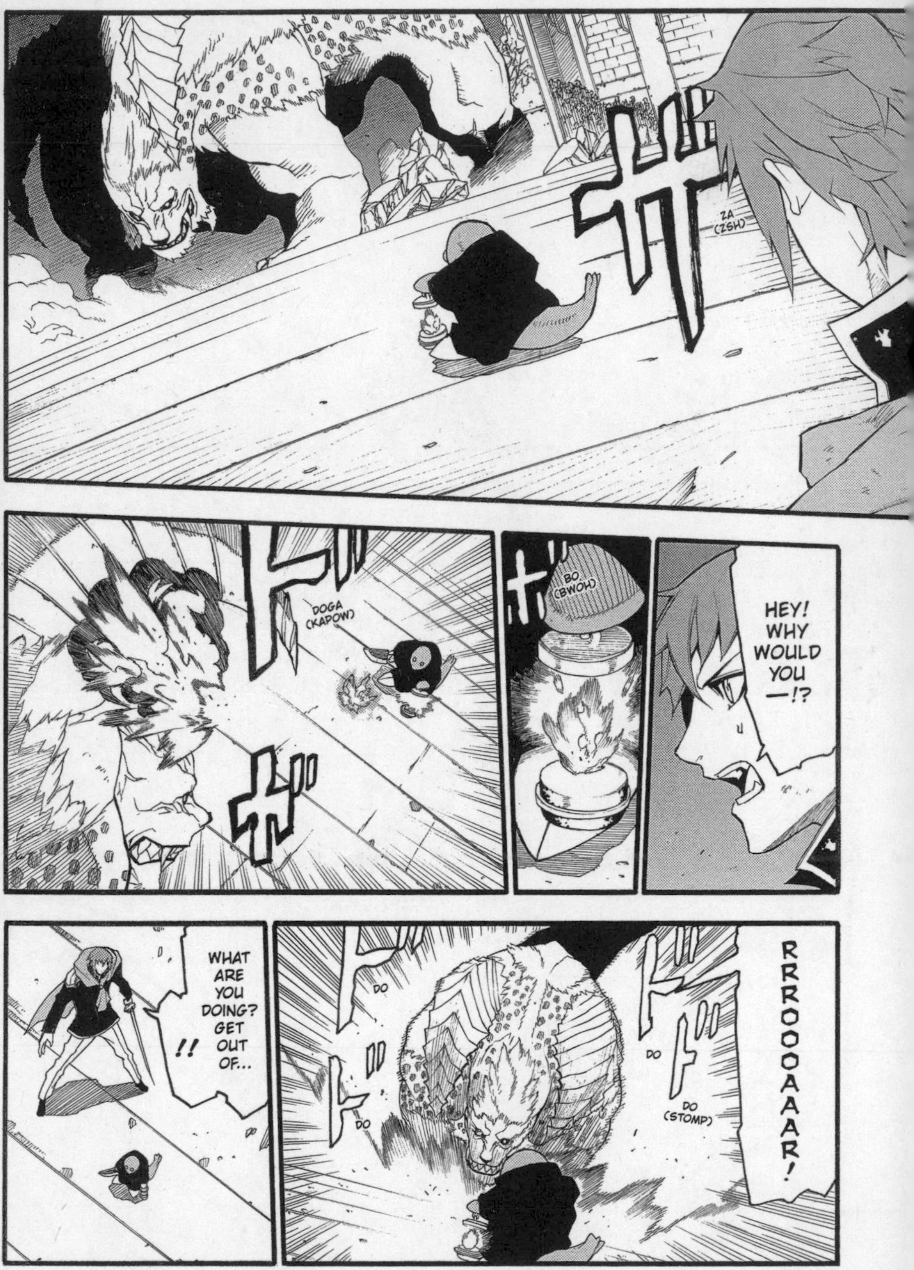
ZA
(ZSH)
HEY! WHY WOULD YOU—!?
BO
(BWOH)
DOGA
(KAPOW)
RRROOOAAAR!
DO
DO
(STOMP)
DO
DO
WHAT ARE YOU DOING? GET OUT OF...
!!

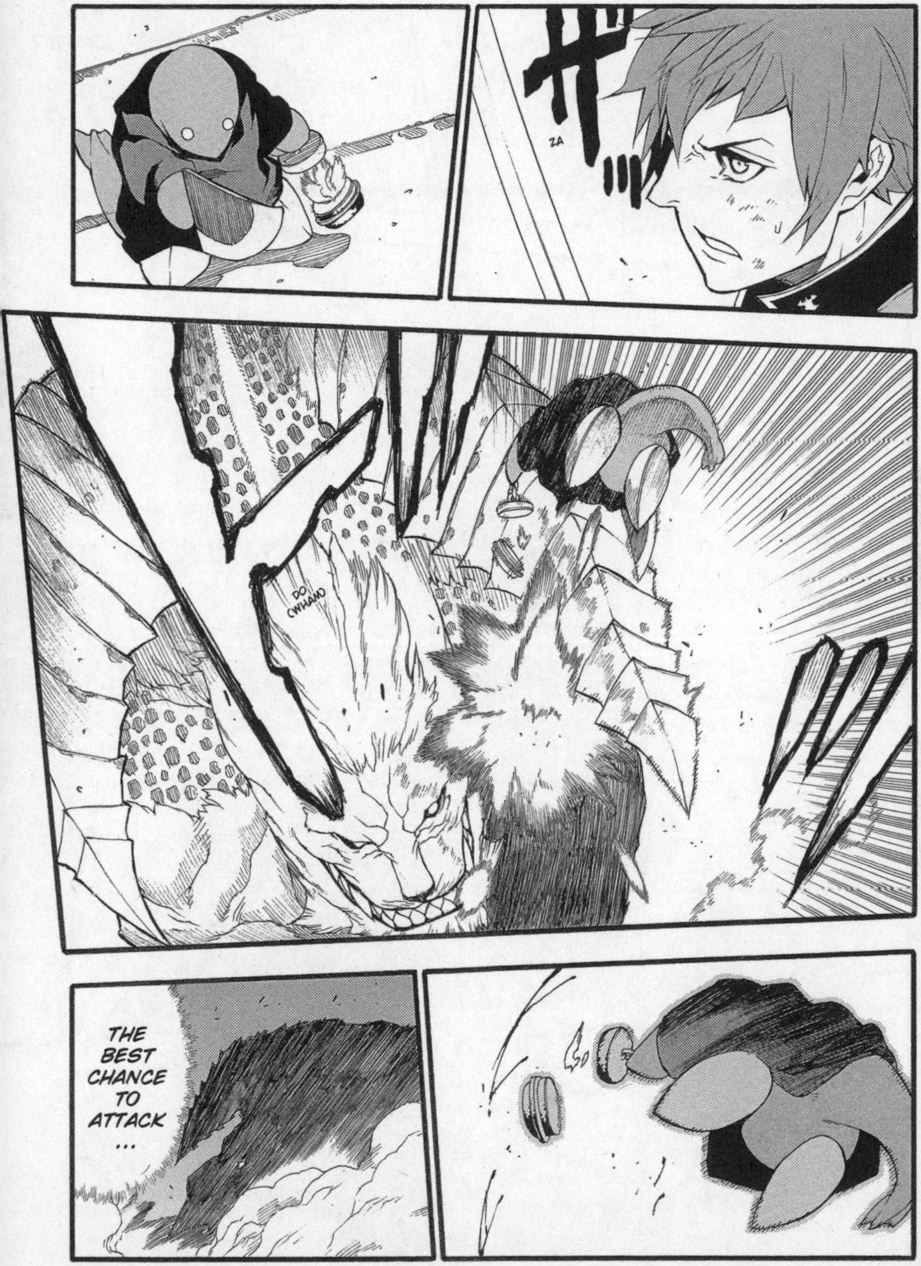
ZA
DO (WHAM)
THE BEST CHANCE TO ATTACK ...

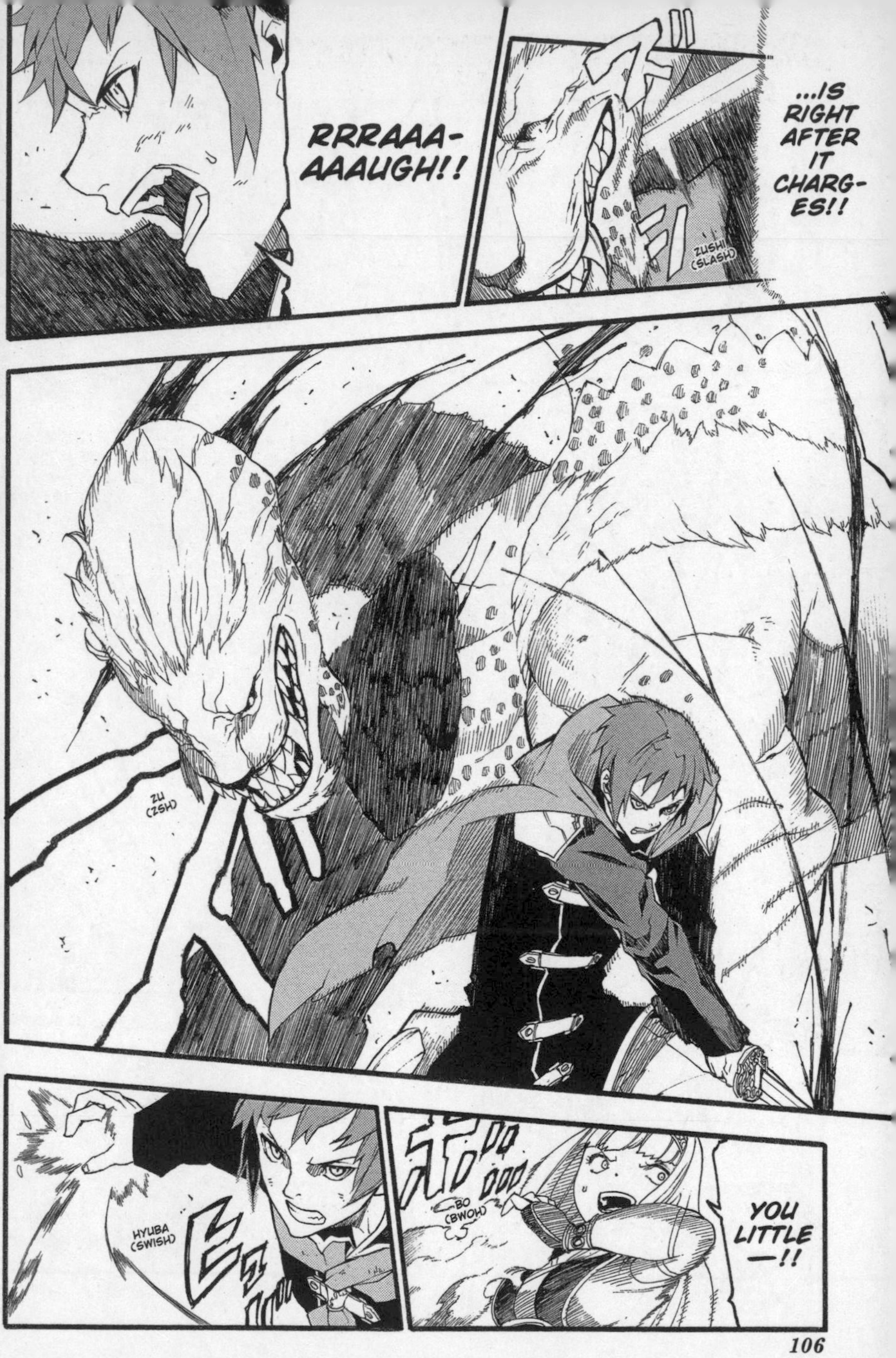
...IS RIGHT AFTER IT CHARG-ES!!
ZUSHI (SLASH)
RRRAAA-AAAUGH!!
ZU (ZSH)
YOU LITTLE—!!
BO (BWOH)
HYUBA (SWISH)

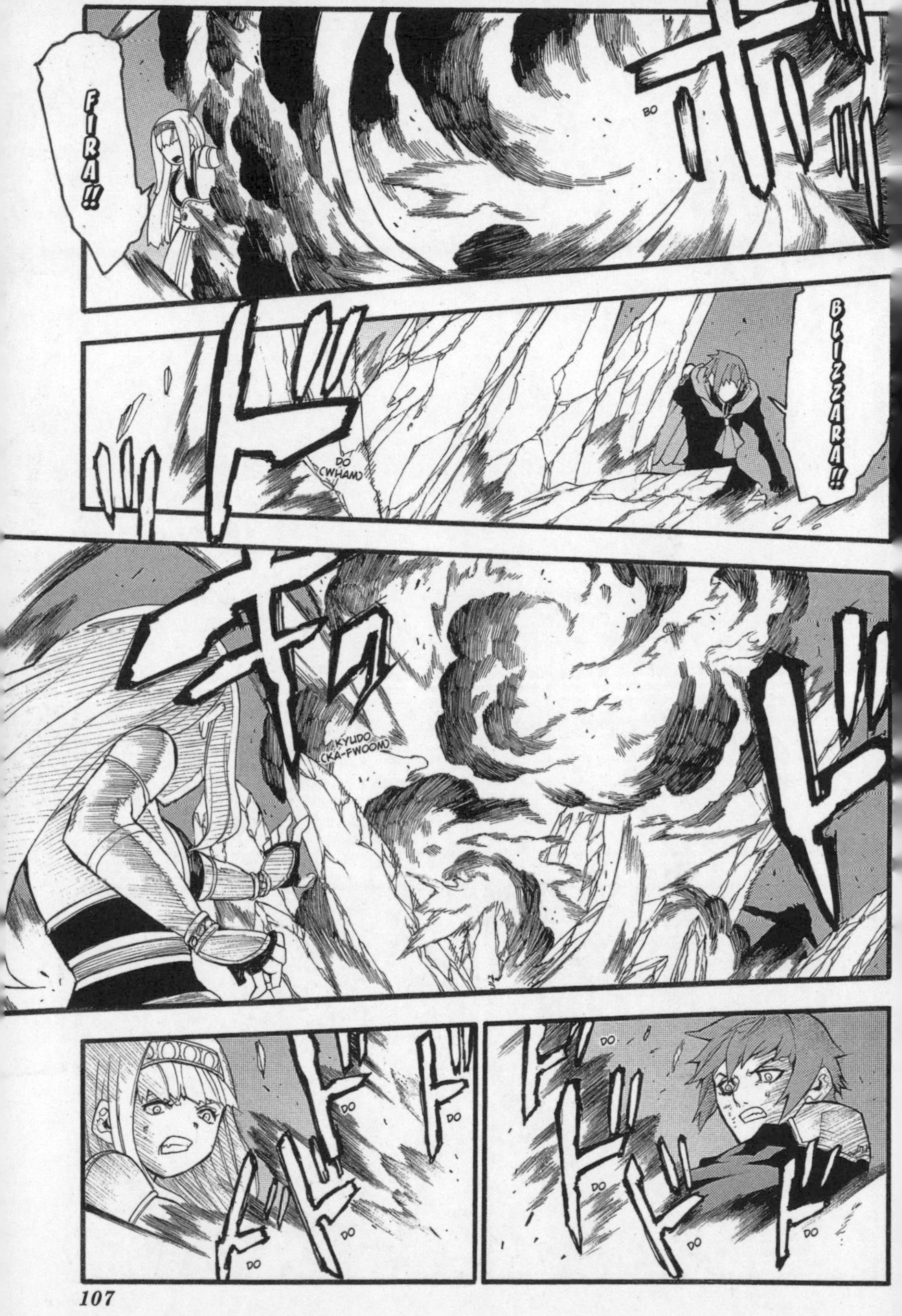
BO
FIRA!!
BLIZZARA!!
DO
(WHAM)
KYUDO
(KA-FWOOM)
DO
DO
DO
DO
DO
DO
DO
DO
DO

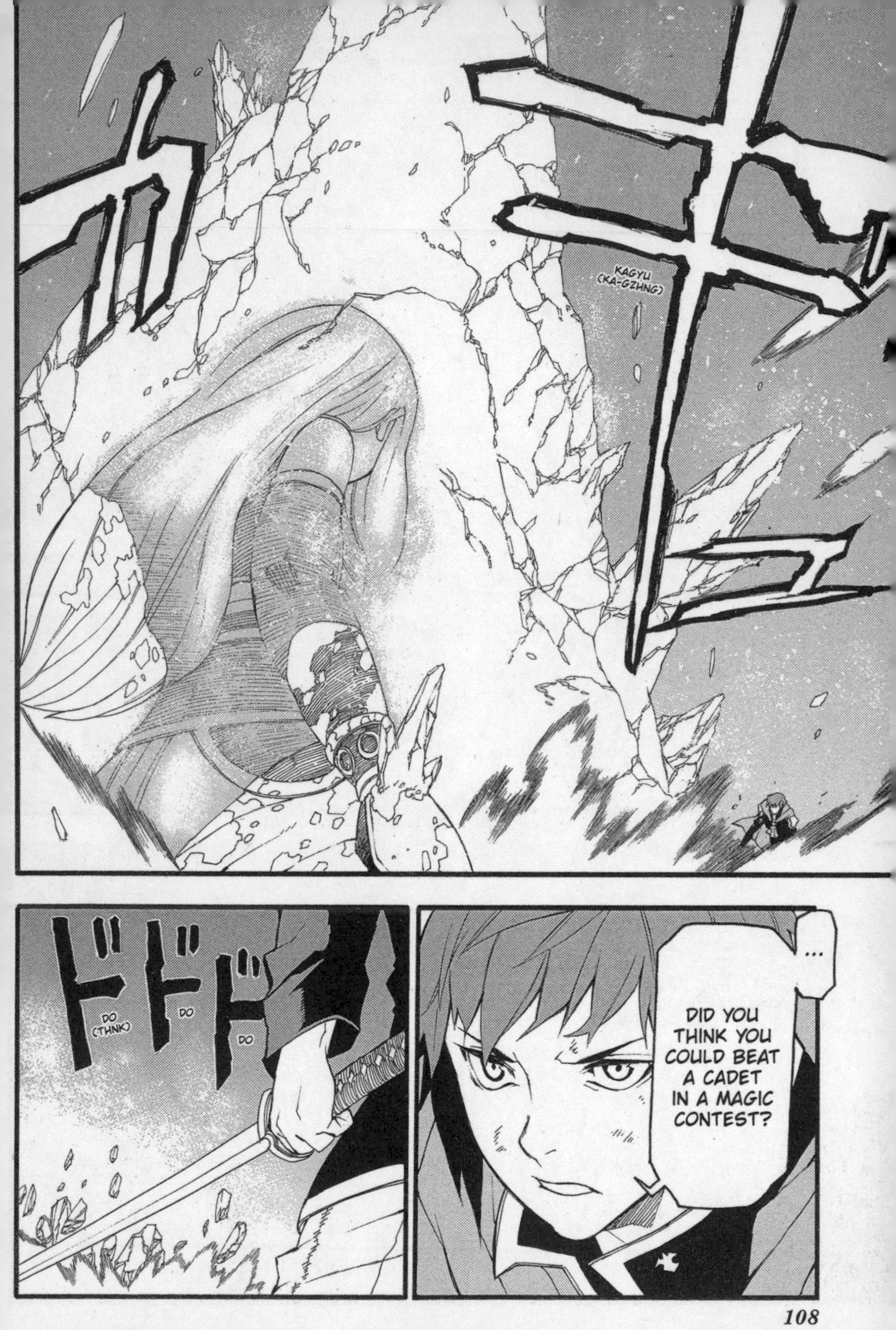
KAGYU (KA-GZHNG)
...
DID YOU THINK YOU COULD BEAT A CADET IN A MAGIC CONTEST?
ドドド
DO (THNK)
DO
DO

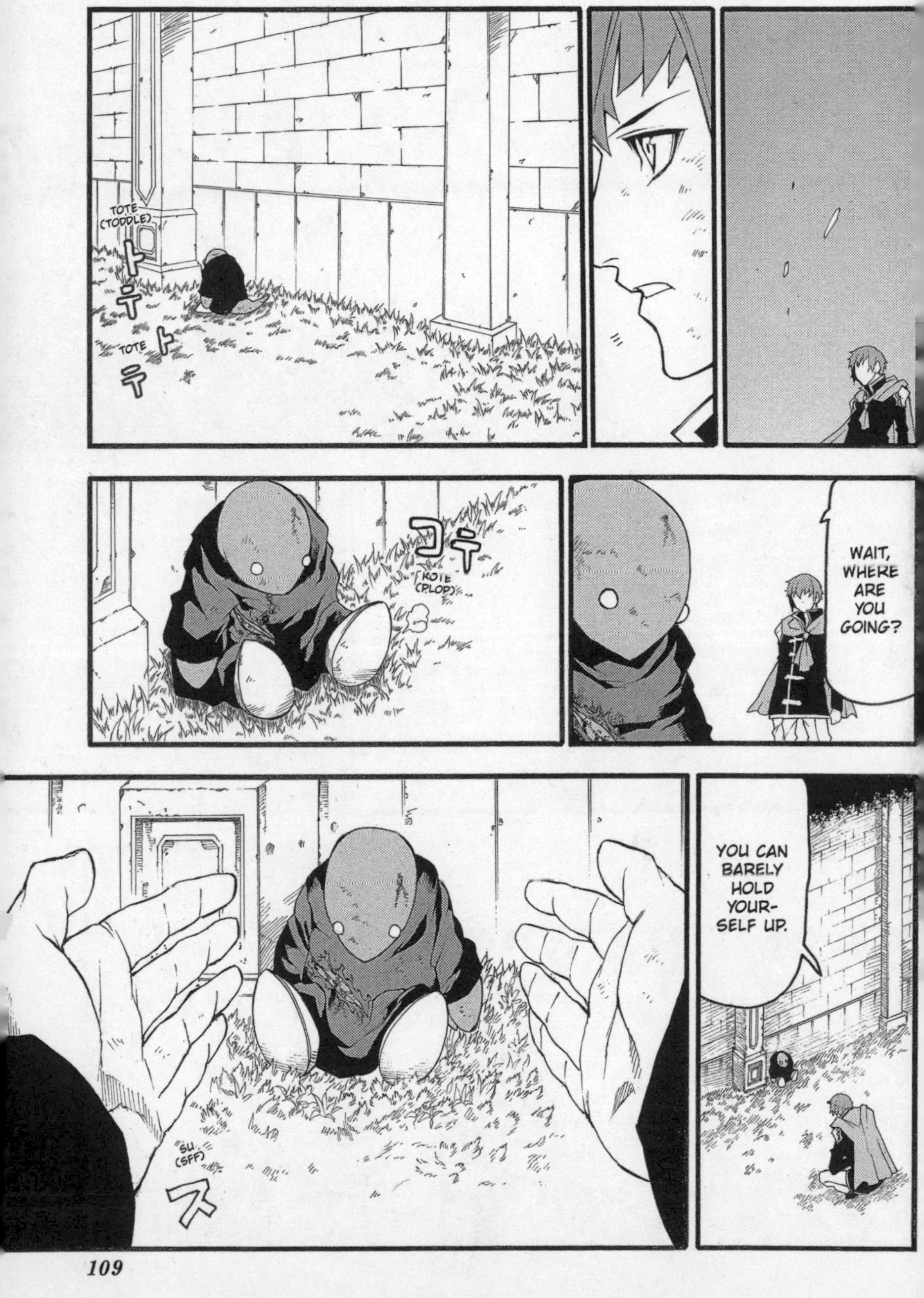

TOTE (TODDLE)
トテ
TOTE
トテ
WAIT, WHERE ARE YOU GOING?
コテ
KOTE (PLOP)
YOU CAN BARELY HOLD YOUR-SELF UP.
SU (SFF)
ス

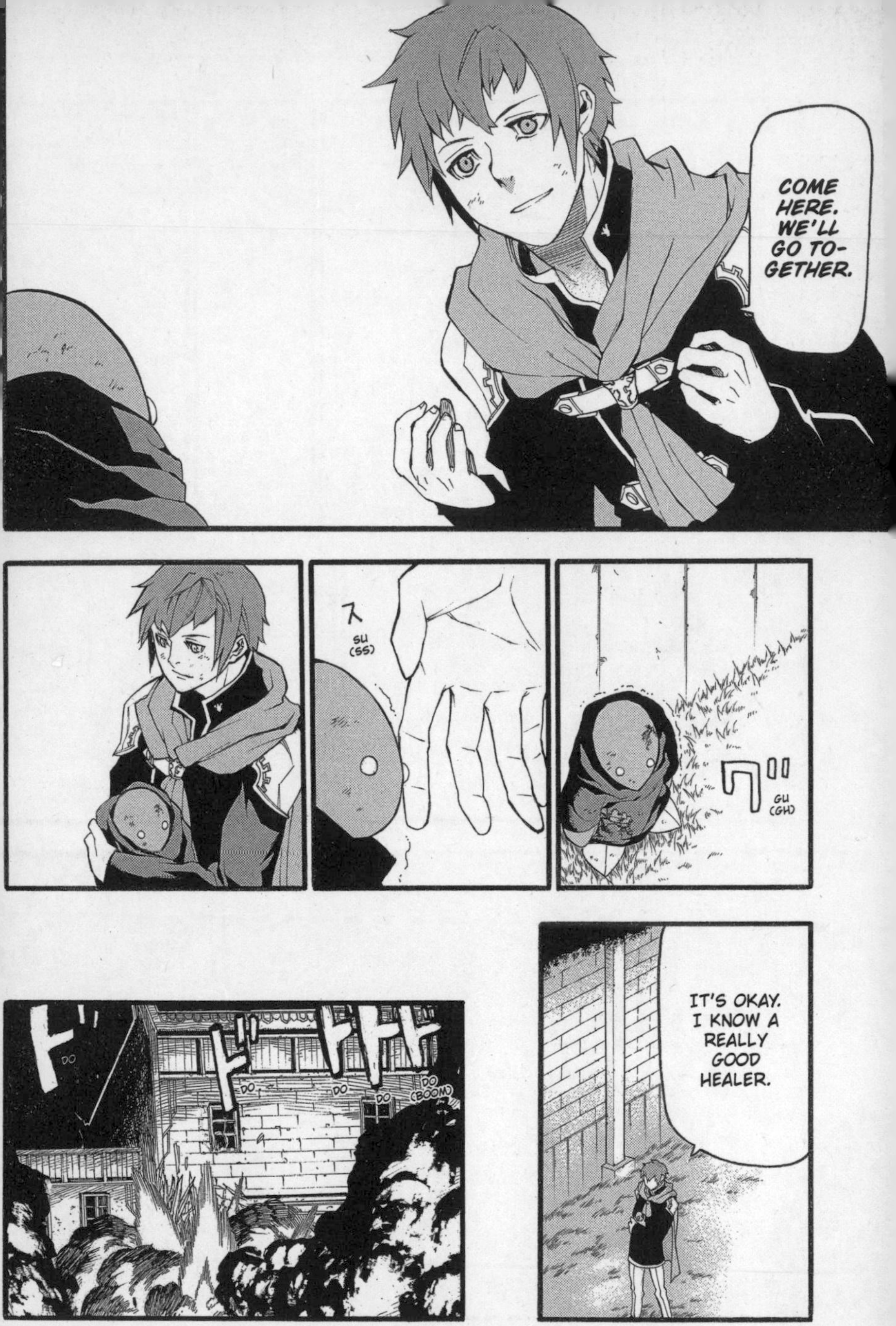
COME HERE. WE'LL GO TO-GETHER.
グ
GU (GH)
ス
SU (SS)
IT'S OKAY. I KNOW A REALLY GOOD HEALER.
ドドドドド
DO
DO
DO
DO
DO (BOOM)

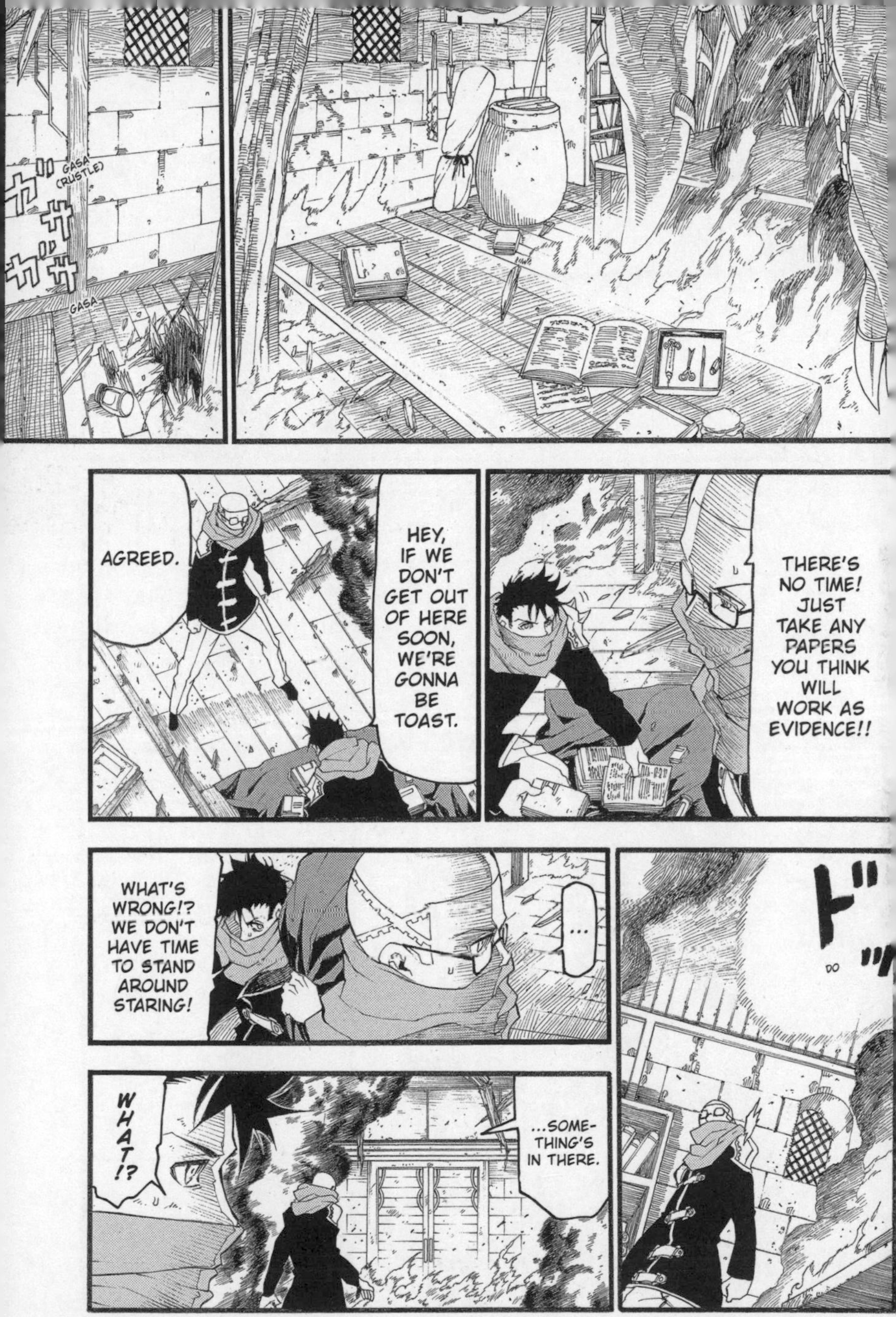
GASA (RUSTLE)
GASA
THERE'S NO TIME! JUST TAKE ANY PAPERS YOU THINK WILL WORK AS EVIDENCE!!
HEY, IF WE DON'T GET OUT OF HERE SOON, WE'RE GONNA BE TOAST.
AGREED.
DO
...
WHAT'S WRONG!? WE DON'T HAVE TIME TO STAND AROUND STARING!
...SOMETHING'S IN THERE.
WHAT!?

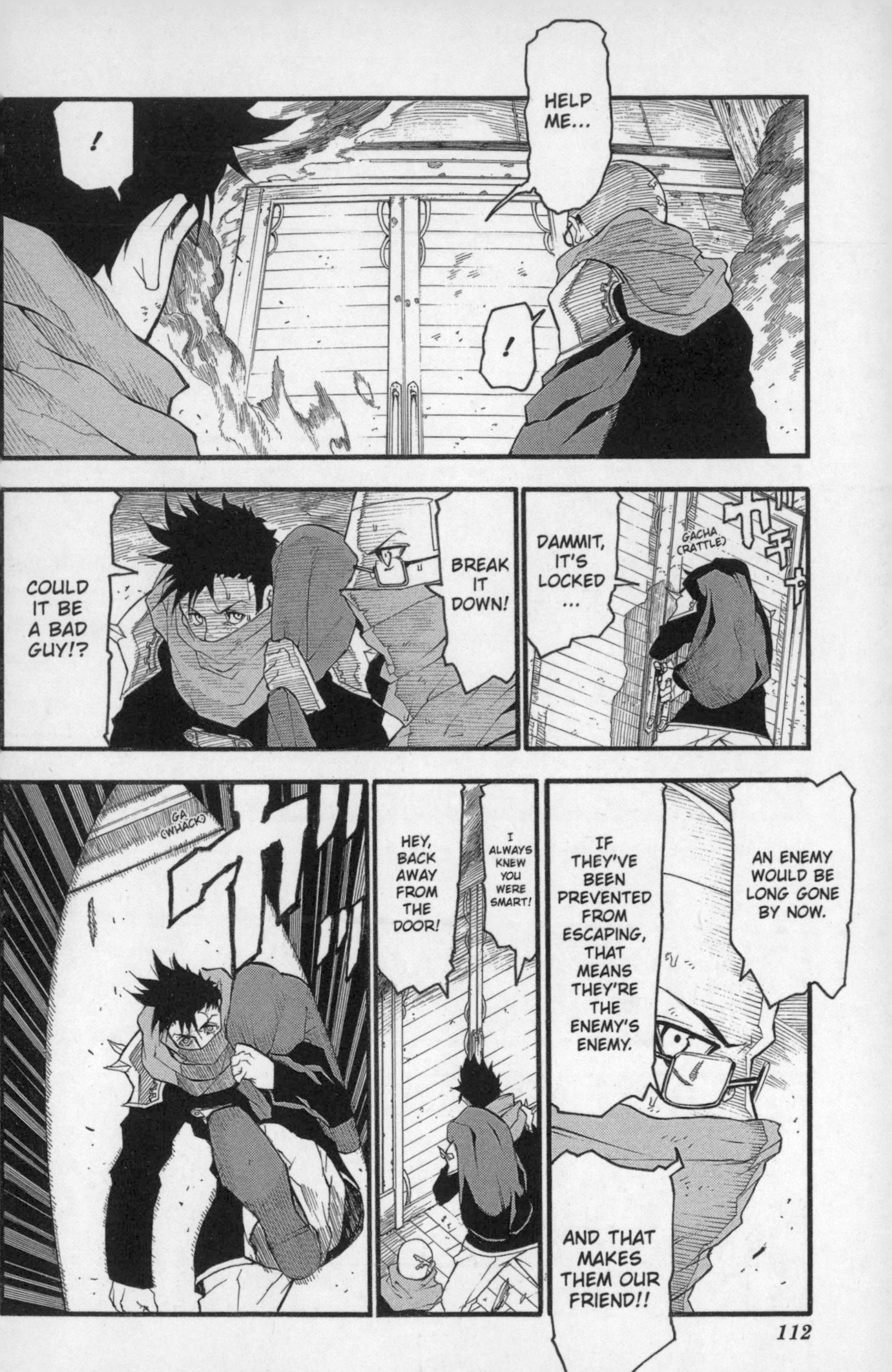
HELP ME...
!
!
DAMMIT, IT'S LOCKED ...
GACHA (RATTLE)
BREAK IT DOWN!
COULD IT BE A BAD GUY!?
AN ENEMY WOULD BE LONG GONE BY NOW.
IF THEY'VE BEEN PREVENTED FROM ESCAPING, THAT MEANS THEY'RE THE ENEMY'S ENEMY.
AND THAT MAKES THEM OUR FRIEND!!
I ALWAYS KNEW YOU WERE SMART!
HEY, BACK AWAY FROM THE DOOR!
GA (WHACK)

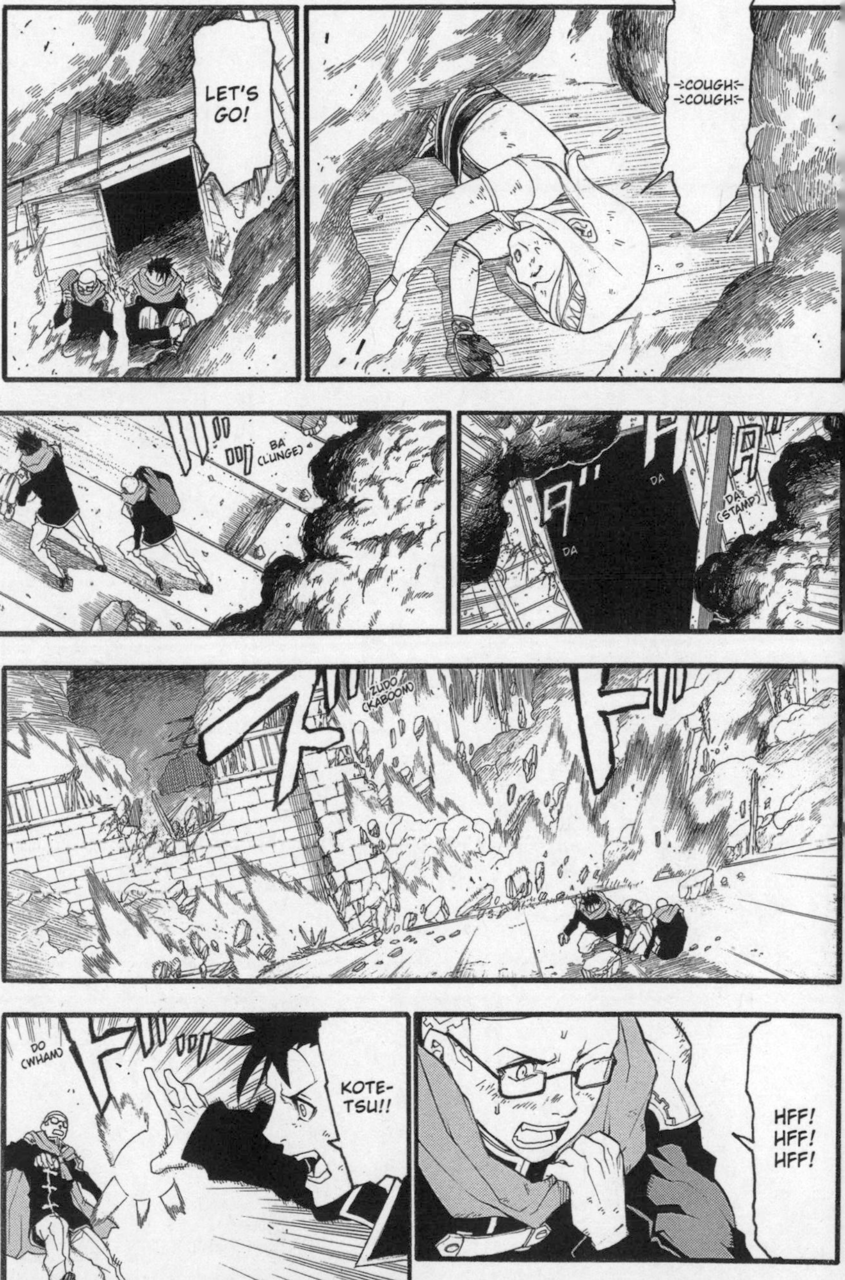
COUGH COUGH
LET'S GO!
DA (STAMP)
DA
DA
BA (LUNGE)
ZUDO (KABOOM)
HFF! HFF! HFF!
KOTE-TSU!!
DO (WHAM)

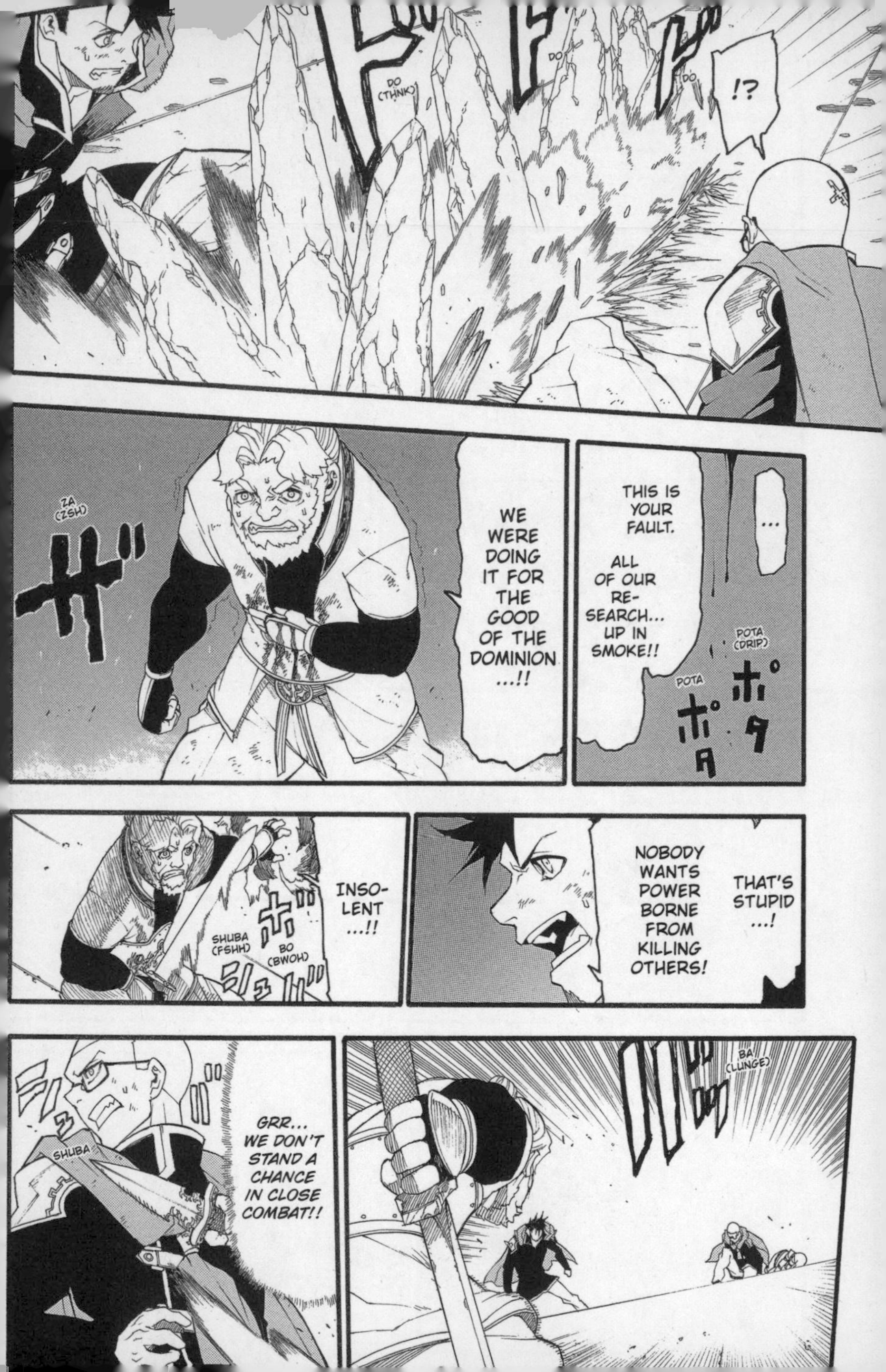
!?
DO
DO
DO (THNK)
...
THIS IS YOUR FAULT.
ALL OF OUR RE-SEARCH... UP IN SMOKE!!
POTA (DRIP)
POTA
WE WERE DOING IT FOR THE GOOD OF THE DOMINION...!!
ZA (ZSH)
THAT'S STUPID...!
NOBODY WANTS POWER BORNE FROM KILLING OTHERS!
INSO-LENT...!!
BO (BWOH)
SHUBA (FSHH)
BA (LUNGE)
GRR... WE DON'T STAND A CHANCE IN CLOSE COMBAT!!
SHUBA

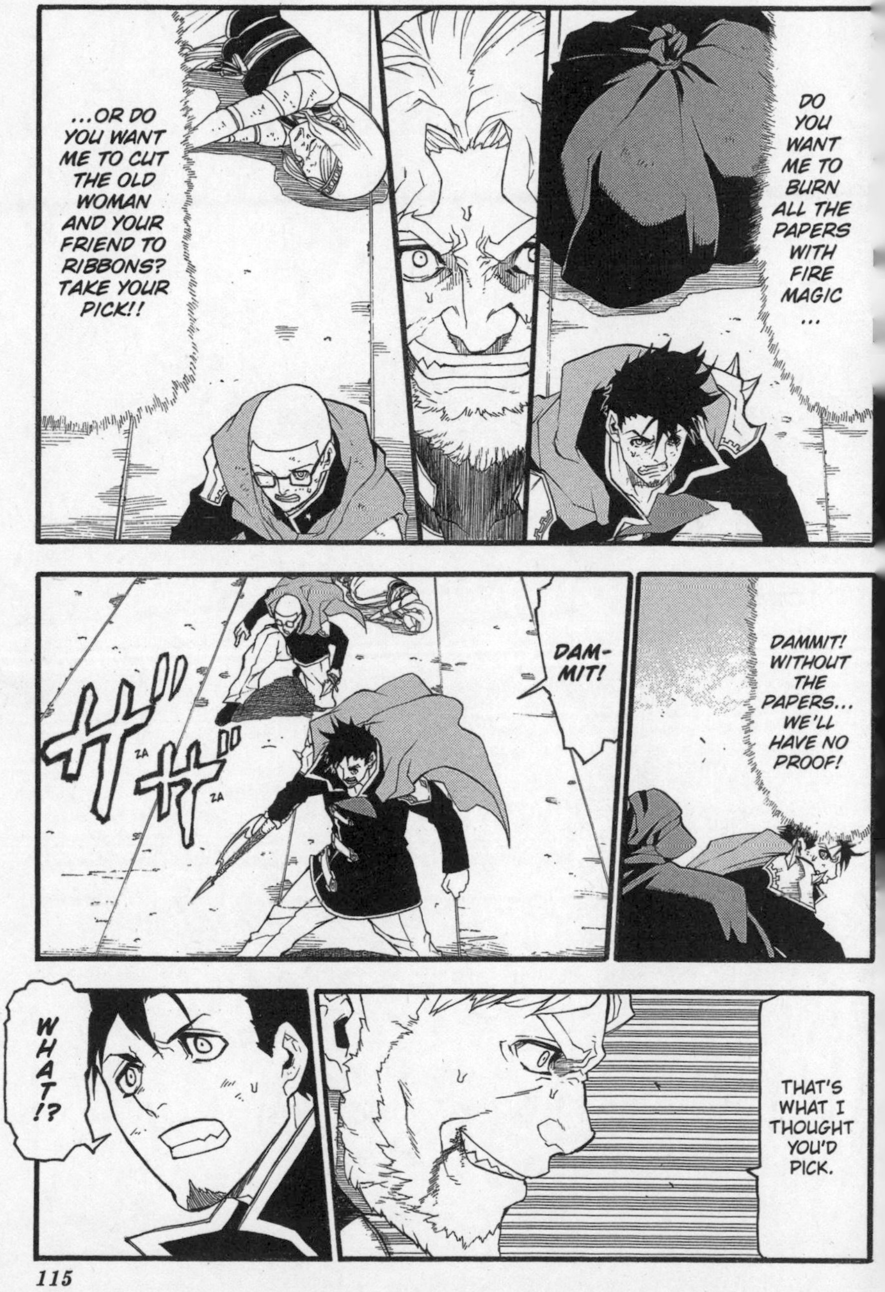
DO YOU WANT ME TO BURN ALL THE PAPERS WITH FIRE MAGIC ...
...OR DO YOU WANT ME TO CUT THE OLD WOMAN AND YOUR FRIEND TO RIBBONS? TAKE YOUR PICK!!
DAMMIT! WITHOUT THE PAPERS... WE'LL HAVE NO PROOF!
DAM-MIT!
ZA
ZA
THAT'S WHAT I THOUGHT YOU'D PICK.
WHAT!?

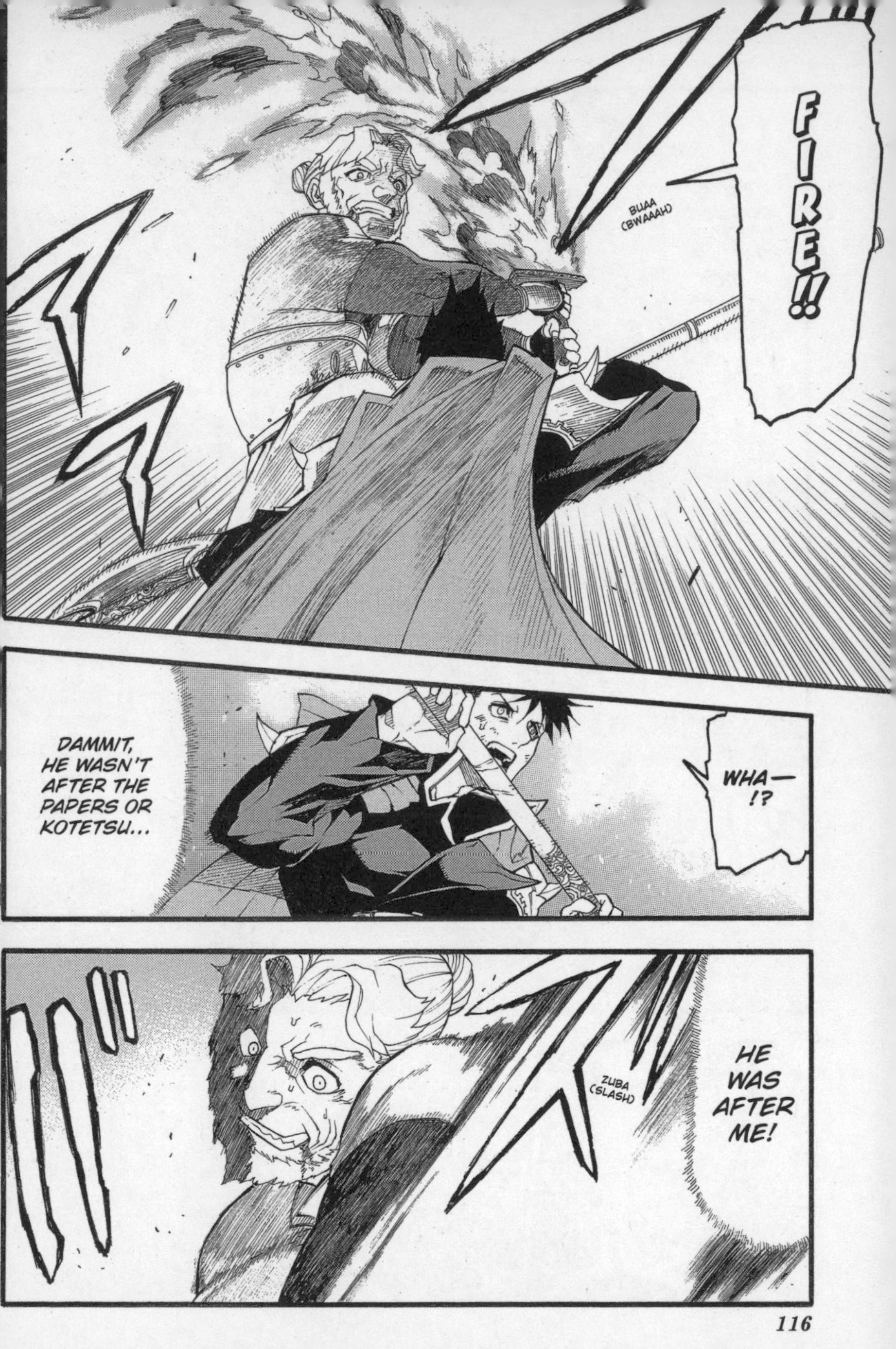
FIRE!!
BUAA (BWAAAH)
WHA— !?
DAMMIT, HE WASN'T AFTER THE PAPERS OR KOTETSU...
HE WAS AFTER ME!
ZUBA (SLASH)

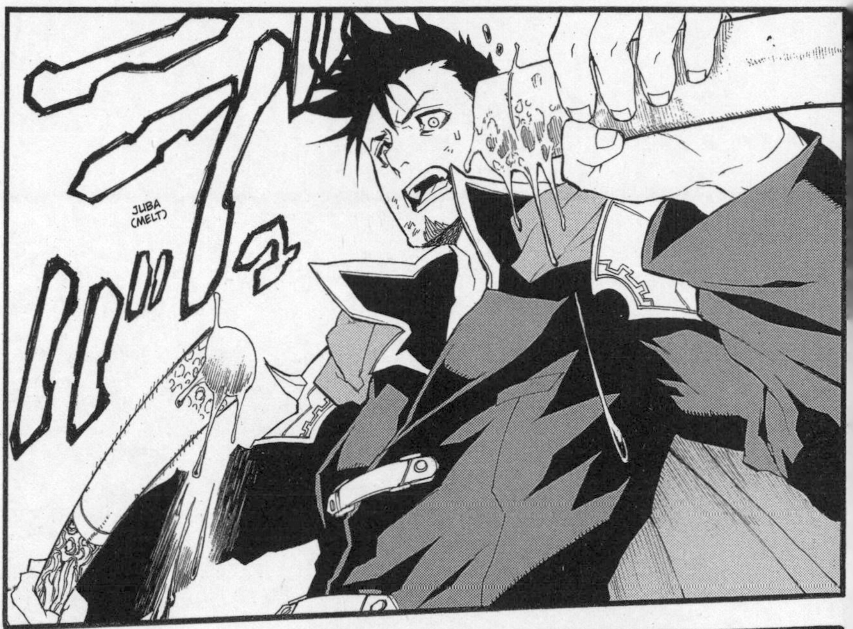
JUBA
(MELT)

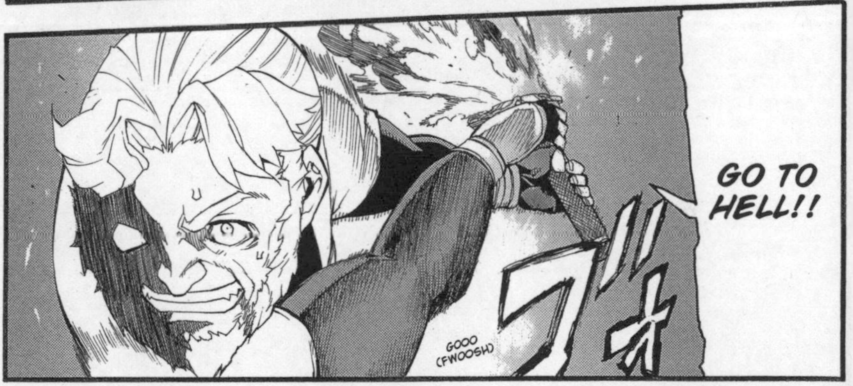
GO TO
HELL!!
GOOO
(FWOOSH)

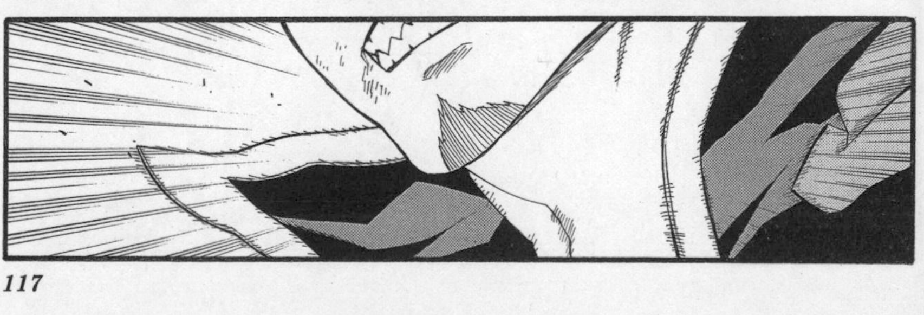

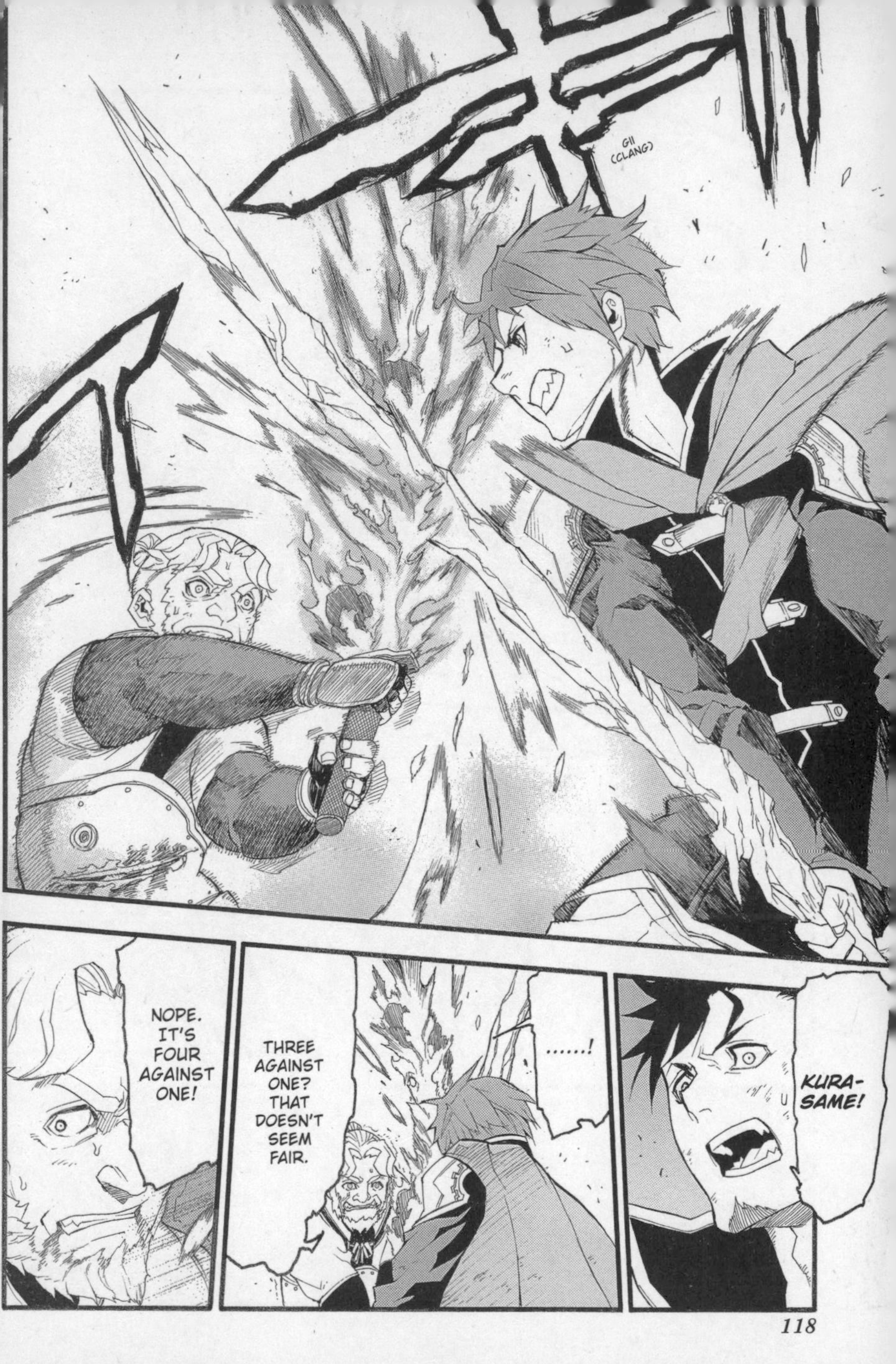
GII (CLANG)
KURA-SAME!
......!
THREE AGAINST ONE? THAT DOESN'T SEEM FAIR.
NOPE. IT'S FOUR AGAINST ONE!

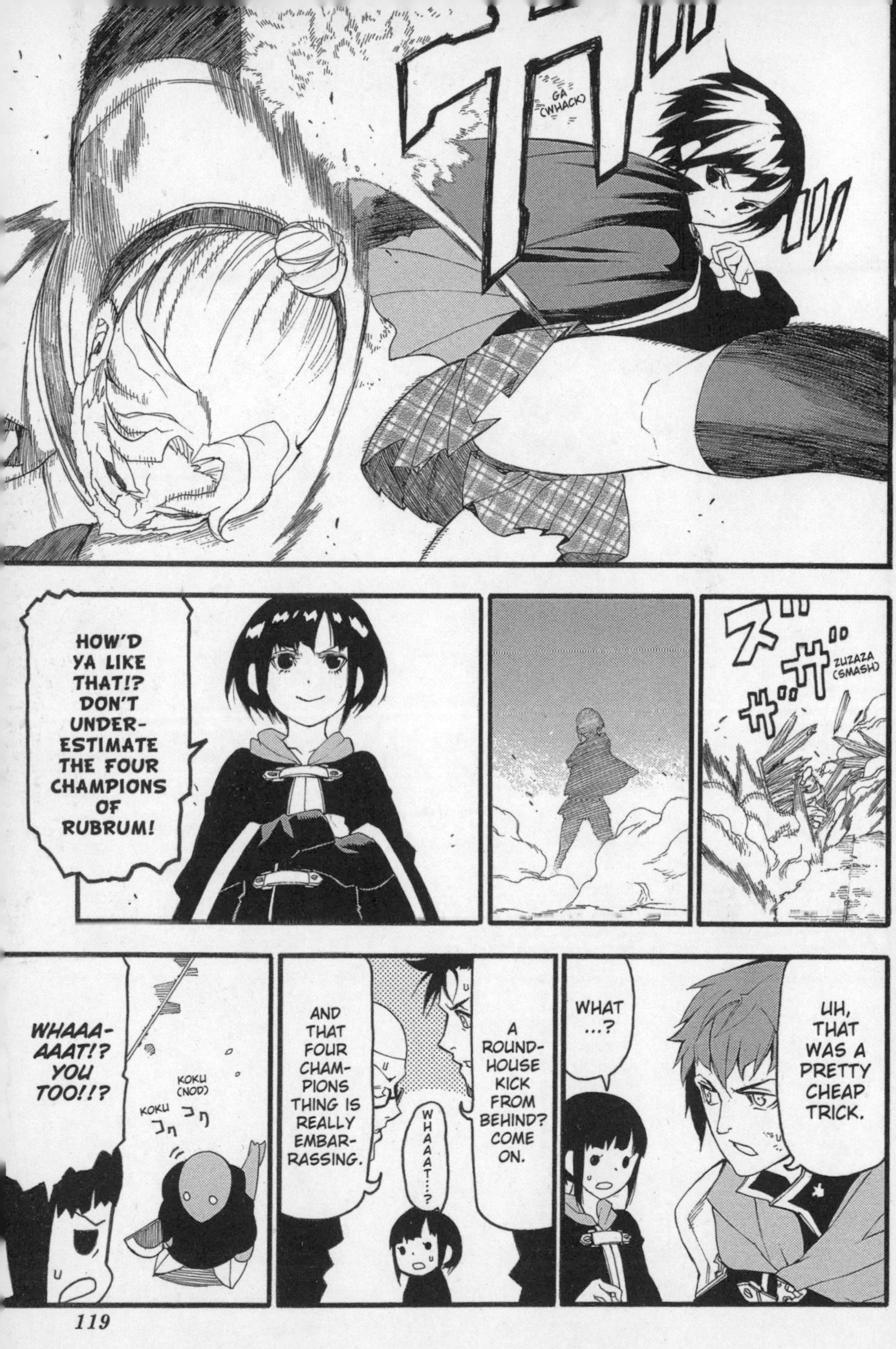
GA (WHACK)
ZUZAZA (SMASH)
HOW'D YA LIKE THAT!? DON'T UNDER-ESTIMATE THE FOUR CHAMPIONS OF RUBRUM!
UH, THAT WAS A PRETTY CHEAP TRICK.
WHAT ...?
A ROUND-HOUSE KICK FROM BEHIND? COME ON.
AND THAT FOUR CHAM-PIONS THING IS REALLY EMBAR-RASSING.
WHAAAT...?
KOKU (NOD)
KOKU
WHAAA-AAAT!? YOU TOO!!?

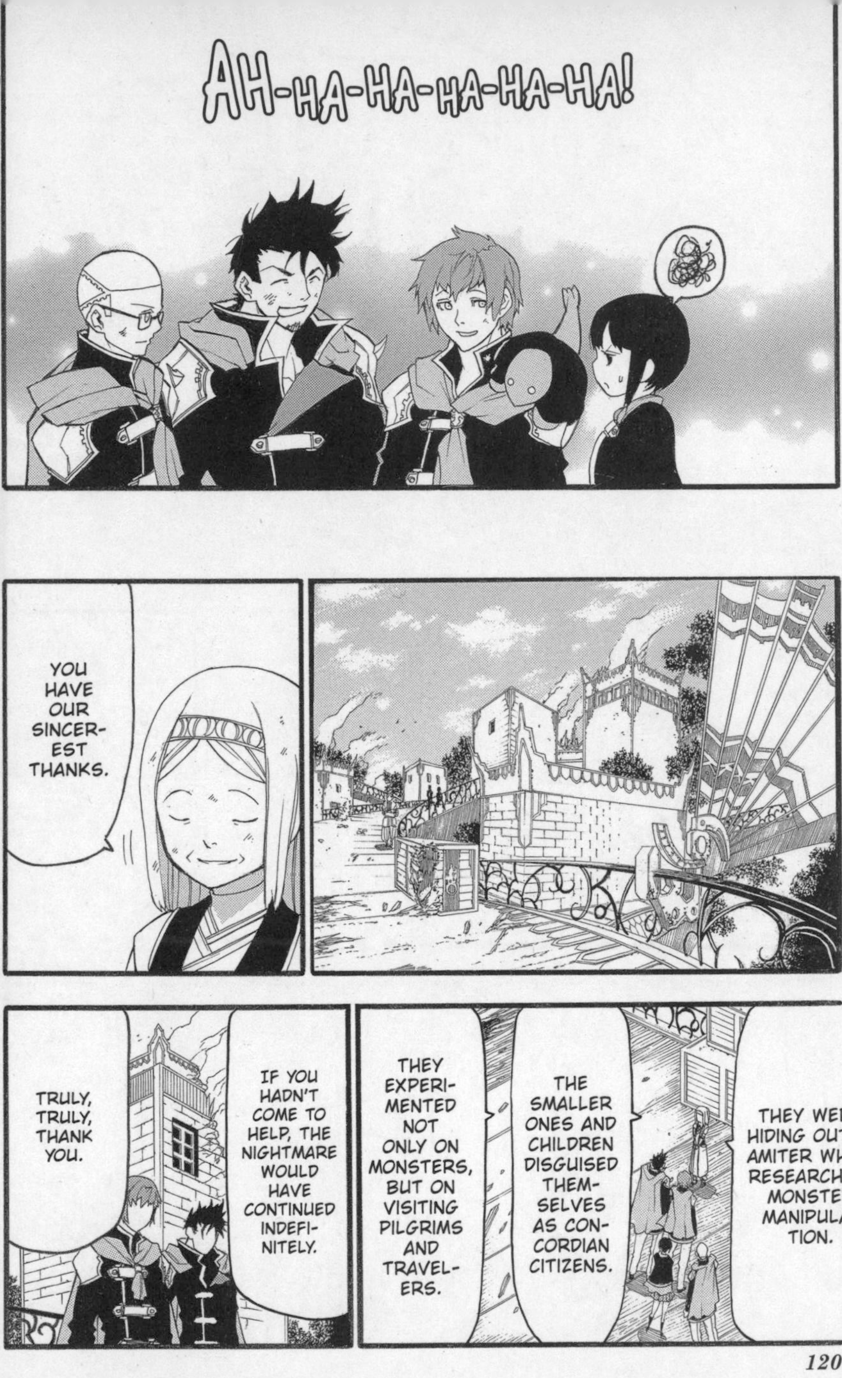
AH-HA-HA-HA-HA-HA!
YOU HAVE OUR SINCEREST THANKS.
THEY WERE HIDING OUT IN AMITER WHILE RESEARCHING MONSTER MANIPULATION.
THE SMALLER ONES AND CHILDREN DISGUISED THEMSELVES AS CONCORDIAN CITIZENS.
THEY EXPERIMENTED NOT ONLY ON MONSTERS, BUT ON VISITING PILGRIMS AND TRAVELERS.
IF YOU HADN'T COME TO HELP, THE NIGHTMARE WOULD HAVE CONTINUED INDEFINITELY.
TRULY, TRULY, THANK YOU.

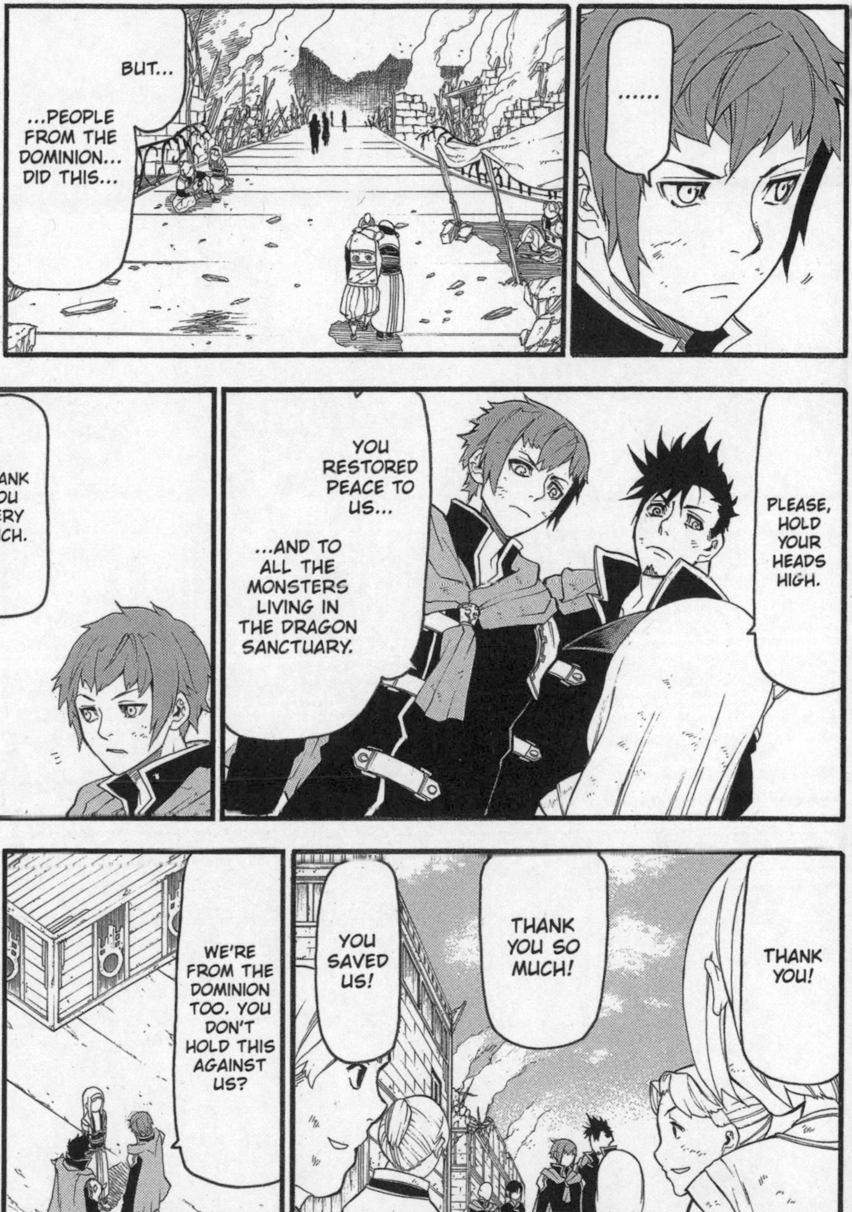
......
BUT...
...PEOPLE FROM THE DOMINION... DID THIS...
PLEASE, HOLD YOUR HEADS HIGH.
YOU RESTORED PEACE TO US...
...AND TO ALL THE MONSTERS LIVING IN THE DRAGON SANCTUARY.
THANK YOU VERY MUCH.
THANK YOU!
THANK YOU SO MUCH!
YOU SAVED US!
WE'RE FROM THE DOMINION TOO. YOU DON'T HOLD THIS AGAINST US?

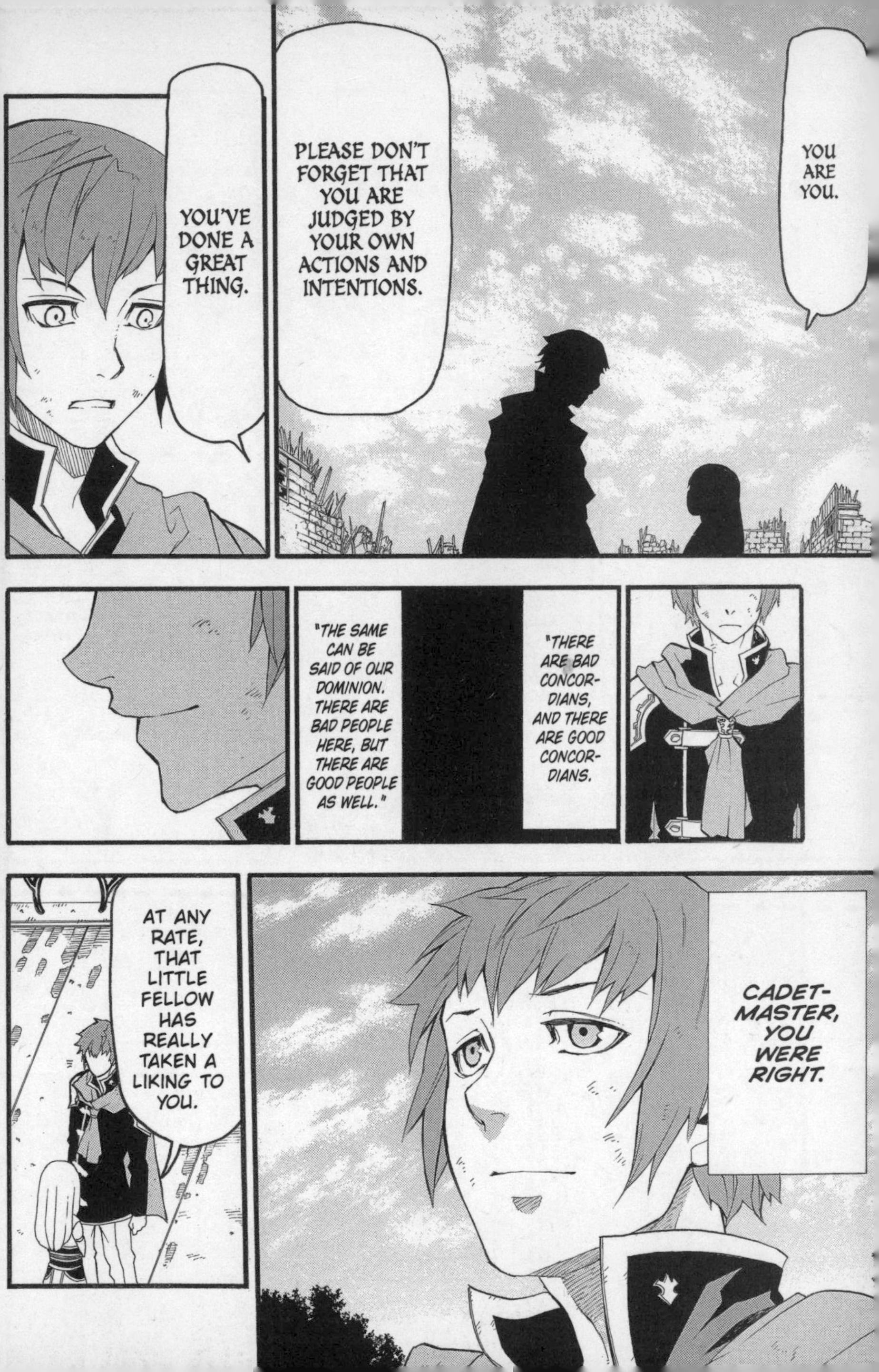
YOU ARE YOU.
PLEASE DON'T FORGET THAT YOU ARE JUDGED BY YOUR OWN ACTIONS AND INTENTIONS.
YOU'VE DONE A GREAT THING.
"THERE ARE BAD CONCOR-DIANS, AND THERE ARE GOOD CONCOR-DIANS.
"THE SAME CAN BE SAID OF OUR DOMINION. THERE ARE BAD PEOPLE HERE, BUT THERE ARE GOOD PEOPLE AS WELL."
CADET-MASTER, YOU WERE RIGHT.
AT ANY RATE, THAT LITTLE FELLOW HAS REALLY TAKEN A LIKING TO YOU.

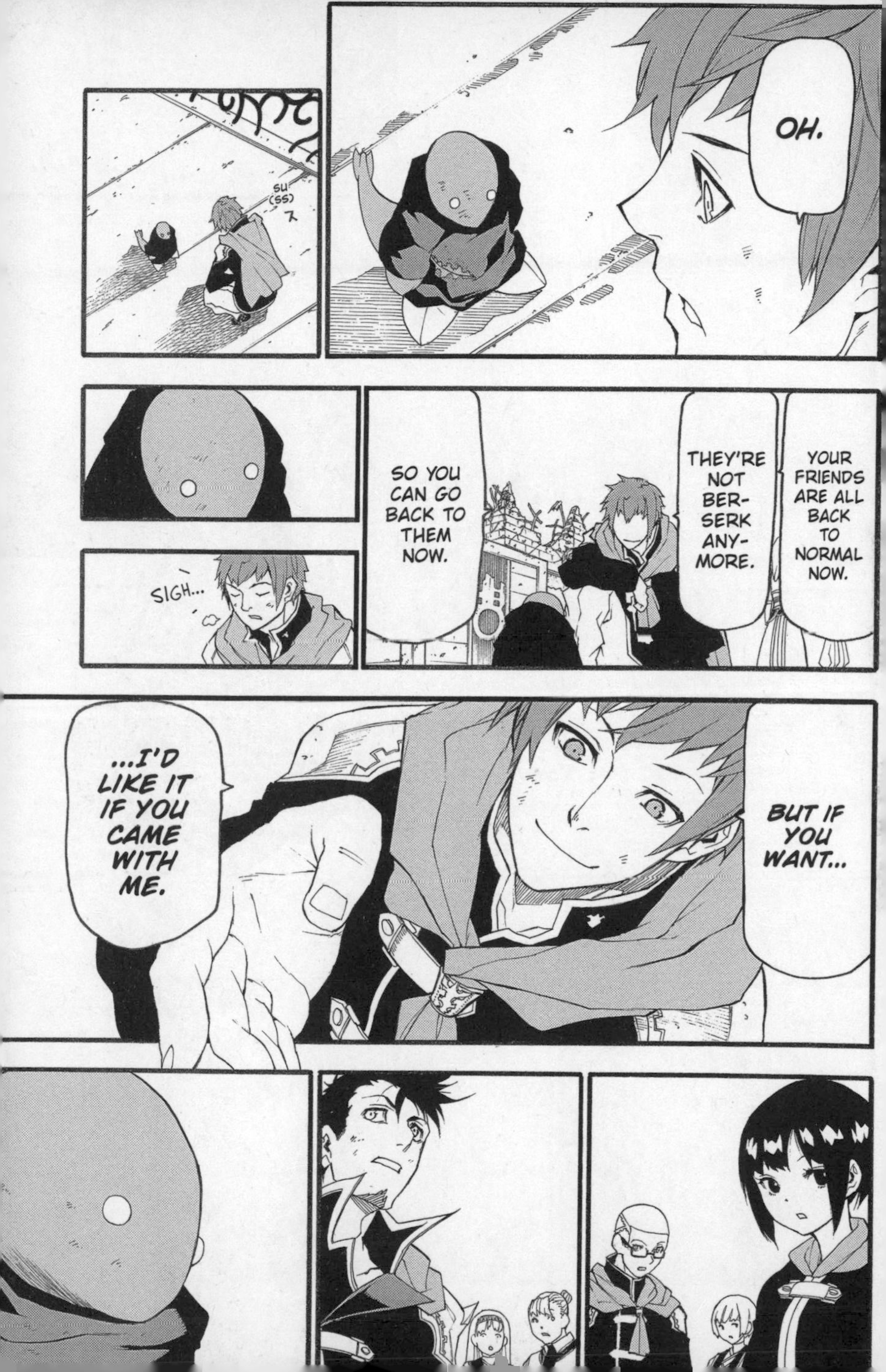
OH.
SU (SS)
ス
YOUR FRIENDS ARE ALL BACK TO NORMAL NOW.
THEY'RE NOT BER-SERK ANY-MORE.
SO YOU CAN GO BACK TO THEM NOW.
SIGH...
BUT IF YOU WANT...
...I'D LIKE IT IF YOU CAME WITH ME.

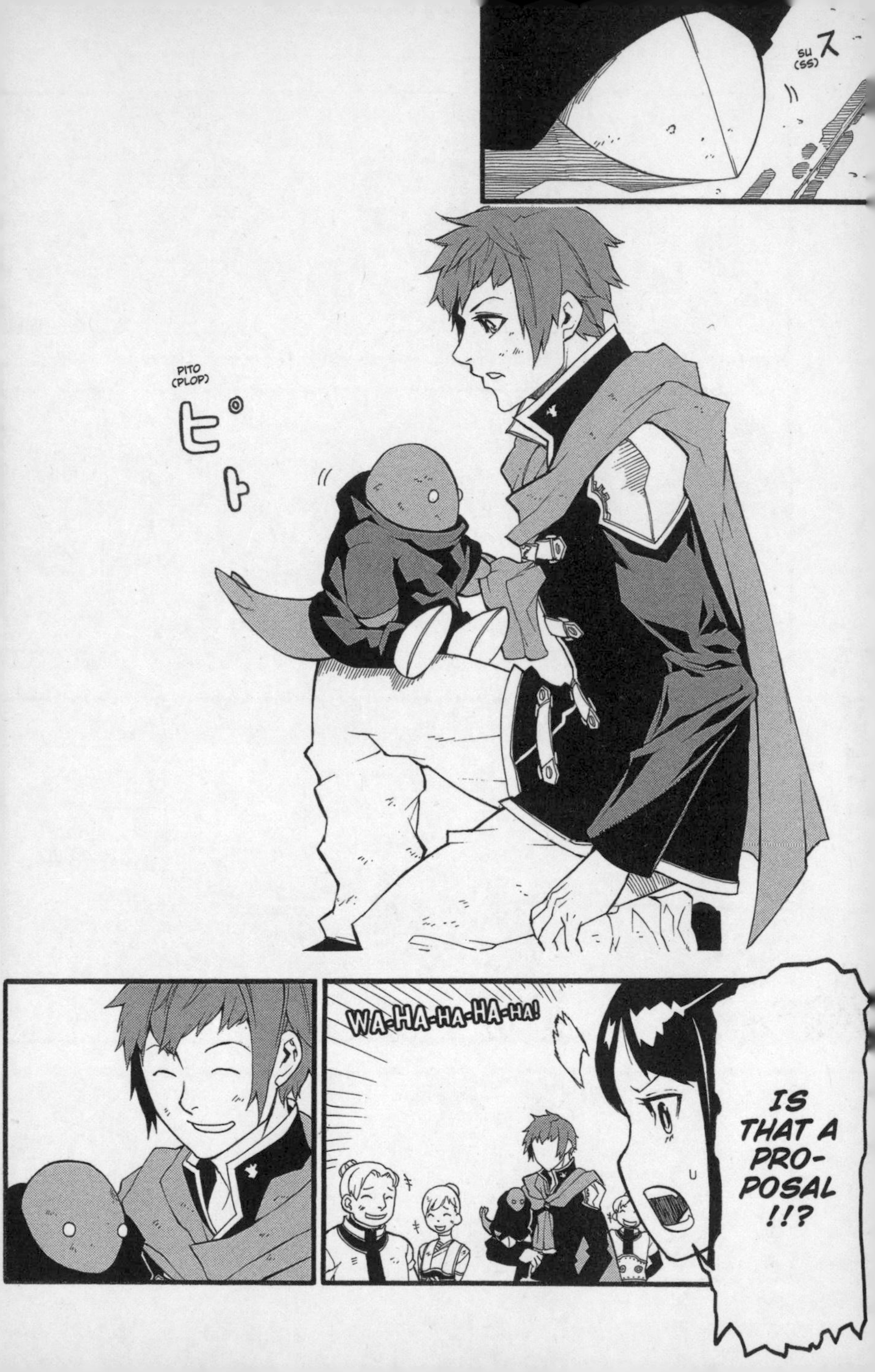
SU (SS)
ス
PITO (PLOP)
ピト
IS THAT A PRO-POSAL!!?
WA-HA-HA-HA-HA!

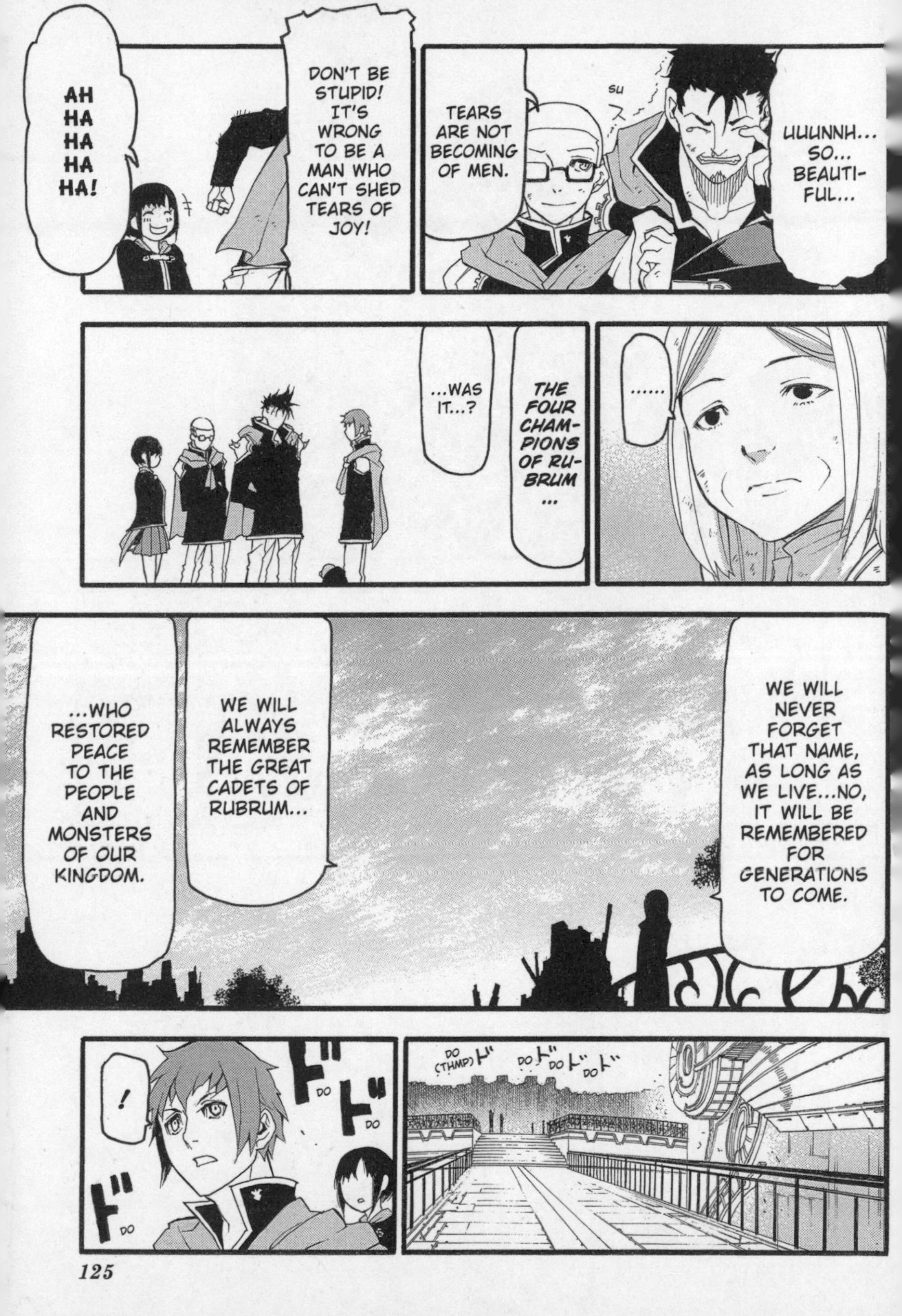
UUUNNH... SO... BEAUTIFUL...
SU
ス
TEARS ARE NOT BECOMING OF MEN.
DON'T BE STUPID! IT'S WRONG TO BE A MAN WHO CAN'T SHED TEARS OF JOY!
AH HA HA HA HA!
......
THE FOUR CHAMPIONS OF RUBRUM...
...WAS IT...?
WE WILL NEVER FORGET THAT NAME, AS LONG AS WE LIVE...NO, IT WILL BE REMEMBERED FOR GENERATIONS TO COME.
WE WILL ALWAYS REMEMBER THE GREAT CADETS OF RUBRUM...
...WHO RESTORED PEACE TO THE PEOPLE AND MONSTERS OF OUR KINGDOM.
DO (THMP) ド
DO ド DO ド DO ド
ド DO
ド DO
!
ド DO

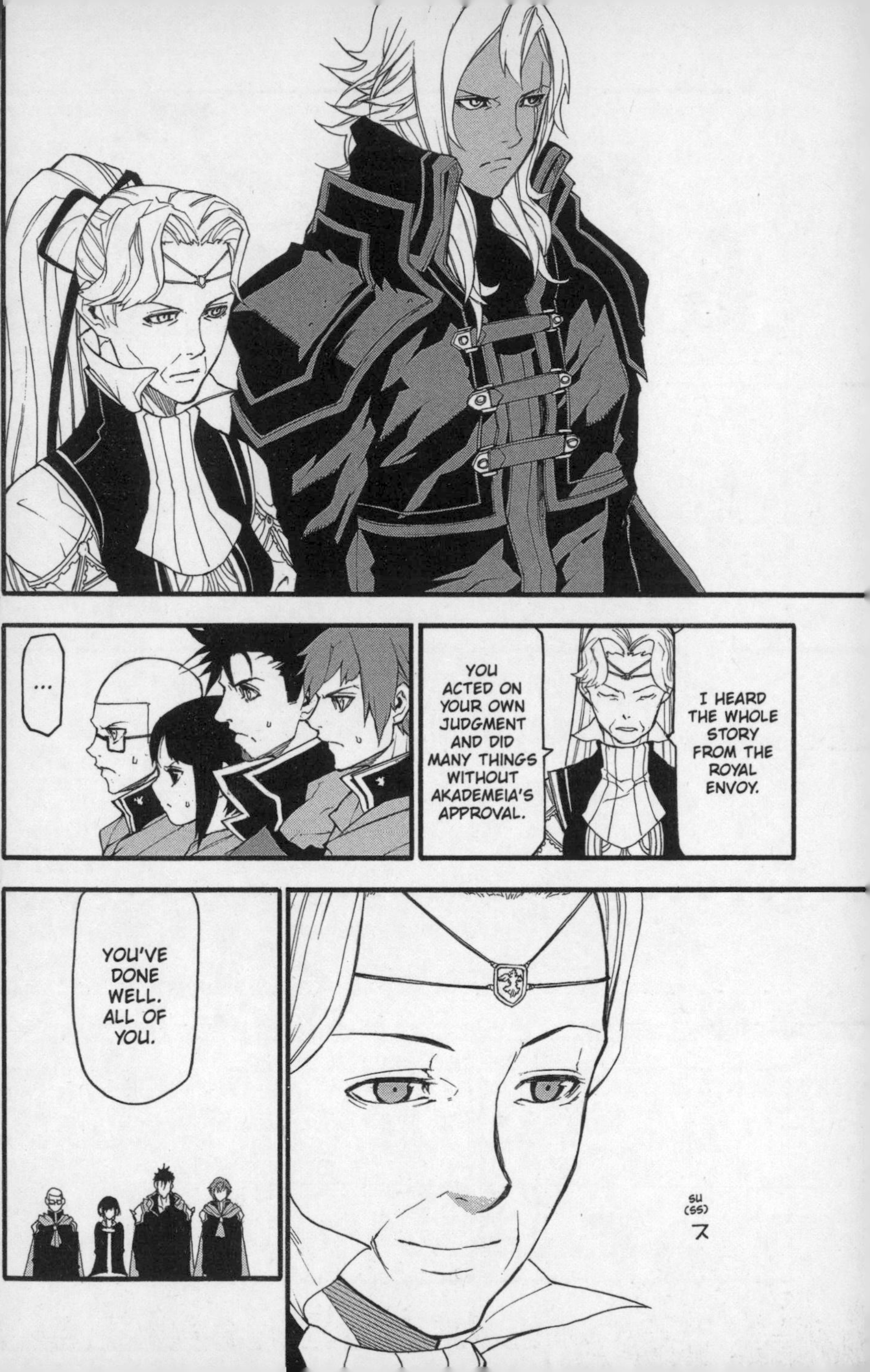
I HEARD THE WHOLE STORY FROM THE ROYAL ENVOY.
YOU ACTED ON YOUR OWN JUDGMENT AND DID MANY THINGS WITHOUT AKADEMEIA'S APPROVAL.
...
SU (SS)
ス
YOU'VE DONE WELL. ALL OF YOU.

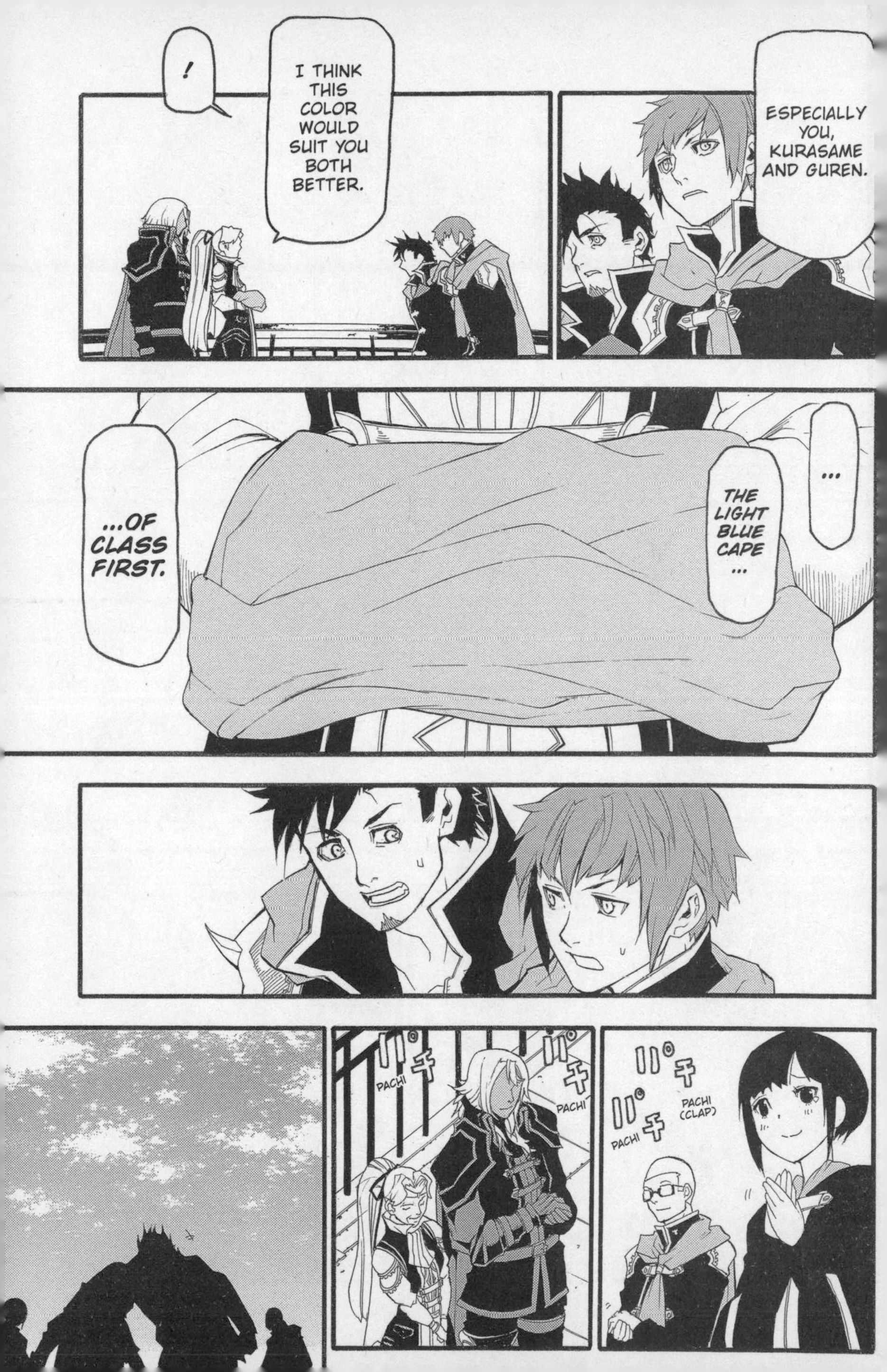
ESPECIALLY YOU, KURASAME AND GUREN.
I THINK THIS COLOR WOULD SUIT YOU BOTH BETTER.
!
...
THE LIGHT BLUE CAPE ...
...OF CLASS FIRST.
PACHI (CLAP)
PACHI
PACHI
PACHI

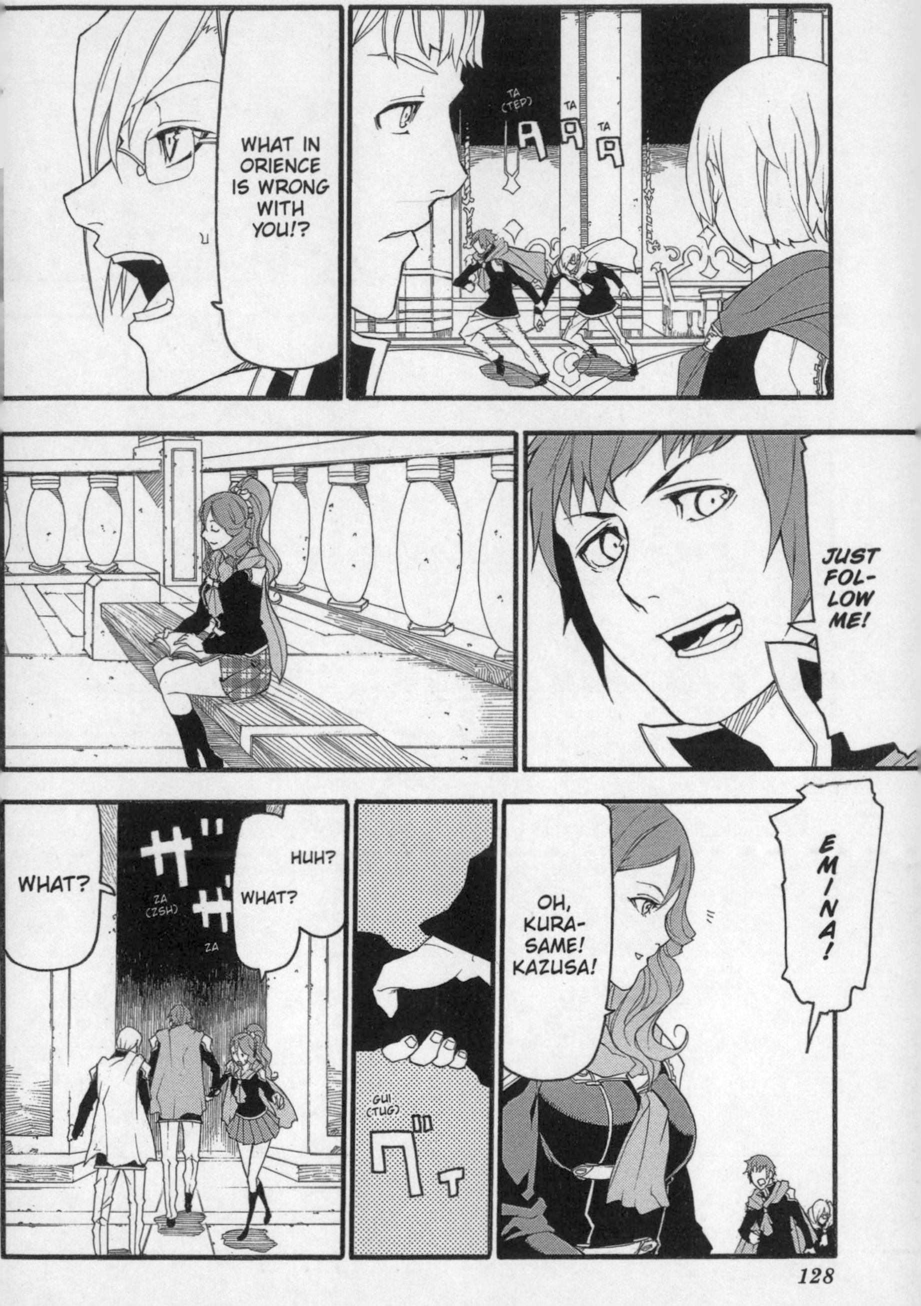
TA (TEP)
TA
TA
WHAT IN ORIENCE IS WRONG WITH YOU!?
JUST FOL-LOW ME!
EMINA!
OH, KURA-SAME! KAZUSA!
GUI (TUG)
HUH?
WHAT?
ZA (ZSH)
ZA
WHAT?

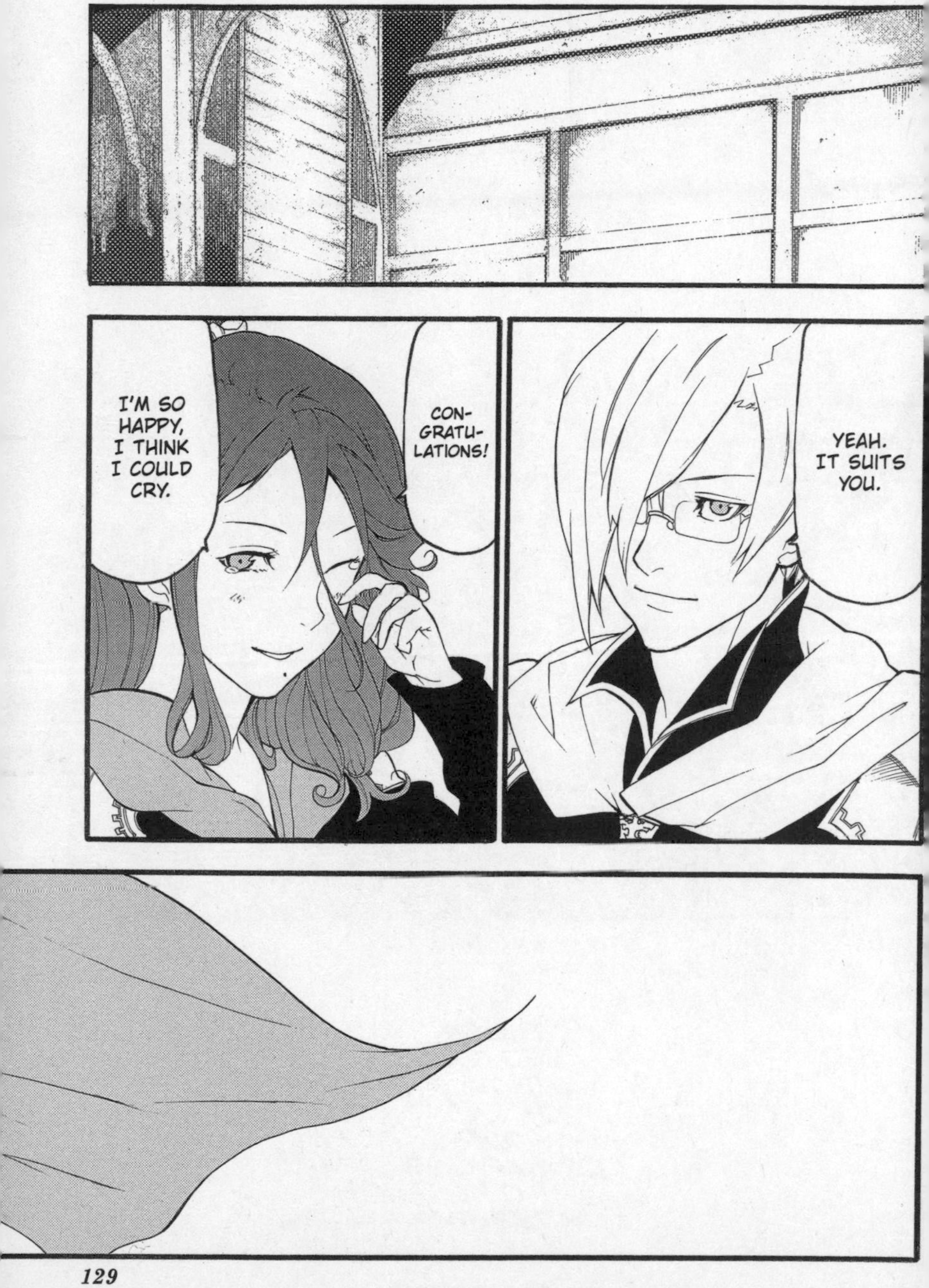
YEAH. IT SUITS YOU.
CON-GRATU-LATIONS!
I'M SO HAPPY, I THINK I COULD CRY.

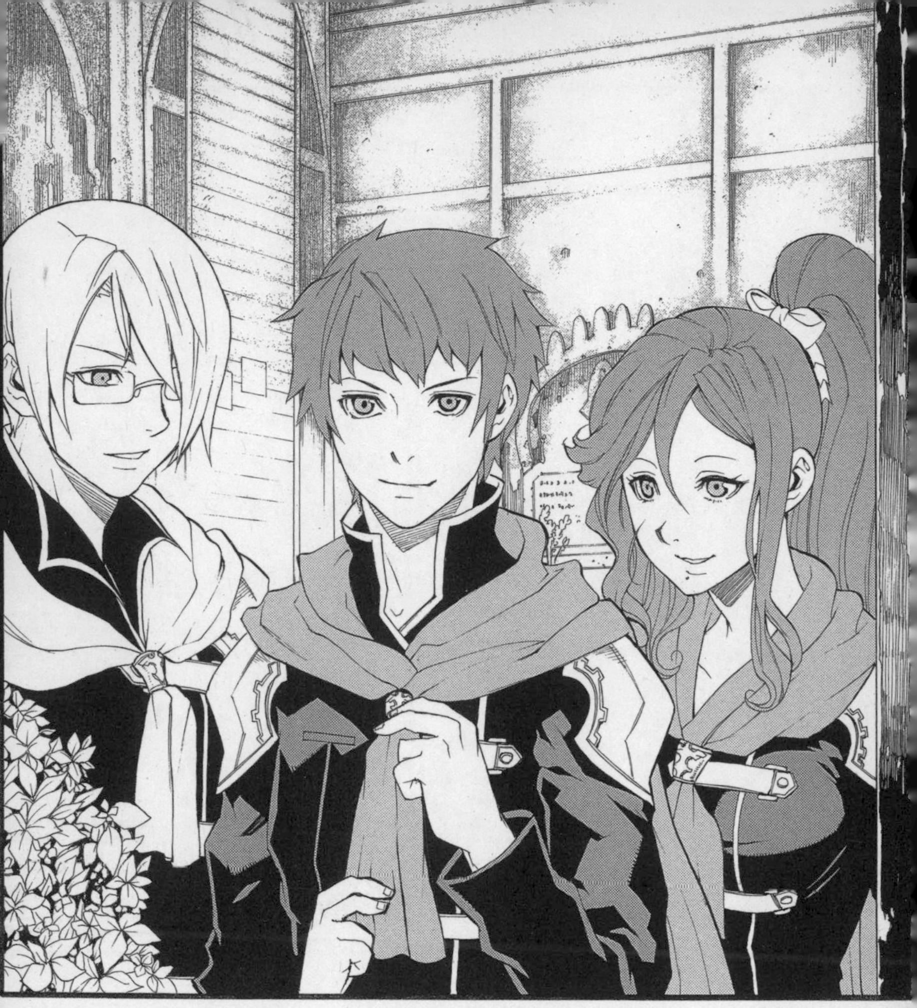

THUS BEGINS THE TALE OF THE FOUR CHAMPIONS OF RUBRUM.

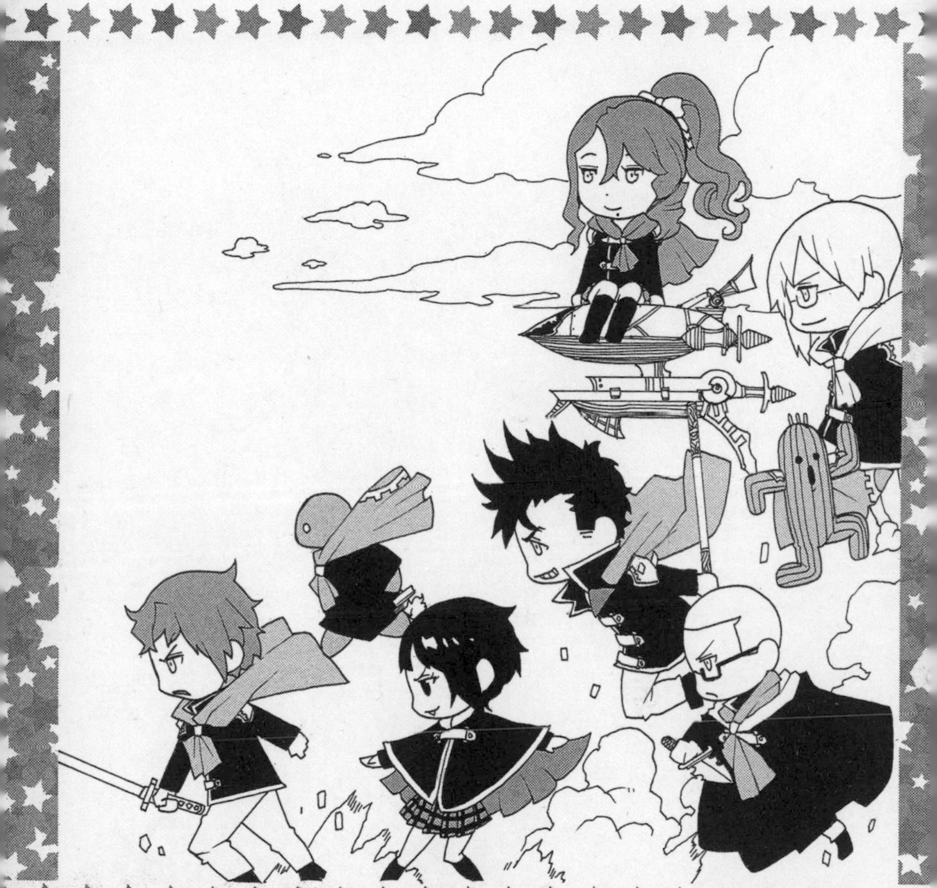

FINAL FANTASY 零式 TYPE-0™
SIDE STORY
The Ice Reaper

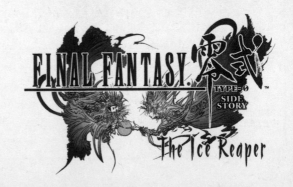

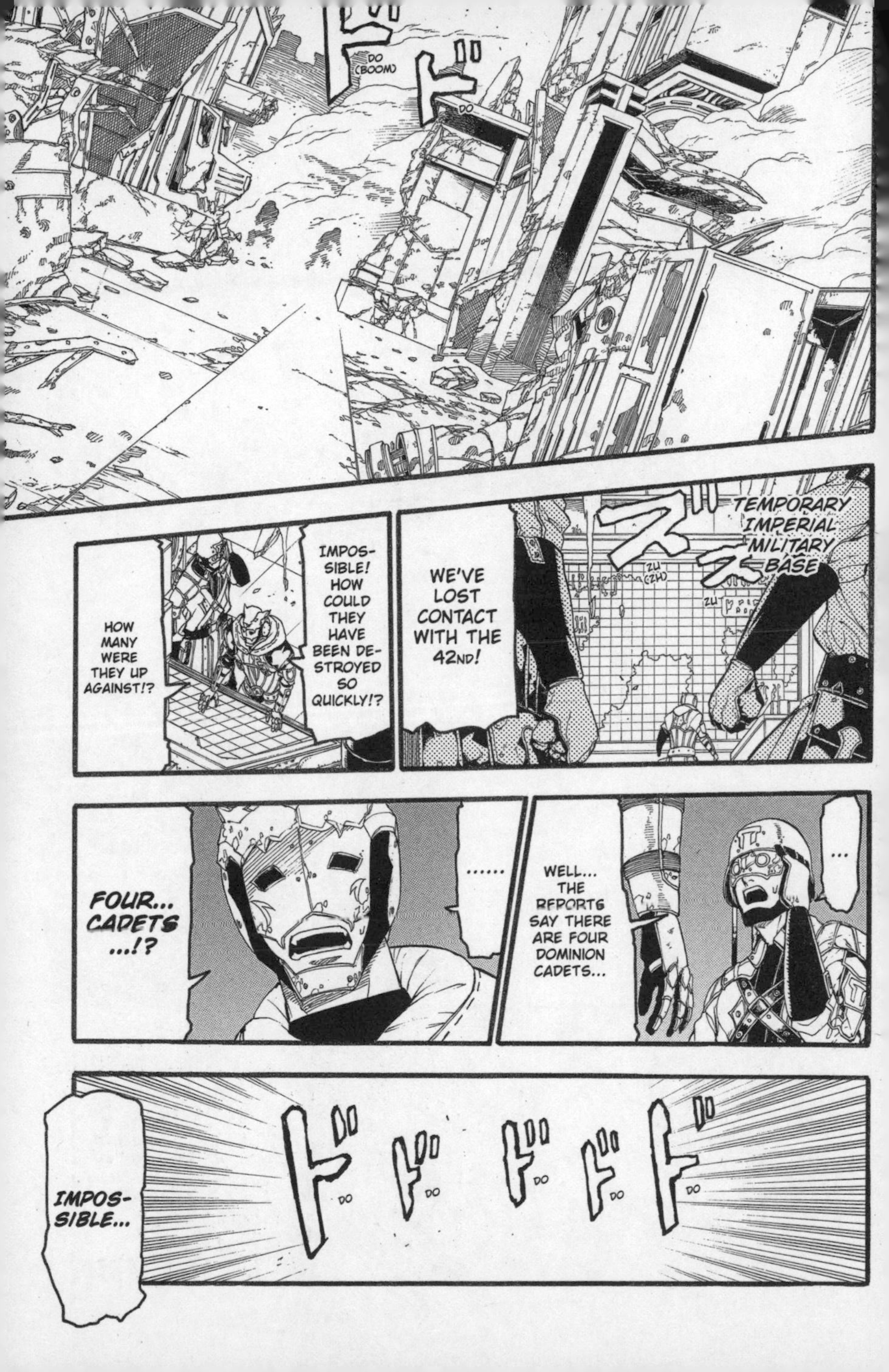
DO
(BOOM)
DO
TEMPORARY IMPERIAL MILITARY BASE
ZU
(ZH)
ZU
WE'VE LOST CONTACT WITH THE 42ND!
IMPOS-SIBLE! HOW COULD THEY HAVE BEEN DE-STROYED SO QUICKLY!?
HOW MANY WERE THEY UP AGAINST!?
...
WELL... THE REPORTS SAY THERE ARE FOUR DOMINION CADETS...
......
FOUR... CADETS ...!?
DO
DO
DO
DO
DO
IMPOS-SIBLE...

CHAPTER 8: ESCORT

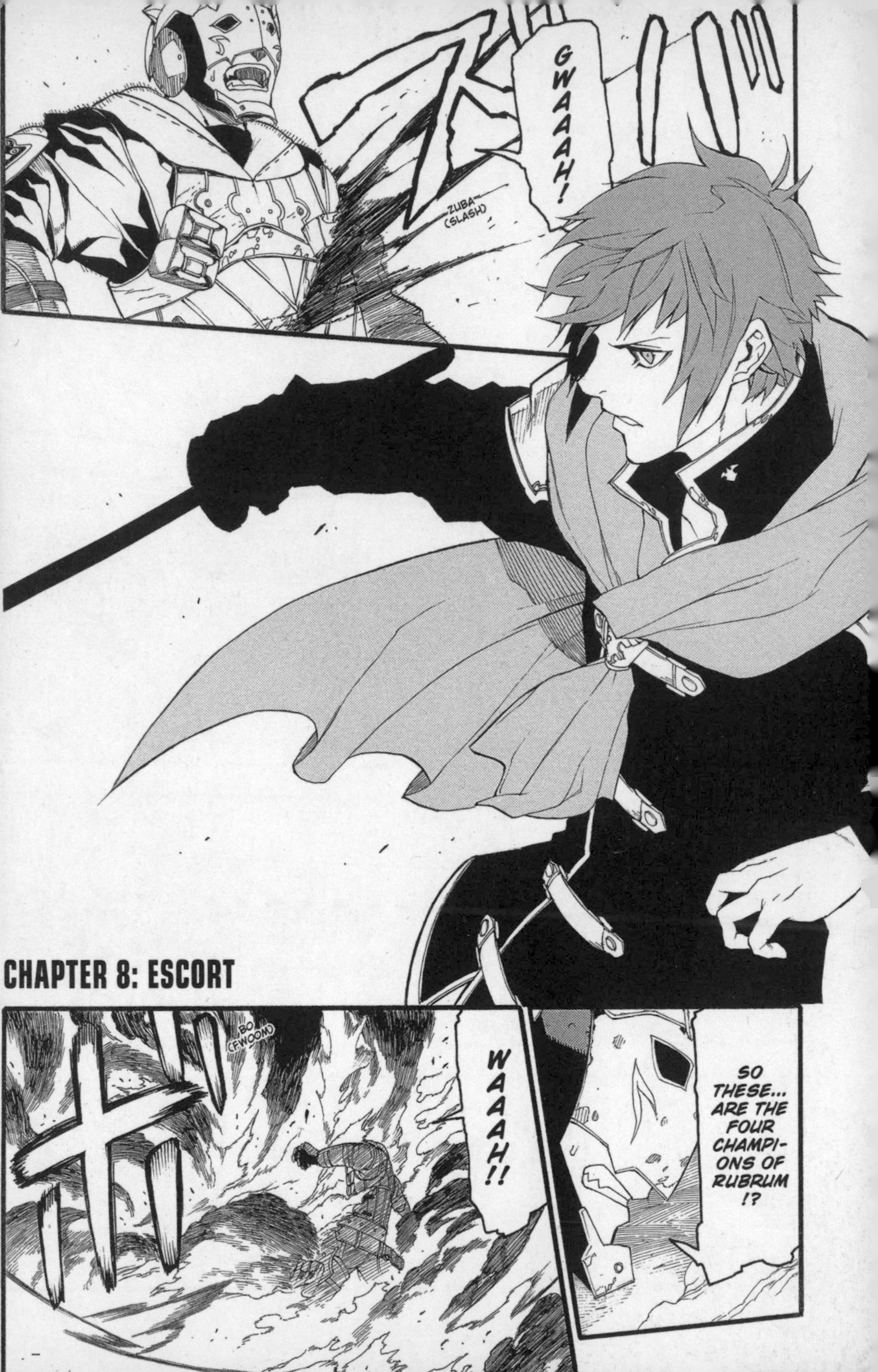
GWAAAAH!
ZUBA (SLASH)
SO THESE... ARE THE FOUR CHAMPIONS OF RUBRUM!?
WAAAAH!!
BO (FWOOM)

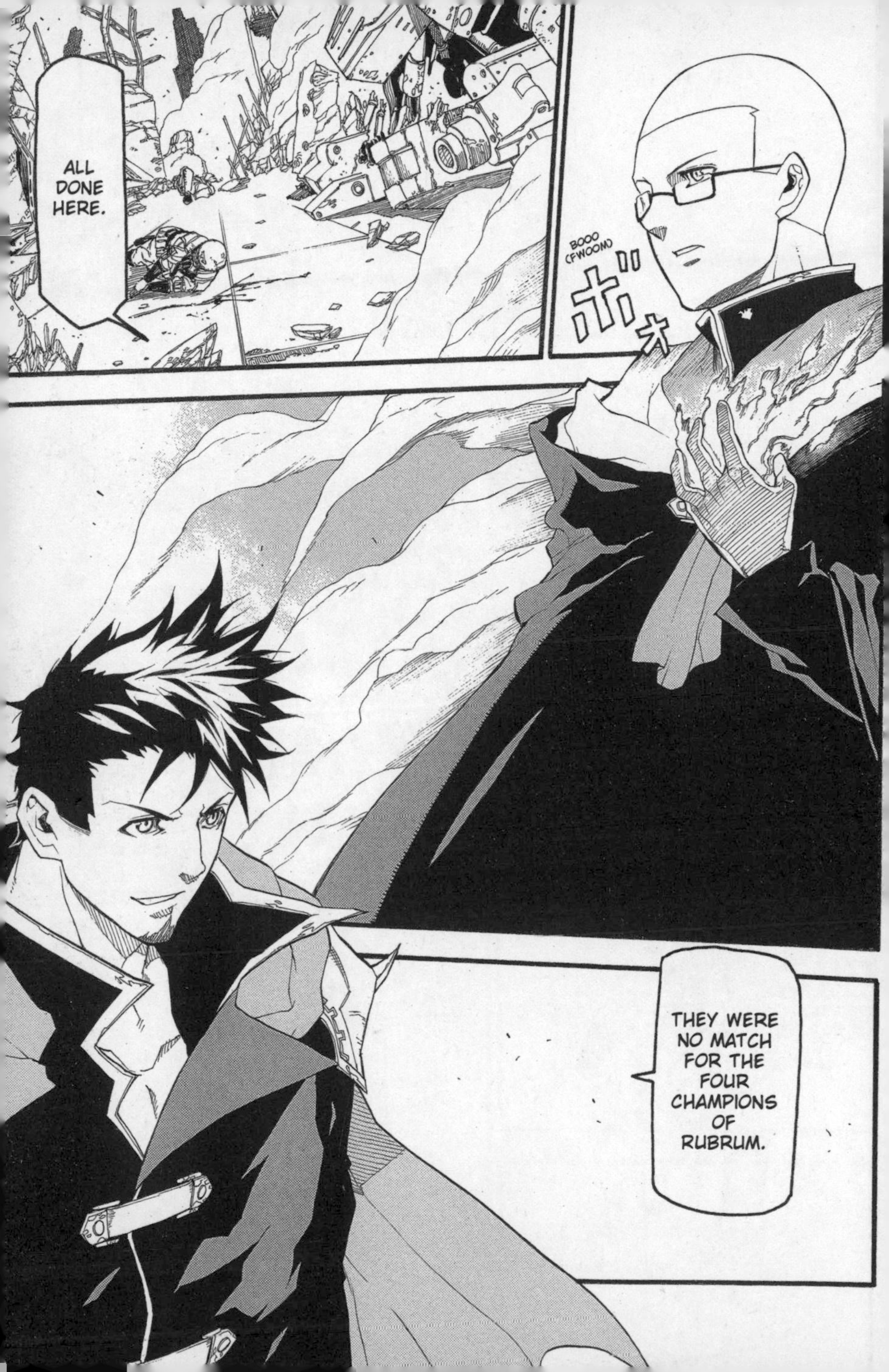

ボォ
BOOO (FWOOM)
ALL DONE HERE.
THEY WERE NO MATCH FOR THE FOUR CHAMPIONS OF RUBRUM.

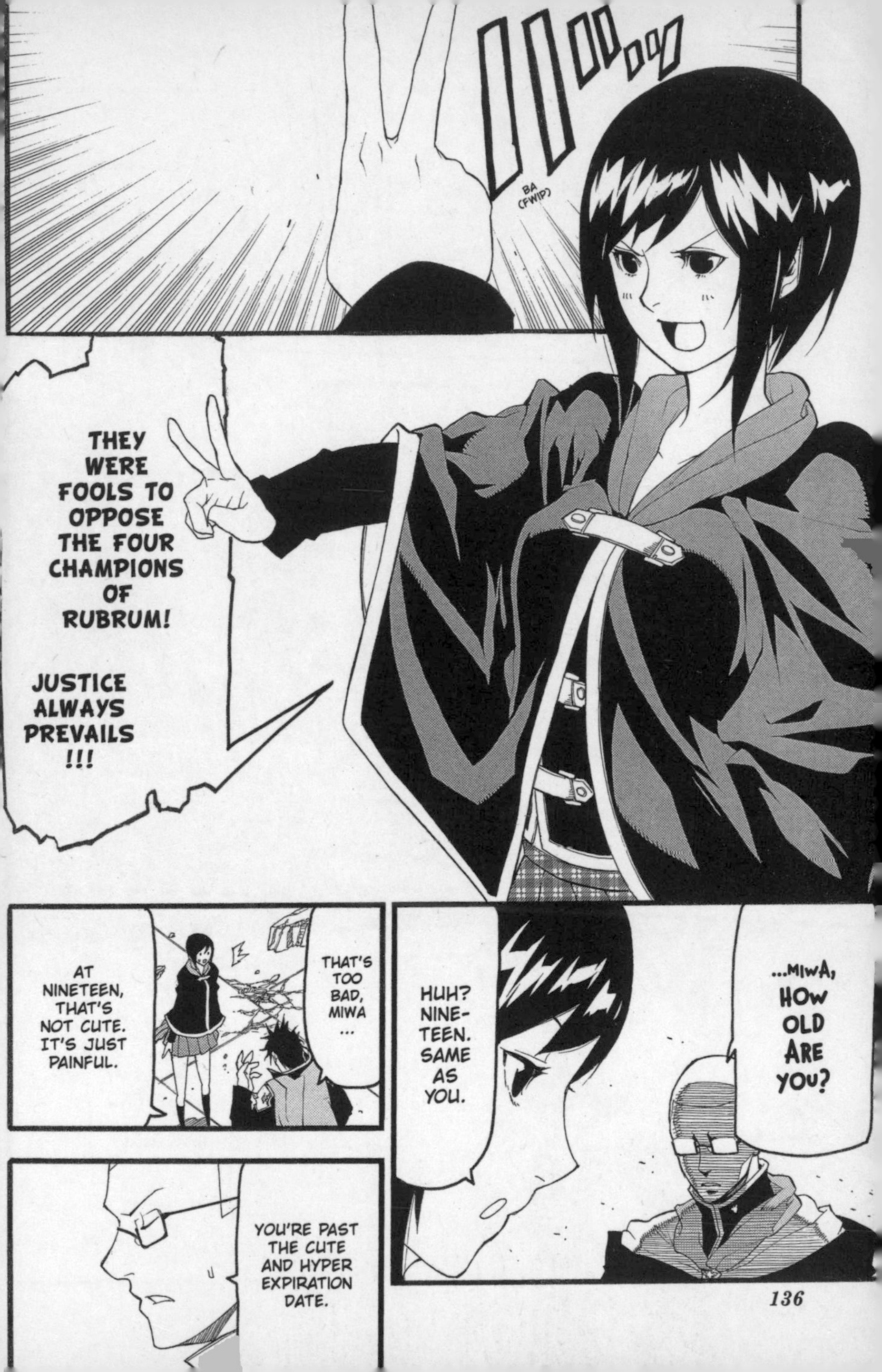
BA (FWIP)
THEY WERE FOOLS TO OPPOSE THE FOUR CHAMPIONS OF RUBRUM!
JUSTICE ALWAYS PREVAILS!!!
...MIWA, HOW OLD ARE YOU?
HUH? NINETEEN. SAME AS YOU.
THAT'S TOO BAD, MIWA...
AT NINETEEN, THAT'S NOT CUTE. IT'S JUST PAINFUL.
YOU'RE PAST THE CUTE AND HYPER EXPIRATION DATE.

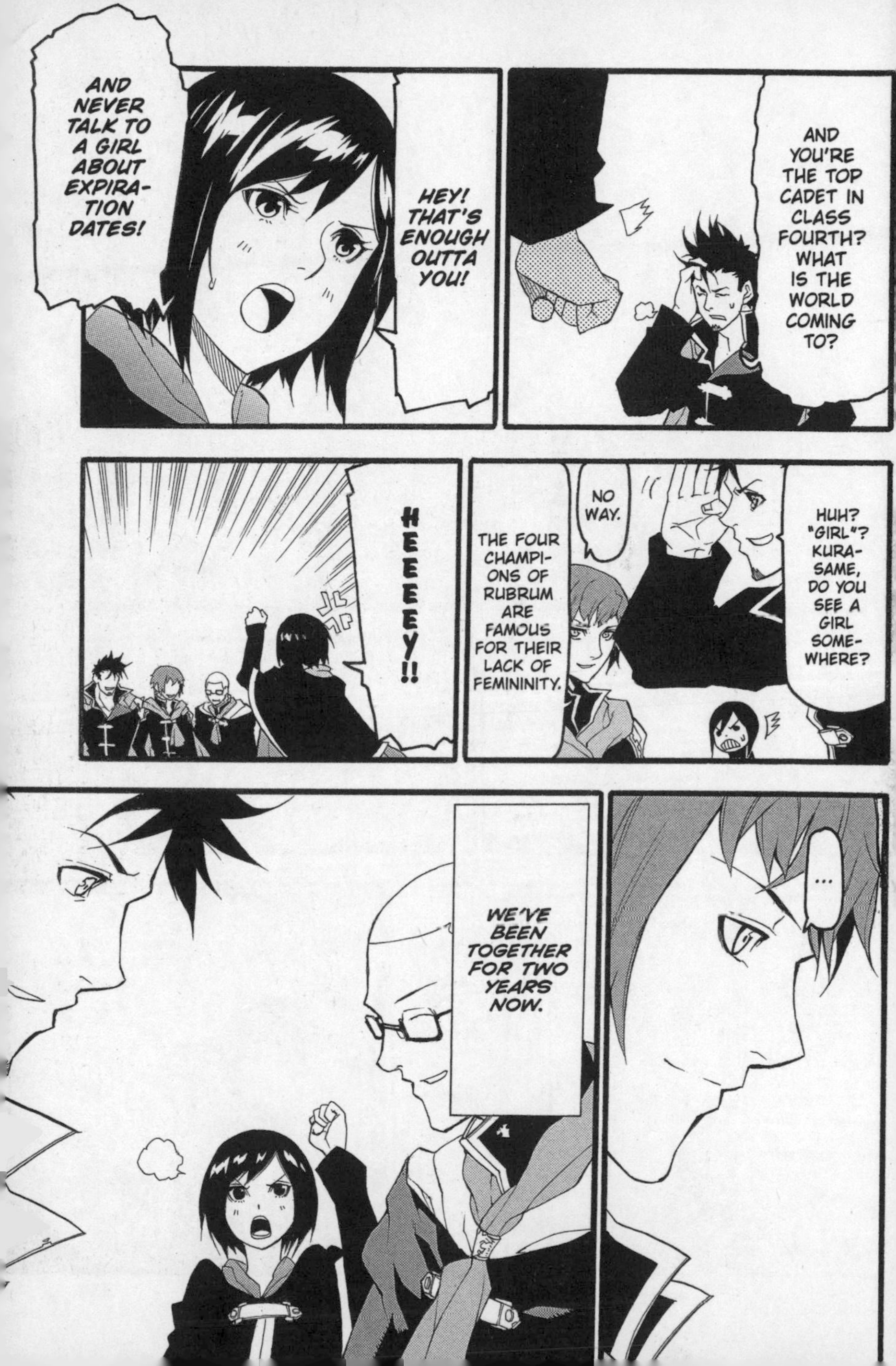
AND YOU'RE THE TOP CADET IN CLASS FOURTH? WHAT IS THE WORLD COMING TO?
HEY! THAT'S ENOUGH OUTTA YOU!
AND NEVER TALK TO A GIRL ABOUT EXPIRATION DATES!
HUH? "GIRL"? KURASAME, DO YOU SEE A GIRL SOMEWHERE?
NO WAY.
THE FOUR CHAMPIONS OF RUBRUM ARE FAMOUS FOR THEIR LACK OF FEMININITY.
HEEEEEY!!
...
WE'VE BEEN TOGETHER FOR TWO YEARS NOW.

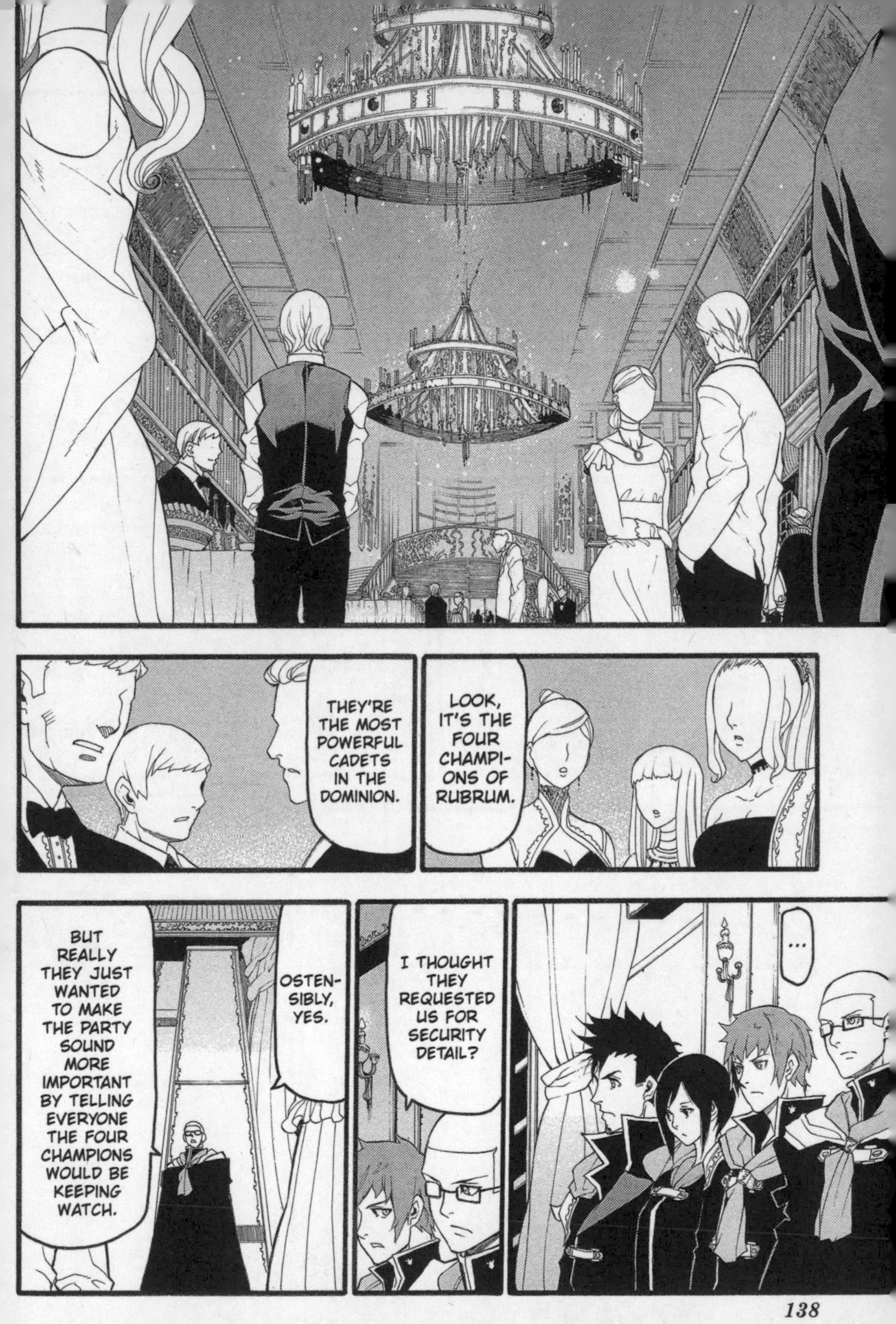
LOOK, IT'S THE FOUR CHAMPIONS OF RUBRUM.
THEY'RE THE MOST POWERFUL CADETS IN THE DOMINION.
...
I THOUGHT THEY REQUESTED US FOR SECURITY DETAIL?
OSTENSIBLY, YES.
BUT REALLY THEY JUST WANTED TO MAKE THE PARTY SOUND MORE IMPORTANT BY TELLING EVERYONE THE FOUR CHAMPIONS WOULD BE KEEPING WATCH.

OKAY.

WELL, I NEED TO GET GOING. THE CADET-MASTER WANTS ME.

THE FOUR CHAMPIONS OF RUBRUM ARE THE FACE OF THE DOMINION, AFTER ALL.

...

THE TWO IDIOTS OF THE FOUR CHAMPIONS.

7 R
SUTA (SHUFFLE)

7 R
SUTA

ALL RIGHT THEN, AS THE FACE OF THE DOMINION, I'M GOING TO EAT SOME YUMMY FOOD!

EH HEH HEH.

OKAY! AND I'M GOING TO GO FLIRT WITH THOSE CUTE GIRLS—AS THE FACE OF THE DOMINION!

OH.

EXCUSE ME.

KOTSUN (TAP)

SU (SS)

THAT'S QUITE ALL RIGHT...

OH... I'M SORRY.

......

IF I'M NOT MISTAKEN, THAT'S THE DEPUTY PRIME LIAISON, FUYOU TOMOSHIBI.

SU
(SS)

!

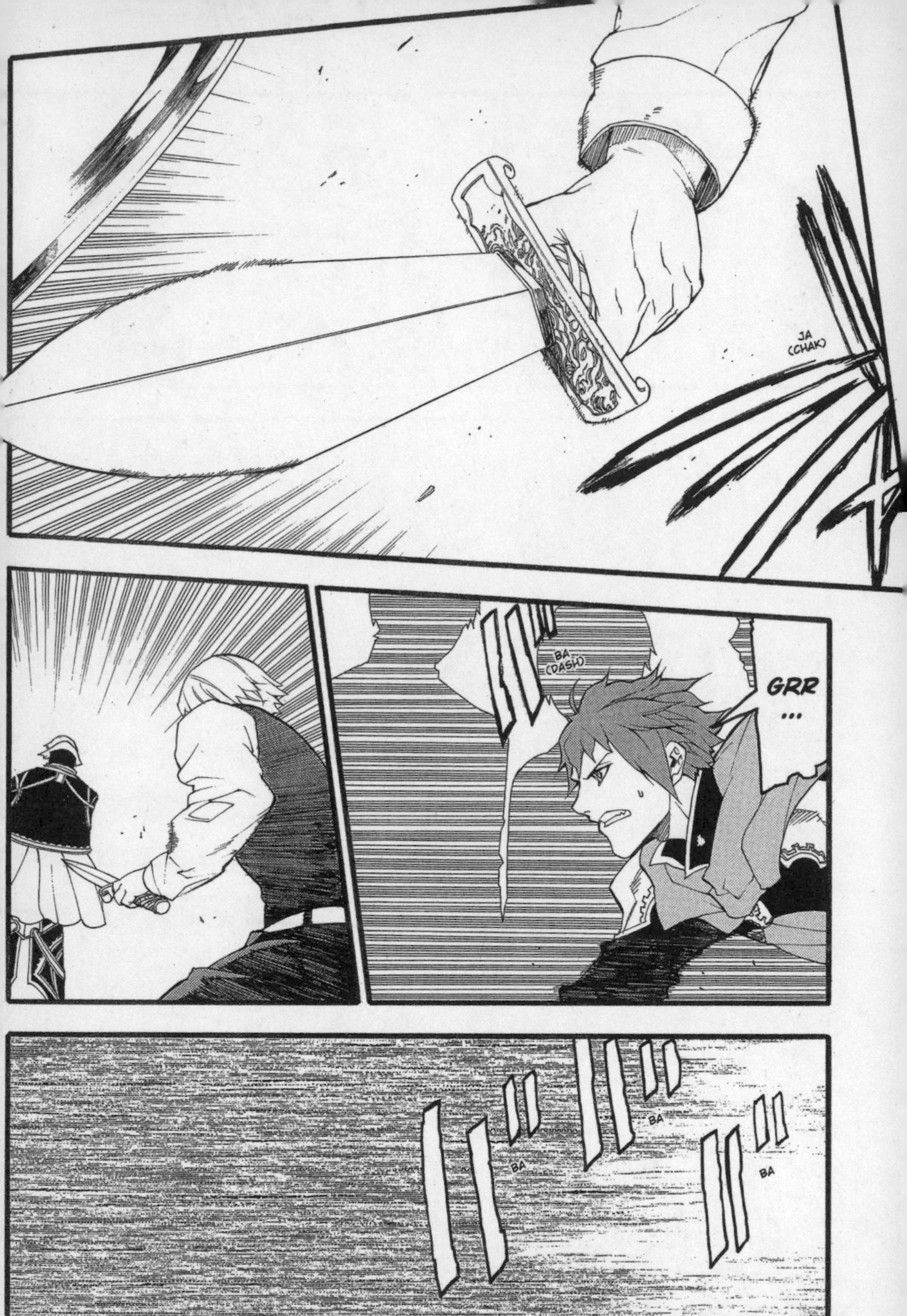
JA
(CHAK)
BA
(DASH)
GRR
...
BA
BA
BA

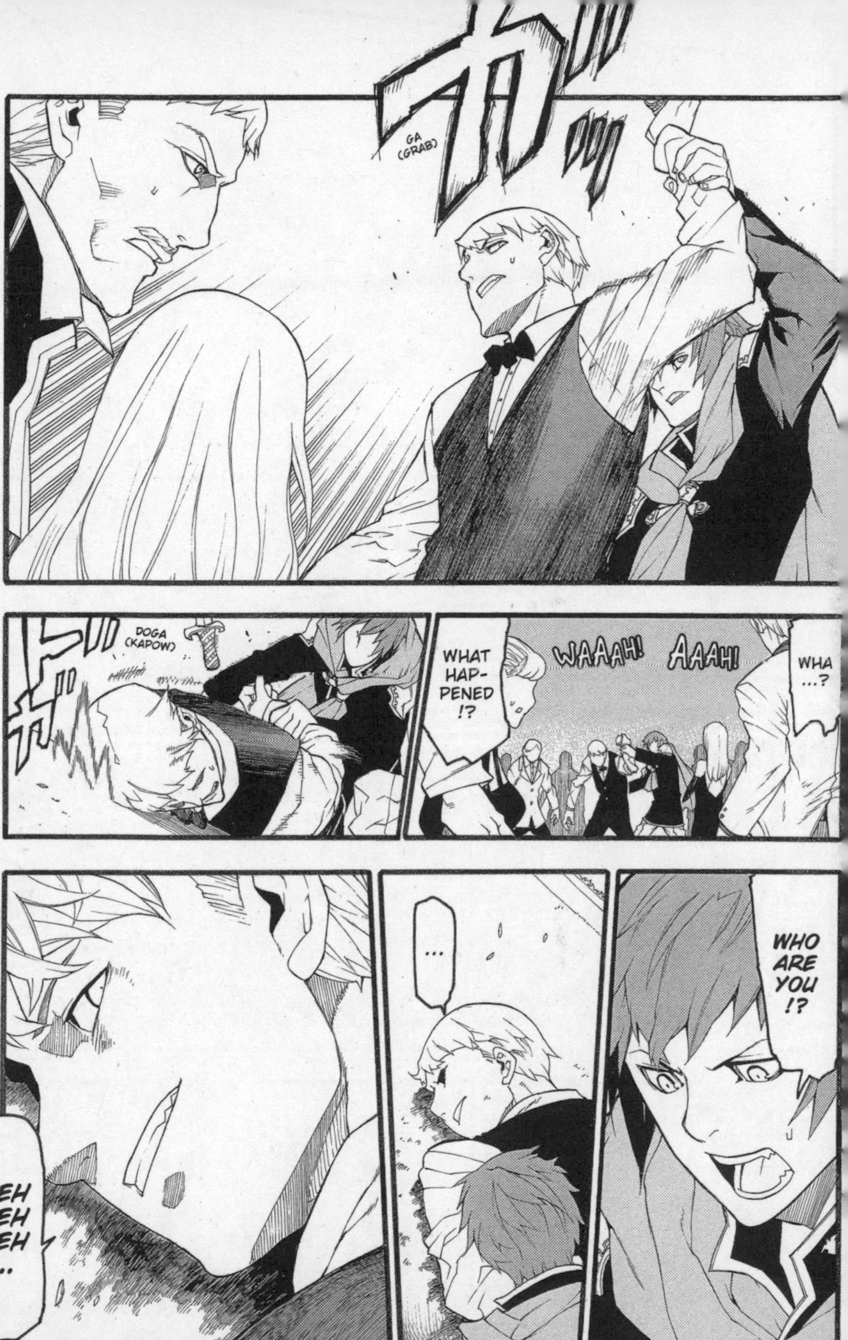

GA (GRAB)
WHA ...?
AAAH!
WAAAH!
WHAT HAP-PENED !?
DOGA (KAPOW)
WHO ARE YOU !?
...
HEH HEH HEH ...

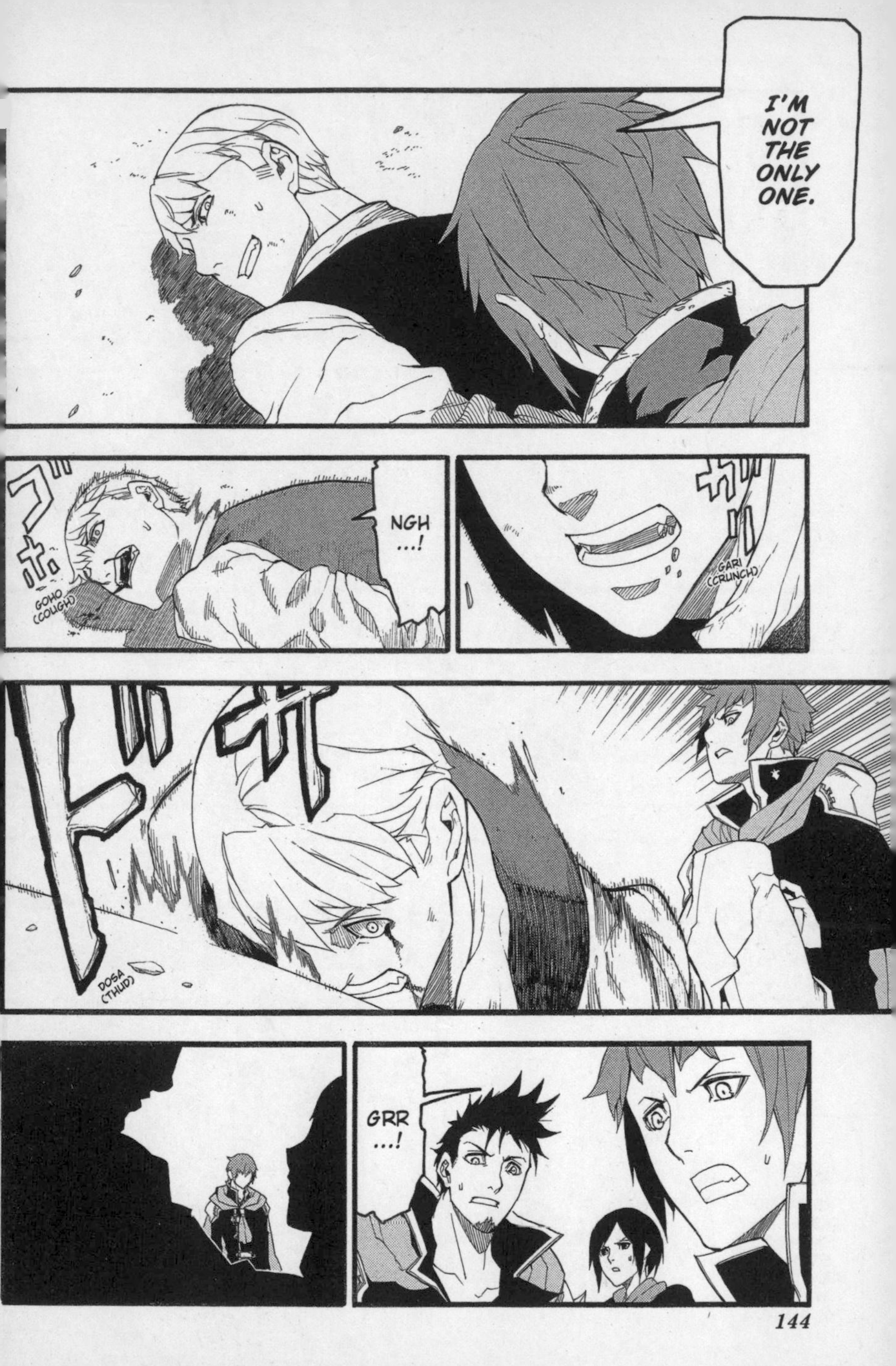
I'M NOT THE ONLY ONE.
GARI (CRUNCH)
NGH ...!
GOHO (COUGH)
DOSA (THUD)
GRR ...!

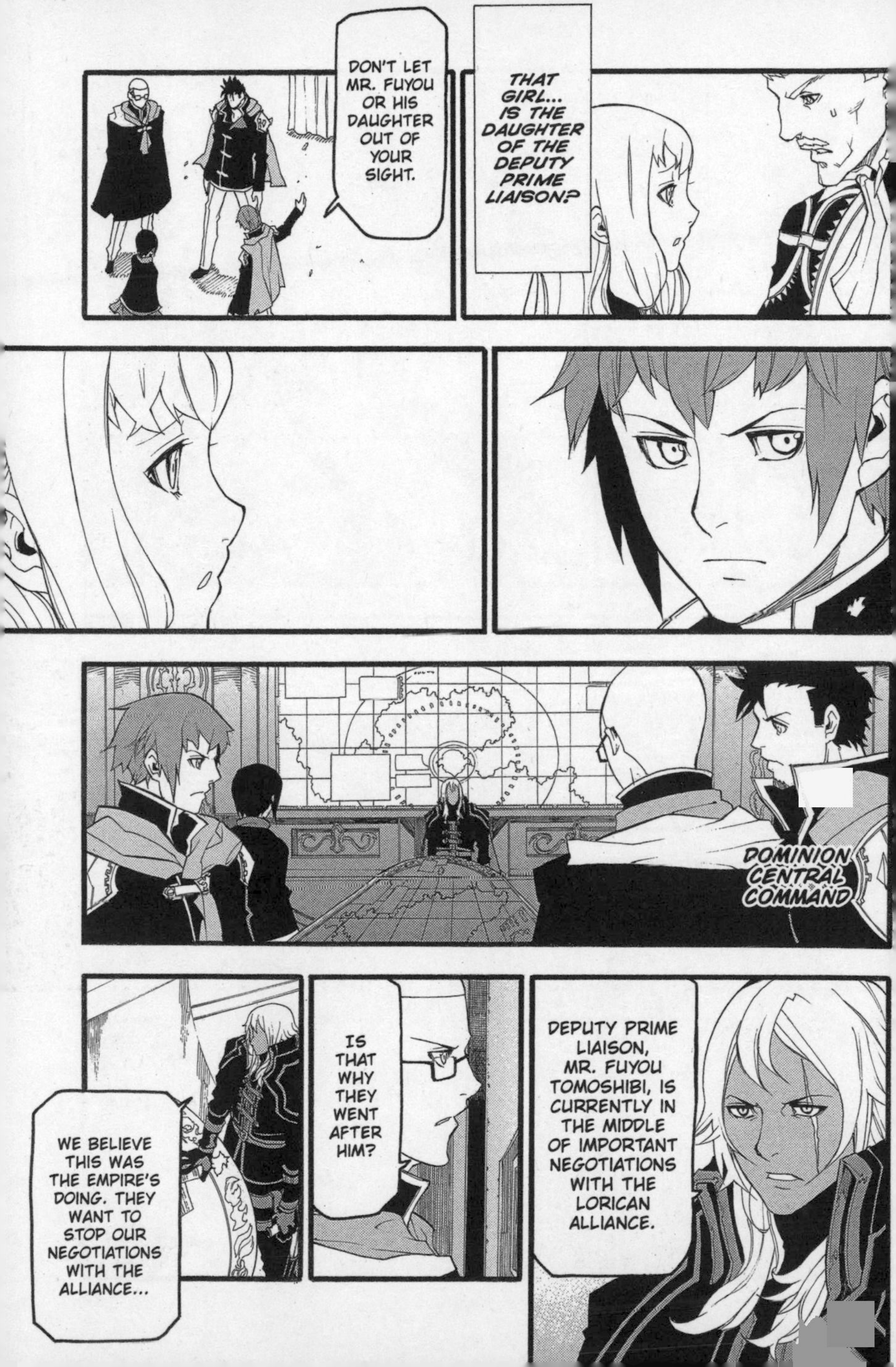
THAT GIRL... IS THE DAUGHTER OF THE DEPUTY PRIME LIAISON?
DON'T LET MR. FUYOU OR HIS DAUGHTER OUT OF YOUR SIGHT.
DOMINION CENTRAL COMMAND
DEPUTY PRIME LIAISON, MR. FUYOU TOMOSHIBI, IS CURRENTLY IN THE MIDDLE OF IMPORTANT NEGOTIATIONS WITH THE LORICAN ALLIANCE.
IS THAT WHY THEY WENT AFTER HIM?
WE BELIEVE THIS WAS THE EMPIRE'S DOING. THEY WANT TO STOP OUR NEGOTIATIONS WITH THE ALLIANCE...

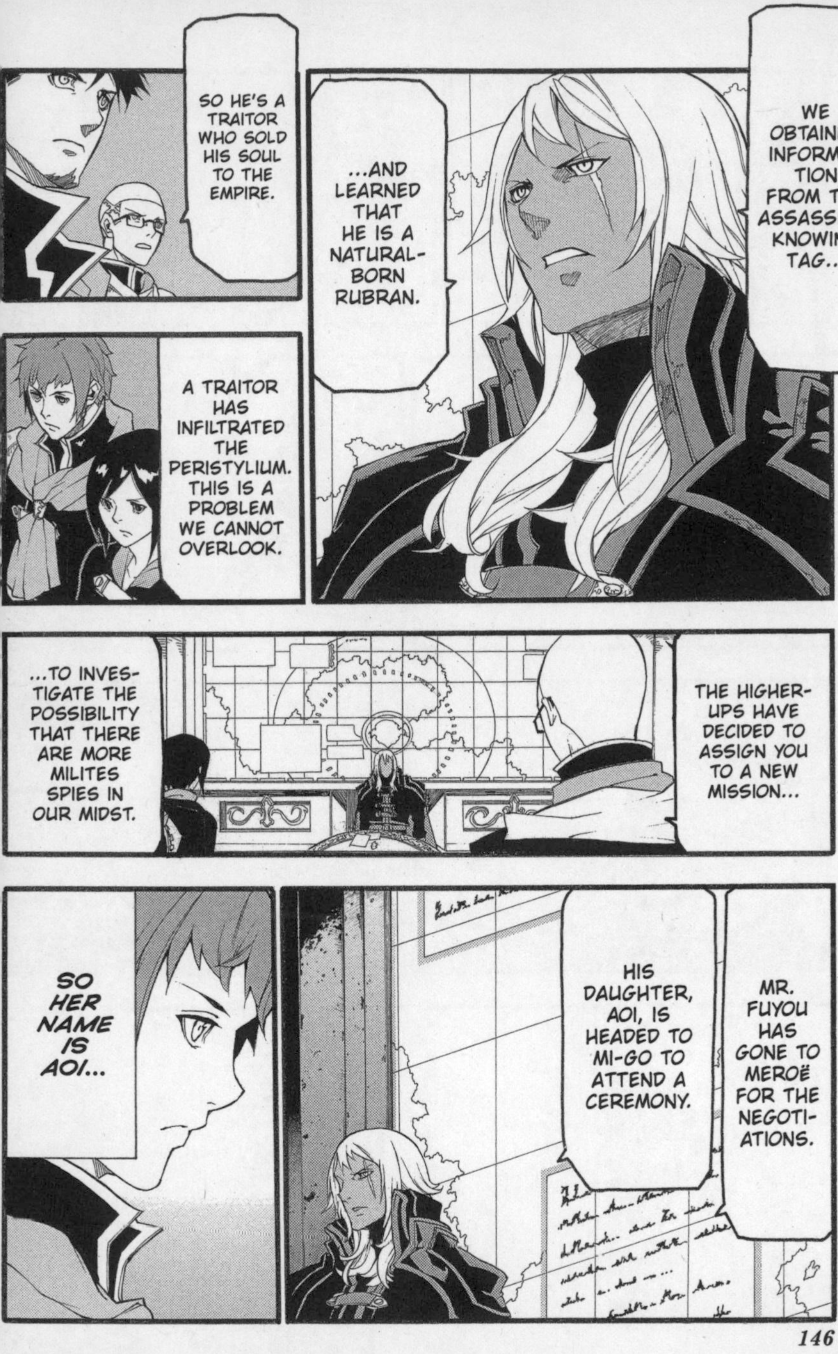
WE OBTAINED INFORMATION FROM THE ASSASSIN'S KNOWING TAG...
...AND LEARNED THAT HE IS A NATURAL-BORN RUBRAN.
SO HE'S A TRAITOR WHO SOLD HIS SOUL TO THE EMPIRE.
A TRAITOR HAS INFILTRATED THE PERISTYLIUM. THIS IS A PROBLEM WE CANNOT OVERLOOK.
THE HIGHER-UPS HAVE DECIDED TO ASSIGN YOU TO A NEW MISSION...
...TO INVESTIGATE THE POSSIBILITY THAT THERE ARE MORE MILITES SPIES IN OUR MIDST.
MR. FUYOU HAS GONE TO MEROË FOR THE NEGOTIATIONS.
HIS DAUGHTER, AOI, IS HEADED TO MI-GO TO ATTEND A CEREMONY.
SO HER NAME IS AOI...

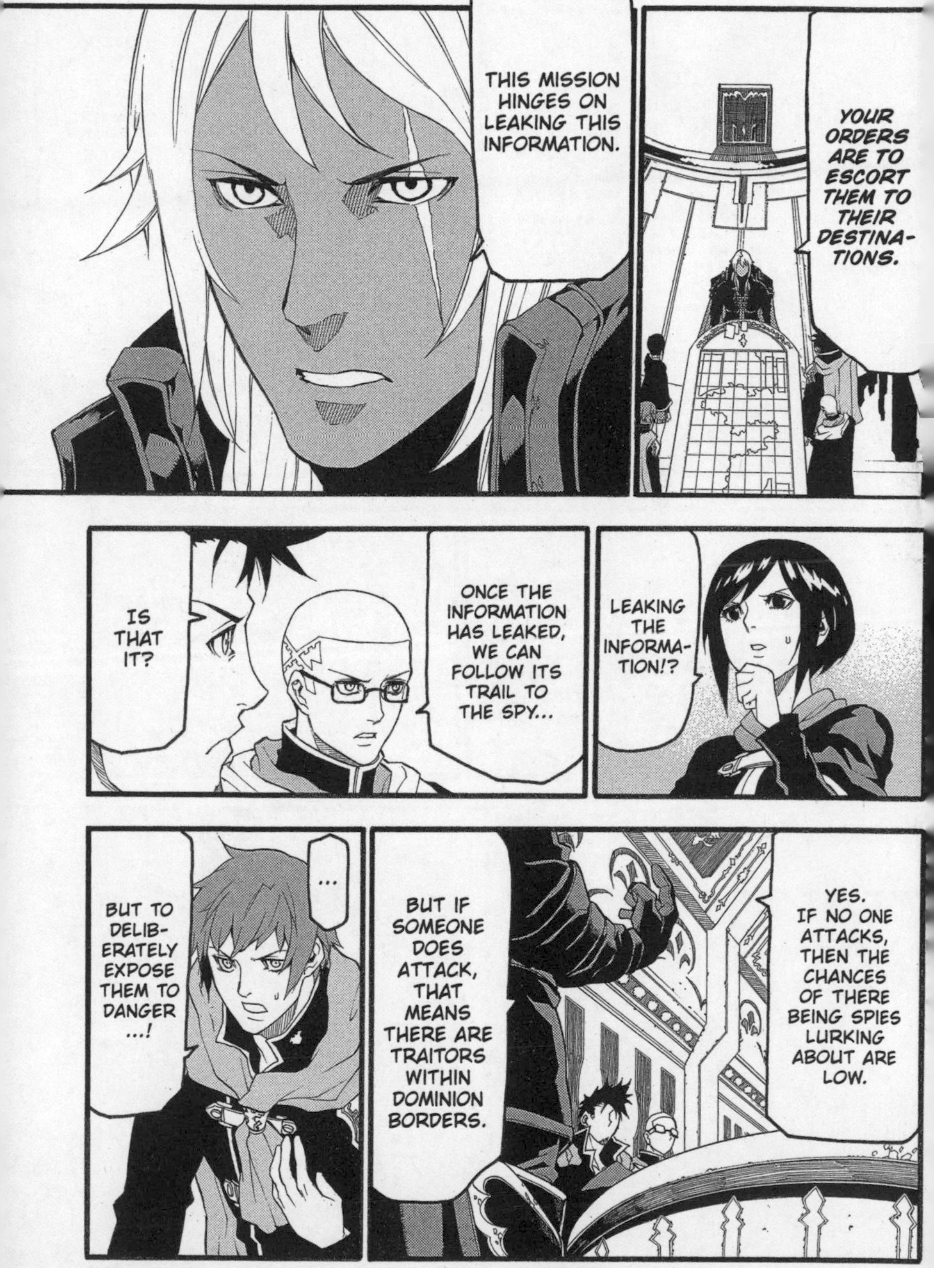
YOUR ORDERS ARE TO ESCORT THEM TO THEIR DESTINATIONS.
THIS MISSION HINGES ON LEAKING THIS INFORMATION.
LEAKING THE INFORMATION!?
ONCE THE INFORMATION HAS LEAKED, WE CAN FOLLOW ITS TRAIL TO THE SPY...
IS THAT IT?
YES. IF NO ONE ATTACKS, THEN THE CHANCES OF THERE BEING SPIES LURKING ABOUT ARE LOW.
BUT IF SOMEONE DOES ATTACK, THAT MEANS THERE ARE TRAITORS WITHIN DOMINION BORDERS.
...
BUT TO DELIBERATELY EXPOSE THEM TO DANGER...!

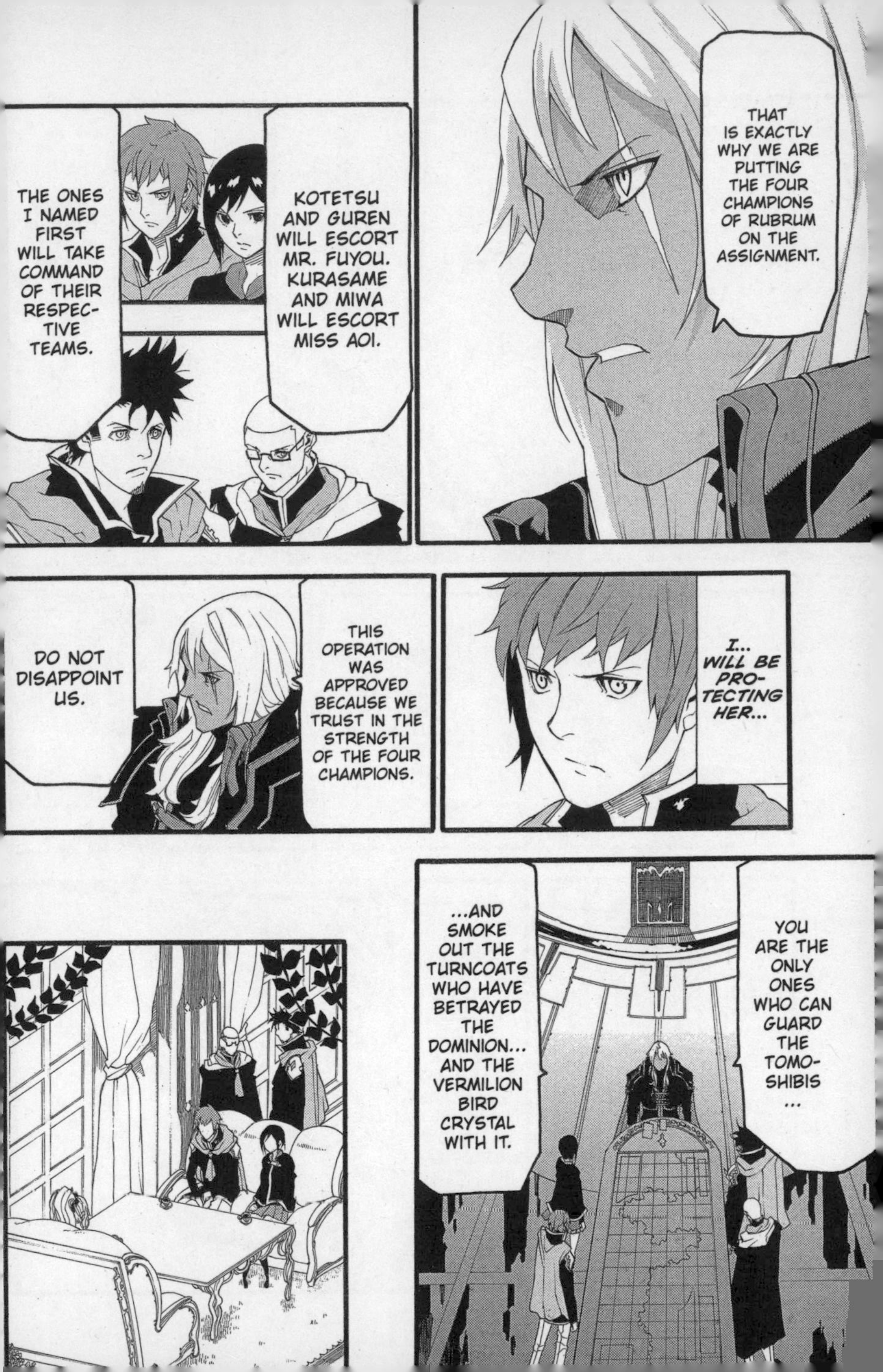
THAT IS EXACTLY WHY WE ARE PUTTING THE FOUR CHAMPIONS OF RUBRUM ON THE ASSIGNMENT.
KOTETSU AND GUREN WILL ESCORT MR. FUYOU. KURASAME AND MIWA WILL ESCORT MISS AOI.
THE ONES I NAMED FIRST WILL TAKE COMMAND OF THEIR RESPECTIVE TEAMS.
I... WILL BE PROTECTING HER...
THIS OPERATION WAS APPROVED BECAUSE WE TRUST IN THE STRENGTH OF THE FOUR CHAMPIONS.
DO NOT DISAPPOINT US.
YOU ARE THE ONLY ONES WHO CAN GUARD THE TOMOSHIBIS...
...AND SMOKE OUT THE TURNCOATS WHO HAVE BETRAYED THE DOMINION... AND THE VERMILION BIRD CRYSTAL WITH IT.

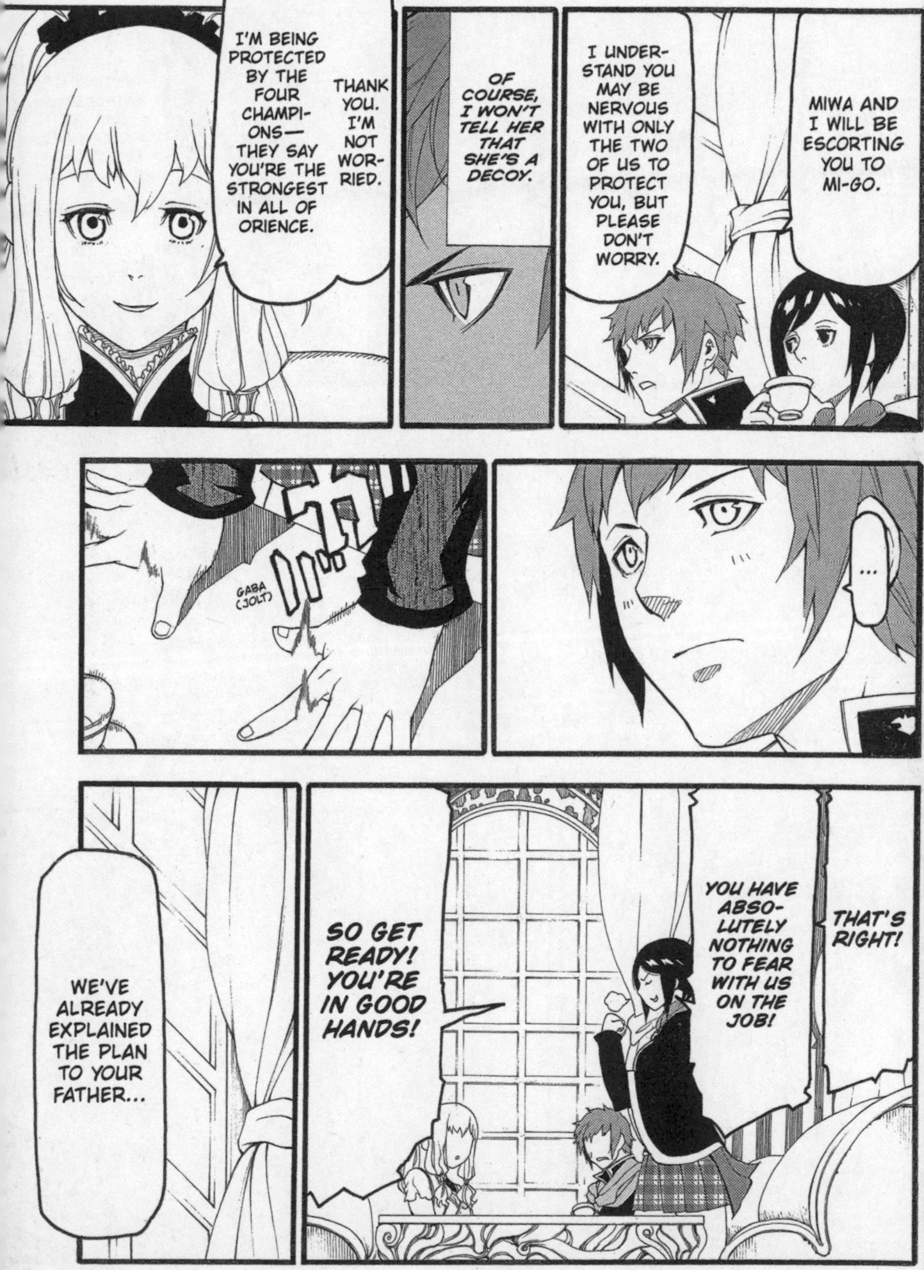
MIWA AND I WILL BE ESCORTING YOU TO MI-GO.
I UNDERSTAND YOU MAY BE NERVOUS WITH ONLY THE TWO OF US TO PROTECT YOU, BUT PLEASE DON'T WORRY.
OF COURSE, I WON'T TELL HER THAT SHE'S A DECOY.
THANK YOU. I'M NOT WORRIED.
I'M BEING PROTECTED BY THE FOUR CHAMPIONS—THEY SAY YOU'RE THE STRONGEST IN ALL OF ORIENCE.
...
GABA (JOLT)
THAT'S RIGHT!
YOU HAVE ABSOLUTELY NOTHING TO FEAR WITH US ON THE JOB!
SO GET READY! YOU'RE IN GOOD HANDS!
WE'VE ALREADY EXPLAINED THE PLAN TO YOUR FATHER...

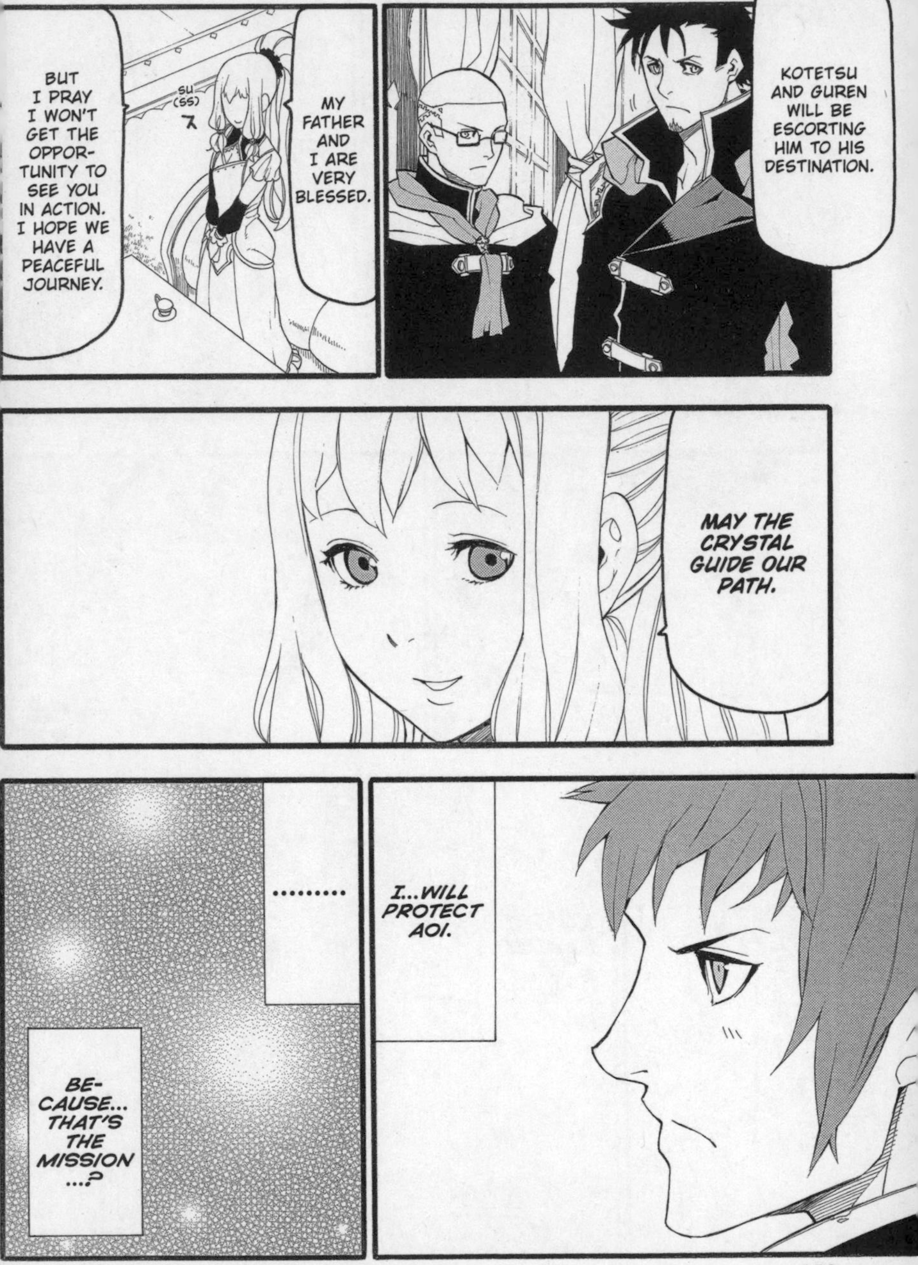
KOTETSU AND GUREN WILL BE ESCORTING HIM TO HIS DESTINATION.
MY FATHER AND I ARE VERY BLESSED.
SU (SS) ス
BUT I PRAY I WON'T GET THE OPPORTUNITY TO SEE YOU IN ACTION. I HOPE WE HAVE A PEACEFUL JOURNEY.
MAY THE CRYSTAL GUIDE OUR PATH.
I...WILL PROTECT AOI.
....
BECAUSE... THAT'S THE MISSION ...?

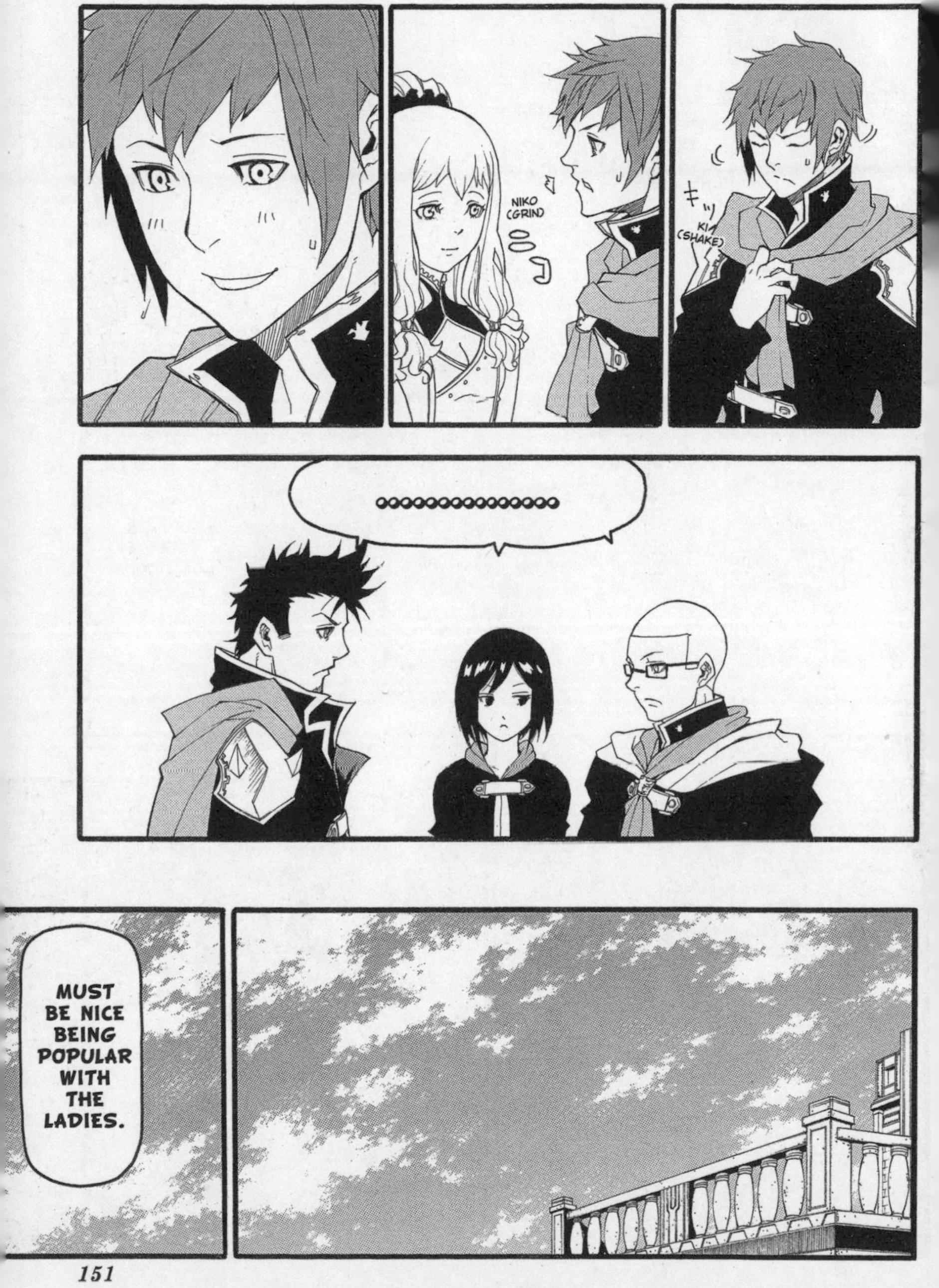
キッ
KI (SHAKE)
ニコ
NIKO (GRIN)
....
MUST BE NICE BEING POPULAR WITH THE LADIES.

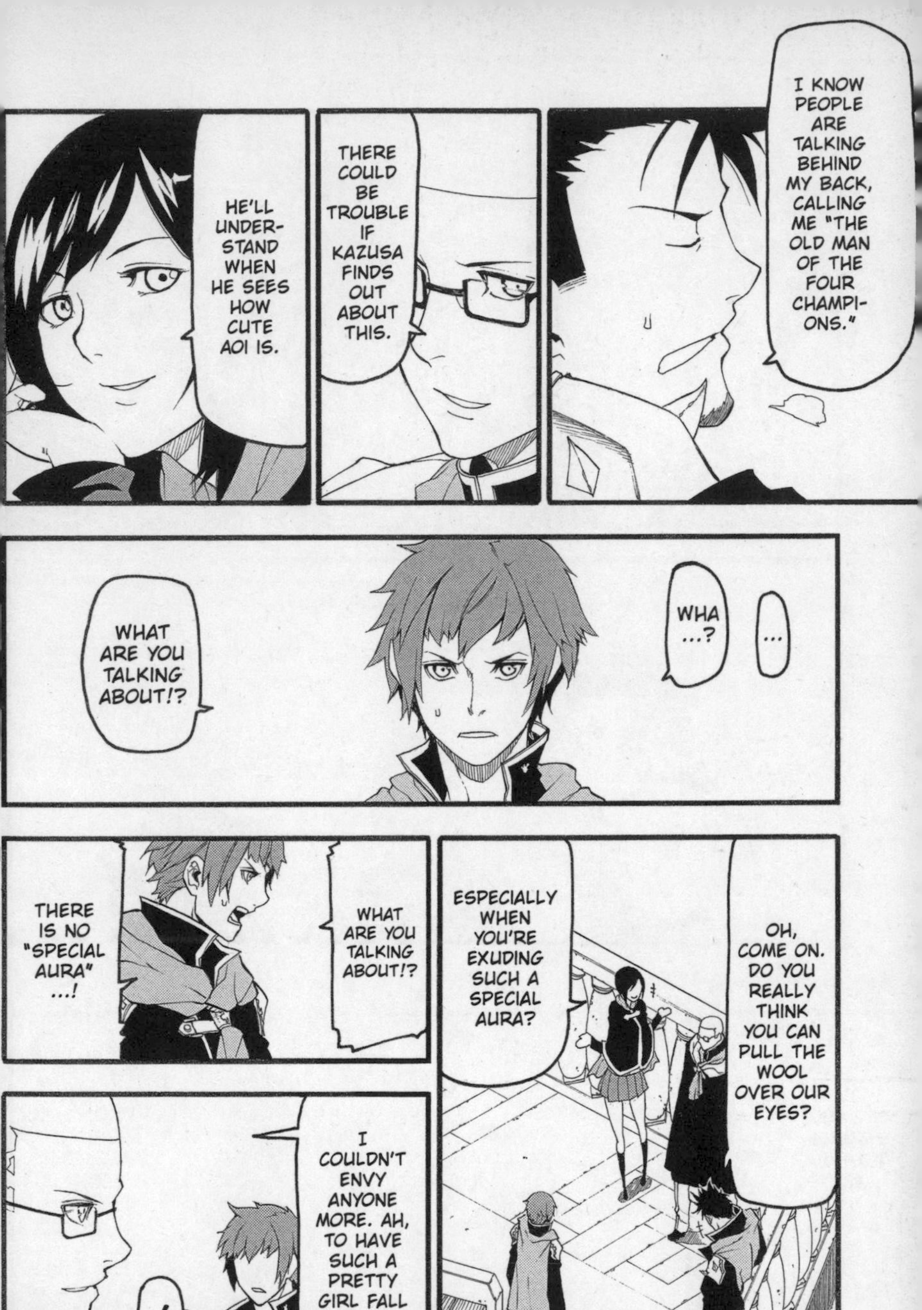
I KNOW PEOPLE ARE TALKING BEHIND MY BACK, CALLING ME "THE OLD MAN OF THE FOUR CHAMPIONS."
THERE COULD BE TROUBLE IF KAZUSA FINDS OUT ABOUT THIS.
HE'LL UNDERSTAND WHEN HE SEES HOW CUTE AOI IS.
...
WHA ...?
WHAT ARE YOU TALKING ABOUT!?
OH, COME ON. DO YOU REALLY THINK YOU CAN PULL THE WOOL OVER OUR EYES?
ESPECIALLY WHEN YOU'RE EXUDING SUCH A SPECIAL AURA?
WHAT ARE YOU TALKING ABOUT!?
THERE IS NO "SPECIAL AURA" ...!
I COULDN'T ENVY ANYONE MORE. AH, TO HAVE SUCH A PRETTY GIRL FALL FOR ME.
!

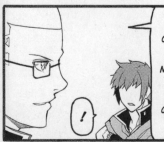

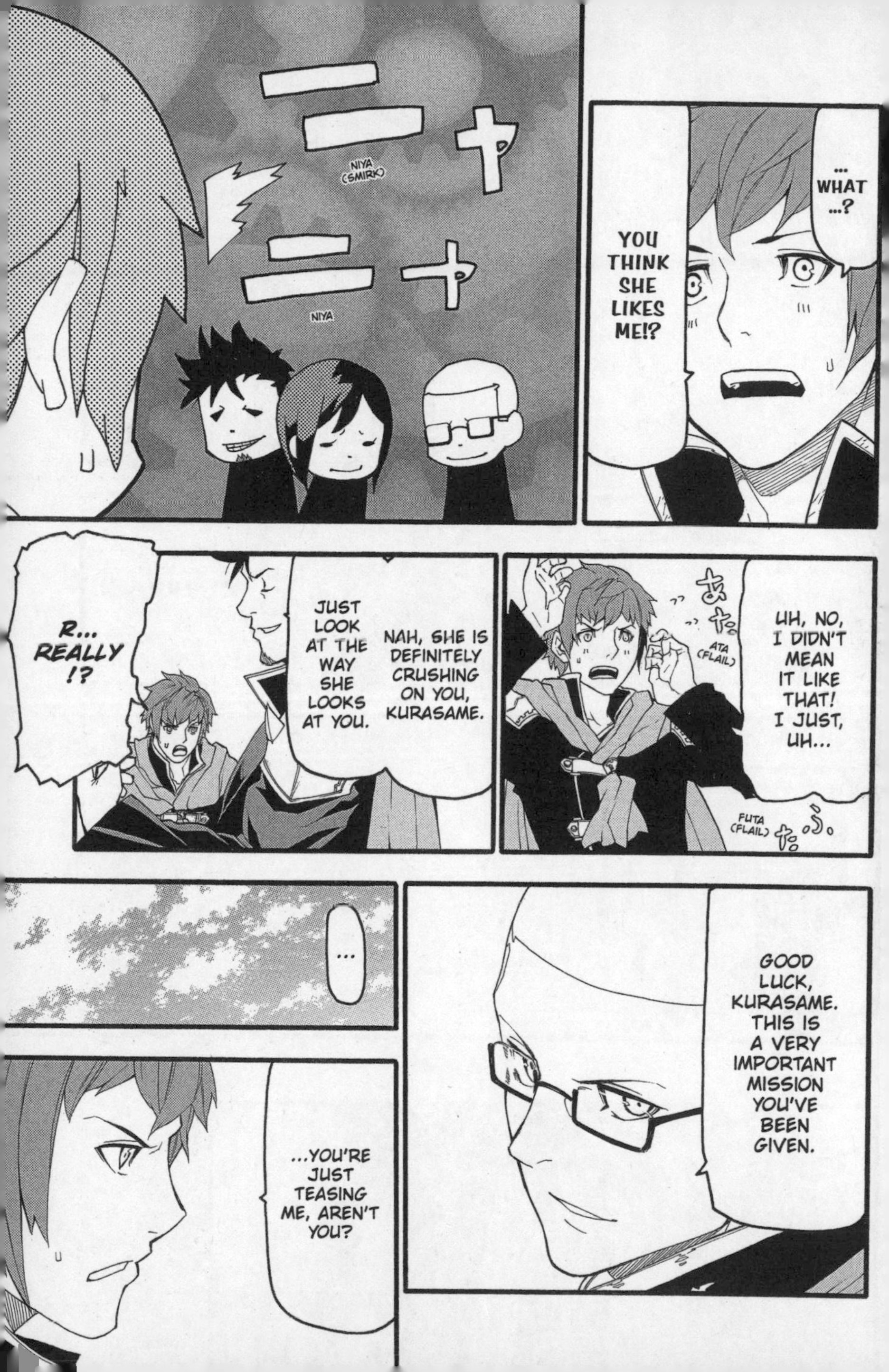

... WHAT ...?
YOU THINK SHE LIKES ME!?
ニヤ
NIYA (SMIRK)
ニヤ
NIYA
あた
ATA (FLAIL)
UH, NO, I DIDN'T MEAN IT LIKE THAT! I JUST, UH...
FUTA (FLAIL)
ふた
NAH, SHE IS DEFINITELY CRUSHING ON YOU, KURASAME.
JUST LOOK AT THE WAY SHE LOOKS AT YOU.
R... REALLY !?
GOOD LUCK, KURASAME. THIS IS A VERY IMPORTANT MISSION YOU'VE BEEN GIVEN.
...
...YOU'RE JUST TEASING ME, AREN'T YOU?

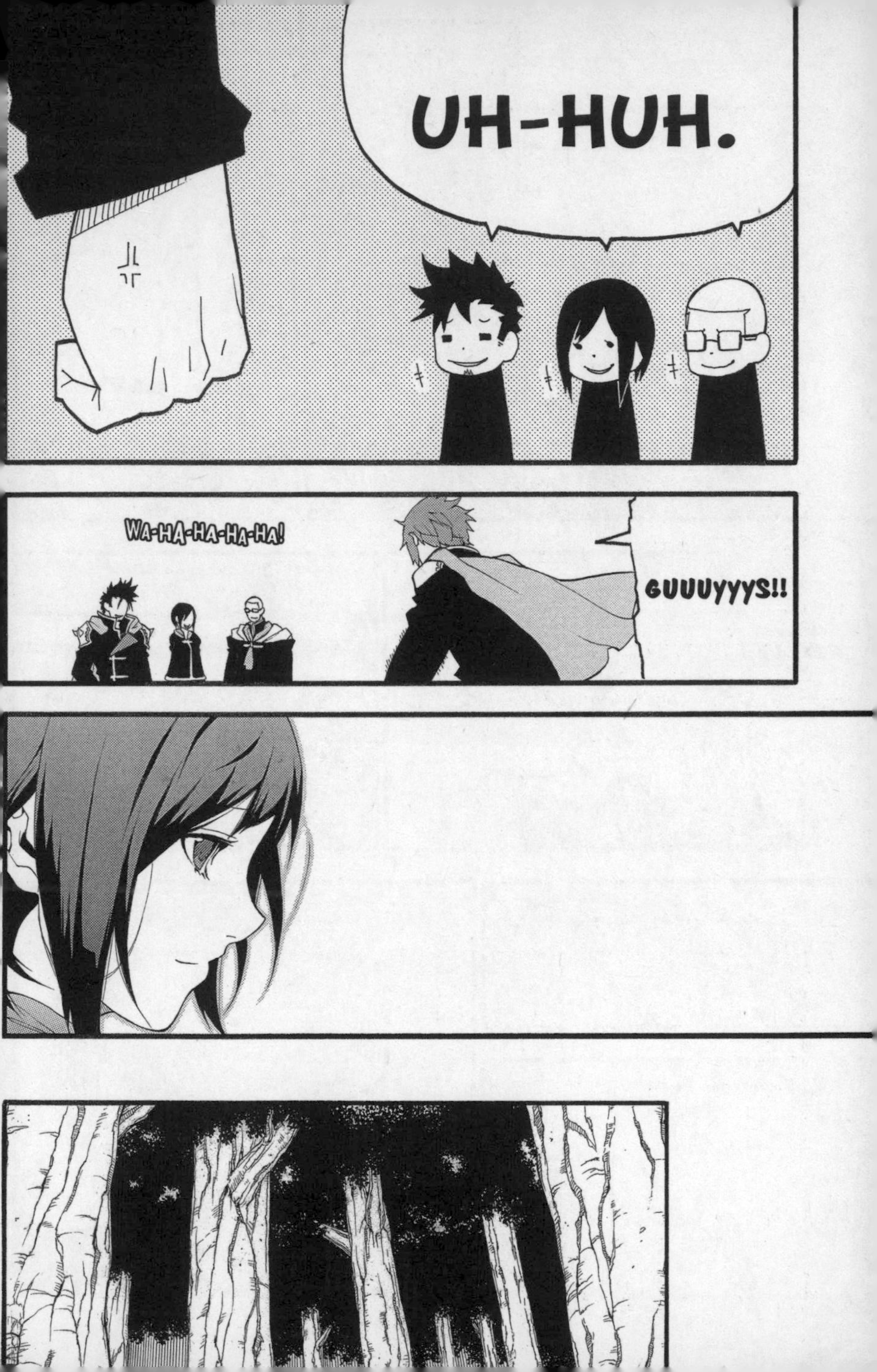
UH-HUH.
GUUUYYYS!!
WA-HA-HA-HA-HA!

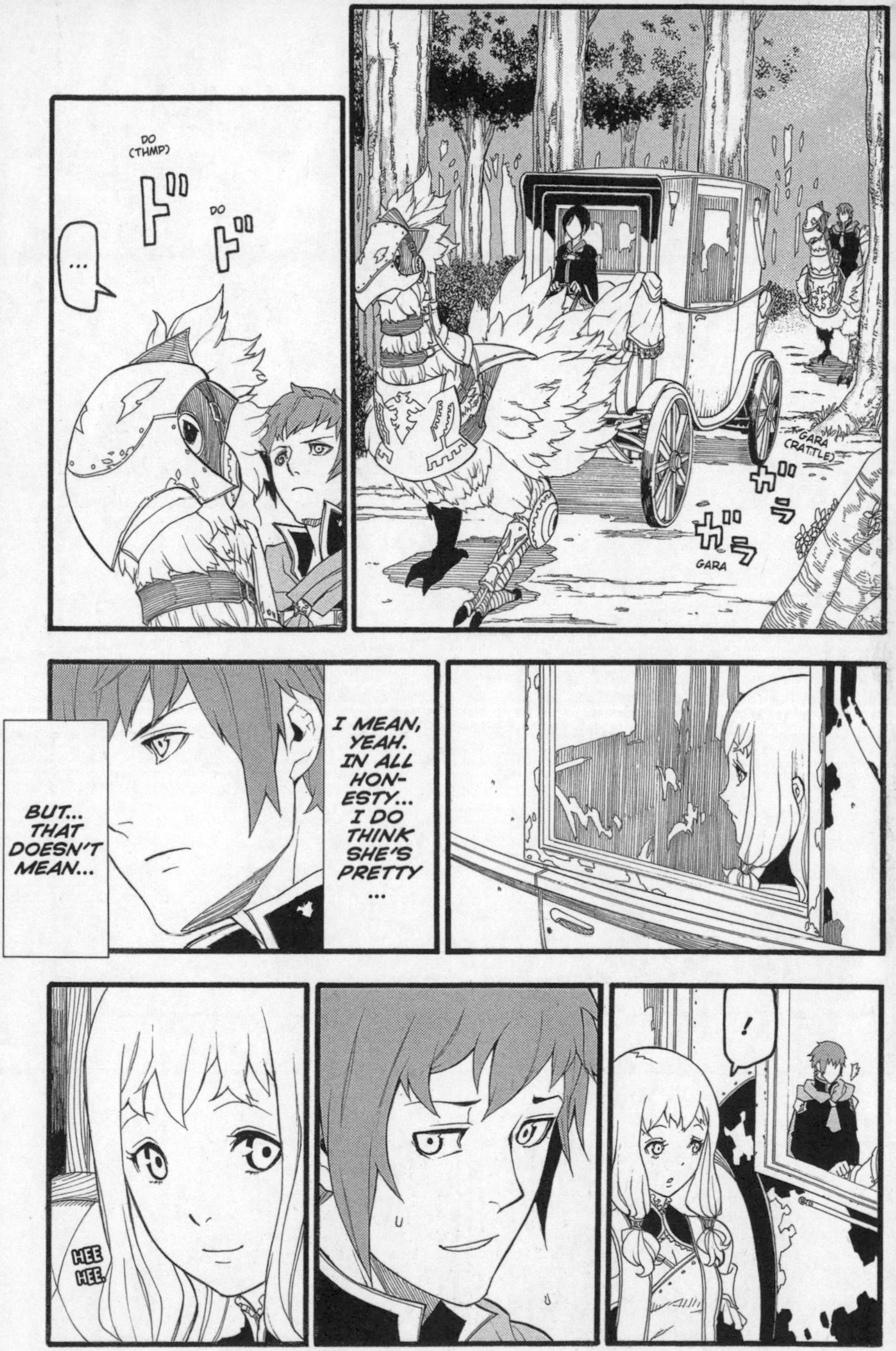
GARA (RATTLE)
ガラ
ガラ
GARA
DO (THMP)
ド
DO
ド
...
I MEAN, YEAH. IN ALL HON-ESTY... I DO THINK SHE'S PRETTY...
BUT... THAT DOESN'T MEAN...
!
HEE HEE.

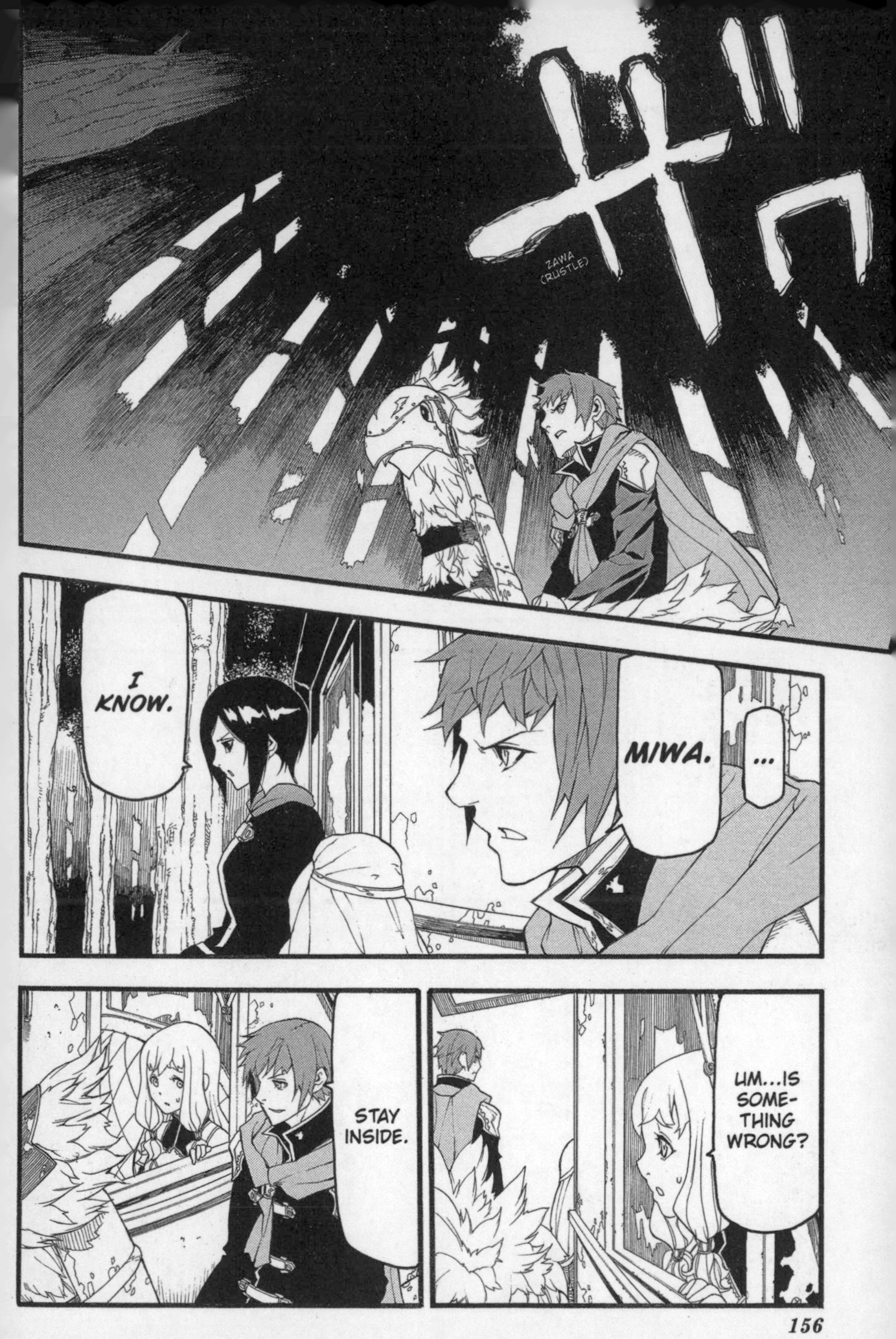
ZAWA
(RUSTLE)
...
MIWA.
I KNOW.
UM...IS SOMETHING WRONG?
STAY INSIDE.

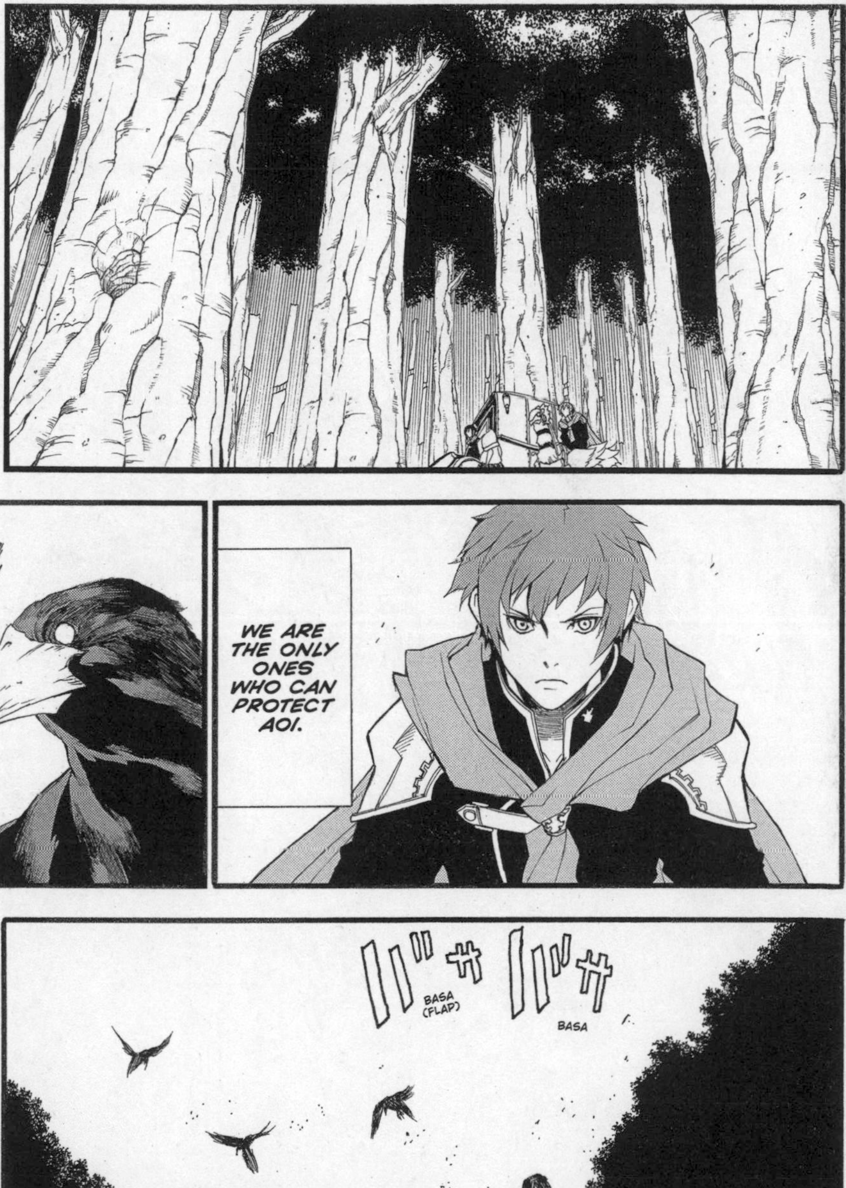
WE ARE THE ONLY ONES WHO CAN PROTECT AOI.
バサ
BASA
バサ
BASA (FLAP)

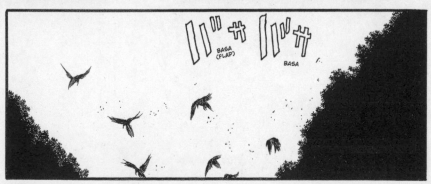

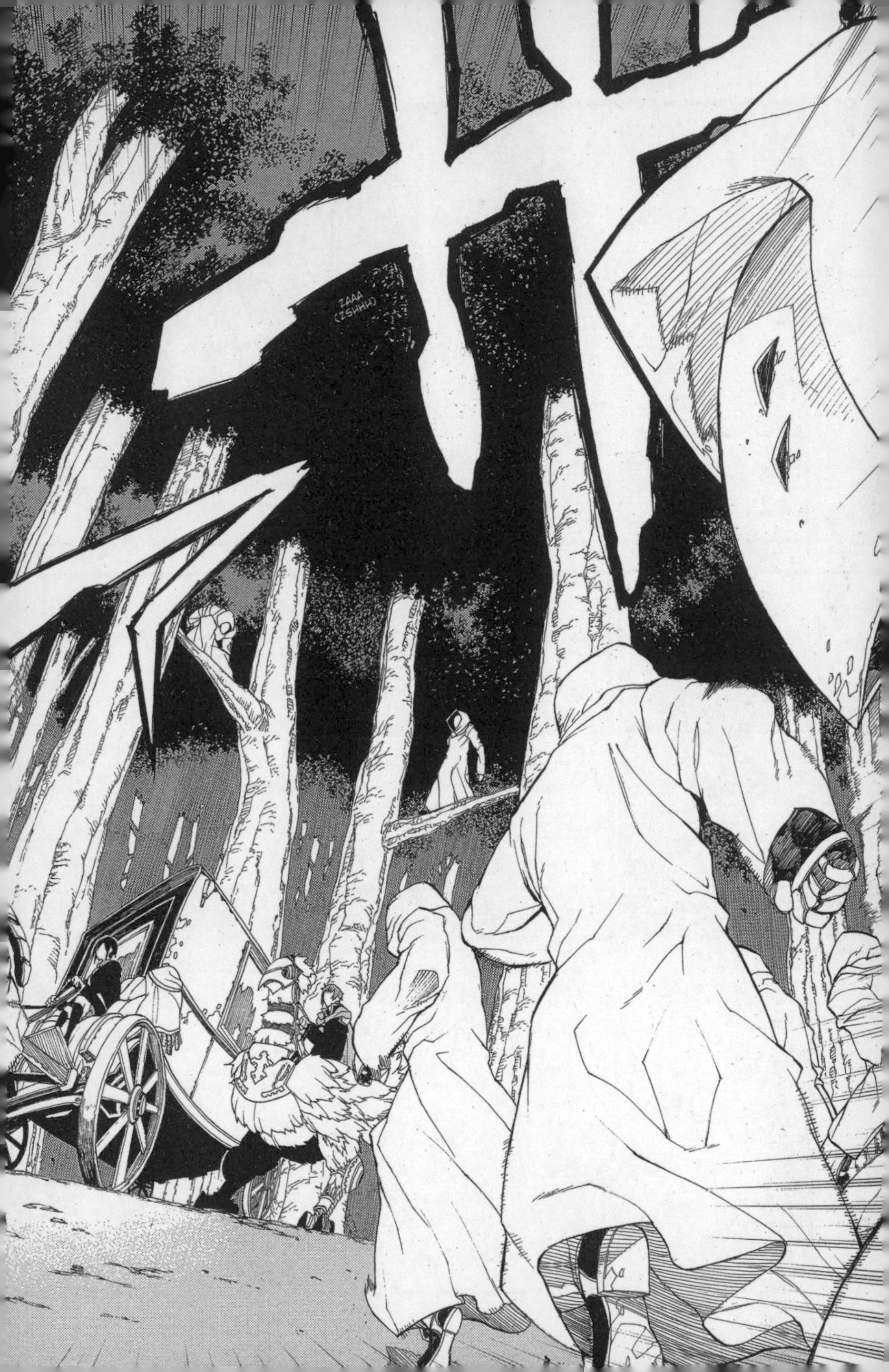
ZAAA
(ZSHHH)

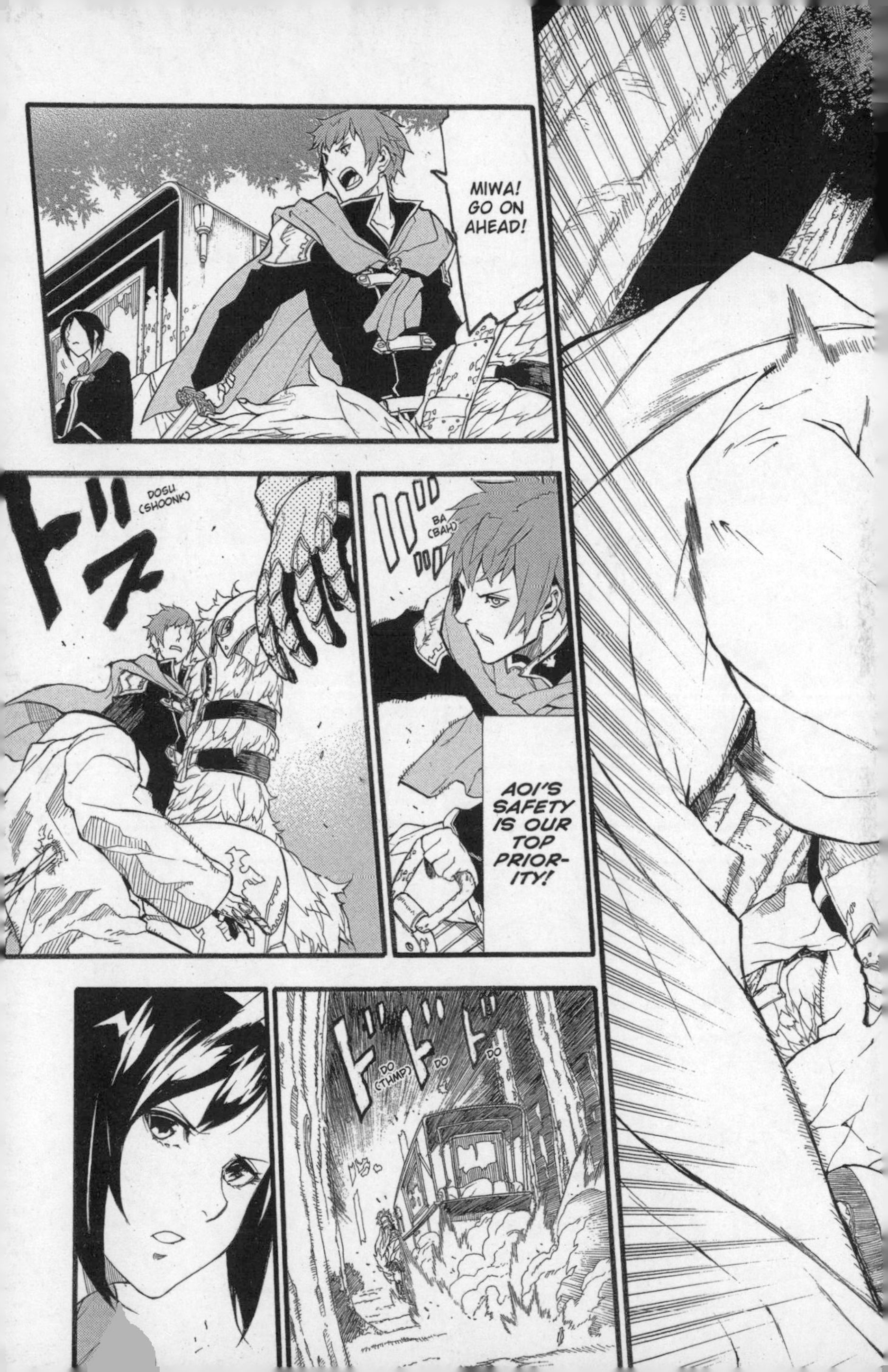
MIWA! GO ON AHEAD!
BA
(BAH)
AOI'S SAFETY IS OUR TOP PRIORITY!
ドス
DOSU
(SHOONK)
ドドドド
DO
(THMP)
DO
DO

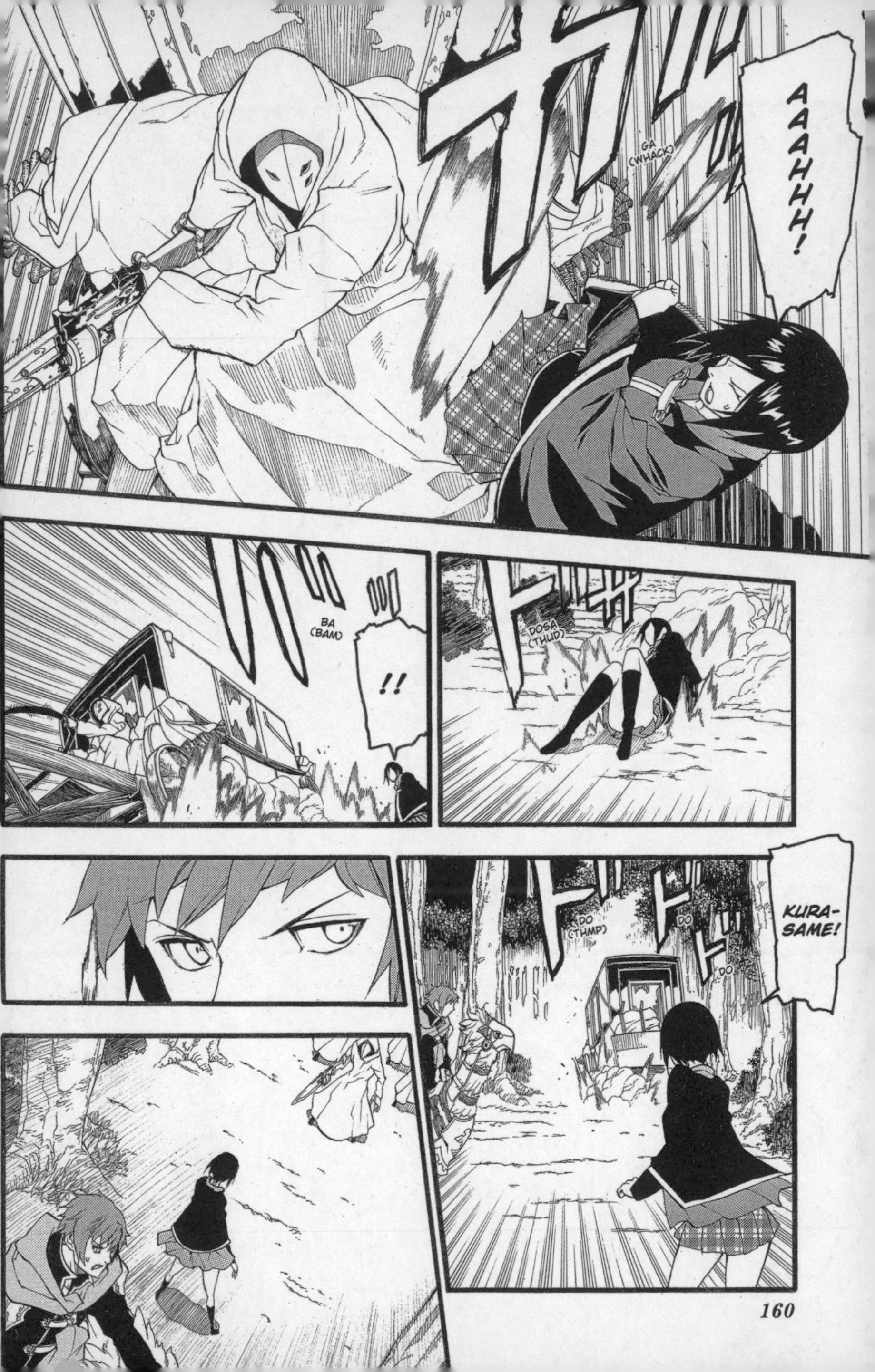
AAAHHH!
GA (WHACK)
DOSA (THUD)
BA (BAM)
!!
KURA-SAME!
DO
DO
DO (THMP)

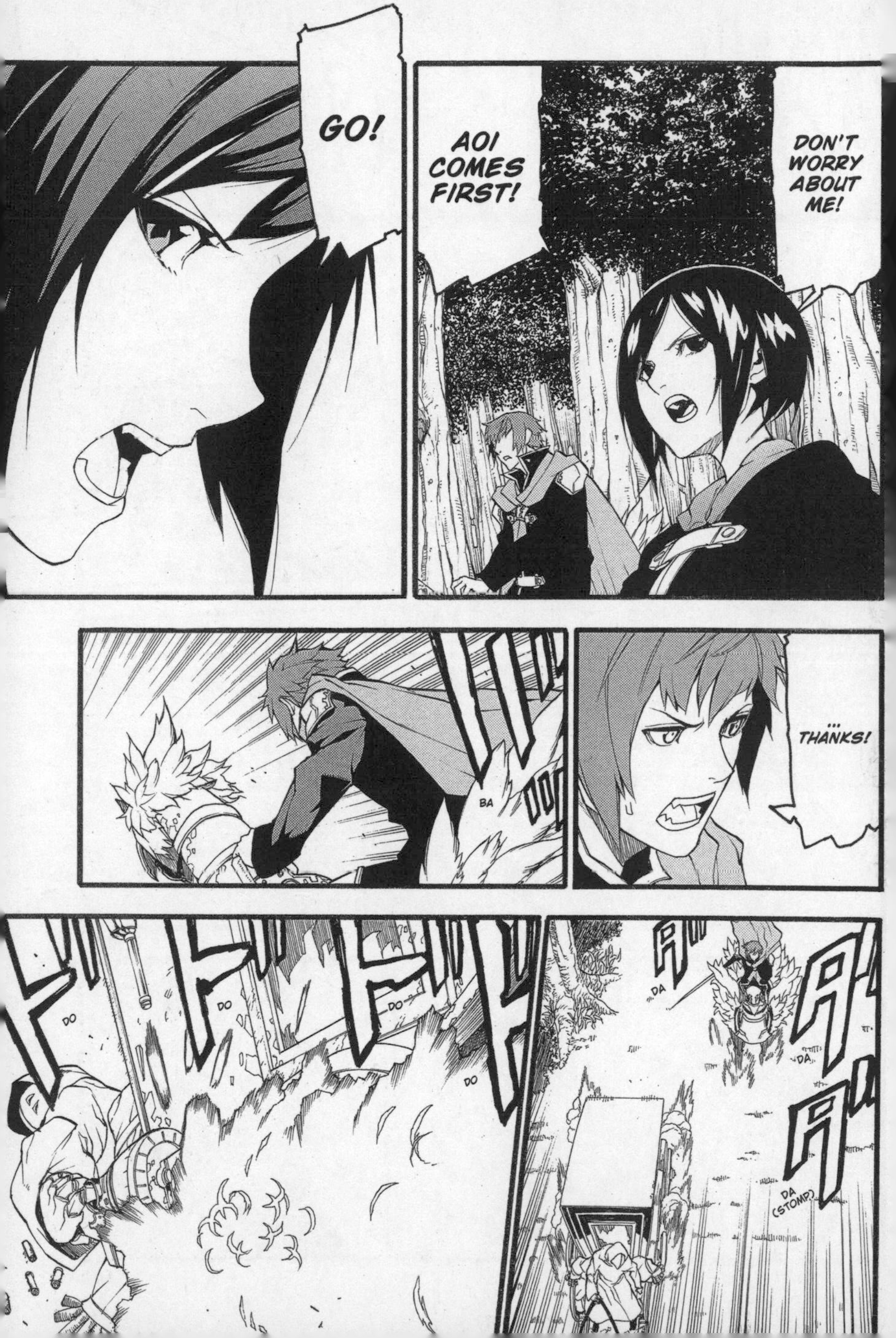
DON'T WORRY ABOUT ME!
AOI COMES FIRST!
GO!
...THANKS!
BA
DA
DA
DA (STOMP)
DO
DO
DO
DO

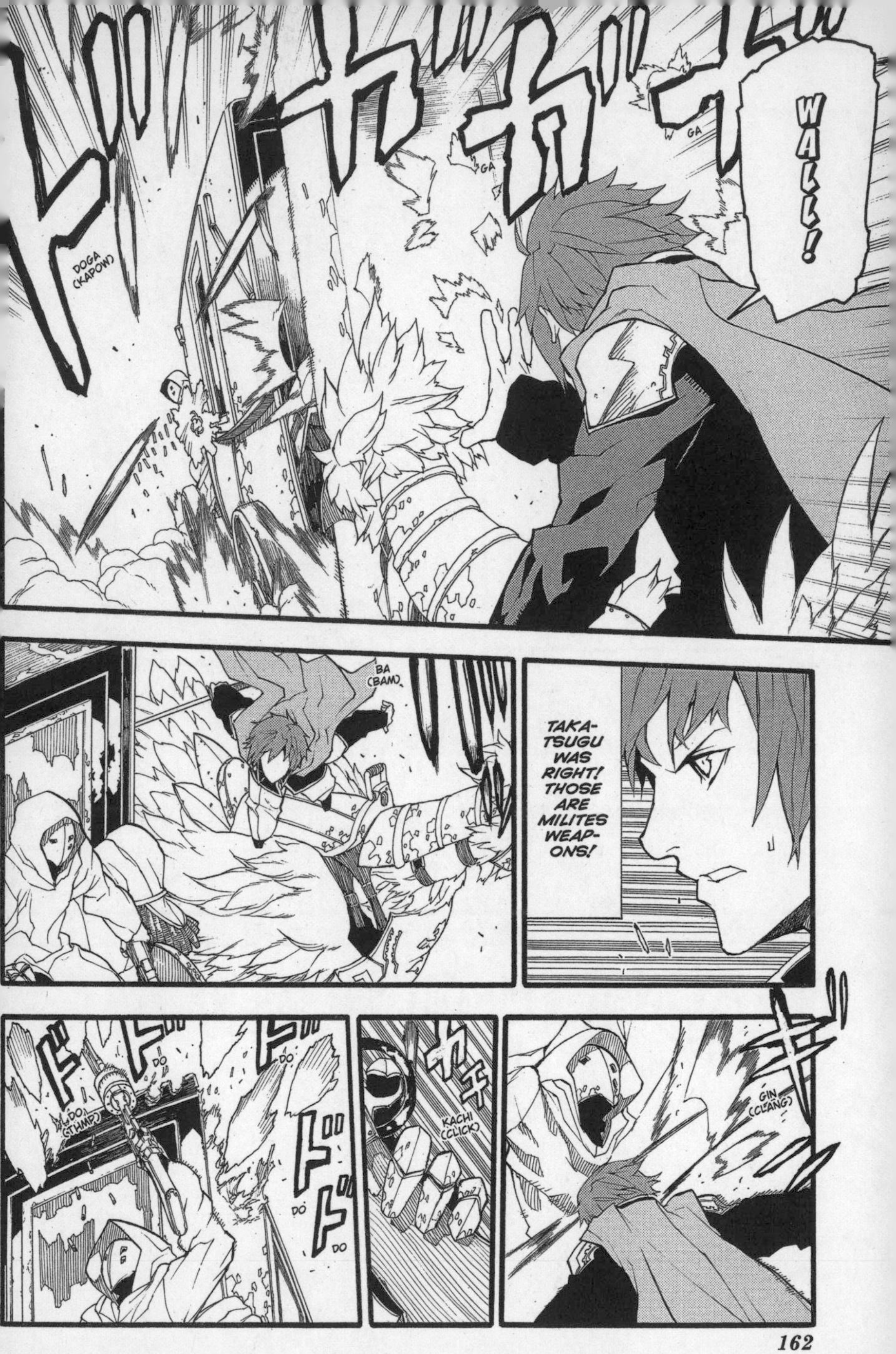
WALL!
GA
GA
DOGA (KAPOW)
TAKA-TSUGU WAS RIGHT! THOSE ARE MILITES WEAP-ONS!
BA (BAM)
GIN (CLANG)
KACHI (CLICK)
DO
DO
DO (THMP)
DO
DO

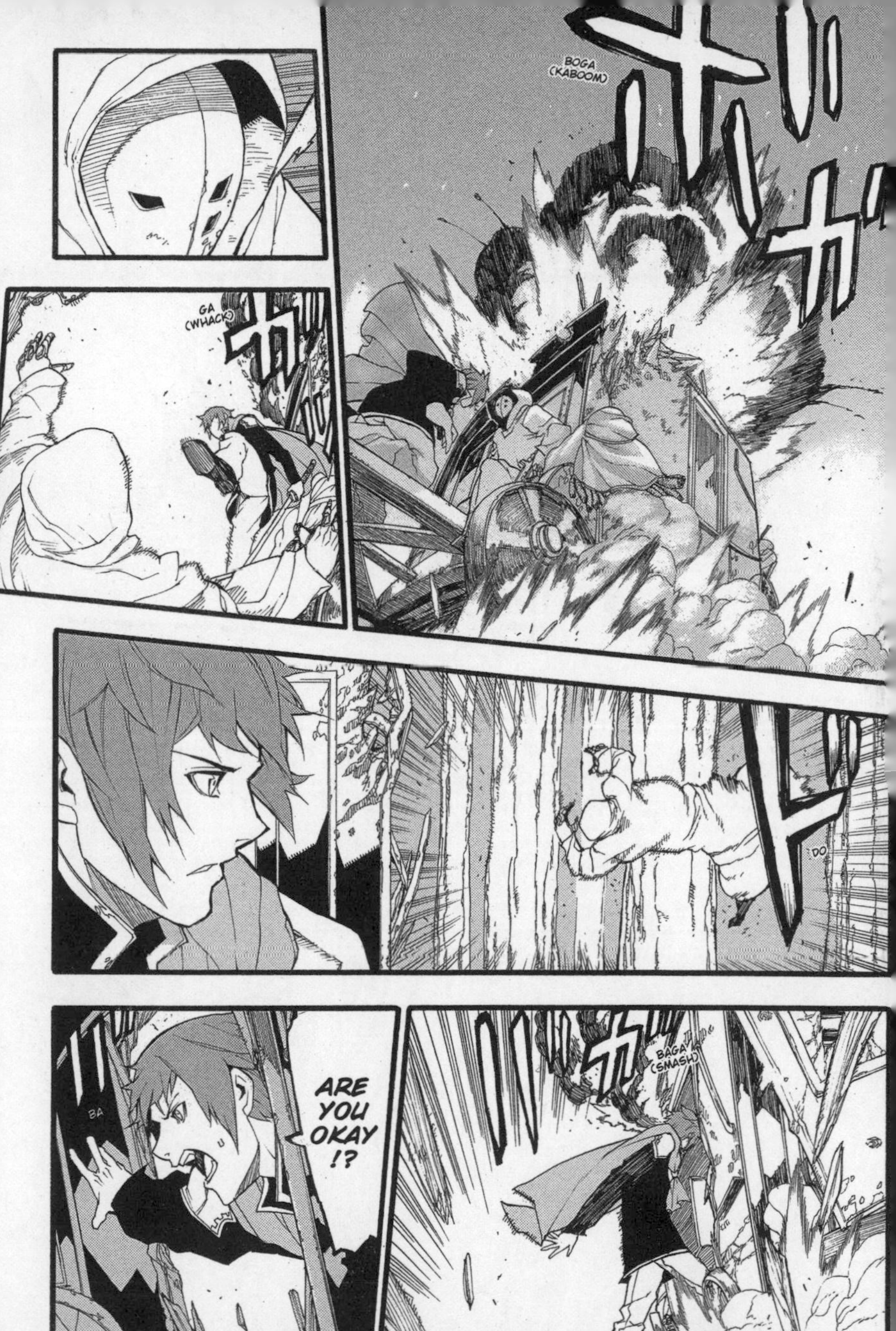
BOGA (KABOOM)
GA (WHACK)
DO
BAGA (SMASH)
BA
ARE YOU OKAY !?

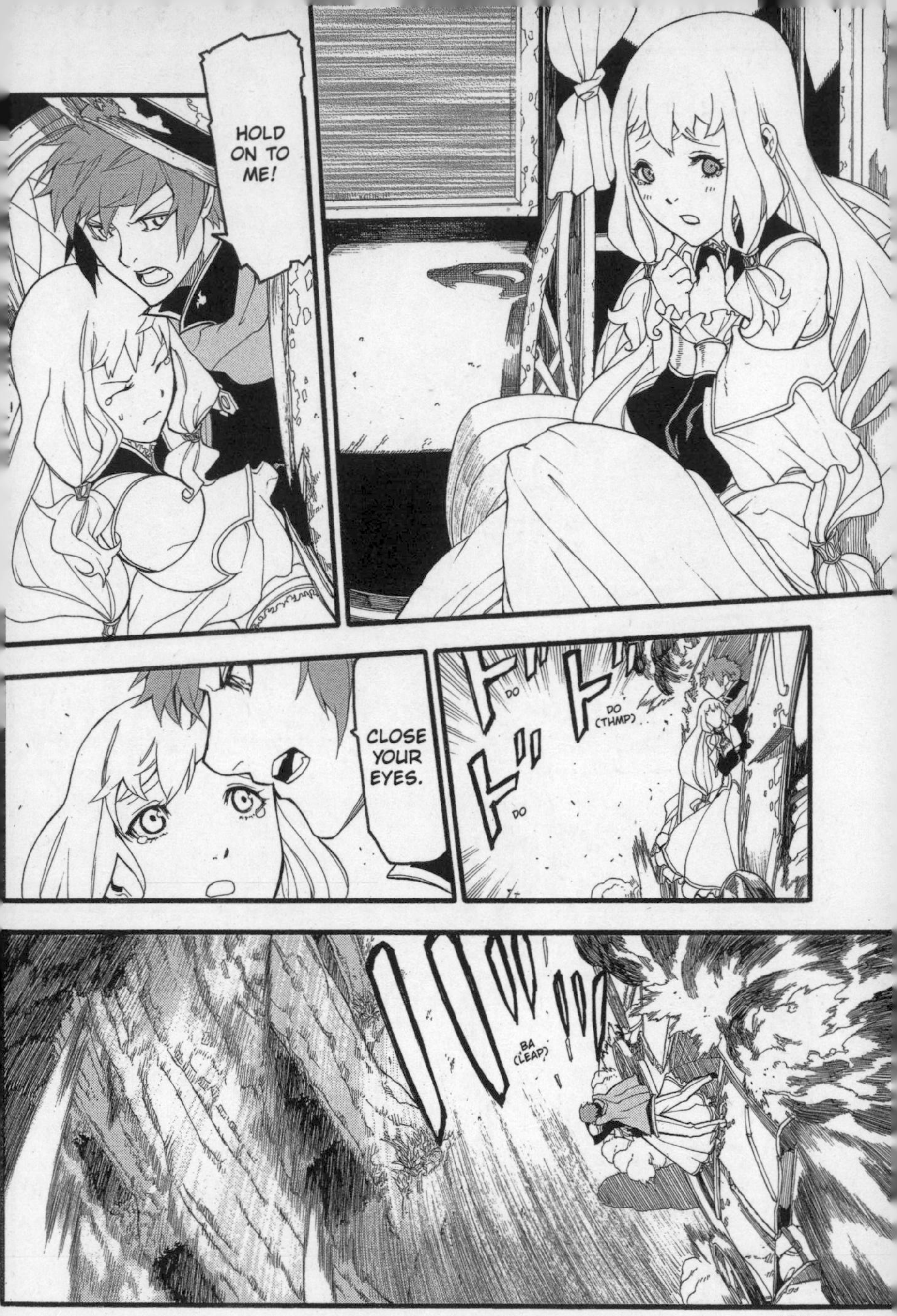
HOLD ON TO ME!
DO (THMP)
DO
DO
CLOSE YOUR EYES.
BA (LEAP)

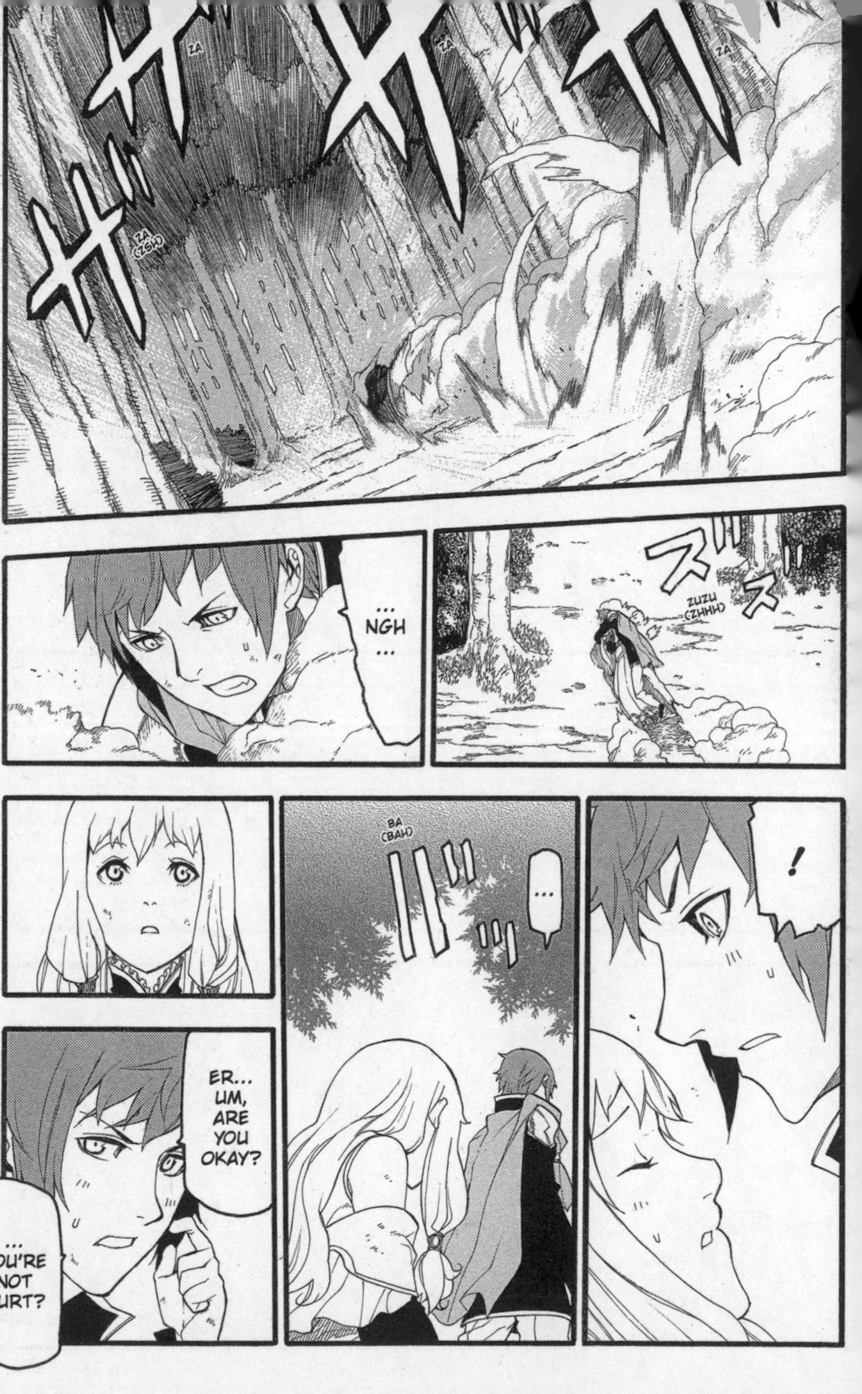
ZA
ZA
ZA
ZA (ZSH)
ZUZU (ZHHH)
... NGH ...
!
BA (BAH)
...
ER... UM, ARE YOU OKAY?
... YOU'RE NOT HURT?

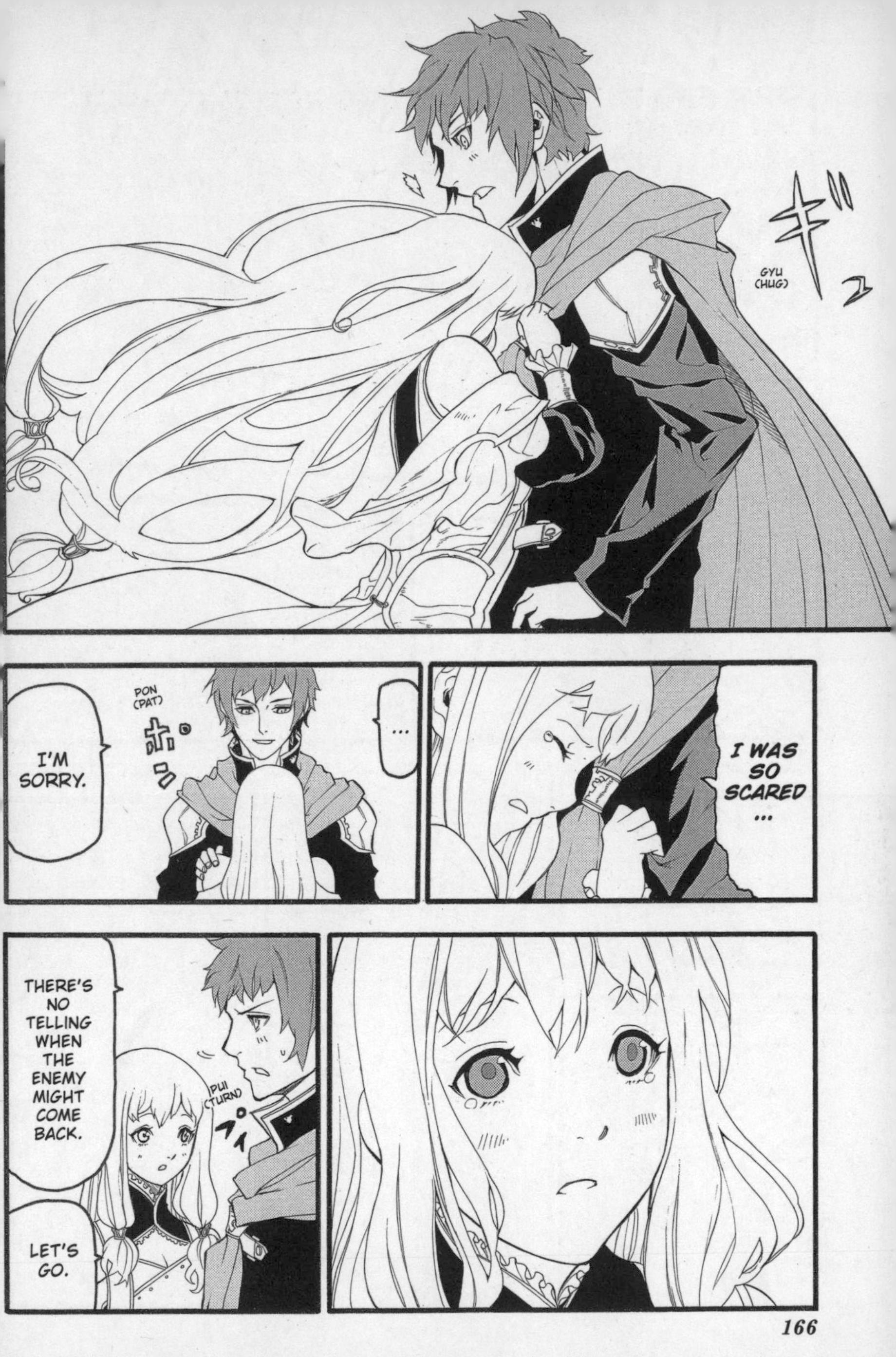
ギュ
GYU (HUG)
I WAS SO SCARED ...
...
ポン
PON (PAT)
I'M SORRY.
プイ
PUI (TURN)
THERE'S NO TELLING WHEN THE ENEMY MIGHT COME BACK.
LET'S GO.

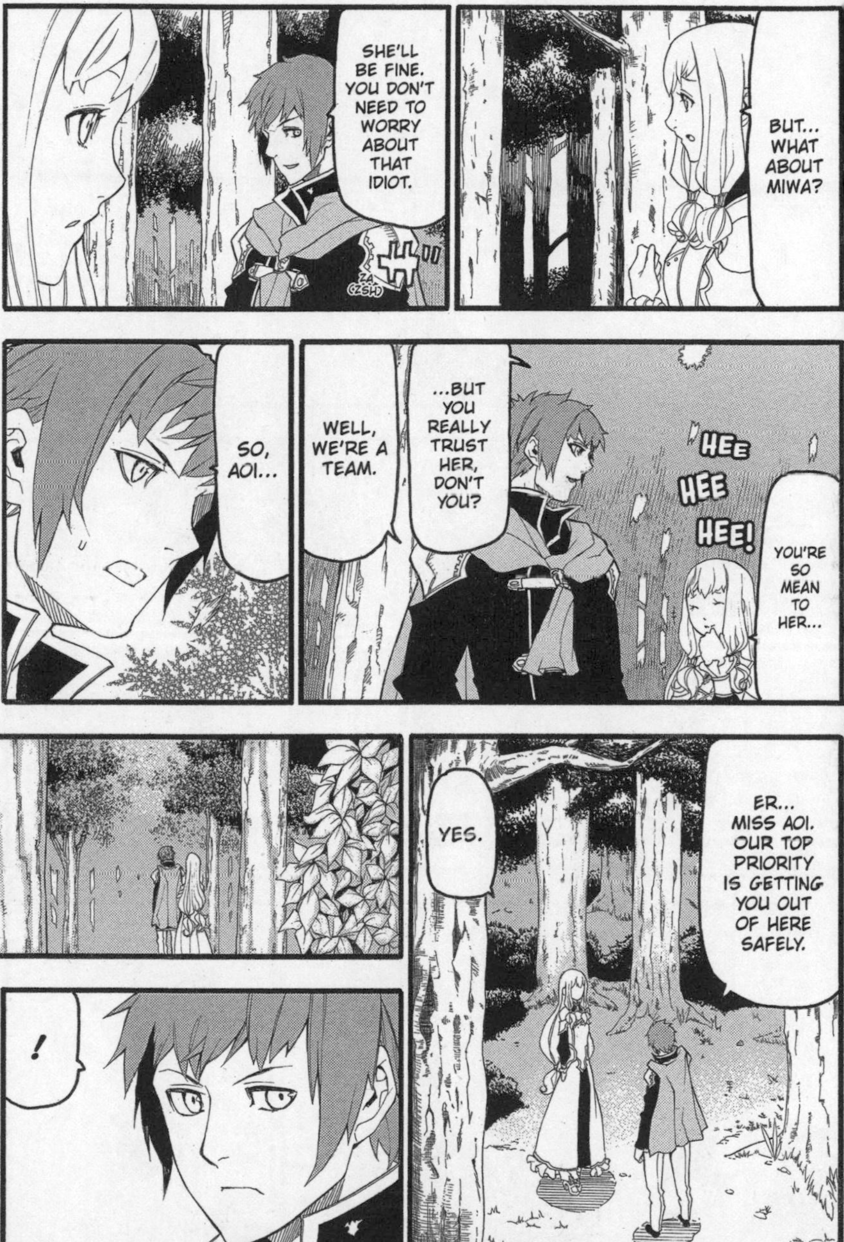
BUT... WHAT ABOUT MIWA?
SHE'LL BE FINE. YOU DON'T NEED TO WORRY ABOUT THAT IDIOT.
ZA (ZSH)
YOU'RE SO MEAN TO HER...
HEE HEE HEE!
...BUT YOU REALLY TRUST HER, DON'T YOU?
WELL, WE'RE A TEAM.
SO, AOI...
ER... MISS AOI. OUR TOP PRIORITY IS GETTING YOU OUT OF HERE SAFELY.
YES.
!

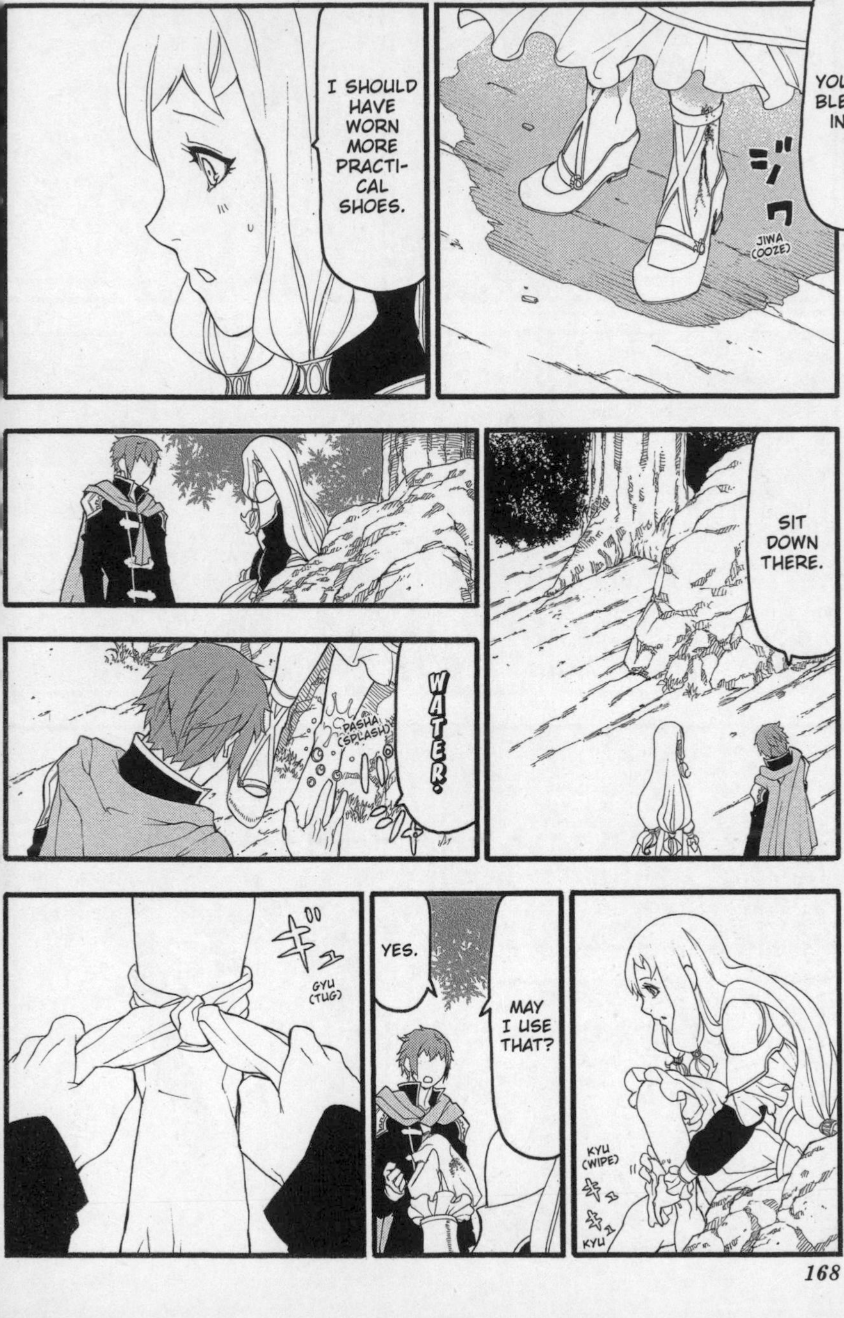
YOU'RE BLEED-ING.
ジワ
JIWA (OOZE)
I SHOULD HAVE WORN MORE PRACTI-CAL SHOES.
SIT DOWN THERE.
WATER.
PASHA (SPLASH)
KYU (WIPE)
KYU
MAY I USE THAT?
YES.
GYU (TUG)

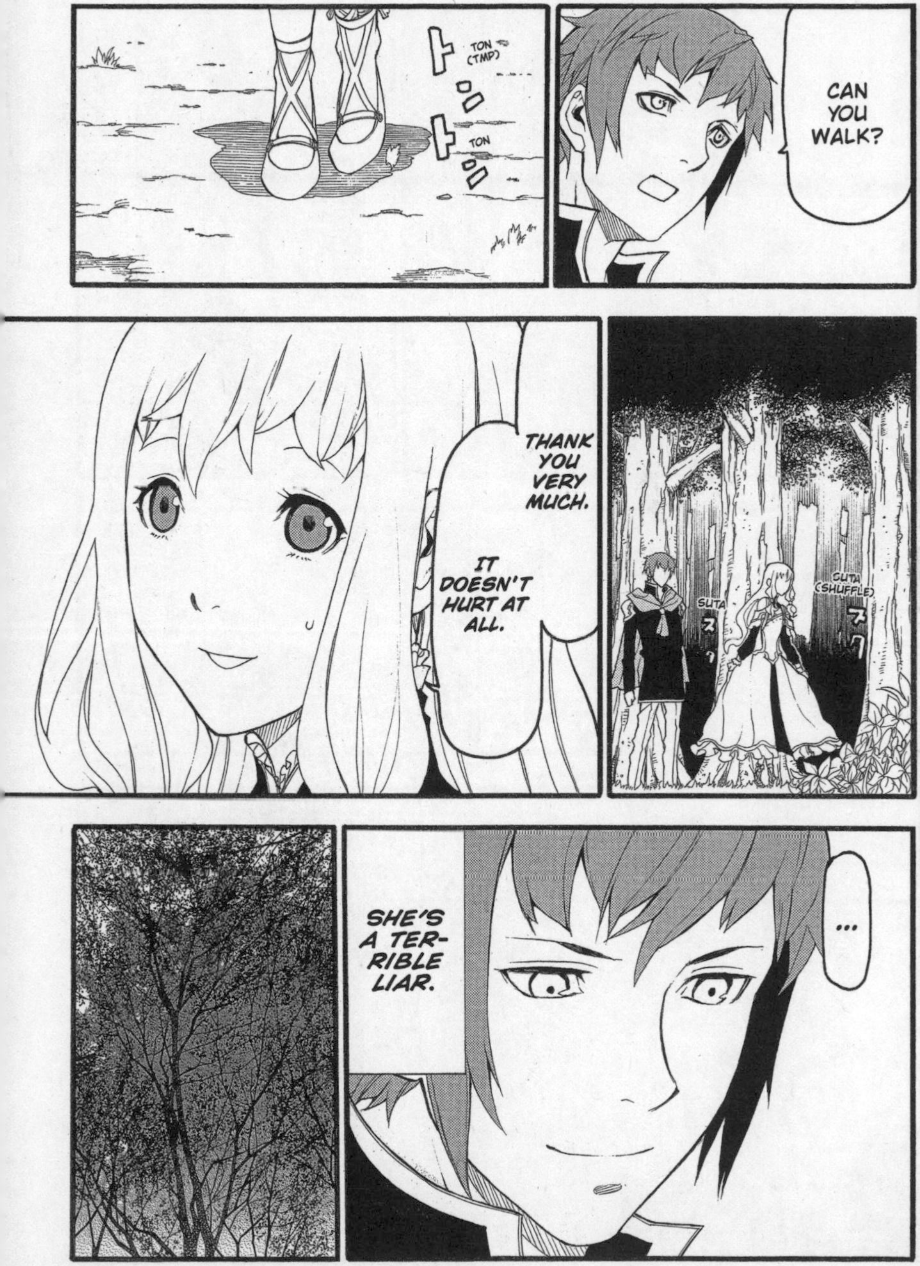
CAN YOU WALK?
TON (TMP)
TON
SUTA (SHUFFLE)
SUTA
THANK YOU VERY MUCH.
IT DOESN'T HURT AT ALL.
...
SHE'S A TERRIBLE LIAR.

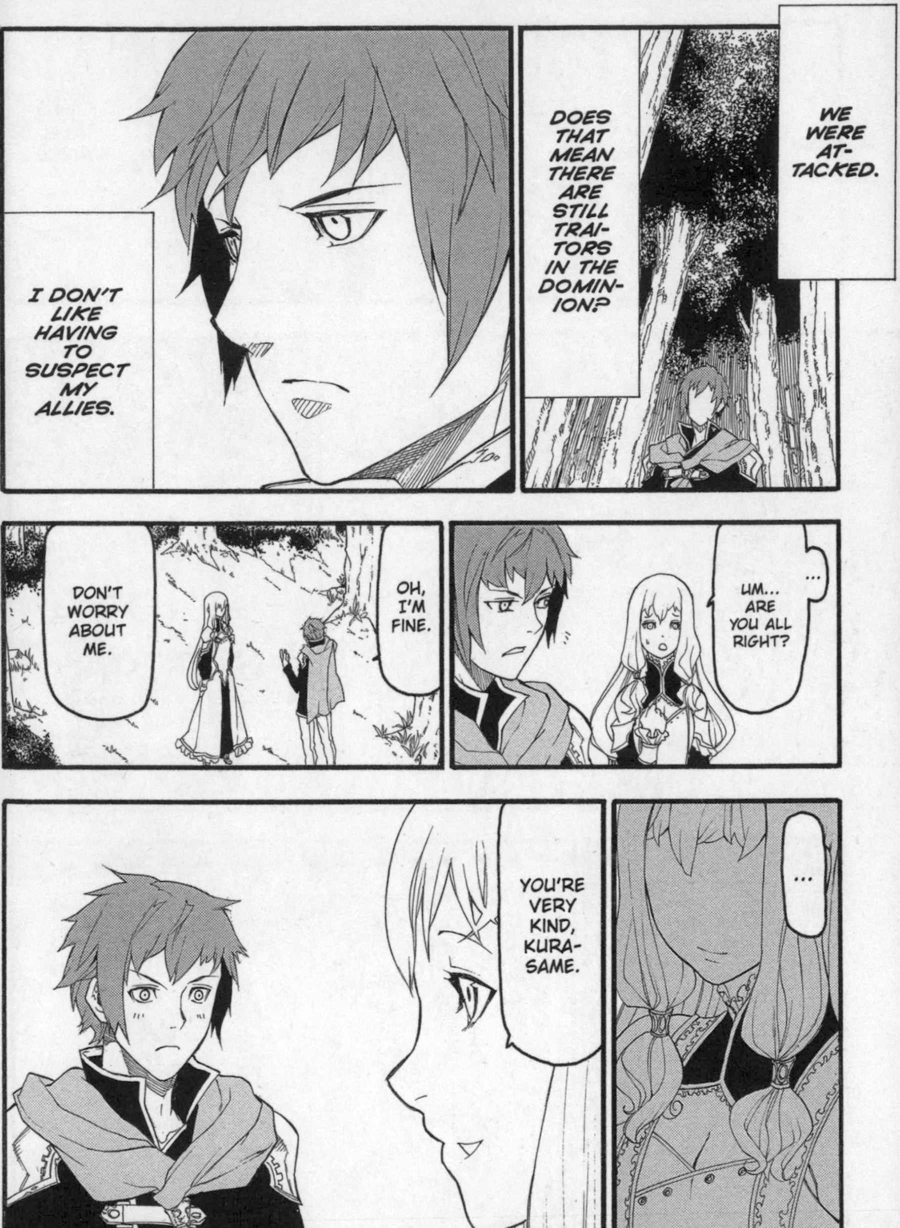
WE WERE AT-TACKED.
DOES THAT MEAN THERE ARE STILL TRAI-TORS IN THE DOMIN-ION?
I DON'T LIKE HAVING TO SUSPECT MY ALLIES.
...
UM... ARE YOU ALL RIGHT?
OH, I'M FINE.
DON'T WORRY ABOUT ME.
...
YOU'RE VERY KIND, KURA-SAME.

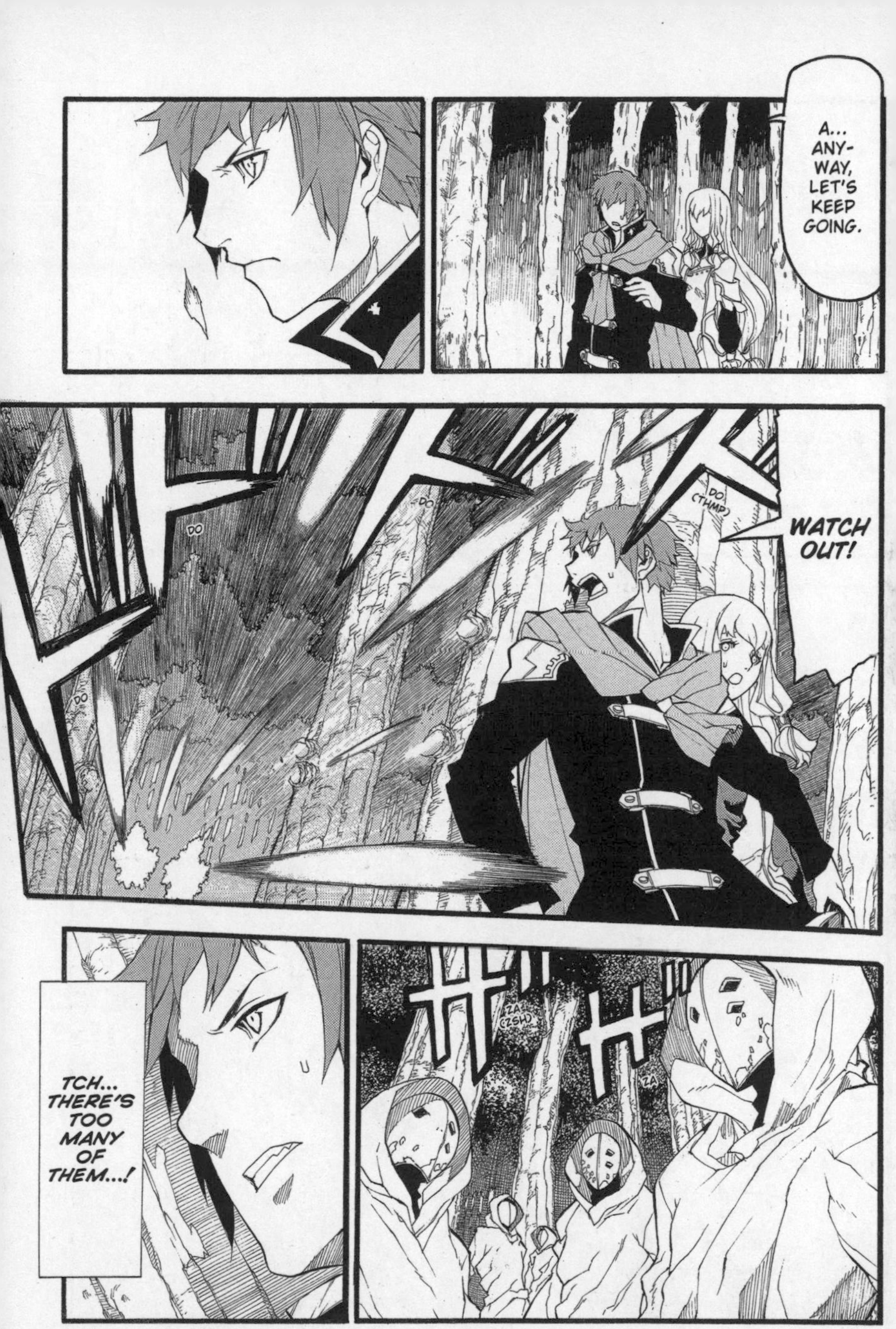
A... ANY-WAY, LET'S KEEP GOING.
WATCH OUT!
DO (THMP)
DO
DO
DO
DO
ZA (ZSH)
ZA
TCH... THERE'S TOO MANY OF THEM...!

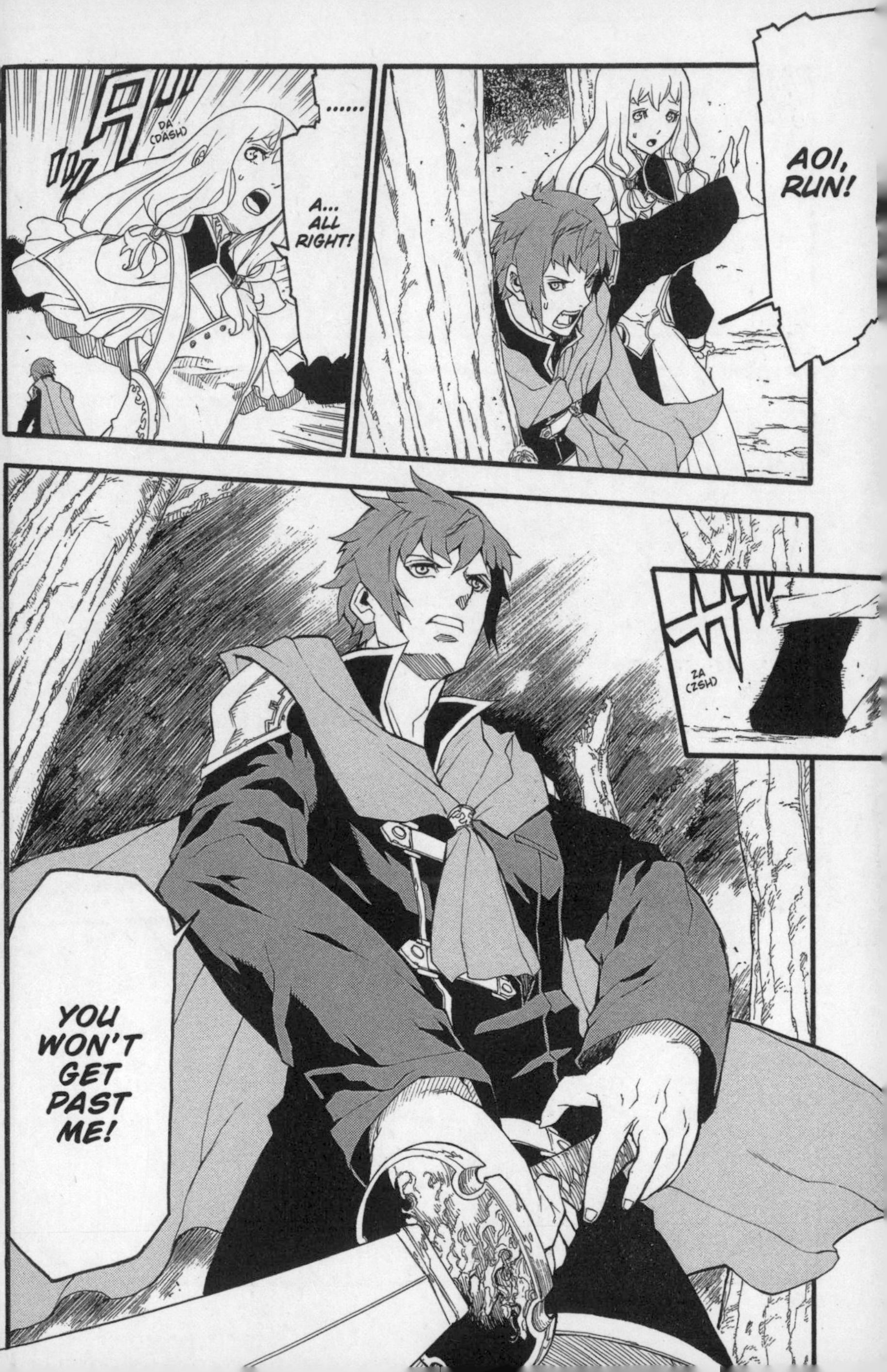
AOI, RUN!
DA (DASH)
......
A... ALL RIGHT!
ZA (ZSH)
YOU WON'T GET PAST ME!

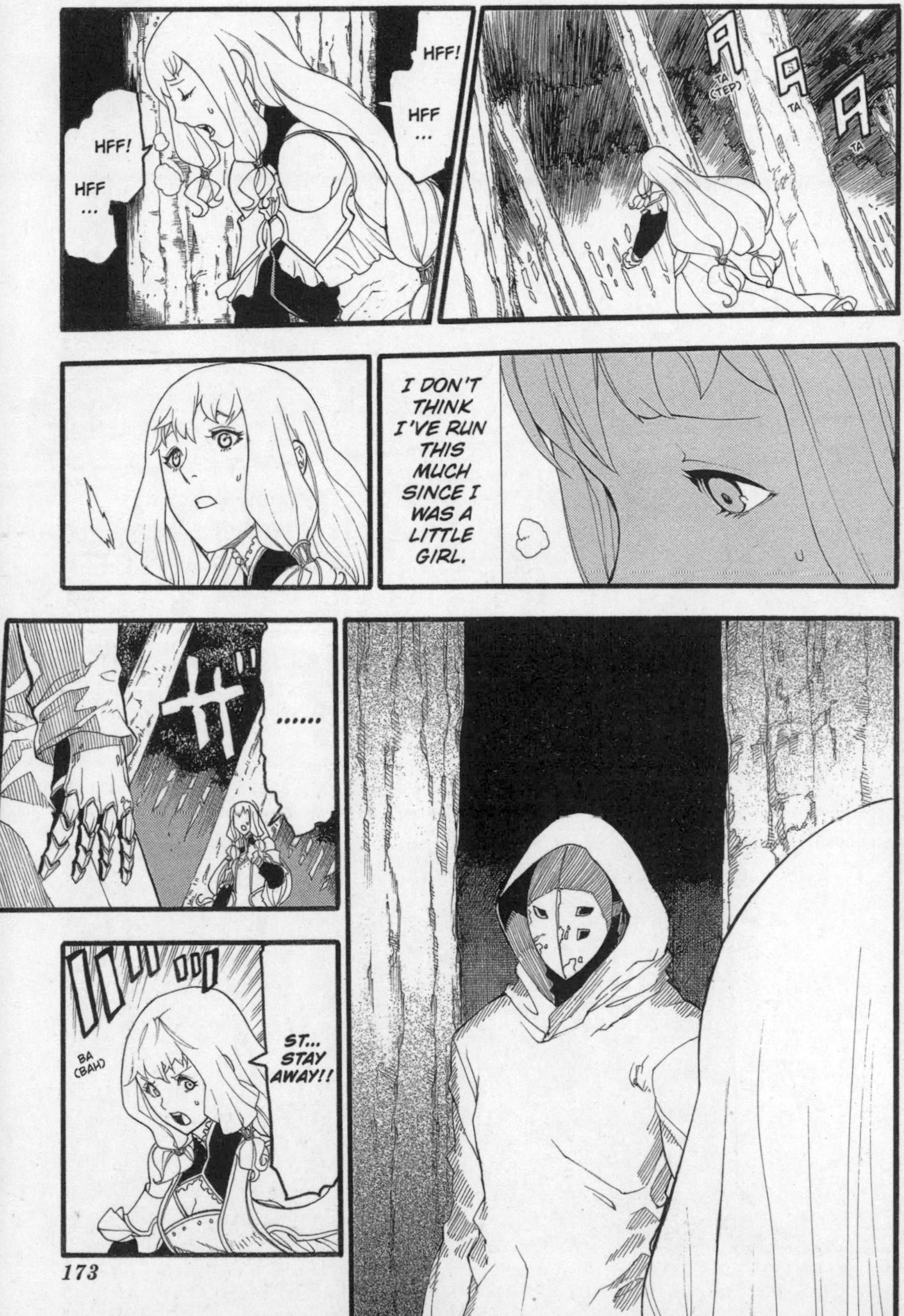

TA (TEP)
TA
TA
HFF!
HFF ...
HFF!
HFF ...
I DON'T THINK I'VE RUN THIS MUCH SINCE I WAS A LITTLE GIRL.
ZA
......
BA (BAH)
ST... STAY AWAY!!

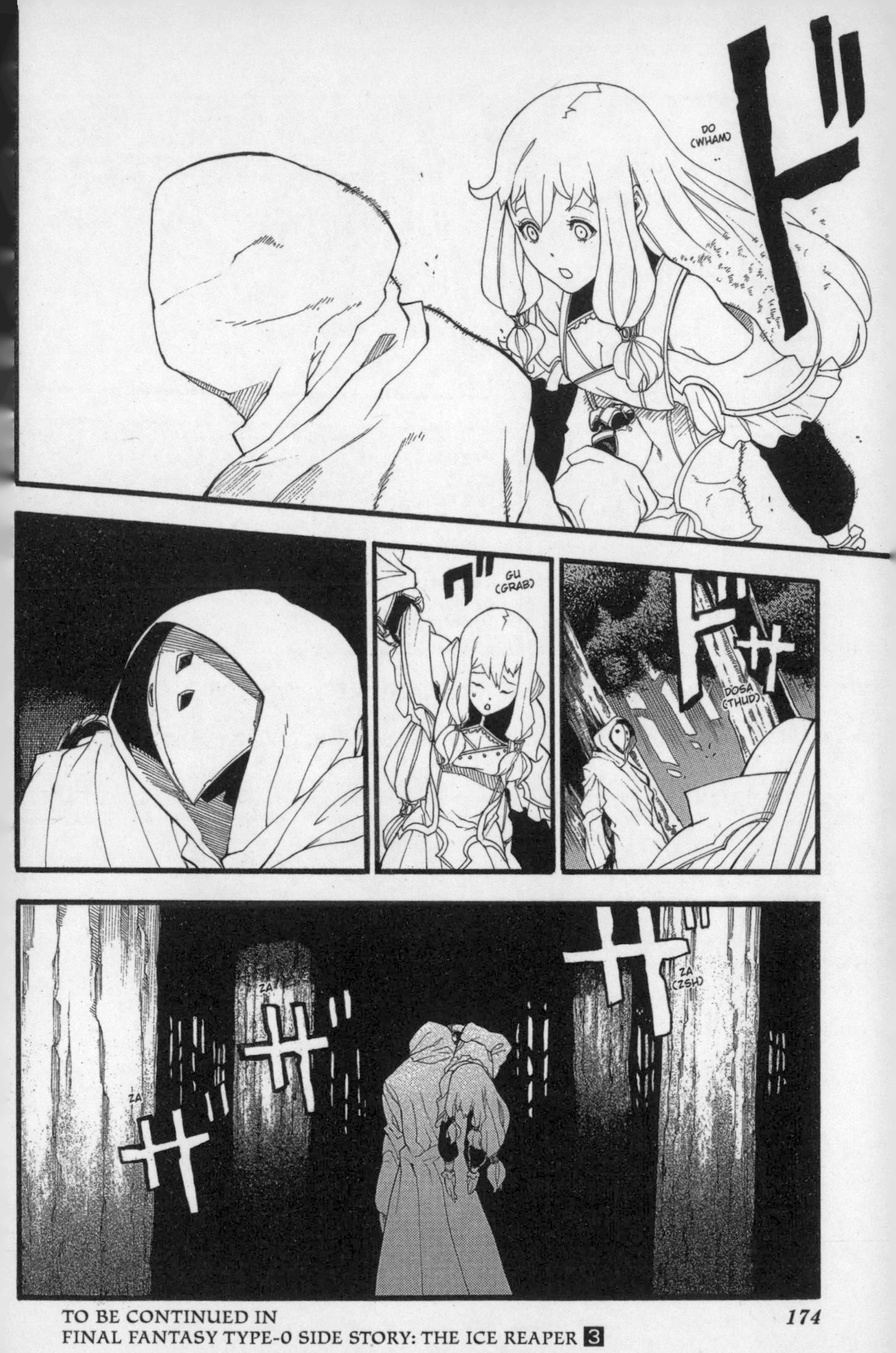
DO
(WHAM)
DOSA
(THUD)
GU
(GRAB)
ZA
(ZSH)
ZA
ZA

TO BE CONTINUED IN
FINAL FANTASY TYPE-0 SIDE STORY: THE ICE REAPER 3

FINAL FANTASY 零式 TYPE-0 ™

SIDE STORY

The Ice Reaper

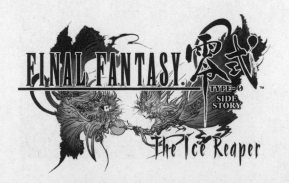

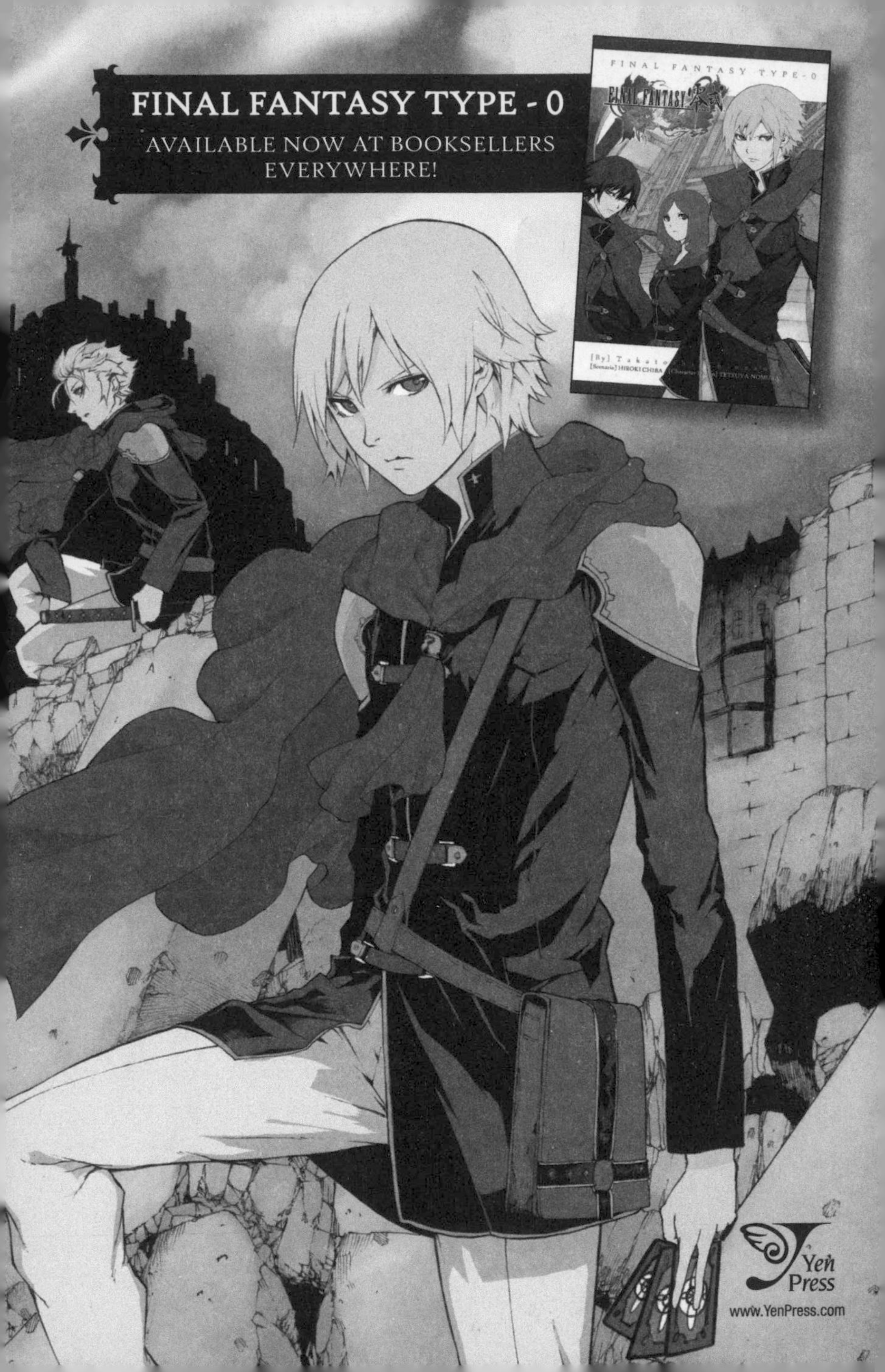
FINAL FANTASY TYPE - 0
AVAILABLE NOW AT BOOKSELLERS EVERYWHERE!
FINAL FANTASY TYPE-0
Yen Press
www.YenPress.com

FINAL FANTASY 零式 TYPE-0

Art: TAKATOSHI SHIOZAWA
Character Design: TETSUYA NOMURA
Scenario: HIROKI CHIBA

The cadets of Akademeia's Class Zero are legends, with strength and magic unrivaled, and crimson capes symbolizing the great Vermilion Bird of the Dominion. But will their elite training be enough to keep them alive when a war breaks out and the Class Zero cadets find themselves at the front and center of a bloody political battlefield?!

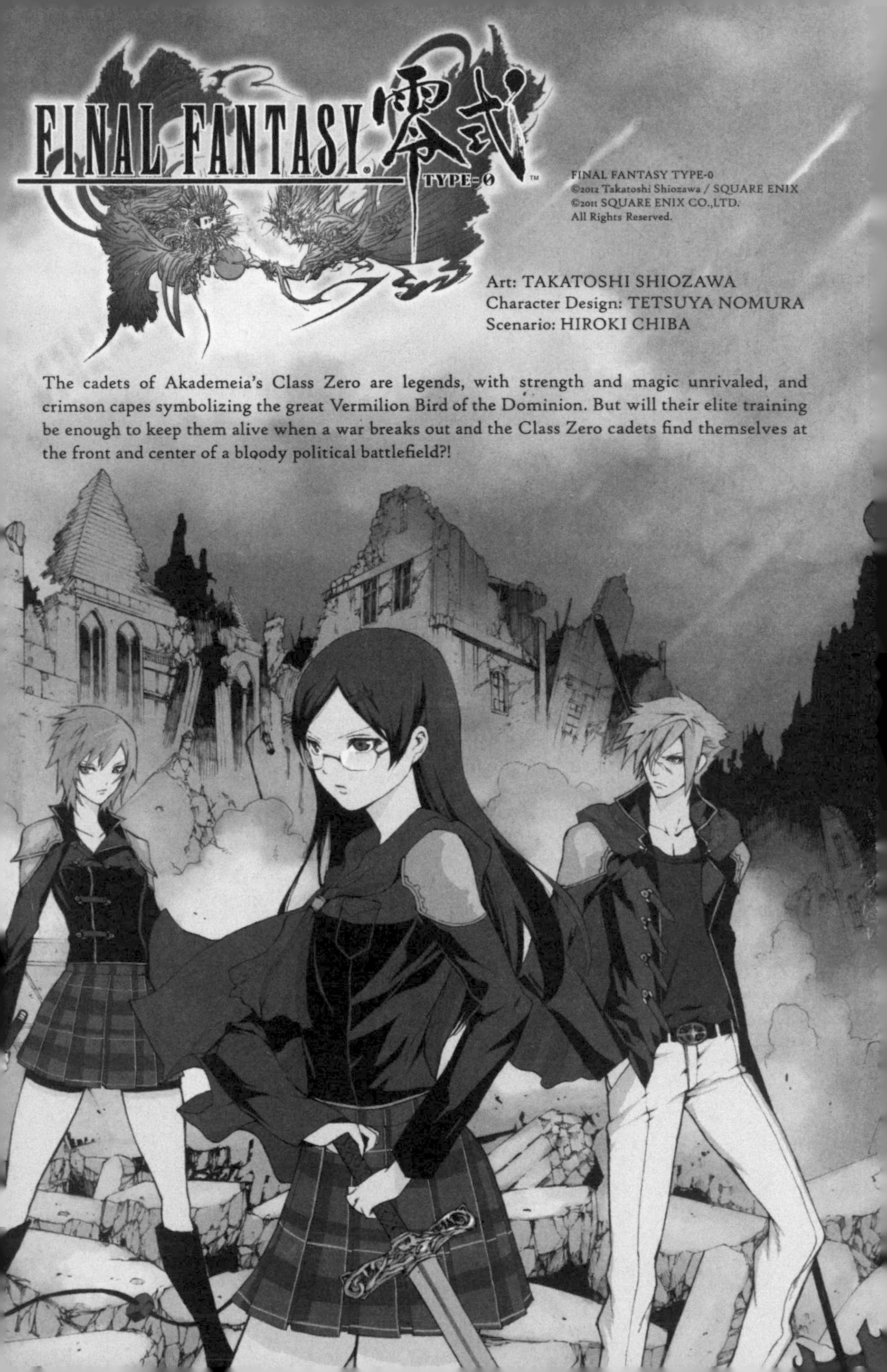

FINAL FANTASY
SIDE STORY:
THE ICE REAPER ❷

TAKATOSHI SHIOZAWA
CHARACTER DESIGN: TETSUYA NOMURA

Translation: Alethea and Athena Nibley

Lettering: Lys Blakeslee

This book is a work of fiction. Names, characters, places, and incidents are the product of the author's imagination or are used fictitiously. Any resemblance to actual events, locales, or persons, living or dead, is coincidental.

FINAL FANTASY TYPE-0 GAIDEN HYOKEN NO SHINIGAMI Vol. 2
© 2013 Takatoshi Shiozawa / SQUARE ENIX CO., LTD.
© 2011 SQUARE ENIX CO., LTD. All rights reserved.
CHARACTER DESIGN: TETSUYA NOMURA
First published in Japan in 2013 by SQUARE ENIX CO., LTD. English translation rights arranged with SQUARE ENIX CO., LTD. and Hachette Book Group through Tuttle-Mori Agency, Inc., Tokyo.

Translation © 2015 by SQUARE ENIX CO., LTD.

Yen Press
Hachette Book Group
1290 Avenue of the Americas
New York, NY 10104

www.HachetteBookGroup.com
www.YenPress.com

Yen Press is an imprint of Hachette Book Group, Inc. The Yen Press name and logo are trademarks of Hachette Book Group, Inc.

The publisher is not responsible for websites (or their content) that are not owned by the publisher.

First Yen Press Edition: October 2015

ISBN: 978-0-316-34877-5

10 9 8 7 6 5 4 3 2 1

BVG

Printed in the United States of America